Authoritarianism and the Elite Origins of Democracy

This book argues that in terms of institutional design, the allocation of power and privilege, and the lived experiences of citizens, democracy often does not restart the political game after displacing authoritarianism. Democratic institutions are frequently designed by the outgoing authoritarian regime to shield incumbent elites from the rule of law and give them an unfair advantage over politics and the economy after democratization. *Authoritarianism and the Elite Origins of Democracy* systematically documents and analyzes the constitutional tools that outgoing authoritarian elites use to accomplish these ends, such as electoral system design, legislative appointments, federalism, legal immunities, constitutional tribunal design, and supermajority thresholds for change. The study provides wide-ranging evidence for these claims using data that span the globe and date from 1800 to the present. Albertus and Menaldo also conduct detailed case studies of Chile and Sweden. In doing so, they explain why some democracies successfully overhaul their elite-biased constitutions for more egalitarian social contracts.

Michael Albertus is an assistant professor of Political Science at the University of Chicago. Albertus's first book, *Autocracy and Redistribution: The Politics of Land Reform* (Cambridge, 2015), won the Gregory Luebbert Award for best book in comparative politics and the LASA Bryce Wood Award for best book on Latin America in the social sciences and humanities.

Victor Menaldo is an associate professor of Political Science at University of Washington and an affiliated faculty member of the Center for Statistics and the Social Sciences, Near and Middle Eastern Studies, and the Center for Environmental Politics. His first book is entitled *The Institutions Curse: Natural Resources, Politics, and Development* (Cambridge, 2016).

Authoritarianism and the Elite Origins of Democracy

MICHAEL ALBERTUS
University of Chicago

VICTOR MENALDO
University of Washington

 CAMBRIDGE
UNIVERSITY PRESS

CAMBRIDGE
UNIVERSITY PRESS

University Printing House, Cambridge CB2 8BS, United Kingdom

One Liberty Plaza, 20th Floor, New York, NY 10006, USA

477 Williamstown Road, Port Melbourne, VIC 3207, Australia

4843/24, 2nd Floor, Ansari Road, Daryaganj, Delhi – 110002, India

79 Anson Road, #06-04/06, Singapore 079906

Cambridge University Press is part of the University of Cambridge.

It furthers the University's mission by disseminating knowledge in the pursuit of education, learning, and research at the highest international levels of excellence.

www.cambridge.org
Information on this title: www.cambridge.org/9781316649039
DOI: 10.1017/9781108185950

© Michael Albertus and Victor Menaldo 2018

First published 2018

Printed in the United States of America by Sheridan Books, Inc.

A catalogue record for this publication is available from the British Library.

ISBN 978-1-107-19982-8 Hardback
ISBN 978-1-316-64903-9 Paperback

Contents

Figures

Tables

Acknowledgments

The driving ideas behind this book date back to our early conversations and work at Stanford University, when one of us (Albertus) was in the final years of his PhD and the other (Menaldo) was a fellow at the Hoover Institution. Both of us coincided on the observation that dictatorship is a dangerous game. When all goes well for ruling political elites and their economic allies, they enrich themselves and lord over their subjects. But when conflicts arise, fortunes can change very quickly – and often dramatically. Years of accumulating power, prestige, and fortunes can be ended in an instant, at the tip of a gun or in a basement prison cell. We began working through bits and pieces of this story, particularly elite infighting and expropriation, and how dictators construct and cohere stable ruling coalitions.

As our work progressed, we began thinking more about how volatility under dictatorship can have consequences for democratization as elites seek safe haven under more predictable institutions. At the same time, we both began uncovering the fingerprints of authoritarianism on many of the democratic countries we were studying for other purposes. In many of these democracies, the livelihoods of citizens had changed very little since their transitions from authoritarianism. And in some, in what seemed like a cruel joke, the democratically elected politicians were powerful elites from the authoritarian era.

We began brainstorming why this was the case and how to systematically measure the persistence of elite power under democracy. It was at this time that Tom Ginsburg invited us to a conference at the University of Chicago Law School on constitution making under authoritarian regimes. Our basic insight was that authoritarian constitutions could be used to delineate power and reduce conflict under dictatorship and that, critically, they could also serve to cement in the influence of authoritarian elites across transitions to democracy. Only later did we unpack this insight, examining a common set of formal and informal tools that outgoing authoritarian elites deploy through constitutions to retain influence and avoid punishment under democracy.

Since those initial insights, many colleagues and mentors have provided us with invaluable feedback that has immensely enriched the ultimate production of this book. Menaldo would like to thank his teachers, mentors, fellow researchers, and parents. He owes a special debt of gratitude to Stephen Haber, who was a superb advisor and mentor at Stanford and is a good friend. Haber's work on the political economy of finance, industrialization, natural resources, democracy, and authoritarianism has profoundly shaped Menaldo's views and therefore greatly influenced this book. Menaldo is also grateful for feedback on parts of his doctoral dissertation and presentations of the coauthored paper with Albertus entitled "Gaming Democracy," both of which were later revised and incorporated in key ways into this book. In particular, he would like to thank Nathaniel Beck, James Caporaso, Stephen Hanson, David Laitin, Ross Levine, Margaret Levi, Noel Maurer, Paul Musgrave, James Robinson, David Stasavage, James Vreeland, Erik Wibbels, Susan Whiting, Dwayne Woods, and Gavin Wright. Menaldo also thanks Jennifer Noveck for invaluable research assistance.

Albertus is similarly indebted to his mentors, advisors, and those scholars who he has the good fortune of knowing. David Laitin, Jim Fearon, Steve Haber, and Jonathan Rodden – his dissertation committee – all provided him with invaluable training and all generously contributed comments on this project that challenged, extended, and deepened the initial ideas. Their enthusiasm in remaining supportive mentors well after Albertus's dissertation was completed is a testament to their laudable dedication to learning and the accumulation of knowledge.

Albertus would also like to thank the many other colleagues who have provided critical and useful feedback on the ideas behind this project, from the hallways at the University of Chicago and at Stanford's Hoover Institution, which provided him precious sabbatical time and funding to work on this book as a National Fellow in 2015–2016, and well beyond: Lisa Blaydes, Brett Carter, Larry Diamond, Frank Fukuyama, Tom Ginsburg, Steph Haggard, Mark Hansen, Will Howell, Bob Kaufman, Aila Matanock, John McCormick, Mike McFaul, Monika Nalepa, Ken Scheve, Dan Slater, Paul Staniland, Nick Stephanopoulos, Milan Svolik, Lisa Wedeen, and Barry Weingast. John McCormick has been an endless fount of discussions regarding the nature of democracy and which social groups it empowers, from ancient Rome to contemporary Latin America.

Both Albertus and Menaldo are particularly thankful to Dan Slater, who read many parts of earlier drafts of this book and provided continually valuable insights that helped us greatly improve our argument and, ultimately, the book.

We are also grateful for helpful feedback we received at a variety of conferences, especially those held at MIT, Harvard, and Northwestern. Thanks to this feedback, we made important revisions with an aim toward broadening the manuscript's appeal, nuancing our claims, and interfacing with a wider range of literature. In particular, we would like to thank Nancy Bermeo, Dan Brinks, Jorge Domínguez, Zach Elkins, Candelaria Garay, Dan Gingerich, Anna Grzymala-Busse, Peter Hall, Alisha Holland, Steve Levitsky, Johannes Lindvall, Vicky Murillo, Rachel Reidl, David Samuels, Kathy Thelen, Joe Wong, Deborah Yashar, and Daniel Ziblatt.

Equally important to the final manuscript were anonymous manuscript reviewers at Cambridge University Press, who provided thoughtful and constructive reviews. The manuscript is without a doubt much better as a result, hopefully to a degree equal to their expectations. We thank Robert Dreesen at Cambridge for soliciting such excellent reviews, and so quickly to boot. Robert has been a fabulous editor – responsive and deft at every stage of the process.

This book draws on elements of several papers that we co-wrote with each other or with others. These include "Dictators as Founding Fathers: The Role of Constitutions in Autocracies" (*Economics & Politics*), "If You're Against Them You're With Us: The Effect of Expropriation on Autocratic Survival" (*Comparative Political Studies*), "Gaming Democracy: The Role of Elite Welfare in Democratic Transition" (*British Journal of Political Science*), "Dealing with Dictators: Negotiated Democratization and the Fate of Outgoing Autocrats" (*International Studies Quarterly*), and "Capital in the Twenty-First Century – in the Rest of the World" (*Annual Review of Political Science*). It also draws on a paper coauthored by Menaldo and Daniel Yoo, "Democracy, Elite Bias, and Financial Development in Latin America" (*World Politics*). Any elements of these papers that appear in the book are reprinted with permission.

Finally, we thank all of our closest personal supporters. Menaldo would like to thank his wife, Nicola, and his two sons, Sebastian and Thomas. Without them and their love, none of the sacrifices associated with writing this book would have been worth it.

Albertus would like to thank his wife, Ally; his parents, Anne and Steve; his siblings, Julie, Paul, Jim, and Daniel; and the wonderful new family that Ally has brought into his life: Karen, Bruce, CD, Emily, Brandon, little Ruthie, Molly, and Mike. They have been behind him every step of the way and provided overflowing love and support beyond words when a nasty bike accident threatened to derail much more than this book. They inspire, encourage reflection, listen to ideas, and most importantly, weave a rich tapestry of life that extends well beyond this book.

Finally, we both would like to thank the internet. Without the ability to talk to each other for hours upon hours at rock-bottom prices, over what turned into weeks, months, and eventually years, over long distances and across different time zones, this book would not have been possible. Thank you, in particular, to Skype, even though it also helped drive our spouses up the wall, because they could often hear our every word.

1

Introduction

In the course of the last half century, democracy has gone from being a relatively rare breed to a form of government under which the majority of countries in the world operate. Scholars, pundits, and citizens alike have hailed this sea change as an advance for freedom, well-being, and opportunity. And an advance it is – like no other the world has previously seen. Starting with the transitions that began in Southern Europe in the late 1970s, the trend toward democracy spread to Latin America. The Latin American democratizations occurred largely in tandem with unexpected transitions in Eastern Europe after the fall of the Iron Curtain. They were then followed by unlikely cases such as Mongolia, Indonesia, Ghana, and even Tunisia.

As a result, citizens across much of the globe are now able to speak and associate freely and elect and replace their representatives while being protected from the arbitrary and often violent dictates of authoritarian rule.[1] Not only do these citizens enjoy the intrinsic benefits of political liberty, but they should also, in theory, enjoy a host of instrumental benefits such as a more responsive government, greater economic opportunities, social mobility, and an expanded safety net. These broad differences between life in democracy and in dictatorship have been enumerated and examined throughout the ages, starting with the first political philosophers up until contemporary democratic scholars.

Fortunately, as the set of democracies has expanded and covered larger portions of the globe, it has become easier to test time-honored beliefs about these differences. Over the past few decades, advances in mathematical modeling and state-of-the-art statistical techniques have allowed scholars to examine the

---

[1] In Chapter 9 we discuss what appears to be an inflection point: this democratizing trend has been interrupted by creeping authoritarianism in countries such as Russia, Hungary, Poland, Turkey, Venezuela, South Africa, and the Philippines.

differences between democracy and dictatorship more carefully and systematically than ever before. The first generation of work using these tools seemed to corroborate the basic intuition that democracy is *of* the people, enacted *by* the people – and, crucially, *for* the people – in opposition to tyranny by one man or oligarchy by the few. But cracks have begun to emerge in the consensus that democracies are actually forged by the people and that their policies are intended to benefit the people.

Take South Africa. During apartheid, its black citizens clamored for the right to vote, for access to land, for access to education and jobs, and for freedom from institutionalized race-based discrimination. Yet when democracy finally came in 1994, it was not necessarily forged by the people: indeed, during the transition process, the outgoing apartheid regime was largely in the driver's seat. The first five years of democracy were governed by a transitional power-sharing agreement in which the newly empowered African National Congress (ANC) agreed that the outgoing apartheid National Party (NP) would be part of the government despite a lack of popular support. Cabinets were to make consensus decisions. Moreover, the transition deal gave provinces – including some designed expressly for domination by whites – the authority to adopt their own constitutions. Whites in these provinces were awarded a veto in local governments over policies that affected them. A sunset clause protected military, police, and civil service members – again, overwhelmingly whites – from replacement once the new government was in power. In short, the NP basically had veto power over the institutional design of the country.

Because South African democracy was not created *by* the people, it is not governed *for* the people. Ownership over major swathes of the economy and control of the education system as well as the judiciary have remained largely in the hands of those elites who reigned under apartheid. Despite two decades of rule by the ANC, inequality in the country is higher now than it was at the end of apartheid. Land reform is shackled by red tape and the resistance of recalcitrant landowners. Blacks make up 80 percent of the population, but they earn one-sixth of what white citizens earn on average. Indeed, with a Gini index above sixty-three, South Africa is the third most unequal place on earth.[2]

To be sure, a nascent black elite has begun to replace the former apartheid-era oligarchy. But these new elites are more intent on guarding their new-found status and wealth than on ushering in a new era of shared prosperity. Corruption, cronyism, and the repression of labor abound. As a result, many South Africans now clamor for much more radical policies, such as large-scale redistribution imposed by the state, even if that means abandoning the democracy they fought so hard to obtain.

Unfortunately, the experience of South Africa is not an uncommon one. Consider the democracies that have been founded in the last several decades.

---

[2] The Gini index ranges from 0, indicating perfect equality, to 100, indicating perfect inequality, in which one individual earns all the income in a society.

Many suffer from high inequality and public spending profiles oriented away from education and other public goods. Social insurance and welfare transfers for the poor are drastically insufficient. While poverty, inequality, and corruption are endemic, crime and violence are often everyday occurrences for a large share of the population. Even more disheartening is the fact that polls conducted across the developing world reveal that the citizens of relatively new democracies are dissatisfied. Many often view bygone eras of authoritarianism with nostalgia, and some support their return.

Why has the quality and breadth of democracy been so disappointing? Why have levels of inequality, poverty, and corruption become alarmingly high, even decades after transitions from authoritarianism? Why have many democracies failed, both today and in the past, to live up to the potential that so many attribute to them?

In addressing these questions, this book strongly challenges the conventional wisdom that democracy is created by and for the people. It poses the bothersome, yet important, possibility that in terms of institutional design, the allocation of power and privilege, the content of public policy, and the lived experiences of citizens, democracy might not reset the political game. Those who benefited under the previous dictatorship often continue to do so well after they formally step down. In short, most democracies might not be all that different than their authoritarian predecessors in terms of material consequences. And while some democracies are indeed created by and for the people, or manage to escape the endemic flaws that they were born with, this is a hard-fought and rare occurrence.

Therefore, in this book we grapple with perhaps the biggest questions in the study of comparative politics: What are the meaningful differences between autocracy and democracy? Where does democracy come from? What are the effects of democracy on human welfare? We conclude that both analysts and citizens must take off their rose-colored glasses if they are to truly understand – and address – the host of imperfections that beset democracies across the globe. Democracy is often an enterprise undertaken by elites and for elites. The timing of democratic transition, as well as the very institutional architecture of democracy itself, is frequently determined by elites prior to exiting dictatorship. As a result, democracy often serves their interests well after transition.

MAJOR EXISTING EXPLANATIONS

Our arguments and evidence in this book depart in crucial ways from how scholars typically think about democracy and its effects. Existing scholarship can be roughly grouped into two camps. The first is composed of researchers who take the orthodox view that democracy is constructed by the people and for the people. The second camp is more clear-eyed about democracy's flaws, admitting that democratic institutions and policies can be distorted and therefore do not always reflect the preferences of the majority. In contradistinc-tion to what we argue in this book, however, this camp does not go so far as to conclude that democracy's flaws are the byproduct of deliberate measures taken by the previous outgoing authoritarian regime: institutions designed by outgoing elites before they exit the stage.

Democracy: Of, By, and For the People

The conventional wisdom is that democracy grows organically from the people and implements their will. It is more politically egalitarian and more responsive to the demands of the majority than dictatorship. Usually, democracy is also theo-rized to be more economically egalitarian, primarily because of this responsiveness.

This is an old view. A very diverse group of celebrated thinkers such as Aristotle, Karl Marx, de Tocqueville, and the American Founding Fathers put forth some of these ideas. Of course, not all of these thinkers believed that unadulterated democracy was necessarily a good thing. Aristotle, for instance, feared that democracy could devolve into tyranny. For his part, Marx believed that the only way to prevent the bourgeoisie from reasserting themselves at the expense of workers was through an empowered proletariat that did not have to bother with the rule of law (a "dictatorship of the proletariat"). And the American Founders worried deeply about a potential tyranny of the majority. All of these luminaries did agree on one point, however: democracy distributes power more evenly than its alternatives, and almost always enables the poor to soak the rich.

A more modern literature formalizes the notion that political equality equals economic equality. This literature builds from the well-established finding that political parties have a tendency to coalesce around the median, or represen-tative, voter in their policy platforms. Because the distribution of pre-tax and transfer income is inevitably unequal throughout the world, this puts class con-flict waged between the rich and poor at the center of political life. That means that under democracy there will be redistribution between social classes: the rich will pay higher taxes than the poor and the poor will receive transfers that will narrow the gap between them and the rich (Meltzer and Richard 1981).

Drawing on this median-voter view of electoral competition, some authors believe that the rich – rightfully – fear democracy and will block it. Specifically, when inequality is high, elites will block a transition to democracy because they anticipate that democracy will yield massive redistribution (Boix 2003; Boix and Stokes 2003). Yet inequality need not be exceptionally low for elites to accept democracy. Some authors argue that at middling rates of inequality, elites will democratize when the poor pose a revolutionary threat; the rich can only placate a sporadically restive populous by handing over political power (see Acemoglu and Robinson 2001, 2006; Przeworski et al. 2000). Whatever their predictions about how inequality ultimately translates into democracy, what unites these views is that they believe democracy is a credible commit-ment to redistribution, hence the fear it instills in the wealthy. Moreover, a parallel literature that does not begin from the median-voter premise finds empirical evidence that democracies dedicate more spending to public goods and have better social and economic outcomes as a result (Bueno de Mesquita et al. 2003; Clague et al. 1996; Lake and Baum 2001).

The history of the advanced Western democracies supports the claim that if a country experiences a transition to democracy, this will increase redistribution from the rich to the poor majority. The steady widening of the franchise across Western Europe and the United States via the removal of income, wealth, and property restrictions on the right to vote for adult men, followed by suffrage for women, stimulated redistribution (Acemoglu and Robinson 2006; Przeworski 2009; Husted and Kenny 1997; Justman and Gradstein 1999; Lott and Kenny 1999). Progressive taxation and high levels of social spending were the warp and woof of this equilibrium. At first, governments raised direct taxes at increasing marginal rates to provide basic public goods in urban areas undergoing rapid industrialization (Acemoglu and Robinson 2006; Aidt, Dutta, and Loukoianova 2006; Lizzeri and Persico 2004). The state's fiscal role then evolved to encompass national programs devoted to welfare, pensions, health care, and housing (Alesina and Glaeser 2004).

The welfare state experienced a gradual, secular increase over the first half of the twentieth century, followed by a veritable quantum leap during the post-war era. Across the developed world, and especially Western Europe, spending on education and social insurance programs skyrocketed (Lindert 1994; 2004; Steinmo 1993). The heyday of this equilibrium was the so-called embedded liberal international order under the Bretton Woods system of fixed exchange rates. During this era, all democratic governments in the developed world – and many developing countries – used capital controls to avail both fiscal and monetary policy for redistribution, full employment, and social insurance (Dailami 2000).

Even during the post-1970s era of increased globalization, policies that benefit the median voter and the poor under democracy have far from vanished (Epifani and Gancia 2009; Rodrik 1998). Public employment still serves as the backbone of the economy in democracies such as Greece. Elected leaders have successfully implemented effective pro-poor conditional cash transfers in developing countries such as Brazil and Mexico (De La O 2013). And robust welfare states in Western and Eastern Europe seem to have mostly weathered calls for austerity in the wake of the Great Recession and have continued to finance generous safety nets and publicly provided services.

One of the main tenets of the median voter–inspired, social conflict view of democracy is that redistribution should not be the exclusive province of the left. Indeed, it seems that pro-poor policies and redistribution in fledgling democracies often cut across ideological orientation, providing evidence that it is the sheer arithmetic of democracy, rather than ideology, that is driving redistribution (e.g., Huber et al. 2008). This pattern is evident in Latin America. Pro-poor policies in Brazil and Mexico were first enacted by centrist presidents and parties. In Chile, Sebastián Piñera, leader of the center-right Alianza coalition who became president in 2010, refrained from reversing progressive social policies adopted since 1990 under Concertación governments.

Democracy Is Of and By the People, but Sometimes Not For the People

Although the consensus view is that democracy is politically and economically egalitarian, other authors argue that certain social and economic factors hamstring its ability to operate as a faithful handmaiden of the majority's economic interests. There is evidence that democracies are no more likely than dictatorships to have better health and education outcomes (Ross 2006; Nelson 2007; Truex forthcoming). Furthermore, there is little evidence that they are less likely to engage in crony capitalism and clientelism (Zingales 2012; Keefer 2007). Indeed, even at the highest levels of inequality, where the demand for redistribution is ostensibly greatest, democracy does not, on average, yield redistribution (Perotti 1996).

In addressing the puzzle that political equality does not necessarily translate into economic equality, many researchers have stressed that politics is often about something other than pocketbook issues. Voter choices are impacted by group consciousness, place-based identity, religion, relative well-being, and priming – all of which can cut against economic self-interest (Bartels 2005; Shapiro 2002; Roemer 1998; Walsh 2012). Regional, ethnic, or religious differences might be more salient than class-based redistributive appeals (Roemer 1998; Walsh 2012). And if poorer citizens are relatively risk acceptant and anticipate upward mobility, they might eschew redistribution to avoid being taxed in the future (Benabou and Ok 2001). Alternatively, framing effects and ignorance about the distribution of income and fiscal policies can blunt demands for redistribution (see Bartels 2005; Shapiro 2002).

The lack of a strong association between democracy and redistribution might instead be due to the fact that the median voter requires specific political and economic tools to aggregate and express his or her interests – tools that are not guaranteed under democracy. Power resources theory, one of the dominant explanations for variation in the size and scope of the welfare state in Organization for Economic Cooperation and Development (OECD) countries, holds that strong unions are needed to compress wage and salary distributions and that social democratic parties will more effectively deliver redistributive social policy (Korpi 1983; Stephens 1979; Iversen and Soskice 2006). Political representatives can also unreliably translate the demands of voters into policy. They might have a greater stake in representing the rich (Gilens and Page 2014; Atkinson 2015). Or perhaps they themselves are much richer and more connected than their constituents (Carnes and Lupu 2015).

Even if citizens do hold strong preferences for redistribution, and these preferences are reflected by their representatives, globalization can tie the hands of policy makers by enabling asset holders to move easily across borders to avoid redistribution (Bates 1991; Boix 2003; Dailami 2000; Freeman and Quinn 2012; Kaufman and Segura-Ubiergo 2001; Piketty 2014; Remmer 1990; Stokes 2001). A government's ability to regulate labor markets and levy progressive taxation is made more difficult by capital mobility (Dailami 2000). As countries compete to attract investment, they might engage in a race to the bottom in which they reduce marginal tax rates on high income earners, adopt flatter tax structures centered on value-added taxes, and cut both corporate tax rates and rates on capital gains (Bird and Zolt 2005).

Indeed, these appear to be key catalysts of the increased inequality that Piketty (2014) documents since the 1970s. Most of the economic gains in recent decades have been concentrated among the top 10 percent of the income distribution – or, more precisely, among the top 1 percent, if not .01 percent. Atkinson (2015) documents a drastic reduction in the top marginal tax rates on income in industrialized countries starting in the mid-1960s. In the United States and Britain, for example, the highest marginal tax rates in the immediate postwar era exceeded 90 percent. They have since dropped by well over half – indeed, by more than 50 percentage points. There is no country in this set for which there has been a significant increase in top marginal tax rates. Atkinson shows that, intuitively, the increased regressivity of the tax code has mapped onto a greater concentration of income at the very top of the distribution.

Moreover, the anemic recovery from the 2007–2009 global financial crash witnessed across these rich countries greatly benefited top earners, notwithstanding the fact that the global economy seemed to turn the corner in 2017. Wage and asset gains have been nearly stagnant for the middle class and poor in the United States and Great Britain, for example, despite booming stock markets.[3] In Spain, Portugal, and Greece, youth unemployment rates surpassed those last seen during the Great Depression.

The bottom line is this: from the vantage of the literature that grapples with the paradox of unequal democracy, democracy is not irreparably broken. Instead, it suffers from a few ailments such as corruption, the inability to process and reconcile multidimensional voter views, agency slack between voters and representatives, or a punishing international environment in which governments have to accept the dictates of global capitalism.

A DEEPER CRITIQUE OF DEMOCRACY

In contrast to the views summarized in the previous sections, we argue that democracy in many cases is not only not *for* the people; it is also not *of* or *by* the people. The aforementioned symptoms are therefore reflective of a much deeper condition that is built into the system itself from the very start.

---

[3] This pattern has been almost entirely reversed in the United States, however. Beginning in 2015, median incomes increased by the largest amount ever recorded and inequality slightly decreased. The pattern has continued since then. Yet, due to slow growth and high levels of workers who remain on the sidelines of the job market, median incomes in the United States remain below their 1999 levels. The same is true for earners in the bottom tenth percentile.

Consider one set of facts that radically challenges received wisdom on the machinery of democracy and its consequences. Democracies are rarely constructed by the representatives of the majority during a movement from below dedicated to political change. Instead, they are often constructed by elites from the former authoritarian regime prior to transition. These elites have little interest in designing institutions that will faithfully represent the majority. To the contrary, they purposefully and explicitly design rules and institutions in a way that blocks the ability of voters to translate their preferences into policy. In other words, democracy is made from above and designed to reflect the interest of former autocratic elites.

At first blush, this might seem like a rather rash accusation. But consider the expression of the social contract at the core of every modern polity: its constitution. From 1800 to 2006, only 34 percent of new democracies began with a constitution that they created themselves or inherited from a past episode of democratic rule in their country. Prominent examples after World War II include Greece, Argentina, the Philippines, and Mongolia. A total of 66 percent of new democracies inherited a constitution that was designed under dictatorship and where outgoing elites dominated the transition process. Chile, Turkey, South Africa, Indonesia, and Thailand illustrate this more common scenario. Indeed, elite-biased democracy becomes more common after World War II. In short, the very DNA of most modern democracies is authoritarian in nature.

We will contend in this book that this simple fact is critical for understanding democracies and for making sense of the puzzle of unequal democracies that do not represent the interests of the median voter. It has enormous practical consequences for the institutional architecture of a democracy, and therefore for what democracy does or does not deliver to its citizens. We will show that many democracies are in fact flawed by design in ways that fundamentally prevent them from addressing social problems, inequalities, and market failures. Before democratization, political elites and their economic allies accumulate wealth, connections, and specialized knowledge about the economy and political system. When the time comes and they bargain their way out of dictatorship to democracy, they then leverage these advantages under elected rule to shape the rules of the game and public policy. Indeed, the advantages of outgoing authoritarian elites are often codified in a constitution that they themselves carefully craft and then impose on a new democracy before exiting. These constitutions pave the way for elites to continue dominating critical political, economic, and cultural institutions.

But why would the political and economic elite who control the political system and the commanding heights of the economy abandon an oligarchic system that deprives the majority of political rights? Elites do not always fare well under dictatorship. In some cases, new factions of political elites ascend to power and expropriate or even destroy longstanding economic elites. Similarly, dictators can be betrayed by their allies and imprisoned, killed, or exiled. These existential threats only provide further reasons for powerful elites to seek stable democratic arrangements on their own terms when they have the capacity to do so.

This insight differs from influential accounts of dictatorship, and thus most explanations of democracy (e.g., Acemoglu and Robinson 2006; Boix 2003), because it relaxes the assumption that political and economic elites are a united front and eschews the idea that regimes and transitions are strictly a class-based affair. We identify splits among elites as key drivers of political change, with the most predominant transitions being those to elite-biased democracy.

A skeptic might argue that an elite-initiated and designed democracy as previously explained stretches the definition of democracy beyond recognition and that we cannot possibly be referring to any authentic democracies. However, it is well known that democracy is defined not by just how closely it expresses the will of the majority but also by how strongly it defends minority rights and provides checks and balances. Interestingly, while we later show that elite-biased democracies score poorly on inclusiveness relative to other democracies, they in fact score quite highly on another critical dimension underscored by prominent theorists such as Dahl (1971): horizontal constraints. Therefore, only by focusing solely on inclusiveness while ignoring other important aspects of democracy might one conclude that these elite-biased democracies do not reach the democratic threshold. Indeed, many modern democracies that are universally recognized as such (e.g., Chile) continue to operate under constitutions penned by their authoritarian predecessors and score highly on all major democratic indices.

In this vein, this book illustrates two important points. First, hardly any regime can conform to the strict Dahlian ideal–type democracy that is purely of the people, by the people, and for the people from its inception. Second, if it comes to approximate this ideal, it is usually because reformers have fought tooth and nail to perfect it over time. As we shall show in the following chapters, even some of the world's most celebrated democracies, such as Sweden and other advanced, industrial democracies, began riddled with illiberal institutions that were introduced by their authoritarian constitutions, only to evolve into highly egalitarian paragons of popular rule after they shed these legacies.

Illiberal institutions also continue to guide some of the world's oldest democracies, even in cases where they penned their own constitutions rather than inheriting them from authoritarian predecessors. Consider the United States, which scores at or near the top of every major index of democracy. The United States boasts a stable republican constitution with strong checks and balances, has a long tradition of free and fair subnational and national elections for two coequal branches of government, and evinces robust judicial review that evaluates legislation and executive decisions against the constitution. Simultaneously, however, the United States continues to hold indirect elections for the presidency, its federal system long protected subnational enclaves in which a majority of citizens in some states were deprived of their basic rights, and until 1913, it maintained an indirectly elected upper chamber that overrepresented state-level oligarchs. Indeed, the American Senate still operates according to rules that require supermajorities to pass ordinary legislation (the filibuster). Gerrymandered electoral districts for the lower chamber alongside high malapportionment in the upper chamber effectively undermine the ideal of one person, one vote.

Throughout this book, we will show that, far from unusual, the United States is typical of the history of most of the world's democracies.

OUR BOOK'S CONTRIBUTIONS

Our book makes several distinct contributions. First, we argue that there are two qualitatively different types of democracy: elite biased and popular. Second, we introduce a new theory and evidence about the causes of democratization. Third, we introduce a new theory and evidence about the scope conditions under which democracy engenders greater egalitarianism. In doing so, we reconcile the paradox that democracies are, on average, not more redistributive than autocracies. Fourth, we challenge idea that capitalism is hardwired to fuel asset and income inequality (Piketty 2014). Instead, capitalism fosters inequality when it is rigged by authoritarian elites to benefit themselves and their economic allies. Crony capitalism of this sort is then sometimes bequeathed to subsequent democracies. Fifth, we bring constitutions back into the study of comparative politics and argue that they matter for explaining the timing, scope, and pace of democratization, as well as outcomes under democracy. Sixth, we challenge the idea that the military is an impartial actor that steps into the political arena to defend the national interest or its own organizational interests and then returns to the barracks (e.g., Geddes 1999). Instead, it is a partisan actor that picks winners and losers and takes its time in doing so.

Finally, we revisit the history of two countries with much scrutinized political regimes – Sweden and Chile – and shift the typical narrative about their political development. This aids in understanding otherwise puzzling aspects of their historical experiences. Of particular note, we demonstrate that Sweden was relatively unequal until the mid-late twentieth century, when its democracy shed the last remnants of elite bias inherited from its autocratic predecessor. We also show that Chile's military dictatorship was not the paragon of neoliberalism it is often portrayed as being; instead, the junta spent its time in office restructuring the political and economic system to benefit its allies and serially violated neoliberal precepts when convenient.

While the remainder of the book is dedicated to developing these contributions, we briefly highlight how some of them differ from existing views here, as we will not always digress into reviews of literatures that appear in our crosshairs – although in both the next chapter and Chapter 3, we identify some of the key works that we draw on or that are similar to ours.

Take the origins of democracy. A vast literature holds that democratization occurs from below. This can take place after a revolution waged by the commercial class and the peasants (Moore 1966). In other cases, wealthy elites that perceive an imminent popular threat in the near future are forced to introduce political change in favor of the masses (Acemoglu and Robinson 2006). In still other cases, a radicalized and energized opposition can weaken an autocratic regime and force it to relinquish power (Mainwaring and Pérez-Liñán 2014).

Alternatively, we argue that it is autocratic elites who tend to introduce democracy when they have an advantageous position that they can leverage to their future benefit. We also argue that these elites are not tantamount to monolithic social classes but instead representatives of different sectors or select segments of the upper class who ally with opportunistic political incumbents who are not necessarily wealthy themselves. In other words, our theory is centered on shifting coalitions between political incumbents and different economic sectors, not a pitched battle between ossified social classes. Our distinctions among elite groups build from and further develop the concept of elite splits found in recent contributions such as Albertus (2015) and Menaldo (2016).[4]

By the same token, we also take issue with the literature that says that democratization is a random and exogenous event (Przeworski et al. 2000), or simply diffused from one country to another passively without elite discretion or strategy (Huntington 1991). Instead, democratic transitions are deliberate decisions that often look alike, not because a new democracy mimics its democratic neighbors, but because the underlying social and political structure is the same between them. To be sure, similar regimes do tend to cluster in time and geographically, but not always because of diffusion. Democracy is not merely a byproduct of global, impersonal forces. Elites in dictatorship have too much at stake. They do not simply roll over or retrench in the face of revolutionary movements or spreading waves of democracy. Instead, they work to shape their own destiny in ways that will benefit them both today and in the future.

Indeed, acknowledging these facts enable us to make better sense of the effects of democracy. Consider the upward trend in inequality since the 1970s and the so-called new Gilded Age that mirrors the inegalitarian pre–World War I world. While Thomas Piketty (2014) argues in *Capital in the Twenty-First Century* that this is partially due to the fact that capitalism is hardwired to exacerbate the gap between the rich and poor, we have an alternative explanation for the long-term U-shaped nature of inequality. Political regime types and the social groups they empower, rather than war and globalization, can account for the sharp fall and then sharp rise in inequality over the twentieth century and beyond.

---

[4] For instance, while we retain the critical difference between political and economic elites, in Chapter 2 we further divide economic elites into two groups: incumbent economic elites and outsider economic elites.

We can also explain inequality patterns beyond the U-shaped one. Capitalists and landholders actually prefer democracy if they can first strike a deal that protects them after transition. This is because dictators are not the loyal servants of the economic elite they are portrayed to be – in fact, they are often responsible for soaking, if not destroying, the rich under autocracy.

Of course, not all democracy scholars believe that regime transitions arise from below, and a number of scholars also admit that outgoing elites often have an outsized role to play in terms of the timing of transitions and even their content.[5] Yet this book differs from more like-minded scholars in its approach to examining the foundations of the social contract that underpins democracy. While so-called transitologists honed in on several pacts forged between authoritarian regime stalwarts and the opposition on the eve of Latin American democratic transitions from military juntas in the 1980s (Karl 1990; O'Donnell and Schmitter 1986), we look at the historical record – including circumstances in which authoritarian regimes *do not* transition – starting around 1800. Unlike much of the prior work on democratic transitions and outcomes, we take a global and historical approach simultaneously rather than a regional approach or an approach rooted in specific time periods. In the process, we take the politics and political economy of dictatorship seriously and uncover the fact that constitutions lie at the heart of elite-biased transitions. Unlike our predecessors working in this tradition, we argue that the prior dictatorial regime is almost invariably the birthplace of democracy.

However, this approach does not imply that democracy is necessarily doomed. Our framework for understanding the deficiencies of democracy also has novel implications for solving some of democracy's thorniest problems. Rather than the majority fighting prolonged, pitched battles over tweaks to key rules and institutions such as the legal system, campaign finance, and the tax system in the face of the exigencies of global finance – important as these issues may be – reformers would be better off focusing their energies on key moments in which large-scale changes can be achieved. These moments tend to cluster on generational transitions during which the old political guard that designed a democracy in their favor dramatically weakens or dies off. During these moments, some societies have been able to upend their authoritarian legacies and amend the institutions under which they live in a way that will benefit the majority.

In the context of demonstrating our main argument and associated points, we also make significant contributions to two additional prominent debates. The first is the debate on the importance of constitutions. Existing scholarship is of two persuasions. One camp tends to view constitutions as mere parchment paper that reflects underlying power balances in society without shaping

---

[5] We discuss in greater depth recent scholarship on elite-led transitions, such as Haggard and Kaufman (2016), Slater and Wong (2013), Riedl (2014), and Ziblatt (2017) in Chapter 3.

them in any fundamental way (Howard 1991; Posner and Young 2007), or at least less influential than meets the eye (Cheibub 2007).

The second camp views constitutions as important, salutary, and in many cases, a panacea for social ills. Some authors have argued that when constitutions are designed, it is often by founding fathers who are preeminently concerned about the future, not their narrow self-interest, and operate as if they are under a veil of ignorance. That means that they concern themselves with the social good and the welfare of future generations (Buchanan and Tullock 1962; Elster 1995).[6] Furthermore, constitutions are considered as more permanent than ordinary legislation (Brennan and Hamilton 2001) and can thus serve to lock in socially desirable outcomes, such as independent judiciary, independent central banks, and individual rights (Myerson 2008; Weingast 1997). Constitutions can also foster desirable citizen values and desirable behavior, such as deliberative decision-making (Sunstein 2001).

We take up a position in the second camp. Constitutions matter, and constitutional design increases the stakes of politics because, in many cases, they can indeed lock policy in – sometimes for decades, if not centuries (Elkins et al. 2009). However, rather than generating magnanimity in founding fathers, this creates a perverse incentive for constitution makers to focus more on their self-interest than they otherwise would (see also Hirschl 2004; Hirschl 2009; Negretto 2013). Instead of a veil of ignorance that militates in favor of the social good and the welfare of future generations, the timing and content of constitutions is, more often than not, opportunistic. We will argue that both political and economic elites design constitutions to protect themselves and to line their pockets while holding down, if not crippling, their opponents and political enemies.[7]

We also challenge the idea that the military is an impartial actor that steps into the political arena to defend the national interest or its own organizational interests and then returns to the barracks as quickly as possible (e.g., Geddes 1999). Coup perpetrators who originate in the armed forces are usually – though not always – allied with key economic elite, enter the political fray to advance an economic agenda, and usually game the political system through constitutional

---

[6] This is not necessarily because constitutional engineers are altruistic but because they often cannot predict the effect that constitutional rules will have on their own interests, or they cannot know what their future roles and interests will be.

[7] This point is somewhat consistent with Linz and Stepan (1996). However, they argue that holdover constitutions are always ticking time bombs: they presage that the new regime will fail to consolidate, either because its institutions will be considered by citizens to be illegitimate, or because they will be poorly designed. One of our goals is to explain variation in when these elite-biased constitutions endure versus when they are reformed to be more popular (see Chapter 5). We should also note that formal constitutions often complement sources of informal power. Ahead we will argue that, above and beyond the rules laid out by the constitution for changing the rules of the game, former autocratic elites can leverage their political networks to forestall or adulterate constitutional change.

engineering and then exit on favorable terms. Furthermore, because they control the state's coercive apparatus, they are uniquely capable of quickly imposing order and then crafting favorable institutional frameworks such as constitutions that will protect their interests after they step down from office.

A NEW THEORETICAL FRAMEWORK FOR UNDERSTANDING DEMOCRACY

Democracies are rarely designed by their founding fathers with the interests of future voters as the preeminent guiding principle. Instead, they are much more commonly "flawed" from inception. There are several reasons why this is the case. First and foremost, the majority of democracies founded throughout human history have been designed by powerful outgoing authoritarian regimes whose interests are often diametrically opposed to those of future voters. Even in circumstances where a new nation is founded from scratch – for instance, due to a successful independence movement – it takes political power, resources, and human capital to design a democracy and implement it. This implies that elites of some sort or another are typically charged with authoring democracy. In a similar fashion to democracies that emerged from dictatorship, these elites have incentives to design institutions and rules while embedding provisions that protect their rights and vital interests. This can include skewed electoral rules, checks and balances designed to impede major policy changes instead of to promote accountability, supermajority thresholds for constitutional change that make it nearly impossible to withdraw advantages bequeathed to elites, selective political party bans, strong forms of federalism, and limits on the popular initiation of legislation.

Such founding flaws distort the structure of decision-making under democracy and condition the likelihood and nature of reforms that occur in the future. One of the most prominent distortions is blanket immunities from prosecution granted to outgoing regime officials for crimes and other transgressions. Indeed, outgoing political elites often spend their last weeks in office ensuring that they will not be prosecuted, imprisoned, killed, or exiled after transferring power. This has profound implications for transitional justice, the rule of law, and even institutional design under democracy. The economic partners of outgoing political elites simultaneously dedicate themselves to safeguarding their property rights and economic interests, usually by reinforcing barriers to entry and similar forms of rent seeking. This has major implications for economic development and the distribution of income, assets, and opportunities under democracy.

Seemingly disparate democracies reveal these common elements across time and place. This is not something that occurs simply by patterns of diffusion or with outgoing elites allowing their fates to be determined by chance and the good intentions of newly elected politicians after a transition. To the contrary, democracies are typically carefully designed – sometimes it can take years for the new regime's founding fathers to hammer out a transitional process and democratic constitution. Moreover, the timing of transition is strategic.

Consider several illustrative examples. In Turkey, the 1982 authoritarian constitution that guided the 1983 transition to democracy created a constitutional court with the ability to ban political parties while stripping the authority of the legislature to make court appointments and instead vesting it in institutions such as the presidency that were heavily influenced by the outgoing military. The result was that under democracy, military generals who had committed human rights violations during the dictatorship were inoculated from prosecution. Furthermore, the military and their allies continued to enjoy economic privileges, such as retaining ownership of key industries.

Bolivia's 1967 constitution was similarly intended to safeguard the interests of incumbent authoritarian elites. Colonel René Barrientos spearheaded a coup against a civilian government in 1964, and three years later, under the aegis of a new constitution, he dismantled the mine workers' union, suppressed strikes, exiled union leaders, and granted private investors preferential treatment. Although key political elites allied to Barrientos were persecuted under short-lived radical leftist military rule after Barrientos died, the 1967 constitution served Barrientos's economic allies well in the lead-up to Bolivia's transitions to democracy in 1979 and 1981 and beyond. Indeed, major business associations such as the powerful Bolivian Confederation of Private Business were key players in calling for – and then benefitting from – Bolivia's ultimate transition to democracy (Albertus and Gay 2017).

Or consider Spain. Adolfo Suárez, who became Spain's first democratically elected prime minister in 1976, was a holdover from the Francisco Franco dictatorship and was the key player in the transition process. He orchestrated democratization on the back of a constitution he enshrined with the help of several of Franco's allies. Provisions that included proportional representation (PR), federalism, bicameralism, and the return of the monarchy helped create a political landscape that subsequently favored the economic interests of oligarchs connected to the Franco regime. Unsurprisingly, Spanish asset and income inequality have remained just as high as they were under dictatorship.

These facts are hard to countenance if we assume, as much of the literature does, that social actors have strong preferences over living under dictatorship or democracy. Much of the recent literature assumes that economic elites necessarily prefer dictatorship, since dictators will act as perfect agents of elites and democrats will faithfully represent the desire of the poor majority to soak the rich (Acemoglu and Robinson 2006; Boix 2003). This is because different regime types are seen as the solution to class struggle: the rich prefer dictatorship and get dictatorship when they are strong, and the poor prefer democracy and obtain it either when they pose a revolutionary threat or when the rich have nothing to lose by conceding it.

At first glance, this account seems to square well with several important facts. Dictatorship has been far more common than democracy in most countries across most of recorded history, and a small minority appears to have been the beneficiary of those arrangements. Indeed, many of the world's countries were dictatorships for decades or even centuries before they democratized, and half of the world's countries remain authoritarian. In many of these places, dictators have created circumstances in which they can reasonably expect to either remain in office for the long haul or step down and hand power over to a successor under autocracy, with their heads on their necks. Consider North Korea under the Kim family, Cuba under the Castros, the monarchies of the Middle East and North Africa, Communist China, and until recently, the single-party dictatorship in Mexico that finally relinquished power in 2000 after seventy-one years of rule. Furthermore, these authoritarian regimes have reliably delivered favorable treatment to economic elites, largely protecting their assets and income flows.

However, the notion that the rich will prefer dictatorship and the poor will prefer democracy is a strong – and not always justifiable – assumption. Dictatorship is potentially fraught with peril for both political elites, who can be killed, jailed, or exiled, and economic elites, who can be expropriated or destroyed.

First, take the position of economic elites. Autocrats sometimes have strong incentives to expropriate and harass segments of the economic elite who do not have recourse to reliable institutions to protect their property rights, even if they occupy the commanding heights of the economy. These rights might include keeping their vast landholdings intact, protectionism, or other rent-generation schemes that involve barriers to entry or securing lucrative government contracts. Because dictators can at times pose potent threats to these segments of the economic elite, if not destroy them entirely, at least a faction of the economic elite might prefer democracy to autocratic rule under the right circumstances.

While economic elites are not always sitting cozy within a dictatorship and can be thrown under the bus by political elites, the latter can also be threatened under autocracy. Indeed, the median tenure of dictators in the post–World War II era is less than two years, and the fate of outgoing dictators is not a particularly desirable one: they tend to be imprisoned, shot, or exiled after a turnover within authoritarian spells.

There are consequently times and places when, just like certain segments of the economic elites, the political elite would rather have democracy if they can protect themselves from criminal prosecution after democratization. Across the board, outgoing dictators also seek to protect their personal fortunes and their families (e.g., via immunity clauses). If the dictator hails from the military, this may be ensured through military autonomy or the creation of a parallel judicial branch for military affairs. If the dictator exits as the head of a powerful political party, he will seek to avoid the party being banned and might even run for political office under democracy.

Democratization is therefore frequently about allaying the fears of political elites and their economic allies. Former authoritarian elites are often quite successful at creating both constitutional and informal roadblocks under democracy, which make democratic institutions more appealing to them and far less effective as tools for the median voter to realize his or her interests. Instead of an economic model that would benefit the majority, outgoing elites can impose crony capitalism and curtail redistribution and social insurance. Elites will therefore spearhead democratization if they can secure a credible commitment to their rights and interests after the transition.

This is consistent with recent work by Haggard and Kaufman (2016). Focusing attention on democracy during and after the so-called Third Wave, they challenge the notion that democratization typically revolves around distributive conflict among classes.[8] These authors argue that many democratic transitions occur from above. Although some involve international actors that impose democracy, most are determined by domestic political factors and tend to center on elite splits and bargains. Haggard and Kaufman identify three main types of transitions from above: (1) elite displacement transitions, in which domestic rivals to incumbent elites push for regime liberalization; (2) preemptive transitions, in which incumbents themselves initiate a transition; and (3) institutional transitions, in which incumbents gradually introduce incremental changes that culminate in democratic transition. What these cases tend to have in common is that they reflect "perceived opportunities" of democratization for elites, typically due to advantages they hold over the opposition such that they can expect favorable political outcomes under democracy (159).

What, then, motivates autocratic elites to sometimes seek to exit dictatorship entirely, ushering in free and fair elections and an ostensibly uncertain future? We argue in this book that the autocratic arrangement that favors political and economic elites can become unviable when a group of outsider economic elites become a sufficiently strong threat. The incumbent political elites and their economic allies might fear that this group will subsequently become stronger in relation to them. This fear is warranted because a rising, nascent economic elite could be emboldened to use their growing de facto power to displace current political elites and their long-established economic allies, in turn constructing a new political economy that favors themselves over those who benefited under the old order. Furthermore, with little recourse to block highly unfavorable policies once they lose power, displaced political incumbents and their economic allies can be viciously attacked – and even destroyed.

---

[8] Even in cases where it does, they find that the role of inequality in driving political change is minimal. In the distributive conflict cases of democratization that these authors identify, mass pressure for regime change stems not from inequality but from the repressiveness of the authoritarian regime, the capacity of the masses for collective action, and poor elite performance, as measured by short-run economic conditions.

The result is that autocratic incumbents and incumbent economic elites might move to exit the dictatorship together. But they will do so on favorable terms, imposing an institutional arrangement on the new democracy that cuts economic outsiders out of the political deal. Therefore, rather than constituting a credible commitment to redistribution, as many in the literature argue (e.g., Acemoglu and Robinson 2006), democracy offers a refuge and credible protection to elites who flee dictatorship when the going gets tough. Even if the position of former authoritarian elites erodes at some point down the line under democracy, they are not likely to be wiped out entirely, as they can lean on the favorable rules they wrote into the transition deal to avert the worst-case scenario.

That democratization is a relatively rare phenomenon historically speaks to the complicated nature of forging transition deals. Democratization does not simply occur when a particular dictator wants a transition, or even when economic elites pull the plug on their support for dictatorship. In addition to the threat posed to incumbent economic and political elites by a rising class of outsider economic elites, political elites and their economic allies *must also coordinate together* to exit the dictatorship on terms that will be broadly favorable and that will endure.

Preexisting focal points, such as a preexisting constitution, a functioning legislature, or established hereditary monarchy, can enable coordination between these two sets of elites. These focal points allow them, as a united front, to forge a beneficial pre-transition deal with opposition forces, or even with the unorganized masses, usually through a formal pact or new constitution. Some examples from recent cases help illustrate this point.

In South Africa, although there was a long-lived authoritarian government that ruled an apartheid regime with an iron fist and seemed stable, it took a host of attacks against the vital interests of both the political and the economic elites to lead them to seek the exits simultaneously when they were still strong enough to choreograph a transition on favorable terms and engineer a political deal through a constitution and related institutional engineering. For political elites, the catalyzing attack was the long-lived insurgency waged by the ANC along with the withdrawal of political support from allies and other international actors. For economic elites, it was the body blow of divestment on the part of international capital that was key to keeping the mines and large agribusinesses producing.

In Myanmar, the military generals at the head of the junta seized the initiative after international opprobrium and sanctions began to bleed the business conglomerates controlled by both the military and important civilian oligarchs. Also from a position of strength, the generals and their business partners were able to coordinate to orchestrate a very gradual and favorable timetable, including staggered elections counterbalanced by appointed senators and other veto points to protect elite interests. With key generals safely lodged in positions of power and privilege, in 2015 free and fair elections gave majority support to the prodemocratic opposition.

Where do the masses fit into this framework? After all, it is the protestors on the streets of Buenos Aires, East Berlin, Warsaw, Manila, and Tunis that galvanized global attention on the eve of their countries' respective democratizations. Are the people not the catalyst of democratic transition? To be sure, the activities of the masses often send a shock to political and economic elites, forcing them to reevaluate their prospects under dictatorship. And in some cases, the masses entirely sweep aside political and economic elites, introducing democracy on their own terms.

The masses, of course, do not always – if ever – act alone. Even in cases of popular revolutions, the masses can be galvanized by outsider economic elites that stand to benefit from undercutting the privileged position of their economic rivals and their political patrons. As in the case of Portugal during the Carnation Revolution, or more recently in Tunisia, outsider economic elites might carry the banner of revolution in tandem with the masses, but they are motivated by narrower ends: the avoidance of an elite-biased transition that permanently places them on the sidelines of the economy. Similarly, in several of the "Color Revolutions" in countries such as Ukraine, Georgia, and Kyrgyzstan in the 2000s, outsider economic elites who were not part of the Communist coalition that governed these countries during the Cold War played a critical role in ousting strongmen. They helped galvanize the masses to overthrow autocratic regimes in mass revolutions and played a critical role in subsequent democratic transitions.

Revolutions that result in popular democracy are surprisingly rare, however. Since the end of World War II, there have been roughly fifty major revolutions that have either toppled autocratic regimes or led to significant political reform in "flawed" democracies. For those revolutions that have occurred under dictatorships, only about a third have resulted in transitions to democracy. Moreover, there has been autocratic backsliding in a host of these cases. Consider Georgia, Ukraine, and Kyrgyzstan, where dictators rose a few years after these countries' respective revolutions. Today, democracy seems to be on the defensive in Hungary and Poland as well.

Why are democratic revolutions so rare if they are putatively in the interests of the people? The answer to this is not as apparent as it seems. The conventional wisdom is that revolutions are rare because it is exceedingly difficult to muster collective action among a sufficient number of citizens under dictatorship. There is little doubt that this is true.

Dictatorships have every interest in forestalling collective action: they hamper freedom of association, monitor citizens' communication, and undermine trust by infiltrating social networks with secret police and informants. In some cases, they physically destroy focal points that are used to coordinate – as witnessed by the tractors that bulldozed the central square in Bahrain during the Arab Spring.

But this is not the only reason revolutions are so rare. Dictatorships not only terrorize their citizens into submission or make it difficult for them to act collectively; they also frequently deliver favorable public policies to blunt their political opposition. One common manifestation of this is rapid economic growth in historically underdeveloped nations. Examples include China, Russia, and historically, Brazil, Mexico, Malaysia, and Indonesia. Indeed, this is the foundation of East Asia's "developmental states": authoritarian regimes that delivered decades of breakneck growth in exchange for political support in countries such as China and Singapore, as well as Taiwan and South Korea before democratization (e.g., Haggard and Kaufman 1995).

This was often on the heels of massive land redistribution that drastically enhanced the well-being and opportunities available to large, historically disadvantaged peasant populations. Indeed, prominent cases of autocratic redistribution of land span the globe. They include Egypt after 1952, Mugabe's expropriations of white landlords in Zimbabwe, and a host of examples from the late 1940s through the 1980s in East and South Asia, including North Vietnam, Pakistan, the Philippines, South Korea, and Taiwan (see Albertus 2015).

Similarly, dictatorships can also deliver targeted benefits to their citizens, including patronage and cognate transfers. This was true under military juntas in Brazil, Argentina, and Uruguay during the 1970s, as well as Mexico under single-party rule before 2000 (see Albertus et al. 2016; Menaldo 2016). The upshot is that average citizens might not be the unequivocal backers of democracy, especially when their economic interests have been well served under dictatorship.

To be sure, and despite intentions to the contrary, there are times in which outgoing political incumbents and their economic allies are not able to get their elite-biased transition deals to stick under democracy. While arranged democratic deals that favor political and economic elites can potentially come undone in several ways, it is economic elites not allied with former authoritarian political elites that sow the seeds of the initial deal's undoing. These actors were either on the sidelines of the initial transition deal as outsiders or did not yet exist.

First, weaker economic actors that were excluded from the transition deal might subsequently become stronger in relation to the economic elites that helped craft the transition. In an effort to peel away rules and institutions that favor their economic competitors tied to the former regime, this rising group of economic actors might partner with the masses to rewrite the social contract. Second, secular shifts within the economy can give rise to a new set of powerful economic actors who were not players in the initial democratic deal. As with the first scenario, these new actors have incentives to rewrite the social contract so that their economic rivals do not have the upper hand.

This insight is consistent with Ansell and Samuels (2014). In their "contractarian" view of democracy, a nascent class of merchants who are distinct and separate from landholding aristocrats spearheads political liberalization. They do so in order to protect their property rights from the narrow incumbent ruling elite. In cases such as nineteenth-century England, the Industrial Revolution birthed a new group of urban-based wealth holders who pushed for limits to arbitrary aristocratic rule as a way to protect against threats to their economic interests. It is by distributing political power more evenly that the rising bourgeoisie can consolidate a new economic order. Crafting a new social contract that empowers the middle class and the masses allows the new bourgeoisie to enshrine a modern political economy based on impersonal property rights and contracts.

The data and case studies we introduce in this book allow us to generate several original empirical findings that support the theoretical framework we outlined above. First, we demonstrate how pervasive the phenomenon of elite-biased democratization has been across time and place. Second, we outline the diverse range of institutional and legal mechanisms that authoritarian elites use to protect their political and economic interests after democratic transition. Third, we document the causes of democratic transitions, both to elite-biased democracy and to popular democracy, and demonstrate that authoritarian regimes in which political incumbents and their economic allies can coordinate to exit the regime on favorable circumstances often usher in elite-biased democracy. Fourth, we highlight the differential consequences of these transitions to show that elite-biased democracies are far less inclusive, pluralistic, and egalitarian than their popular counterparts. Fifth, we document and explain the reasons behind the annulments and amendments of long-standing elite-biased constitutions inherited by democracies and show that it is typically rising economic elites that opportunistically spearhead genuine reforms that set their country on a new, more egalitarian political and economic course.

ROADMAP FOR THE BOOK

Chapter 2 provides an elite-centric framework to explain both the causes and the consequences of democracies that are flawed by design. We outline why both economic and political elites under authoritarianism at times prefer to transition to democracy over clinging to the status quo. We then detail the circumstances under which they can effectively exit dictatorship together and bring about a democracy that serves their ends. Chapter 2 also outlines under what conditions non-elite-biased democracies – those with popular institutions that benefit the majority of the population – are born and endure. Finally, this chapter addresses how, when, and why elite-designed democracies can shed their authoritarian baggage and become more responsive to the majority of citizens.

Chapter 3 provides a broad descriptive overview of democracies that are rigged by elites under dictatorship. It covers a long historical period – from 1800 to 2006 – and spans the entire globe. We illustrate this phenomenon using constitutions inherited by democracies from previous autocratic regimes, which serve as our main measure of elite manipulation throughout the book. We show how pervasive this phenomenon has been across time and place, exploring the timing of authoritarian constitution making as well as these constitutions' institutional and legal details.

Chapter 4 tests many of our theory's empirical implications. We empirically model the democratic transition process by unpacking democratizations into two distinct types: those that are elite biased, as measured by inheriting a constitution from their autocratic predecessor, and those that are more popular, as measured by freely and fairly elected leaders writing their own democratic constitutions. We find that high levels of state capacity and the presence of a legislature under autocracy are more likely to culminate in transitions to elite-biased democracy. We also show that the interaction of these structural factors and precipitating factors, such as natural disasters, revolutions, and economic crises, is crucial for predicting why some regimes transition to elite-biased democracy versus popular democracy. These factors also help explain the timing of those transitions.

Chapter 4 also documents the scope conditions under which democratization induces greater representation, pluralism, inclusiveness, redistribution, and justice. There is an association between democracy and more egalitarian political and economic outcomes, but only if authoritarian elites are unable to impose a constitution on the new democracy before exiting power. This finding holds across a host of measures of democratic governance and fiscal, monetary, and material outcomes. By contrast, democracies that inherit authoritarian constitutions are much more similar to their authoritarian counterparts across these outcomes – and far from the median voter's ideal point. We also find that outgoing dictators who are able to impose a holdover constitution during democratization and beyond are less likely to face severe punishment upon relinquishing rule. These dictators also live longer.

In Chapters 5, we explore patterns of change in which there have been major political reforms or even the annulments of long-standing elite-biased constitutions. We demonstrate that elite-biased constitutions are more likely to be overturned once the old guard from the former authoritarian regime is dead and buried. Similar to the ideas expressed in Chapter 4, while this paves the way for potential change, precipitating factors such as dramatic slowdowns in economic growth and major shifts in trade openness tilt the balance of power among major social actors and catalyze coordination among outsider economic elites and the masses to push for political change. We also demonstrate that once an elite-biased democracy sheds its authoritarian baggage by annulling or amending the constitution it inherited from the previous regime, policy making becomes more inclusive and pluralistic and economic outcomes more egalitarian.

Chapter 6 looks at Sweden's democratization to show that our theory is not relegated to the most recent democratizations in the developing world.

We reevaluate conventional wisdom about this celebrated case of democratic government. It has been widely proffered that mass enfranchisement at the turn of the twentieth century (1) was a reaction to threats to national security and was not influenced by the concerns of oligarchs to protect their rights and interests and (2) immediately ushered in an egalitarian regime rooted in social democracy.

We instead show that political elites granted democracy from above. While they believed that conscription would be more palatable if it was accompanied by political rights, these rights were effectively muzzled by constitutional engineering. The primary instruments used by the elites to control the transition process were restrictions on the franchise, an indirectly elected upper chamber, and proportional representation that allowed conservative parties to survive despite the fact that their base of support had become a minority portion of the overall electorate. Elite biases were strongest in the first decade after Sweden's democratic transition; they eroded substantially around 1921 and in the early 1930s. This ushered in centralized wage bargaining, a muscular social insurance regime, and the hegemony of the Social Democrats. But the last major vestige of elite bias – an indirectly elected upper chamber – was only eliminated in 1970. Only then did Sweden become exceptionally egalitarian; before that point, its distributional outcomes were much closer to those of Germany or France than those of Denmark.

Chapter 7 explores the case of Chile, which shows the power of constitutional design in allowing former regime elites and their economic allies to protect their interests and also helps illustrate the timing of when institutional legacies from a former authoritarian regime are most likely to erode. In 1973, General Augusto Pinochet displaced a popular democracy, presided over by President Salvador Allende, that was quite egalitarian and centered on import substitution industrialization. Pinochet and other military generals then imposed a constitution in 1980 and began empowering their economic allies by adopting policies that ushered in a self-styled system of export-oriented crony capitalism. This elevated agricultural interests, the mining sector, and a nascent financial sector to the pinnacle of the Chilean economy. After almost two decades of repressive military rule, in 1990 Chile experienced a democratic transition that was shepherded by General Pinochet's 1980 constitution.

This document provided a host of safeguards for the military and key authoritarian elites, including the appointment of autocratic elites as senators for life, endowing the military with the ability to choose the head of armed forces and to retain considerable autonomy over its affairs, and the shielding of General Pinochet and other generals from prosecution for the crimes they committed under autocracy. It also included the banning of parties on the extreme left and a tailor-made binomial electoral system that overrepresented conservative parties and favored the creation of umbrella coalitions that incentivized the left to partner with centrist political parties. The constitution also prescribed supermajority thresholds in both chambers as requirements to change the constitution, cementing the conservative status quo. These elite-biased measures were eroded for the first time in 2005, when Pinochet was on his deathbed. Now that Pinochet and several of his generals have died, there is talk of replacing the 1980 constitution entirely and starting fresh.

Chapter 8 theorizes and examines legacies from colonial rule or foreign occupying powers. Whereas Chapters 3 and 4 treat countries that transition to democracy with constitutions penned under dictatorship as elite-biased democracies and other democracies as popular democracies, the category of popular democracy contains two quite different sets of countries: those that operate with constitutions that they write themselves upon transition and those that are democratic from their inception. Many countries that win independence as democracies, however, remain subject to the influences or dictates of their former colonial occupier in ways that mimic what happens under elite-biased democracy.

Chapter 8 unpacks the legacies imposed by occupiers. It not only classifies the countries that have been subject to such legacies but also presents a set of common pathologies that many newly independent democracies inherit from their former colonial occupiers. This chapter draws a parallel between these pathologies and the forms of elite bias detailed in earlier chapters. It then discusses the pathologies of two prominent democracies (Canada and the Philippines) that arose from colonial occupation as well as one democracy (Ukraine) that was cleaved off of a geographically larger authoritarian predecessor state (the Soviet Union). Chapter 8 therefore adds greater nuance – and generalizability – to the concept of elite-biased democracy developed earlier in the book.

Chapter 9 briefly summarizes the book and then moves on to drawing out additional implications implied by our theory. First, we discuss democratic breakdown from the perspective of our theoretical framework, inspecting the relevant empirical patterns and attempting to shine light on the causes of these patterns. We also discuss shifts from popular democracy to elite-biased democracy: how a democracy that is created from below, or an elite-biased democracy that is subsequently reformed, can nonetheless succumb to capture by economic elites. Finally, we draw lessons from our theoretical framework for democratic reformers. We argue that instead of focusing on drawn-out efforts to strengthen civil society and undercut illiberal elements in democracies around the world, reformists and activists would be better served by focusing on critical periods when large-scale change is possible. These moments tend to cluster on generational transitions during which the old political guard that introduced elite biases through democratization dramatically weakens or dies off. During these moments, some societies have been able to upend their authoritarian legacies and amend the institutions under which they live to seek an improved form of government – one that is actually of, by, and for the people.

2

Elites and the Causes and Consequences of Democracy

This chapter introduces a theory about the causes and consequences of political regimes. Our framework addresses several long-standing questions about the causes of democracy. Who spearheads a democratic transition, why do they do so, and how do they do it? Why do some autocracies endure while others transition to a democracy gamed by elites? Why do some democracies start out more popular, or become so over time?

Our framework also addresses major issues associated with the consequences of democracy. Why do many democracies operate under arcane, sometimes labyrinthine, elite-biased institutions? Why are some democracies more redistributive than others? Why do some democracies shed their founding constitutions while others keep them? Finally, why do some democracies transition back to dictatorships?

Like most theories of political regimes, ours distinguishes between dictatorships and democracies. The fundamental difference between these regimes is how leaders are selected and who has a say over this selection. In short, for a regime to be considered democratic, free and fair elections must determine legislative and executive office holders, losers must hand over power, and suffrage must be broadly distributed.

While there is nothing controversial about abiding by this minimalist definition of democracy, we make important distinctions within the two main regime types. Many observers have noted the wide variation in institutional forms and outcomes in both democracies and dictatorships. Few, however, have drawn clear-cut analytical lines in the sand within these regime categories.[1]

---

[1] Prior scholarship, however, does problematize a simple dichotomous regime distinction. For instance, both Boix (2003) and Acemoglu and Robinson (2006) sometimes relax the assumption that there are only two types of regimes and, harkening back to Aristotle, entertain the possibility that there can be republics governed by the aristocracy. Other authors make the case that there are hybrid regimes, or anocracies, that mix attributes of democracy and dictatorship (e.g.,

We do precisely this, and we do so in a novel way that helps to explain a host of important outcomes in a parsimonious fashion. Dictatorships come in two varieties: (1) those that are stable and consolidated, consistently funneling rents to political and economic elites and using those rents as a reliable source of revenues, and (2) those that are volatile, in which elite infighting and turnover prevails and the state cycles through different political economy models and suffers from unreliable revenues.[2] Democracies also come in two types: (1) those gamed by elites, both political and economic, on the eve of democratic transition, and (2) those that are popular because the masses are able to write the rules of the game, usually with the help of a select group of outsider economic elites. Each of these arrangements is centered on different political arrangements that create distinct winners and losers.

In a consolidated dictatorship, a powerful faction of economic elites is united with the incumbent authoritarian political elite against the masses, and another, distinct set of outsider economic elites remain on the sidelines. Political elites create a stable distributional arrangement in which they partner with a subset of economic elites to create an economy that serves their interests and engenders political quiescence. They extract revenues from those privileged elites in exchange for rents. This is a quid pro quo in which favorable policies, such as barriers to entry that produce rents, are exchanged for political support and revenues that can finance the state. Incumbent political elites also typically extract revenues from other economic groups and the masses, who get little, if anything, in return. This reflects a harsh reality: outsider economic elites are more vulnerable than those that ally with the regime. Of course, while political elites might attempt to tax these outsiders or even expropriate them, they can also ignore them altogether.

In a volatile dictatorship, regime insiders and a faction of economic elites collude with a dictator to cut out politically expendable segments of the economic elite, and there is turnover within the political economy. Therefore, there is no stable distributional arrangement in which incumbent political elites are seamlessly extracting revenues from a stable group of economic incumbents in exchange for a share of the latter's rents to finance the government. Instead, political elites' economic partnerships are contested, with different factions of economic elites vying for a privileged position and specific factions rising into and falling out of power. By extension, political instability is typically the norm; economic elite factions that are left on the sidelines or threatened by political incumbents have incentives to attempt coups, assassinate their enemies, and foment rebellion in an effort to unseat those incumbents. The nature

Levitsky and Way 2010). And the widely used and referenced Polity database categorizes and codes several dimensions and gradations of democracy.
[2] Other authors have similarly distinguished between dictatorships that are established versus contested (e.g., Svolik 2012).

of the economy can change quite drastically as losing sectors are cut out of the deal or destroyed.

Now consider a popular democracy in which the median voter is faithfully represented by elected officials. Under this arrangement, political elites from the former authoritarian regime along with their former incumbent economic elite allies are cut out of the deal. The regime's institutions will favor inclusivity and wide participation, competition, and pluralism. It will therefore not overrepresent any one narrow group, such as moneyed special interests. Not only will the provision of public goods match its demand by the citizenry and economic regulation maximize social welfare, but the degree of progressivity in public policy will be relatively high because the democracy's electoral and representative institutions will approach the preferences of the median voter and the majority. For these reasons, the popular hue of the democracy will be consistent over time, in that it will be eminently hard for any single actor to arrogate the rules of the game to advance his or her own interests.

By contrast, consider a democracy captured by elites. Elite-biased democracy is a regime in which free and fair elections are paired with institutional devices that codify the rights and interests of the economic elites that were favored under the former authoritarian period. These devices are intended to create an economy that suppresses redistribution to the masses and benefits the economic elites from the previous authoritarian regime at the expense of the outsider economic elites. They are also designed to protect the political elites from the former authoritarian period, shielding them from prosecution and revanchism. These tools are explicitly designed by elites under the previous authoritarian regime, or in the intervening transition period, to protect those who were powerful under that regime. Such peculiar political arrangements, though they have authoritarian origins, are fully implemented and enforced under the succeeding democratic regime.

Because these outgoing elites differ from society to society and time period to time period, the devices they engineer to vouchsafe their rights, interests, and security are heterogeneous. Some tools with a historic pedigree include unelected or indirectly elected upper chambers that overrepresent moneyed interests and strong forms of federalism. They also include restrictions on the franchise. More recent examples include biased electoral rules, de facto restrictions on the franchise such as voter ID laws, and malapportionment. More extreme examples are cases in which elements of the former autocratic regime win veto points over select policy domains, gain permanent appointments in the upper chamber or other political bodies, and erect parallel judicial organs that exempt them from prosecution under mainstream prevailing law. Requiring supermajorities to reform institutions ensures that the median voter and unorganized business interests cannot simply rewrite the social contract in a way that imposes their preferences on the policy agenda.

Political regimes can of course shift between these types. Volatile dictatorships can become consolidated. Elite-biased democracies inherited by newly elected governments from outgoing authoritarian elites can be reformed to be more inclusive and responsive to the demands of the majority. Indeed, the main contribution of our theory is to explain the causes and consequences of these shifts.

This chapter, therefore, generates a series of powerful new insights into political regime dynamics. Perhaps the most important is that while a democracy might be responsive to popular interests, there is nothing inevitable about the relationship between democracy and the welfare of the majority of citizens. It is possible for authoritarian political elites and their economic allies to negotiate a democratic transition that can not only insulate them from punishment but allow them to thrive economically. Democracy is therefore often a continuation of the same political dynamic that characterizes the previous authoritarian period. The same actors who mattered under autocracy and their concerns endure beyond dictatorship.

BASIC ASSUMPTIONS

In this chapter, readers might find our distinctions simplistic and not reflective of the real world. In some important ways, this is true. As with any theory, the conceptual terms are ideal types. For the purposes of tendering explanations and predictions that can travel across widely different places and times, we must sacrifice some real-world complexity for generalizable terms and ideal-type distinctions. Along the way, we will inevitably be wrong, or at least incomplete, in some instances. The goal, however, is to be correct much more often in a way that illuminates key dynamics that other scholars have not previously recognized.

Our guiding assumptions are as follows. Most fundamentally, politics is an elite-driven affair, and if the masses become critical participants, it is typically because they are responding to cues from other actors who can help them solve their collective action problems. These other actors (typically outsider economic elites) are usually endowed with political or economic power that provide leadership or focal points that aid political coordination.

Both economic and political elites seek first and foremost to protect their rights and interests. They will therefore support the regime most likely to deliver their favored policies. The key actors in our theory, therefore, do not have a preference for dictatorship or democracy per se. As one regime type becomes more threatening, they strategically push for another type and, if conditions allow, can exit in a way that preserves what was best about the previous one.[3]

---

[3] In other words, we do not assume that political and economic elites shift from risk loving under dictatorship to risk averse as they seek out democracy. Indeed, elites who seemingly evidence risk-loving behavior under dictatorship often face grave threats and thus avail the strategies that are best suited to mitigating these threats, which appear to be risky to outside observers because they are often centered on threats, coercion, and violence.

This is a less restrictive set of assumptions than what is used in existing theory (e.g., Acemoglu and Robinson 2006).

We treat the following actors in our theory as unitary in nature: authoritarian political elites, authoritarian economic elites allied with authoritarian political elites, outsider economic elites not allied with authoritarian political elites, and the masses. To be sure, these are not the only social groups that impact political regimes and regime change. Furthermore, these groups can sometimes set against themselves from within, riven by factions in a way that forestalls their ability to act in an effective and unified manner. We do not deny these political realities. But to model each and every eventuality would be far too complex and not especially helpful. Simply splitting economic elites by their relationship with political elites under dictatorship is already a departure – and a step toward greater nuance – than existing theory admits.

We also assume that political and economic elites do not have to be attorneys, judges, or advocates to effectively design and enact a constitution, related institutions, and public policies that advance their interests. They are perfectly capable of conducting these activities under both democracy and dictatorship – and, if need be, can hire professionals to do their bidding. We also assume that if they convoke a constitutional convention they can typically guide, if not control, this process in an attempt to yield their desired outcomes.

We also do not dismiss the possibility that unforeseen circumstances or mistakes can occur. Consider the constitution-making process. A revolution could emerge during a choreographed transition from above that undermines outgoing authoritarian elites' intentions and machinations. Indeed, in a later section, we incorporate this contingency into our framework. More prosaically, constitutional engineers can miscalculate. The representatives selected to participate in a constitutional assembly might find a way to introduce and win support for a document that strays from the elites' original intent. Elites might also misfire in their ability to control the timing of the elections that mark their exit from power and even be surprised by the results of the democracy's founding election. We revisit two examples of how this occurred – in South Africa and Egypt – in the conclusion to this book.

These outcomes can and do occur, as with any policy intervention, but rarely so. Constitutional engineers are successful in their designs much more often than not. Consequently, when legal and political changes happen under democracy after the transition, they overwhelmingly occur under a new process, and one that is inherently guided by the institutions that democratic actors are made to live under. Politicians under democracy are therefore limited in their ability to escape the box they have been put in. They cannot unilaterally rewrite the rules of the game.

By extension, we assume that formal institutions matter enough for their designers to invest time and energy in manipulating them, and subsequently to be confident to exit dictatorship and live under them. We do not discount the importance of informal institutions such as political culture, patronage, religious practices, or ideas that are in vogue internationally. Informal institutions or ideas such as these can work in tandem with formal institutions or bolster them; however, we do not believe that authoritarian elites invest in designing formal institutions to guide democracy that have no correspondence with how they hope democracy will function. The vast variation in institutions within democracies, and even dictatorships, is not arbitrary or a reflection of fashionable trends. They are not simply diffused between borders or created by wise and enlightened founding figures to promote the general good.

Finally, we agree with the emerging consensus in political economy about the relationship between political institutions and economic outcomes. An economy is more often than not the reflection of political strategies and exigencies (Acemoglu, Johnson, and Robinson 2005). So if given the possibility, powerful economic actors will design both the political and the economic institutions that are most convenient to them. This can impact the progressivity of the fiscal and public spending system, as well as its geographic incidence; the nature of monetary and trade policy; competition policy; and government regulation in general. The bottom line is that politicians are not looking to maximize social welfare, at least not explicitly; they are looking to hang on to power and implement a distributional arrangement that benefits them, even if it comes at the expense of overall development or a more egalitarian distribution of benefits.

With these assumptions in hand, we now move to a discussion of the key actors that drive the formation and disintegration of regimes.

KEY ACTORS IN THE THEORY

Different political deals create distinct winners and losers. Economic and political elites try to bargain for institutions that can safeguard their rights and interests. These actors are therefore the key players in forging the political deals and designing the institutions and outcomes we will explain.

Authoritarian political elites and their economic elite partners are the key actors in shifts between types of dictatorship and, typically, shifts from dictatorship to democracy as well. They often continue to operate in the background under democracy after a transition from dictatorship, securing a political role and continuing to win favorable economic policies.

Among authoritarian elites, we make several distinctions. First, we distinguish between political elites and economic elites. Second, among the economic elite, we distinguish between those who partner with the incumbent political elite and those who remain on the sidelines as outsiders.[4]

Of course, political elites under democracy, such as elected representatives and party leaders, are hardly unimportant figures. While they serve at the behest of voters, they are elected through the prism of existing electoral and

---

[4] These distinctions build on and further develop the concept of elite splits in our earlier work (e.g., Albertus 2015; Albertus and Menaldo 2012a; Menaldo 2016).

other institutions. In the event that voters under democracy are able to entirely upend authoritarian legacies, democratically elected political elites will effectively act as agents of the masses. However, political institutions under democracy do not necessarily reflect the electoral voice or interests of the majority. In other words, institutions that are biased in favor of elites can give rise to elected officials and bureaucrats who are more interested in representing the interests of former authoritarian elites than those of the masses.

Authoritarian Political Elites

Among authoritarian political elites, we relegate attention to the dictator and the dictator's inner circle, the individuals who hold power and govern the country. Depending on the place and time, this might mean a military junta and top military brass, party apparatchiks, an extended family linked to the dictator, or even a roundtable of mullahs.

Incumbent political elites under dictatorship are not merely the puppets or predators that scholars usually assume them to be. Political elites are instead autonomous agents; they have their own interests and political agendas (Albertus 2015; Albertus and Menaldo 2012a; Menaldo 2016). They sometimes ally with a set of economic elites and they sometimes betray them in favor of a new set. Sometimes, they partner with incumbent economic elites to exit a dictatorship on favorable terms. Other times, they are themselves displaced by outsider economic elites in a palace coup under dictatorship. They therefore have to be leery of economic elites, even though they team up with them – or at least some segment of them – when it is in their interest to do so.

Though political elites have their own objectives, they can differ across place and time and among individuals. Sometimes, political elites simply want a cut of the rents that can be generated through economic policy. Other times, especially if they have a military background, they want to protect their organizational interests or the nation's interests. Still others have sincere ideological agendas.

What each of these political elites share in common, however, is that more often than not, the way to implement their objectives is to directly or indirectly hold power. When political elites can marshal a tight grip on power under dictatorship, they can achieve their objectives through force or the implicit threat of force.

Yet dictatorship also carries risks; political elites can be attacked by rivals and even displaced. Consequently, in some circumstances they will prefer to influence politics indirectly by designing favorable institutions or lurking behind the scenes – either acting as puppet masters of a de jure ruler or exercising soft veto power under democracy. Political elites might opt for either dictatorship or democracy when indirectly influencing politics, depending on the context. When they opt for democracy, this necessitates designing and enforcing the political institutions and selection mechanisms that elevate individuals into political office.

Incumbent Economic Elites

The second set of key actors in our theory is incumbent economic elites. These are the manufacturers, large landowners, firm managers, and other private actors whose participation in economic activity generates rents and tax revenues that can be shared with incumbent political elites. Incumbent economic elites are rarely monolithic representatives of the upper class writ large; more often than not, they are a coalition of distinct sectors of the economy.[5]

While the incumbent economic elites have many shared interests with the incumbent political elite, they are a distinct group that should not be collapsed into the same category. Both dictatorships and democracies have a group of incumbent economic elites and – as we shall make clear in the sections to come – they both also have a group of outsider economic elites. Not only are incumbent economic elites private actors who make goods and services and run enterprises rather than government across both regime types, but they also do not automatically and effectively coordinate with political elites. This autonomy is particularly salient vis-à-vis the ability to exit a dictatorship on favorable terms, an issue we will take up again later in the chapter.

Incumbent economic elites have their own objectives, and these can differ somewhat across place and time and between individuals, but they typically boil down to favorable policies that protect their assets and income flows and translate into additional rents. These policies differ according to what sector the incumbent economic elites operate in. They can come in the form of barriers to entry in the domestic nontradables sector, protectionist policies that defend them against cheaper imports, export subsidies and favorable exchange rates if they generate profits by selling agricultural commodities abroad, or access to cheap and ample credit. These rents are, in short, created through regulations that generate winners and losers through distortions and the manipulation of markets. The price of these favorable policies is sharing a cut of the rents with their political benefactors and, similarly, producing revenues that can be taxed to finance government operations.

Although incumbent economic elites are autonomous agents with their own interests and political agendas, they partner with political elites because they require favorable institutions and policies to thrive. They sometimes ally with political elites to attack or even eliminate outsider economic elites who are left to fend for themselves. Other times, they partner with political elites to exit a dictatorship on favorable terms. Consequently, they do not prefer one regime

---

[5] For a detailed discussion of large landowners as an elite group and their relation to other economic elites such as industrialists, see Albertus (2015, chs. 2–3). For a discussion of industrialists as an elite group, see Menaldo (2016, ch. 3).

type over the other as such; they opt for whatever form of government secures them favorable policies, be it a dictatorship or a democracy.

Outsider Economic Elites

Outsider economic elites are similar to incumbent political elites in certain ways. They can also be manufacturers, large landowners, firm managers, and other private actors whose participation in economic activity generates tax revenues. The key distinction vis-à-vis incumbent economic elites is that they do not depend on the political elites for their market share and rents – at least not in a direct sense. Their incomes and profits are not the by-products of rigged markets.

Outsider economic elites actors can constitute a distinct source of power and influence. This leaves two options for the political incumbents. First, they can leave outsider economic elites alone. Alternatively, they can try to expropriate outsider economic elites, fearing that their power will only grow stronger into the future. This reaction can be goaded by incumbent economic elites who might fear losing favorable property rights and regulations if their political partners abandon them in favor of partnering with outsider economic elites. Outsider economic elites under dictatorship, therefore, have an uneasy and possibly volatile relationship with both incumbent political elites and incumbent economic elites.

Where do outsider economic elites come from? They are the by-products of benign neglect or structural economic change. This is because there are often large portions of the economy that remain unregulated and untaxed. This leaves different regions or sectors free to potentially develop linkages within the domestic economy or with foreign countries and to specialize in providing capital, inputs, or even finished products to their economic partners.

Indeed, outsider economic elites can be very productive and generate large stocks of savings and outputs, which allow them to be big players in the capital markets. Alternatively, they can function as intermediaries that channel capital and facilitate trading and other transactions among disparate groups in society. Their ability to provide credit and liquidity, whether directly or indirectly, can be a source of strength and independence, needed by the political elites and incumbent economic elites to finance some of their operations. An important historical example of this phenomenon is the Chinese minority that formed the backbone of the private financial system in countries such as Malaysia, Indonesia, and the Philippines.

Another catalyst of outsider economic elites is economic change. Urbanization and industrialization can create a new capitalist class (Ansell and Samuels 2014). This educated and landless class can use human capital and access to physical capital to create new stocks of wealth and opportunities to capture market share in new products and services. They can therefore generate new profits.[6]

---

[6] Historically, these outsider elites have emerged due to technological or secular changes. New ideas and inventions can reach commercial value suddenly and unexpectedly due to a technological

There are several possible reasons for the benign neglect that helps nurture outsider economic elites. First, rent seeking and taxation require costly up-front investments and infrastructural power. Political elites in many countries have limited resources, requiring them to pick and choose where they spend their valuable political and coercive capital. Second, political incumbents can benefit from the economic activity generated by outsider economic elites, but that activity might be disrupted or entirely squelched if the former attempt to tax or regulate it. Furthermore, in such cases, political elites might find it impossible or very costly to replace or replicate these activities themselves because they lack the knowledge, competence, or capital necessary to do so.

Like incumbent economic elites, outsider economic elites are not passive bystanders. But unlike incumbent economic elites, they are in a much more precarious position. There are often good strategic and political reasons for dictators to predate on them. This is because dictators require the assistance of incumbent economic elites to hold power and govern the country. The latter provide a steady source of revenues and rents, and if they have a conflict of interest with the outsider economic elites, then the incumbent political elites invariably choose to support their partners. This is not to say that outsider economic elites will not also be forced to provide revenues and rents to political elites. Indeed, when they can be pinned down, they can be forced to pay higher revenues than incumbent economic elites. Regardless, they are able to remain autonomous and solvent despite being taxed, even if they remain in a more precarious position than their incumbent counterparts.

The distinction between incumbent and outsider economic elites is important for several reasons. First, they pose unique threats to each other. On the one hand, incumbent economic elites pose a lethal threat to outsider economic elites because they can lean on their political allies to attack them. On the other hand, incumbent economic elites have to be leery of outsider economic elites because outsider economic elites have a separate and autonomous source of economic power. The latter can marshal this power to strike against the alliance of incumbent political elites and incumbent economic elites.[7] Or, as we will explore in the sections that follow, incumbent political and economic elites can be left in the lurch after a transition to popular democracy orchestrated by outsider economic elites and the masses. The bottom line is that incumbent economic elites need secure property rights and regulation-induced rates of

---

breakthrough or a change in relative prices. The invention of a manufacturing process that reduces the need for labor, for instance, could give nascent industries a competitive edge over incumbent economic elites that are allied with unionized wage laborers. Possible examples from history include looms, refrigeration, and electrification.

[7] Incumbent economic elites can also turn against political elites if the latter substantially contravene their interests or pose a threat of future predation. In this case, incumbent economic elites would seek a new dictator to act on their behalf. This does not, however, undermine our basic logic and predictions that follow.

return; without favorable policies, they simply cannot compete in the market-place, if they can even survive at all.

Second, what might seem like a predatory dictatorship to some observers might not be an entirely dysfunctional one if the predation is surgical and actually benefits incumbent economic elites. Our view therefore diverges from two canonical, if not competing, treatments of dictatorship in the literature. Incumbent economic elites under dictatorship are not merely the masters of political elites as many scholars assume (e.g., Acemoglu and Robinson 2006; Boix 2003; Marx 1848). Instead, they are partners. This is because incumbent economic elites rely on the political elites for favorable policies and regulations. Moreover, economic elites are not passive victims (e.g., Levi 1989; Wintrobe 1990). Although dictators are sometimes predatory and seek to seize private actors' assets and incomes, they do not and cannot destroy an economy entirely. They always require help from some faction of the economic elites to hold power and govern the country because they require revenues, and more often than not, these revenues are centered on generating and taxing rents.

The Masses

The last important actor is the masses. This group constitutes a majority of the population, and therefore they outnumber the elites. They tend to be generally poorer than the incumbent political elites. Furthermore, they are by definition poorer than incumbent and outsider economic elites. When incumbent economic elites have a privileged position under either dictatorship or elite-biased democracy, the masses tend to suffer from regressive public policies. Conversely, the masses can benefit from a volatile dictatorship in which incumbent economic elites are attacked and their assets redistributed to them. They can also receive favorable public policies under popular democracy, a point we return to later.

As a matter of sheer statistics, the masses are a variegated group that differs on a host of dimensions. Within this group, there are differences not only in assets and income but in their economic roles and interests. They can also be divided by religion, race, ethnicity, or other ascriptive characteristics. Regardless – and crucially – they are geographically dispersed.

The key implication is that the members of this group suffer from a serious collective action problem. They therefore typically depend on mobilization from above. Even if they can solve their collective action problem, there are limits to their ability to follow through and orchestrate long-lasting political change on their own. They might be able to spearhead a revolution by amassing in public squares and organizing popular protests that induce gridlock and even topple incumbents, but they lack the human, social, and physical capital, as well as the organizational capacity, to design constitutions and implement institutions such as political parties, elections, and bureaucracies. At the very least, their diversity along a range of dimensions makes it difficult for them to coordinate on a single focal point or solution to translate their preferences into national political power – that is, unless they have help from outsider economic elites.

OUTCOMES

This section outlines four main political outcomes. Two occur under dictatorship: (1) consolidated dictatorship, in which political elites and their economic allies create a stable arrangement, consistently creating rents and funneling these to themselves, and (2) volatile dictatorship, in which fighting among different elite factions and economic volatility prevail. The other two occur under democracy: (1) elite-biased democracy, which is tilted in favor of former authoritarian elites, and (2) popular democracy, which more faithfully represents the median voter.

The key to understanding the causes and consequences of each of these regime types is identifying how the preferences of authoritarian political elites, incumbent economic elites, outsider economic elites, and the masses are translated into action. This depends on how these actors interact with each other on the political stage. Conflicts among groups can present threats to vital interests or generate fears that interests will be undermined in the future, catalyzing an attempt by the threatened group(s) to push for an alternative political arrangement that they can better control. While this might mean replacing one dictatorship with another, it might also entail strategically transitioning to democracy.

This section is therefore a fundamental building block for the rest of the book: it outlines exactly when, why, and how we should observe democratization. Most importantly, it details why some democracies are biased in structure and content to benefit elites, such as South Africa and Chile, while others are popular democracies that more faithfully represent the interests of the people, such as Sweden. These are the two types of democracy that have existed in the modern world, a point that we will empirically document in the next chapter.

To understand the conditions under which different regime outcomes come about, we identify the preferences of each of the actors outlined in the previous sections over the various outcomes and elucidate these outcomes.

Consolidated Dictatorship

Incumbent authoritarian political elites always prefer a consolidated dictatorship over its alternatives, everything else equal. Their economic elite partners have similar preferences. For outsider economic elites, consolidated dictatorship can also be an acceptable outcome, provided that they are left alone. However, if the vital interests of outsider elites are threatened, they might opt to orchestrate a coup and take over power under a new autocratic order in which they are represented politically. Outsider economic elites might alternatively attempt to bankroll a revolution to usher in a popular democracy in which their interests are represented in exchange for some redistribution. The masses are hardly happy with consolidated dictatorship, but their collective action problem typically – though not always – forestalls their ability to dismantle it via revolution.

Authoritarian political elites and their economic allies prefer consolidated dictatorship above all else because they are able to generate a stable arrangement in which they have a steady flow of revenues and rents available by dominating economic policy. They can control the masses and hold outsider economic elites at bay. This preference is conditioned, however, by the strength of the outsider economic elites and their ability to, for example, finance and organize a revolution instituting a popular democracy.

What position do outsider economic elites take vis-à-vis consolidated dictatorship? As explained previously, these economic elites are beyond the reach of the state, might not interest the state, or might benefit the state if the state treats them with a light touch. At times, however, outsider economic elites face potent threats. They are constantly at risk of being sold down the river because they are not part of the ruling cabal: their property can be expropriated or they might be subject to stringent regulations or onerous taxation.

Outsider economic elites must therefore invest in strategies that protect them from these threats. One option is to exit. Whether with their capital or with their families, these elites can seek out friendlier countries that would be much less likely to harm their core interests. Another option is to cultivate a separate base of political power rooted in their autonomous source of economic power. They could finance and groom an alternative set of political allies under dictatorship that can remain in the wings but potentially take over power if their vital interests are threatened. This usually deters the incumbent political and economic elites from predating on them.

Dictatorship is therefore a very uncertain road for outsider economic elites: while a dictatorship that leaves them untouched can be acceptable, they very much hate an unfriendly one. However, they cannot always arrange a more beneficial outcome under dictatorship in which they replace the incumbent political and economic elites.

The masses are typically pawns under consolidated dictatorship. Although they would prefer a popular democracy, their collective action problem usually prevents them from acting on this desire. Instead, they often enable the political elite and their economic allies to protract autocracy by acquiescing to targeted transfers or other goodies. In other cases, they are simply divided and conquered through fear and intimidation.

Volatile Dictatorship

None of the elites in our framework prefer volatile dictatorship as their first choice, but it can nonetheless occur. Volatile dictatorship occurs when something has changed in the political equilibrium to upset the balance of forces between the incumbents under consolidated dictatorship – political elites and their economic allies – and outsider economic elites.

There are several scenarios in which a dictatorship can become volatile and thus constitute a suboptimal alternative for political elites and their economic allies to consolidated dictatorship or even elite-biased democracy. Incumbent economic elites might have clear rivals and will want the political elites to attempt to undercut or destroy those rivals. In this case, they will push the dictator to destroy those foes – often through expropriation – as a way of signaling exclusive reliance on them.

When will incumbent economic elites have clear foes that they wish to see destroyed? This occurs when outsider economic elites see their star rising, whether due to secular changes in the economy or the changing political opportunities and constraints on the part of political elites. This makes incumbent economic elites nervous.

There are good reasons for this mistrust. A sufficiently strong and emboldened group of outsider economic elites, who themselves do not trust that political incumbents will continue to treat them with a light touch, could seek to displace both incumbent economic elites and their political patrons. And they might succeed, marking a period in which there is cycling among different ruling groups. Outsider economic elites would prefer not to make waves but cannot credibly promise not to challenge the status quo when an underlying shift in the balance of power occurs. Neither can incumbent political elites, who could choose to cozy up to outsider economic elites at the expense of incumbent economic elites. Incumbent economic elites, therefore, can be backed into a corner and push their political elite allies to attack outsider economic elites, both to reduce the power of the latter and to win a credible signal of loyalty from the incumbent political elites.

For outsider economic elites, volatile dictatorship poses both attractive possibilities and risks. If these outsiders supplant incumbent economic elites, ushering in a volatile dictatorship, they can potentially arrogate the fruits of new regulation that they themselves help craft. In other words, these outsiders can become the new insiders and reap the associated benefits. However, as previously outlined, in other circumstances, volatile dictatorship is the byproduct of insecure incumbent economic elites who fear the rise of outsider economic elites and therefore push incumbent political elites to destroy these outsiders. For obvious reasons, this is a nightmare scenario for outsider economic elites.

For the masses, volatile dictatorship can at times deliver more material benefits than even a popular democracy is likely to deliver – for instance, through the repartitioning of the assets of outsider economic elites. A good example is the aftermath of Bolivia's 1952 revolution. Poor peasants and miners swarmed into the streets to topple a consolidated dictatorship, yielding a new, entrenched political party, the Movimiento Nacionalista Revolucionario (MNR; Revolutionary Nationalist Movement), that redistributed massive tracts of land to peasants and nationalized large- and medium-sized mines. In such cases, the masses are not simply defanged or repressed by authoritarianism; they actively support it. Even if volatile dictatorship does not deliver benefits to the masses, outsider economic elites can leverage their dissatisfaction with consolidated dictatorships to enlist their help in toppling incumbent political and economic elites.

Elite-Biased Democracy

The preferences of the primary actors over elite-biased democracy are as follows. Incumbent authoritarian political elites prefer an elite-biased democracy if they can coordinate with incumbent economic elites on orchestrating such an outcome when they are threatened by rising outsider economic elites.[8] Incumbent economic elites are similar: they prefer elite-biased democracy if they can coordinate with political elites and if they are threatened by rising outsider economic elites. For their part, outsider economic elites would prefer to avoid this outcome because it blunts the possibility that they can translate their economic rise into greater political power. At the same time, a volatile dictatorship in which they lose out is worse. Therefore, they prefer either a status quo dictatorship where they are left alone or a popular democracy. The masses, for their part, chafe under elite-biased democracy. While they have greater political freedoms than under dictatorship, those freedoms cannot be effectively translated into improved material outcomes.

Political elites cannot always effectively consolidate their power under dictatorship. In fact, throughout history, there have been a host of risks to sitting dictators. They are subject to assassinations, palace coups, civil insurrections, popular revolts, and betrayals and mutinies of all sorts. Furthermore, the fate of outgoing dictators who are replaced by a succeeding dictator is not desirable: they tend to be imprisoned, shot, or exiled (Goemans et al. 2009).

There are consequently circumstances under which incumbent political elites would rather have democracy, especially if they can protect themselves from criminal prosecution after democratization or even be reelected to political office. Political elites that help steer a transition to an elite-biased democracy can avail a host of tools to realize these outcomes: they can embed immunity clauses in the constitution, underwrite military autonomy or the creation of a parallel judicial branch for military affairs if the military is their staunch ally, make it difficult to ban erstwhile authoritarian political parties, and create favorable electoral rules that enhance the likelihood that they will be elected to political office.

For incumbent economic elites, dictatorship can also prove over time to be less than a guarantee to their rights and interests, which depend on incumbent

---

[8] Rising outsider economic elites can pose a further threat by also helping to catalyze the masses to foment a popular revolution.

political elites exercising power and manipulating the economy to their benefit. The policies that regulate the economy to the benefit of incumbent economic elites might become unsustainable as the economy changes. Barriers to trade and international investment, overvalued exchange rates, large trade and fiscal deficits, and distortions to domestic markets and capital formation might eventually unravel, bankrupting the state and threatening the balance sheets of incumbent economic elites. Similarly, incumbent economic elites might not be able to forestall a challenge from rising outsider economic elites under dictatorship.

There are times, then, when incumbent economic elites fear that they will lose control of the regulations that give them advantages under dictatorship. Most perniciously, they might fear that a different set of political elites bankrolled by outsider economic elites will displace them.[9] It is under these circumstances that they might team up with incumbent political elites and exit the dictatorship.[10] Democracy, ironically, may allow them to better address any structural changes they need to make to the economy together with the former authoritarian political incumbents. This can solidify their advantages and dictate to the outsider economic elites how the new game will be played – namely, in a way that mitigates the existential threat that the latter poses to them.

Incumbent economic elites' preference for elite-biased democracy is stronger if they can reliably protect their property rights and economic interests from expropriation and unfriendly regulation after democratization. They will therefore seek political overrepresentation, pursue campaign finance laws that allow them to bankroll compliant candidates, target seats on the central bank, and pursue control over import-export agencies and dominance over bureaucratic organs that implement barriers to entry and raise their rate of return. Therefore, provided that incumbent economic elites can coordinate with incumbent political elites to exit the dictatorship on favorable terms when they face threats from outsider economic elites or the masses, they will do so.

When incumbent political elites and their economic allies exit the dictatorship on favorable terms, this short changes outsider economic elites. In particular, elite-biased democracy can introduce institutions, rules, and regulations that stunt the capacity of outsider economic elites to strengthen economically. This, in turn, blunts their political power. For this reason, they do not like elite-biased democracy.

Ultimately, the political-economic outcomes that these three parties prefer is necessary but not sufficient for obtaining it, a point we will elaborate later

---

[9] For a further discussion of the role of uncertainty over the policy implemented by a future dictator and its implications for regime change, see Albertus and Gay (2017).

[10] Freeman and Quinn (2012) generate a similar prediction regarding the relationship between portfolio diversification and democratization, but for a very different reason: by increasing the mobility of asset holders, they have less of an incentive to support dictatorship, since democracy poses less of a threat to them.

in this book. For explaining why some dictatorships end and are replaced with elite-biased democracies rather than popular democracies, coordination issues are critical. Authoritarian political elites and their economic allies might both prefer at any given time to exit the dictatorship on favorable terms but might not be able to do so, despite their greatest hopes.

How do the preferences of the masses figure into elite-biased democracy? Elite-biased democracy is created by elites, for elites. The masses prefer popular democracy far and away. However, their influence is marginal at best when it comes to opposing elite-biased democracy. The masses might win greater political voice and freedom from repression, but they will have difficulty translating their political voice into policies that meet their economic interests. For this reason, the masses can sometimes prefer a volatile dictatorship that delivers material benefits to them over an elite-biased democracy.

Why Elite-Biased Democracy Is a Sustainable Regime Type
Much of elite-biased democracy is about locking in the institutions and laws that protect former authoritarian elites by placing restrictions on either redistribution or punishment. Lock-in occurs either directly through the de jure institutions created during the transition or through de facto elite power that is enhanced due to these institutions and the policies they produce.

First, elite-biased electoral rules created during democratic transition can effectively consolidate existing power structures as economic elites push for rules after democratization that further cement their electoral advantage. For example, elites can engineer a mapping of votes to seats in a way that favors them; they can also help draw favorable district boundaries or gerrymander districts to produce even more skewed malapportionment to their advantage.

Second, elites can use the power they have gained from institutions biased in their favor to exercise greater influence than non-elites over the political system. Because the public policies adopted serve to widen inequality, this gives economic elites an advantage in terms of collective action, resources, and de facto power over the less well off. Elites can then gain favorable policies, either via legal means (such as lobbying and financing campaigns) or illegally, via corruption. Moreover, if economic elites can finance and support political parties and social actors such as the media, they can mobilize coalitions around issues that benefit them economically and politically.

How do political elites in particular protect themselves from criminal prosecution under democracy or parry the threat to the vital interests of their support organizations, such as the military budget? After all, these actors are those most likely to be called to task for their crimes and malfeasance under dictatorship. There are several ways in which the evasion of prosecution can occur. Key politicians and the military can gain positions for life in the legislature or bureaucracy. Similarly, they can retain veto power over critical policies. Or, alternatively, outgoing dictators can pack the courts with their lackeys on the eve of democratization, and these justices can strike down new laws that threaten to prosecute politicians from the authoritarian period. Of course, these devices can protect the rights and interests of their economic allies as well.

Popular Democracy

The preferences of each of the main actors over popular democracy are as follows. In contrast to elite-biased democracy, authoritarian political elites fear popular democracy, as do their economic elite partners. This outcome can be tantamount to a volatile dictatorship. Former autocratic political incumbents might be criminally prosecuted for their misdeeds and repression; former incumbent economic elites might be expropriated or sidelined. Outsider economic elites, by contrast, might benefit under popular democracy as regulations and taxes that unfavorably singled them out under dictatorship are dismantled. The masses always want popular democracy over gamed democracy and consolidated dictatorship. Their preference between popular democracy and volatile dictatorship is more ambiguous.

Outsider economic elites are very particular in their support for democracy. They prefer to avoid an elite-biased democracy designed to favor formerly empowered political and economic elites. In such a scenario, outsider elites would lack favorable rules and regulations and might be no better off than if they were in a consolidated dictatorship that excluded them from policy making. By contrast, outsider economic elites support building a democracy from scratch that sidelines former authoritarian political and economic incumbents. Under these circumstances, the majority of the population can be used as a bulwark of support for more liberal policies in which greater redistribution is exchanged for more secure property rights and freer markets that bar former incumbent economic elites from retaining their unfair advantages. If outsider elites nonetheless find themselves in an elite-biased democracy, they would prefer to unravel its biases – even if it means ushering in a more popular democracy that requires them to finance a greater degree of redistribution to the masses.

For the masses, there is a discrepancy between what they want in the short run and the long run. While the masses get both redistribution and political rights under popular democracy, they might – in expectation – benefit from large-scale redistribution under volatile dictatorship to a greater degree than regularized, and more muted, taxes and transfers under popular democracy.[11]

---

[11] Consequently, the preference of the masses over these two regime types depends on their relative weighting over political rights versus economic benefits. It also depends on the anticipated level of material benefits the masses receive under volatile dictatorship versus popular democracy. It is important to note, however, that even if citizens benefit from greater material redistribution under volatile dictatorship, other political and economic distortions deployed to ensure citizen quiescence can stunt the ability of citizens to leverage that redistribution for growth in the

Their optimal outcome over the long run, however, is popular democracy because it faithfully represents the interests of the median voter and common citizens.[12]

Coordination is key to translating preferences over popular democracy into reality: preferences are, as with elite-biased democracy, necessary but not sufficient. The masses can hold the most fervent and sincere desires for democracy, but that alone does achieve it. Outsider economic elites typically play a critical strategic role in bringing forth popular democracy, albeit for their own self-interested reasons. Anticipating that their state of ascendancy will threaten the vital interests of their potential enemies, outsider economic elites might reach out to, fund, and even take the lead in organizing opposition groups among the population to topple dictatorship and exit to democracy on favorable terms. That is, they will coordinate with the masses to exit dictatorship on favorable terms.

Similarly, the masses need help from the outsider economic elites to codify a new democratic constitution. They require resources, human capital, and organizational wherewithal. And they will typically lean on outsider economic elites to pull off this feat. In short, to achieve democracy, both of these groups must forge a marriage of convenience.

For their part, incumbent political elites and their economic partners both fear popular democracy and stand to lose if it is installed. Former authoritarian incumbent political elites can be dragged into court and prosecuted for the crimes they perpetrated under dictatorship. Former authoritarian incumbent economic elites can lose favorable regulatory and institutional frameworks that assign them lucrative property rights, funnel rents to them, and provide them access to markets on favorable terms. A popular democracy might elect politicians who can divide and conquer these political and economic actors, moving to destroy or winnow them down selectively or setting factions against one another. These incumbents therefore prefer elite-biased democracy or consolidated dictatorship to a popular democracy.

COMMON PATHS TO OUTCOMES

Now that we have outlined the key political actors and outcomes, what explains changes from one political equilibrium to another? In prior work, we have taken up aspects of this question. Specifically, we have outlined the conditions under which there are transitions from consolidated dictatorship to

---

longer term. For an example in the context of Mexico, see, e.g., Albertus et al. (2016). See also Menaldo and Yoo (2015).

[12] As we will demonstrate in Chapter 3, however, popular democracy is empirically rarer than elite-biased democracy in which institutional constraints to large-scale policy change are higher. This is consistent with Albertus (2015), who documents generally high institutional constraints to rule under democracy in Latin America. There is greater variation in institutional constraints across democracies outside of this region. Relative to Albertus (2015), we shed important light on the origins and structure of institutional constraints.

volatile dictatorship and vice versa (see Albertus 2015; Albertus and Menaldo 2012a; Menaldo 2012). There, consistent with what we outlined above, we have argued that elite coalitions and coalition building are the cornerstones of such transitions. When political elites draw their key supporters from new groups distinct from incumbent economic elites (e.g., from middle-class military officers or a nascent group of economic outsiders), they will be forced to signal their exclusive loyalty to their new supporters over former incumbent economic elites. One major way to credibly signal loyalty is through attacking and expropriating these rival economic elite groups.

Once rival elites are destroyed, political elites can enshrine their core supporters as a new base of power, carving up control of the economy anew and creating a stable distributional arrangement. This might call for adopting a constitution that institutionalizes the authoritarian bargain or for legislatures, courts, and other institutions that superficially appear democratic but that are intended to consolidate the deal between elites.

At other times, a consolidated dictatorship can devolve into a volatile one. Flash points between different elite factions can arise – for example, conflicting views over foreign policy – or authoritarian institutions can become so gridlocked as to be rendered dysfunctional. In this case, these institutions become a coordination point that does not resolve elite differences but rather serves as a battlefield for attempting to vanquish different-minded foes. Outsider economic elites might seize the initiative and help propel a transition to popular democracy – a phenomenon that we will explore in Chapter 7 when we explicate the political history of Chile.

In Chapter 5, we explore transitions from elite-biased democracy to popular democracy. If incumbent political elites and their economic allies choose to exit dictatorship on their own terms and introduce an elite-biased democracy, then outsider economic elites have no choice but to deal with the consequences. One option is to hunker down and protect themselves under the new democratic regime. This might mean remaining in the political opposition or striking against the conservative elements in the manipulated democracy when the time is right. The latter can involve funding political parties, organizing dissenting media, running for office themselves, or agitating for constitutional change and other political reforms. In some cases, new groups of outsider economic elites might arise after democratization with similar interests as those that existed at the time of transition: like their predecessors, they chafe under a political and economic order that favors incumbent economic elites from the former episode of dictatorship.

The common focus of outsider economic elites, both vintage and new groups, is therefore to unwind the authoritarian legacies that democracy inherits in the form of elite-biased rules and institutions. Under certain conditions, they can succeed and usher in a popular democracy that replaces the elite-biased one. In Chapter 5, we both outline these conditions and test whether they are associated with a transition from elite-biased to popular democracy empirically.

In later chapters, we take up other issues pertaining to regime dynamics involving shifts from democracy to dictatorship. In Chapter 7, we specify how popular democracy was overthrown by disgruntled economic elites that lacked political voice in the case of Chile; this democracy was replaced with a consolidated dictatorship. In the book's conclusion, we broach broader circumstances under which democracy can collapse.

We relegate the remainder of our attention here to transitions from autocracy to either elite-biased democracy or, alternatively, popular democracy. To explain transitions to democracy, we heed calls by prior research to separate deeper, structural factors from proximate ones (see, e.g., Mainwaring and Pérez-Liñán 2014).[13] In Chapter 4, we empirically test the major claims we make in the remainder of this chapter.

Elite-Biased Democracy

We begin with an elite-biased transition. A move to a democracy gamed by elites is usually jointly initiated by political incumbents and incumbent economic elites. In terms of opportunity, if these actors can coordinate to exit dictatorship by setting a timetable for transition and crafting a series of extrication deals – preferably culminating in a constitution that protects their rights and interests under democracy – they will do so. Two broad features of a dictatorship allow these actors to accomplish these tasks.

The first is strong state capacity. If political incumbents can avail powerful and competent fiscal, administrative, legal, and military bureaucracies, then they should have an enhanced ability to team up with their economic allies to exit the dictatorship on favorable terms.[14] By contrast, dictators who head states that cannot project power into the periphery, administer censuses, collect taxes, and provide public goods should have a hard time imposing the constitutions that shepherd elite-biased transitions relative to dictators who preside over strong states. Indeed, drafting a constitution intended to manage a political transition structured to protect outgoing dictators' personal well being and interests, as well as the rights and interests of their economic allies, is quite costly and risky and presupposes considerable administrative and political wherewithal. The process of constitutional adoption by a dictator often calls for controlling and manipulating constitutional delegates to prevent them from shirking and creating a document that challenges or embarrasses the regime.

---

[13] Mainwaring and Pérez-Liñán (2014) go beyond this distinction and even introduce "mid-range" factors impacting transitions, such as normative preferences about regimes and the radicalism of policy preferences.

[14] The broader literature on state capacity and democratization writ large has reached mixed results. On the one hand, Hariri (2012) argues that states with a longer history of sovereignty and administrative capacity can use that capacity to maintain stable authoritarian rule. By contrast, and focusing on former Soviet states, Fortin (2012) argues that a strong state is a necessary precondition for democratic transition.

Similarly, if political incumbents have the luxury of ruling with the aid of a legislature, then they should also enjoy higher odds of exiting the dictatorship under propitious circumstances. Indeed, it is more likely than not that the legislature will be the forum that allows them to plan their extrication in the first place, hammer out the deals needed to get the job done on their terms, and serve as the venue for the constituent assembly that is commissioned to draft the constitution they will use to exit autocracy and set up the ensuing regime.

To see how this is the case, consider the special role that legislatures play in some dictatorships. They allow political incumbents to formally institutionalize their political power by defining who qualifies as a regime insider and who does not, what political insiders' rights are, and what tools they can avail to defend their rights and pursue their interests. Along these lines, legislatures allow a dictator to do two important things. First, a legislature aids a dictator in ushering in a stable distributional arrangement in terms of who will benefit from rents produced by the coercive power of the state and its politicized regulation of the economy. Second, it helps a dictator credibly commit to protecting the property rights and vital interests of regime insiders – not only in the immediate present but in the uncertain future, and even when the identity of key individuals who helped launched the regime into existence has changed.[15]

A legislature helps achieve these functions because it provides a concrete and transparent set of rules and a predictable structure of political authority beyond the raw power possessed by regime insiders. A legislature provides a forum for political and economic elites to come together and coordinate. This disciplines the dictator and deters opportunism against regime insiders. A legislature also allows for information to flow from the dictator to political and economic elites and for feedback from the latter to the dictator.

Indeed, it might be the case that the law and who crafts the law matters as much or more in a dictatorship vis-à-vis a democracy. Membership in the legislature and its committees allows political elites to have an opportunity to craft or at least modify the bills that define their rents. So does the ability to lobby legislators in the halls of the legislative assembly. By having direct input into the laws that are crafted, regime insiders have a say over monetary and financial policy, fiscal policy, trade policy, and regulatory policy. Economic elites who are allied to the regime often seek protectionist measures that create barriers to entry and attendant monopoly rights, as well as tax breaks and subsidies. In many ways, autocratic legislatures are not too different from legislatures in "gamed" democracies captured by special interests that, while freely and fairly

---

[15] Some scholars have noted the role of legislatures in autocracies as venues for power sharing and distributing rents (e.g., Gandhi 2008; Lust-Okar 2006). Others have argued that legislatures can serve as a stepping stone to democratization, albeit for a different reason than what we argue – namely, that they enable transition more easily once incumbent autocrats are overthrown (Brownlee 2009).

elected, nonetheless end up doing the bidding of the politically powerful, even if this damages the interests of the average citizen.

Because of the aforementioned functions of autocratic legislatures, these forums enable political and economic elite incumbents under dictatorship to coordinate on protecting themselves in the face of exogenous shocks and unforeseen events. Rather than pursuing a narrowly self-interested path in which each member attempts to save his or her own skin, legislatures encourage actors to coordinate a response to threats from outsider economic elites and the masses, or even from abroad, in a way that allows them to continue to secure their rights and interests. Because legislatures help codify a stable distributional arrangement, it is in the best interest of regime insiders to respond to a challenge to the regime's authority by remaining loyal to the regime. In other words, legislatures incentivize and allow for elite incumbents to circle the wagons and project a unified front against adversity.

Most importantly, dictators can rely on legislative institutions under autocracy to impose constitutions that should stick after democratic transition, provided that their legislatures are relatively strong and autonomous. These elite-driven constitutions are key tools in creating an ecosystem of institutions that enable former authoritarian elites to thrive under democracy. New constitutions most often call for the election of a constituent assembly, and dictators are able to more smoothly call, operate, and control such an assembly when it is rooted in an existing and well-functioning legislature.

When constituent assemblies are called for in the absence of an effective legislature, it is more difficult for dictators to impose resilient constitutions. Indeed, they might not be able to impose a constitution at all. Instead, the absence of a legislature might make it more likely that authoritarian political incumbents will be caught off guard, possibly during a moment of weakness, and be dragged kicking and screaming into a popular democracy spearheaded by an opposition composed of outsider economic elites and the galvanized masses. Furthermore, institutions such as a long-lived monarchy can complement the benefits of autocratic legislatures; a constitutional monarchy, especially, can provide several time-tested forums for coordination between political incumbents and economic incumbents (Menaldo 2016). This allows monarchs to set a timetable for popular elections and constitutional changes that liberalize the political system while continuing to vouchsafe the rights and privileges of the elite – when this becomes necessary in the face of exogenous shocks and unforeseen events. Indeed, because monarchs are often able to achieve a politically neutral image, at least in the eyes of many, this can help legitimize a transition to an elite-biased democracy – a point we will revisit in Chapter 6, when we discuss Sweden's transition to elite-biased democracy.

Finally, there are a host of precipitating factors that can stimulate political incumbents and their economic allies to exit the regime. To be sure, many precipitating factors are idiosyncratic in nature and differ by country and time period. While in some autocratic settings, these idiosyncratic factors can motivate elites to head for the exits – provided that they can count on some-thing like reliable state capacity or a legislature to guide the democratization process – in other settings, they might have less bite.

Consider policies that regulate the economy to the benefit of incumbent economic elites and that can become unsustainable as the economy changes. Barriers to trade and international investment, overvalued exchange rates, large trade and fiscal deficits, and distortions to domestic markets and capital forma-tion might eventually unravel, bankrupting the state and threatening the bal-ance sheets of incumbent economic elites. Similarly, incumbent economic elites might not be able to forestall a rising challenge from outsider economic elites under dictatorship, tilting them toward supporting an elite-biased democracy. This can occur because outsider economic elites have liquid forms of capital or diversified portfolios that refuse to be easily destroyed. What these factors have in common is that incumbent economic elites fear that they will lose control of the policies and regulations that give them advantages under dictatorship or fear that a different set of political elites bankrolled by the outsider economic elites will displace them from their position of domination over the economy.

On the other hand, not all precipitating factors are idiosyncratic or country- or time period–specific in nature. Natural disasters are one proximate factor that can provide the final trigger for a regime transition to democracy that is elite biased – provided that political incumbents and their incumbent economic elites have *the opportunity* to exit on favorable terms because they can coordi-nate to get the deal that they want. While any given natural disaster is idiosyn-cratic, all countries face them at one point or another.

Of course, in the absence of a legislature or similar institution that facilitates coordination by regime insiders, a shock caused by a natural disaster might instead create a focal point that the opposition can exploit to organize collec-tively. This is especially the case if a natural disaster destroys the presidential palace or other symbols of regime strength and prestige or kills top regime officials. This can quickly reset the political game, creating a succession crisis and upending expectations about what will come next under dictatorship. Not only can the security apparatus be in disarray if lines of command become con-tested, but destruction, death, and chaos can drive citizens to protest against the regime. This makes it less likely that the political incumbents and their economic allies will be able to orchestrate a transition on favorable terms.

However, all bets are off if a natural disaster occurs in a context in which regime insiders can count on a legislature to confront the political and eco-nomic fallout and, more importantly, counteract any threats to the status quo from citizens galvanized by regime incompetence or indifference to citizens' plights.

The chief empirical implications that we can deduce from this discussion of elite-biased democratization are threefold. First, there should be a strong, positive relationship between state capacity and a transition to an elite-biased democracy. Second, there should also be a strong, positive relationship between the presence of a legislature under dictatorship and a transition to an elite-biased democracy. The reason for both of these "reduced-form" predictions is that although it is difficult to pin down the precipitating factors that galvanize the political incumbents and their economic allies to head for the exits together across time and place, we can say with considerable confidence that whatever the ultimate catalyst, when the day comes, these parties will be more likely to coordinate and democratize on friendly terms when they possess tailor-made administrative infrastructures and political forums. Third, even though from a researcher's standpoint it is hard to establish a covering law that can accommodate disparate transitions to elite-biased democracy, there is one common factor that does precipitate these transitions: natural disasters. Moreover, natural disasters have the benefit of being exogenous to political regimes.

Popular Democracy

A move to a popular democracy is usually jointly initiated by outsider economic elites and the masses. These actors can use changes in the balance of power or changes in expectations about the regime's strength and durability to demand a timetable for transition that forces political incumbents and their economic allies into extricating the regime. This is particularly effective if they can seize the initiative provided by an unexpected shock to push the political incumbents from power without much forethought or planning. This should culminate in a popular democracy that faithfully represents their interests after the first steps to democracy are undertaken, such as writing a constitution that cuts authoritarian elites out of the deal.

For this strategy to succeed, it is eminently helpful to outsider economic elites and the masses to exploit a lack of coordination potential among the regime's political incumbents and their economic allies. Consistent with the logic outlined previously, if authoritarian political incumbents lack a legislature, then this should make it easier for outsider elites and the masses to exit the dictatorship under propitious circumstances. In the absence of institutionalized focal points that trigger coordination by political incumbents and their economic allies, outsider economic elites and the masses will be able to exploit the vacuum and coordinate to bring down the regime and usher in a popular democracy.

As with the transition to elite-biased democracy, the precipitating factors that can catalyze a transition to popular democracy differ by country and time period. Nonetheless, we explore three proximate factors that can bring down an autocratic regime while ushering in popular democracy. These factors are sufficiently common across place and time to enable us to exploit them in the service of deducing general hypotheses about transitions to popular democracy.

The first precipitating factor that can help usher in popular democracy is a revolution. Incumbent elites are caught off balance when a revolution occurs. Fear of being swept from office by popular fervor pressures elites to rush into a transition bargain more quickly than they would otherwise have done, thus decreasing their ability to manipulate the transition process to safeguard their interests after democratization. This is particularly the case when elites cannot coordinate and must instead scramble individually to save their own hides. In some cases, authoritarian political incumbents and their economic allies are entirely steamrolled as the masses and outsider elites coordinate to bring daily life to a standstill and strip state assets and perhaps even physically overrun major political offices and businesses. A revolution that successfully establishes democracy presents the masses and the outsider economic elites who help bank-roll the revolution with a blank slate, which they can use to codify a new demo-cratic constitution and banish the influence of the former authoritarian regime.

Even in the best-case scenario, in which incumbent political elites and their economic allies are able to thwart a revolution, they might be forced to rush into a transition bargain more quickly than they would have otherwise done, decreasing their ability to manipulate the transition process to safeguard their interests after democratization. Indeed, a failed revolutionary attempt can sig-nal the possibility of future violence and the ability of a subset of the masses to overcome its collective action problem in the foreseeable future. Even attempts at revolution that fall short of actual revolution will therefore tilt the scale in favor of the masses and outsider economic elites.

On the other hand, political and incumbent economic elites who have a legislature at their disposal that they can avail to coordinate to repress a revo-lutionary threat have every incentive to do so – and to brutally crack down on the opposition, lest they lose everything in a successful revolution. History is replete with examples of entrenched and institutionalized authoritarian regimes successfully repressing revolutionaries. Take several of the 2011 Arab Spring revolts: in Egypt, Iran, and Syria, incumbents brutally suppressed revo-lutionary movements and used their legislatures and other state institutions such as the police and judiciary to retard any progress made by outside forces toward greater political liberalization. In other words, a revolution can back-fire against revolutionaries, a point we revisit in Chapter 9.

A second proximate factor that can sweep incumbents from power is an economic growth collapse. Scholars have long recognized that steady economic growth helps stabilize authoritarian regimes (e.g., Przeworski et al. 2000). Consider the so-called Asian Tigers. A host of East Asian "developmental states" struck on such a reliable growth formula that the regimes heading many of these states staked their legitimacy on continual, broad-based economic growth (Slater and Wong 2013). This was true for decades in authoritarian countries such as Singapore, Taiwan, and South Korea and later in Indonesia and China. Conversely, economic slowdowns have long been pointed to as undermining both democratic and authoritarian political regimes (e.g., Gasiorowski 1995; Haggard and Kaufman 1995).

Yet a sudden negative shock to growth strikes at the heart of regimes that legitimize themselves as technocratic developmentalists, or even of regimes that cynically use economic growth in exchange for popular quiescence. Such a shock can allow outsider economic elites to organize the masses as their disenchantment with the authoritarian regime grows in tandem with citizens' shrinking wallets. In other words, outsider economic elites can leverage mass discontent to help foment popular action such as demonstrations, which can culminate in toppling the regime and ushering in democracy.

Yet another shock that can affect the viability of a sitting authoritarian regime and hasten its collapse in a way that empowers the masses and the outsider economic elites is an economic crisis that is precipitated, if not initially created, by outside events. This is particularly true of sovereign debt and currency crises. While their genesis often lies in unsustainable macroeconomic policies, such as ballooning trade deficits or runaway budget deficits and high debt loads (Frankel and Rose 1996), the actual timing of these types of crises is more often the result of unforeseen speculative attacks by foreign investors or precipitous declines in the international price of commodities (Krugman 1979).

It bears reemphasizing that coordination issues are critical in ultimate regime outcomes. As previously outlined, it should be more likely for political incumbents and their economic allies to exit the regime on auspicious terms if a legislature is in place. By the same token, the absence of a legislature complicates the ability of political elites and their economic allies to transition on favorable terms. Take, for example, a financial crash and economic crisis that hits because the economic model chosen by the political elites and their economic allies proves unsustainable. Such a pressing scenario will make it difficult for political elites to spend their time crafting the ideal exit strategy with incumbent economic elites. Absent a forum for quickly hammering out a bulwark against change, the authoritarian status quo should end with a transition to popular democracy. By contrast, if a similar economic shock happens in the presence of a legislature, the ruling group should be able to avoid the worst possible outcome: suffering a transition to popular democracy. A legislature should enable the incumbent authoritarian elites to coordinate to effectively bed down crises and forestall an unanticipated transition.

Summarizing Our Key Theoretical Predictions for Regime Outcomes

In this section, we summarize our theoretical framework, discuss causal mechanisms, and tender key predictions for regime outcomes that will be empirically tested in Chapter 4. Table 2.1 displays the theory's predicted outcomes on the basis of how structural underpinnings and proximate factors operate on the key actors. It also gives readers a sense of the mechanisms at work behind the predictions outlined previously.

The table begins on the left-hand side with how the presence or absence of proximate factors that can destabilize dictatorship impact incumbent economic elites and outsider economic elites. When proximate factors are present, this weakens incumbent economic elites and strengthens outsider economic

TABLE 2.1. *Theoretical Mechanics and Key Predictions*

Presence of Proximate Factors That Destabilize Dictatorship	Impact of Proximate Factors on Strength of Incumbent Economic Elites	Impact of Proximate Factors on Strength of Outsider Economic Elites	Presence of Structural Underpinnings	Economic Elite Interaction with Political Elites and Masses	Outcome
Proximate factors active (e.g., natural disaster)	Weakens	Strengthens	Structural underpinnings present (e.g., legislatures and strong bureaucracies)	Coordination between incumbent economic elites and political incumbents to exit due to fear of being eclipsed by outsider economic elites	*Elite-biased democracy*
Proximate factors inactive	Strengthens	Indeterminate	Structural underpinnings present (e.g., legislatures and strong bureaucracies)	Incumbent economic elites team up with political incumbents to neglect or repress outsider economic elites and the masses	*Consolidated dictatorship*
Proximate factors active (revolution, economic crisis, currency or debt crisis)	Weakens	Strengthens	No structural underpinnings present	Coordination between outsider economic elites and the masses to overthrow political and economic incumbent	*Popular democracy*
Proximate factors inactive	Strengthens	Indeterminate	No structural underpinnings present	Creates possibility for betrayal of incumbent economic elites by political incumbents and opening for masses to be recruited	*Volatile dictatorship*

elites. By contrast, when they are absent, incumbent economic elites can enrich themselves without a serious threat, entrenching their power. But the absence of proximate factors has an indeterminate effect on outsider economic elites. In some circumstances, secular changes in the economy cultivate a stronger outsider economic elite. By contrast, the strength of outsiders can also wane if their economic opportunities and fortunes are choked off by their incumbent economic elite rivals.

Moving to the right, Table 2.1 then outlines the ways in which the presence or absence of structural underpinnings – legislatures and strong state institutions – condition how the key actors interact in light of the proximate factors. These interactions, in turn, produce the key outcomes of interest: elite-biased democracy, consolidated dictatorship, popular democracy, and volatile dictatorship.

In the first row, structural underpinnings support an exit to democracy spearheaded by elites when a proximate factor unsettles dictatorship and generates a threat by outsider economic elites. In the second row, structural underpinnings support consolidated dictatorship as incumbent political elites and their economic allies team up to repress outsider economic elites and the masses. Ceteris paribus, these latter actors are relatively disadvantaged in the absence of destabilizing shocks to the regime. In the third row, proximate factors again unsettle dictatorship, but authoritarian elites do not have structural factors that could support dictatorship on their side. In this case, outsider economic elites and the masses team up to topple dictatorship and impose a popular democracy. Finally, in the fourth row, both proximate factors that destabilize dictatorship and structural factors that could underpin it are absent. Dictatorship is unlikely to give way to democracy, but it is also unstable as political and economic elites clash. Volatile dictatorship ensues.

Figure 2.1 summarizes the theoretical framework in a different way. This figure is a simple and stylized extensive form representation of the interactions between the key actors in the theory and how these interactions map onto different regime outcomes. Before tracing out the game, we provide some caveats. The representation of incumbent political and economic elites is collapsed together in Figure 2.1; the discussion unpacks their interactions and, previously, we discussed at length the coordination dilemma they face and how structural underpinnings act as focal points to help them solve this dilemma. Similarly, we remind readers that the activation of the masses to act against an incumbent authoritarian regime also depends on the existence of a focal point, which allows them to coordinate with the outsider economic elite in anticipation that the outsider economic elite will strike against the regime. We therefore note that a key modeling choice (see Figure 2.1) attests to the fact that such a focal point may be necessary but is not sufficient: given their collective action problem, the masses may still fail to join the economic elites in challenging the incumbent regime, even if a focal point helps them solve the coordination issue. In other words, the collective action challenge that the masses face is distinct

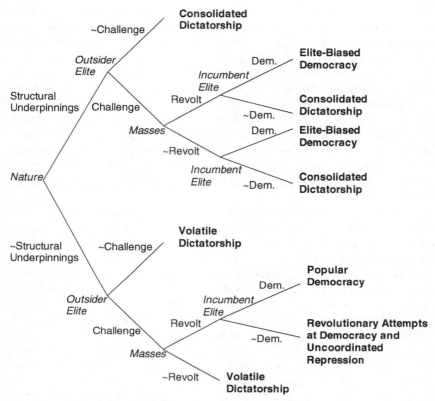

FIGURE 2.1. Extensive Form Representation of the Democracy Game.
Note: Players are indicated in italics and outcomes are in bold.

from their coordination with outsider economic elites; sometimes the masses simply cannot act in a cohesive manner. Because what follows below is a stylized depiction of the democracy game rather than a fully specified one, we do not incorporate that strategic dilemma ex ante into probabilities. Instead, we flesh it out explicitly, as a choice, after the masses first observe how the outsider economic elites react to incumbents in the presence or absence of structural underpinnings.

The game begins under dictatorship, in which incumbent political and economic elites hold power. Nature determines whether there are structural underpinnings present (e.g., a legislature) that can enable incumbent political and economic elites to coordinate their actions, whether those actions are repression under dictatorship or a joint move to elite-biased democracy.

Consider first the case in which structural underpinnings are present. Outsider economic elites make the first move, deciding whether to challenge authoritarian incumbents or not. Their choices are critical; absent activation by outsider economic elites, the masses cannot easily overcome their collective action problem to revolt against the regime. If outsider economic elites do not challenge incumbents, consolidated dictatorship results.

If outsider elites do challenge the regime, perhaps because they are ascendant economically and some proximate factor strengthens them, then the masses can choose whether to join their challenge by revolting. Whether incumbent political and economic elites face a joint or singular threat, they must choose whether or not to initiate moves toward democracy. This choice can be conditioned probabilistically by factors such as repression costs, the strength of the threat they face today and in the future (impacted by "proximate factors" that destabilize dictatorship), and their ability to construct favorable democratic institutions. In that sense, the dice may be loaded in their favor or against them. If incumbent elites choose to democratize, they first coordinate on a transition framework that yields elite-biased democracy. If, on the other hand, they have the capacity to dig in and remain strong, then they will team up to repress outsider economic elites and the masses. This is true regardless of whether the masses join in the challenge that outsider economic elites make against the incumbent authoritarian regime. Of course, if the masses do join outsider economic elites in challenging the regime and incumbent elites choose to democratize, the nature of the democratic bargain may incorporate specific institutions and provisions intended to blunt the capacity of the masses to achieve their demands under democracy.

Next consider the case in which structural underpinnings are absent. Again, outsider economic elites make the first move, challenging authoritarian incumbents or not. And again, their choice is particularly important because absent a challenge by outsider elites, the masses will rarely be able to singularly challenge the regime. Absent a challenge by these actors, incumbent political and economic elites will engage alternatively in collusion and competition, and outsider economic elites can rise as a potential threat to incumbent economic elites. Volatile dictatorship results when incumbent political elites cannot – or will not – strike a stable arrangement with a group of economic elites, whether they be the incumbents who have been privileged in the past or a new group of outsiders. This differs from an institutionalized bargain in which the political incumbents ally with a discrete group of economic elites under the auspices of a stable autocracy with features such as a legislature or dynastic monarchy.

If outsider elites challenge the incumbent authoritarian regime, for instance because they rapidly gather strength, the masses choose whether to join their challenge by revolting. Absent a popular revolt, democracy will not obtain. On the one hand, incumbent elites have no incentives to democratize, given that they lack the tools to impose a favorable and enduring democratic bargain. Instead, they will either attack or ignore outsider elites. On the other hand, if outsider elites prevail in their challenge, they will impose their own dictatorship, and attack former incumbent economic elite rivals. Democracy will obtain, however, if the masses revolt as proximate factors strengthen their hand and that of the outsider economic elites. Incumbents may be forcefully toppled or forced to democratize. Regardless, they do not have the structural underpinnings to impose their will, and popular democracy results. Finally, if incumbent elites have the wherewithal to dig in, they may face periodic revolutionary attempts that seek to impose popular democracy, and have little choice but to attempt to repress uprisings where possible.

How Our Theory Relates to Long-Standing Theories of Democratization

Some of the structural factors that have long been highlighted in the literature as being favorable to democracy parallel the logic implied by our framework. Take modernization theory, the argument that wealthier and, by the same token, more urbanized and educated nations are more likely to transition to democracy. We agree with this notion in principle but propose a different causal channel. Rather than operating directly on the likelihood of transition through the presence of a middle class or a more educated populace, wealth is usually tied to infrastructural capacity and state strength, and a subset of institutions and practices associated with these transformations can enable an authoritarian regime to more predictably orchestrate and subsequently manage a transition favorable to their interests.

Indeed, this could help explain why the empirical evidence for modernization theory has hitherto been mixed (see Acemoglu et al. 2008). To the extent that modernization matters for democratization, it is by enabling incumbent political and economic elites to coordinate for a favorable transition from dictatorship and endowing them with the tools to realize it. There might not be a strong correlation between income per capita (or urbanization and education) and transitions to popular democracy, however. That is because it is not necessarily the case that the structural factors we have outlined allow a combination of outsider economic elites and the masses to coordinate to oust an autocratic regime. Indeed, as we will discuss later on, mass revolutions that usher in democracies unbiased by elites have happened in many poor countries, including the Philippines, Nicaragua, Mongolia, and some Eastern European countries after the fall of the Iron Curtain. One possible reason for this is that incumbent elites were simply not able to get their act together and head off a movement to democracy from below: they lacked the administrative and legislative infrastructure necessary to exit on terms favorable to their interests.

There is also mixed evidence on another structural factor mattering for democratization that has been widely highlighted in the literature: economic inequality (see Albertus and Menaldo 2012b). Our theoretical framework can help make sense of the fact that the correlation between the distribution of income and democratization is, at best, weak. Economic inequality in our framework is irrelevant for elite-biased transitions; it does not impact the administrative and legislative infrastructure that is key to allowing elites to exit on terms favorable to their interests; moreover, as we will discuss, the incumbent political elites and the plutocrats who support them are usually motivated to bail out of dictatorship when they are threatened by economic rivals in a different economic sector, not a different economic class.

Economic inequality is more important, at least in theory, for transitions to popular democracy, given that it can fuel strong demands for redistribution that can be effected via representation. However, the chief obstacles to such transitions – and formidable ones at that – are barriers to collective action. Solving the collective action problem among the masses, however, is not strongly tied to inequality. Instead, it might be more closely tied to international diffusion effects or domestic technological changes – proximate rather than structural factors highlighted in the literature on democratization.

Our predictions regarding a null relationship between economic inequality and democratic transition do not imply that our theory is agnostic about distributive outcomes after democratization. While the exit from dictatorship to elite-biased democracy is usually about the fear of one sector of the economy losing its privileged position to a rising rival sector and is therefore not driven by the distribution of income or wealth per se, once democracy is instituted, the economic elite that monopolized economic policy under the previous dictatorship will have to grapple with the masses that have been granted a political voice. Economic elites will therefore want to block vertical redistribution in the form of progressive taxes and transfers. They will also want to block rival economic groups from getting their say over economic affairs. Economic elites will block reforms that would limit their rents; they will uphold barriers to entry, allow for cartels and conglomerates to suppress competition, and defend policies that confer them with cheap credit, favorable subsidies and tariffs, tax breaks, and light regulation.

PUBLIC POLICY AND INSTITUTIONAL CONSEQUENCES OF DIFFERENT TYPES OF DEMOCRACIES

Given our discussion about the dramatically different origins of elite-biased democracy versus its popular counterpart, it should not be surprising that these types of democracies favor fundamentally different actors in their basic institutions, governance, public policies, transitional justice decisions, and distributional outcomes. All our actors should expect to have differing fates under these two distinct regime types.

Governance Outcomes

In terms of governance under democracies that inherit constitutions from their autocratic predecessors, we expect that these regimes will be less pluralistic, inclusive, and representative than popular democracies with their own constitutions. The reason is that the median voter will not be as politically empowered and faithfully represented in an elite-biased democracy as in a popular democracy. Instead, the previous political incumbents and their economic allies will carve out entire policy domains for themselves, ushering in laws and regulations that protect their rights and interests. As a result, the masses will get the short end of the stick. In the next two chapters, we outline the means by which this has been accomplished across places and time.

Fiscal and Material Outcomes

In terms of the fiscal and material outcomes under elite-biased democracy, we expect an increase in redistribution from economic elites to the masses after democratization *only* when an incoming democratic regime overturns the old order by writing a new constitution that empowers the majority. Under these circumstances, democracy will be redistributive because it faithfully represents the preferences of the median voter. Yet when former authoritarian political and economic elites remain strong under democracy because they have been able to impose a constitution before exiting the outgoing dictatorship, the subsequent elite-biased democracy will be less redistributive than it would have been under popular democracy. In some cases, it might even be less redistributive than under the previous autocratic period – especially if it prevents the chances of a populist dictator arising.

We therefore expect to find across places and time periods that elite-biased democracies will have smaller governments in general; allocate less public money to education, healthcare, and housing; and have more regressive tax structures. This will be especially true after 1972, when the relationship between democracy and fiscal and monetary policy became complicated by the post–Bretton Woods global political and economic order. Globalization ties the hands of policy makers by enabling asset holders to move easily across borders to avoid redistribution (e.g., Dailami 2000; Freeman and Quinn 2012; Remmer 1990). In an international regime where capital-account liberalization is the order of the day and investors search for the highest returns across all marketplaces, no regime, democratic or autocratic, can fully close their borders and soak the rich easily. That globalization also engenders investment portfolio diversification and foreign investment, therefore eroding the specificity of all asset classes, reduces the resistance of wealthy individuals to democratization by putting them beyond the redistributive reach of the state (Freeman and Quinn 2012).

Several policy tools that facilitate redistribution are restricted by capital mobility. These include a government's ability to regulate labor markets and levy progressive taxation (Dailami 2000). Almost universally, countries have reduced marginal tax rates on high-income earners, adopted flatter tax structures centered on value-added taxes, and cut both corporate tax rates and rates on capital gains. Other barriers to direct, progressive taxation include the proliferation of shadow economies, hard-to-tax sectors, and a global policy agenda rooted in free markets and neoclassical economics (Chwieroth 2007).

Even in countries that have not fully liberalized their capital accounts, there have been formidable obstacles to conducting traditional fiscal redistribution. One is the relatively large size of the informal economy in most developing countries. On the one hand, this has made it more difficult to tax business ventures and an important segment of the upper middle class (Alm, Martínez-Vazquez, and Wallace 2004). On the other hand, many partnerships, trusts, and businesses manage to keep the bulk of their earnings in foreign currencies and sometimes hold these assets offshore. The increasingly multinational nature of medium to large corporations has engendered a cat-and-mouse game among governments seeking to tax profits and firms seeking to shield them through complex accounting procedures (e.g., transfer pricing) and a plethora of offshore tax havens. It has proven quite difficult for countries to develop an international framework aimed at limiting tax avoidance and evasion on a global scale. Finally, tax evasion by all classes decreases tax morale and reduces the size of the tax pool, therefore making it harder to reach economies of scale in tax collection and increasing the transaction costs of progressive taxation.

Therefore, even popular democracies that more fully represent the interests of the median voter should have a difficult time engaging in meaningful redistribution during the post–Bretton Woods era. Indeed, as we report in Chapter 4, the degree of tax progressivity under democracy between 1972 and 2006 is much lower than one would expect in a world in which income inequality has skyrocketed (Piketty 2014; Atkinson 2015). While in that chapter we corroborate our intuition that popular democracies should have more progressive tax structures than elite-biased ones, the difference is not huge. So how do policy makers under popular democracy get around these constraints?

They avail unorthodox measures to redistribute. The most prominent mechanism to conduct redistribution "off the government's balance sheet" is for the state to retain autonomy over its currency, thus allowing policy makers to raise revenues via the inflation tax. By leveraging its control of interest rates and the money supply to compel the central bank, deposit banks, and investment banks to hold government notes at lower than market interest rates, it can fund budget deficits oriented toward redistribution.

Of course, there are important scope conditions that influence the viability and potency of these macroeconomic tools. Flexible exchange rate policy allows for monetary autonomy to occur in an environment in which capital is internationally mobile. In that context, governments face a trade-off between domestic monetary policy and exchange rate stability (Cohen 1998). Alternatively, governments can maintain both monetary policy autonomy and exchange rate stability, but only if they regulate the flow of capital across their borders. This was the equilibrium that obtained during the so-called embedded liberal international order under the Bretton Woods system of fixed exchange rates. During this era, all democratic governments in the developed world – and many developing countries – used capital controls to avail both fiscal and monetary policy for redistribution, full employment, and social insurance (see Dailami 2000, 5).

Therefore, our intuition that macroeconomic policy can be deployed to satisfy redistributive pressures in democracy assumes an international regime of unrestricted capital mobility and is consistent with recent contributions that extend the median-voter approach (Meltzer and Richard 1981) to monetary policy. Bearce and Hallerberg (2011) deduce that the median voter under democracy tends to prefer monetary autonomy over fixed exchange rates in the post–Bretton Woods era. Because citizens occupy the domestic production sector of the economy, they are indifferent to exchange rate stability. Instead, they prefer monetary autonomy because money creation provides the government with a tool to finance redistributive transfers (Desai, Olofsgård, and Yousef 2003).

There are, of course, two qualifications to using monetary policy to redistribute income. First, monetary policy works only up to the point at which distortions reduce the level of transfers.[16] Second, running the printing presses to pay for redistributive spending and transfers is of course more difficult if the central bank has de facto independence. Yet it remains common enough under popular democracy.

In short, we expect that democracies in which the median voter has a strong hand in writing the rules of the game – democracies that adopt their own constitution after democratization – should indulge in macroeconomic policies that have the potential to redistribute in favor of the median voter. Specifically, they should adopt flexible exchange rates that give them monetary autonomy. By contrast, democracies in which outgoing autocratic elites have imposed the rules of the game, marked by a constitution inherited from the previous autocracy, are more likely to have fixed exchange rates. By extension, they should defend the value of their currency and rely less on inflationary finance.

Outcomes for Former Political Elites

Elite-biased democracies and popular democracies should again differ dramatically in their approaches to transitional justice. Because outgoing authoritarian political incumbents are key players in crafting the rules of the game under an elite-biased democracy, they should be much more likely to construct institutions that will help shield them from prosecution against crimes and transgressions committed under autocracy. They might pass explicit laws that

---

[16] Although at first blush, this might seem to rule out the heavy use of seigniorage revenues to finance redistribution, given its correlation to price increases, considerable research has shown that the deadweight costs of moderate inflation are negligible. Indeed, the effect of inflation on growth – provided the former remains below a certain threshold – can actually be positive. At high inflation levels, however, the costs associated with distortions might outweigh the benefits to the median voter (see Stiglitz 1998).

TABLE 2.2. *Distributional Consequences under Different Regimes*

		Proximate Factors That Destabilize Dictatorship Active	
		Yes	No
Presence of structural underpinnings	Yes	Crony capitalism and inequality under elite-biased democracy	Crony capitalism under consolidated dictatorship
	No	Free market capitalism moderated by social safety nets and redistribution under popular democracy	Chronic underdevelopment and swings between different sectoral winners and losers under volatile dictatorship

proscribe attempts to pursue transitional justice – or laws that grant them direct representation such as legislative seats that come with immunity. In the next chapter, we outline these tools in detail.

Outgoing authoritarian political elites – and especially outgoing dictators, who are the potential lightning rods of the authoritarian past – should therefore avoid punishment in democracies that inherit constitutions from autocracies. They should be more likely to avoid being imprisoned for crimes they committed under dictatorship (e.g., human rights abuses and corruption) and similarly less likely to face exile or the death penalty. At the same time, their "golden parachutes" should give them access to goods, services, and lifestyles that outpace those of their fellow citizens. They should live out the rest of their days in a more carefree manner and thus experience less stress, have access to better healthcare and amenities, enjoy better nutrition, and have access to and afford imported medications and medical procedures that others are deprived of. All of this should translate into longer, healthier lifespans. Conversely, democracies that adopt new constitutions can create new rules for the political game that will favor punishing former authoritarian political elites and that will reduce their longevity – for instance, by depriving them of their fortunes, honor, and even proper healthcare.

Summary of the Argument and Key Predictions

Table 2.2 is a two-by-two matrix that demonstrates how structural underpinnings that support dictatorship – such as legislatures and strong state capacity – interact with proximate factors that can destabilize dictatorships to drive distributional consequences. When structural underpinnings are present and a proximate factor materializes, one should expect crony capitalism and high inequality under elite-biased democracy. When structural underpinnings to dictatorship are present but no proximate factors that could spur a transition are present, the anticipated outcome is again crony capitalism. But the difference this time is that this will occur under consolidated dictatorship.

What if there are no structural underpinnings present and proximate factors that destabilize dictatorship are activated? The most likely outcome is a popular democracy in which capitalism is balanced with a social safety net and progressive taxes and transfers, equalizing the distribution of income and opportunities. Finally, the absence of both structural underpinnings and proximate factors yields chronic underdevelopment and swings between different sectoral winners and losers under volatile dictatorship. This could, but need not, lead to large swings in the distribution of assets and income.

CONCLUSION

In laying out a theory of political regimes, regime change, and the distributional consequences of regimes, this chapter provides the foundation for the rest of the book.

One of the main takeaways from this chapter is that there are common reasons across place and time for incumbent authoritarian elites to strategically choose democracy over dictatorship – that is, if they are fortunate enough to live in a regime with the necessary tools for pulling off this sometimes risky feat. This decision is fundamentally rooted in the internecine competition between economic rivals and not, as much of the existing literature would have us believe, a timeless struggle between social classes. Even for elites, life under dictatorship can be nasty, brutish, and short.

Orchestrating an orderly democratic transition in which outgoing political elites and their economic allies can impose their institutional preferences can be rife with difficulties. Caretaker governments tasked with overseeing a transition might attempt to abrogate an exit pact and seek justice for an autocrat's misdeeds, even if doing so brings their downfall. Or defections by lower-level elites could lead to a countercoup that reverses the transition and punishes outgoing elites for risking the welfare of other regime elements. Alternatively, the first steps toward a transition might embolden the democratic opposition to go to the streets to push for a better deal – one that the autocratic incumbents are unwilling to accept.

Nonetheless, when these obstacles can be overcome, it is possible for political elites and their economic allies to negotiate a democratic transition that can not only insulate them from punishment but allow them to thrive economically. As the next chapter will make clear, this is phenomenon is much more pervasive than both researchers and publics have previously thought. The history of democracy is largely the history of gamed democracy.

3

Constitutions as Elite Deal Making

Content and Trends

Incumbent authoritarian political elites and their economic allies at times face joint threats, especially from ascendant outsider economic elites and from the masses. How do they negotiate these shifting sands, and how do their reactions impact the potential for democracy? Incumbent authoritarian elites and their economic allies are often able to successfully design a roadmap for regime transition. This chapter argues that the most successful approach – and a quite common one – is to construct a constitutional document that protects their vital rights and interests, and that they can impose on a new democracy. Constitutional Machiavellianism of this sort allows elites to exit the dictatorship on their terms and to continue to benefit well after democratization.

Holdover authoritarian constitutions can be incredibly intricate and effective documents. They can encode a host of biases that favor former authoritarian elites: tailor-made electoral rules, selected political party bans, devolution of authority to subnational units, guarantees to private property rights, military vetoes over key national policies, and numerous veto points to block consequential institutional redesign. Indeed, their effectiveness in this regard perhaps helps account for the fact that an incredible 70 percent of countries that have transitioned to democracy since WWII have done so under the aegis of an authoritarian constitution.

But why would authoritarian elites who seek to protect their hides under democracy through a constitution expect that such a strategy would work? After all, couldn't newly elected leaders under democracy simply rewrite the rules once in office? Outgoing authoritarian elites are all too aware of this potential threat and deftly design constitutions to prevent it from coming to fruition. By combining elements such as favorable electoral rules or malapportionment *along with* obstacles to constitutional change, such as requiring large supermajorities to scrap the constitution, they can replicate their de facto strength in new ways that derive explicitly from de jure protections.

Newly elected representatives under democracy, for their part, are typically hamstrung by this constitutional one-two punch. Yet having a seat at the table, even with a constitution that is far from ideal, is preferable to complete exclusion. Succeeding democrats are forced to hold their noses and hope that generational change, along with broad social and economic shifts, can enable them to tweak and perhaps ultimately replace an authoritarian constitution in the future. This typically occurs after the original authoritarian stakeholders have died or been dramatically weakened, a point we will elucidate in Chapter 5 and also revisit in the conclusion.

This chapter first lays out why constitutions can be an effective vehicle for vouchsafing the interests of outgoing authoritarian elites after a transition to democracy. It unpacks the contents of these constitutions to demonstrate what elements are doing the work. We do not argue that all elements of a constitution serve to further elite interests – or have any effect, for that matter. Aspirational statements, for instance, often remain just that. But institutional design and explicit provisions to protect former authoritarian elites can and do carry bite. We explain why this is the case and what design elements are most effective. Furthermore, we outline the patterns of democratic transition and constitutional adoption since 1800 in order to convey how common this phenomenon is.

CONSTITUTIONS AS A VEHICLE OF ELITE DEAL MAKING

As we outlined in Chapter 2, when the balance of power in a consolidated dictatorship promises to shift, or there is a looming threat to the regime, autocratic incumbents might seek to get ahead of the curve and hand over power through a democratic transition – that is, if they are able to successfully bargain for the transition on favorable terms.

A recent example of a roadmap to democracy imposed from above throws this strategy into high relief. In Myanmar in late 2015 and early 2016, President Thein Sein, along with the military dominated legislature, passed a flurry of legislation that benefited themselves on the eve of democratization. The military had ruled the country for several decades, and in the process enriched generals and key officers before losing free and fair elections in November 2015 to the opposition, the National League for Democracy. Now they seized the chance to ensure that life would be good for them under elected government too. Their eleventh-hour legislation included promises of amnesty to military generals who have been accused of human rights abuses, a generous pension plan for departing lawmakers, the awarding of lucrative business contracts slated to benefit outgoing generals and other elites, and the transfer of manufacturing plants from the ministry of industry to the ministry of defense (see Mahtani and Paddock 2015).

Democratic transitions such as Myanmar's are frequently complicated affairs. What ensures that an arrangement crafted by outgoing authoritarian elites will continue to stick under democracy? How can these arrangements be credibly binding once a new regime takes root? Outgoing authoritarian elites are acutely aware that the opposition and future politicians face strong incentives to renege on a regime transition pact and, in the extreme, completely overturn it. This awareness, and the credible commitment problem it reflects, therefore dominates their terms of extrication and the actual design of a new democracy's institutions.

O'Donnell and Schmitter (1986) and Przeworski (1991) illustrate how militaries that support autocratic rule manipulate the terms of transition in their favor and then maintain resources and autonomy post-transition to protect their interests. This was a key tactic employed by Turkey's National Security Council and Egypt's military following the fall of Mubarak. Sutter (1995) indicates one way these interests can be credibly enforced: "The possibility of reintervention allows the military to ensure compliance by other parties and overcome the punishment dilemma" (110).

Another way outgoing elites can protect their interests after transition is through the endurance of dominant parties that survive the transition and afford them a greater likelihood of recapturing office after democratization. Ziblatt (2017), for instance, outlines how conservative parties in nineteenth- and early twentieth-century Western Europe that were dominant under authoritarian or oligarchic rule were able to use their organizational prowess to navigate increasing electoral competition and even open up new issue dimensions. This sometimes allowed them to win office with the support of selective working-class workers. Slater and Wong (2013) argue that authoritarian parties in some countries in East Asia and Southeast Asia have effectively introduced democracy from a position of strength, leveraging their records of economic performance to win beyond the founding of competitive elections. Riedl (2014) similarly argues that authoritarian parties in sub-Saharan Africa that are deeply rooted in existing social structures have been more willing to introduce democratic reforms, knowing they have the capacity to win free and fair elections. Relegating attention to democratic transitions since 1980, Haggard and Kaufman (2016) uncover a similarly important role for political parties across place: they provide incumbents with a distinct electoral edge.

In other cases, key players in the outgoing authoritarian regime can leverage advantages and information that they have accumulated under dictatorship to secure beneficial policies under democracy or even regain power. Some authoritarian regimes can exploit their past experience, reputation, symbols, and political expertise to renovate themselves into formidable democratic competitors (Grzymala-Busse 2002).[1] Others can use compromising knowledge about opposition collaboration with the regime to blackmail competitors into quiescence, enabling regime officials to skate free of punishment and even compete under democracy (Nalepa 2010).

---

[1] In a somewhat similar vein, Acemoglu and Robinson (2008) argue that outgoing elites can choose to invest in de facto power to offset the de jure loss of power that comes with democratization.

Finally, consider Michels's (1911) classic "iron law of oligarchy." This axiom states that the exigencies of governance vested in modern bureaucracies ultimately limits how pluralistic, inclusive, and egalitarian a new democracy can become. The idea is that the imperatives of specialization, delegation, and professionalization mean that a small faction inevitably comes to control a society's political organizations and agencies. The upshot is that this phenomenon limits a government's democratic intentions and aspirations; moreover, the cadre of experts who dominates policy making is able to hijack the collective decision-making process to satisfy its own ends. To the extent that the power brokers and experts who come to dominate a democracy's policy-making organs are holdovers from the previous autocratic regime, they can insulate themselves from sanctions and secure their own material and political interests.

While former autocratic elites can certainly use the host of measures outlined previously to protect themselves from the credible commitment problem tied to democratization, they can rely on de jure protections and institutions as well. Indeed, they might prefer to focus on the latter approach. As the types of de facto power that elites possessed upon transition fade over time, former elites need to replicate their de facto strength in new ways that derive explicitly from de jure protections. For instance, the threat that revanchist elements within society will launch a reactionary coup might fade with military churn and socialization under democracy, the meaning of authoritarian-era symbols of progress or solidarity can fade for new generations, and new scandals under democracy can incentivize opposition parties to cast a narrative that former authoritarian parties have retained more of their untoward past practices than they have actually renovated.

Indeed, returning to the recent example of Myanmar's first steps toward transition, the military imposed a constitution and transition plan before losing parliamentary elections in November 2015, which awarded it 25 percent of the seats in parliament – precisely the figure needed to block constitutional reform.

In the following sections, we demonstrate that Myanmar is not exceptional: elites quite often codify their outsized influence in a constitution prior to transition that is subsequently bequeathed to a new democracy. By designing a favorable constitution that is adopted by the new democratic regime as part of a transition pact, former autocratic leaders increase the likelihood that the representatives of the new political order will not implement harmful policies. This insight builds on earlier work on these issues (Wood 2000; Alexander 2002a; Negretto 2006; Albertus and Menaldo 2014a; Albertus and Menaldo 2014b).

Although elite-biased institutions and rules are typically forged through constitutions, in some cases, legal and political tools separate from constitutions can also enshrine biases. This is especially true in older democracies that

---

This de facto power can be used to influence policy outcomes in ways that are favorable to them despite elections and checks and balances under democracy.

were once monarchies and became more "republican" through the strategic use of statutes that simultaneously protected older aristocratic elements or incumbent economic sectors (usually landholders). At the extreme, a handful of countries (most famously, the United Kingdom) do not operate under a formal constitution and therefore only resorted to extraconstitutional measures to promulgate elite biases such as franchise restrictions. We revisit this issue later in the book, especially in our analysis of Sweden's elite-biased democratic transition in Chapter 6 and in our exploration of how colonial legacies distorted democratization efforts in Chapter 8.

Crafting the Deal

The democratic transition process is often fluid and unpredictable in nature. In this context, how are pacts and informal deals negotiated between incumbents about to step down and an opposition hungry to obtain power for the first time translated into a more formalized constitutional process? One key in this dynamic is that incumbent authoritarian elites typically have powerful advantages over the opposition. By controlling the state apparatus and the security apparatus, for instance, they often set the initial terms for convoking an assembly charged with formalizing a negotiated deal. They are the first movers in electing or appointing delegates to a constitutional assembly – and they themselves are often delegates at the convention. Furthermore, their initial agenda control enables them to wield disproportionate influence over voting rules within constituent assemblies to ensure favorable content. In other words, they outline the rules for *how* decisions about the structure and content of the constitution are made. This includes crucial processes such as proffering constitutional provisions for consideration and rules for voting them up or down. They may also name and dominate the committees within the convention that are deputized with hammering out the charter's details.

Indeed, the constitutional assembly is the gateway to a favorable democratic experience for outgoing authoritarian elites for several reasons. First and foremost, this is the forum for constructing the institutional architecture under which democracy will operate. Elites in the constituent assembly will seek to ensure that this architecture is favorable to them. Second, the constitutional assembly sets the concrete terms of the actual handover of political power. It sets conditions and terms for the first and most consequential round of elections to the legislature and presidency. Furthermore, and crucially, it also sets the timing of these elections. Depending on the contemporaneous strength of the opposition, outgoing elites might have incentives to jump quickly to elections before the opposition can congeal into coherent political parties.

Consider Tunisia's constitutional creation experience in the wake of the Arab Spring. Although the transition occurred quickly and in an unanticipated fashion, leaving little time for authoritarian elites to plan in advance, elites nonetheless circled the wagons in an attempt to preserve their influence. Upon fleeing the country in January 2011, President Ben Ali deputized his long-serving prime minister Rached Ghannouchi from the ruling Democratic Constitutional Rally (CDR) Party as president. Ghannouchi's cabinet contained twelve members of the CDR. When Ghannouchi was forced from power shortly thereafter, he handed the torch to Beji Caid Essebsi, who had served in several key positions under the republic's founder and was a key legislator under Ben Ali (indeed, he served as the head of the Chamber of Deputies from 1990 to 1991).

Essebsi played a key role in determining the nature of the democratic transition and held power until handing it over to the Ennahda Party leader in December 2011. Indeed, he even liquidated the CDR, only to draw from it a host of leaders for a new party he created for the 2014 legislative elections. More importantly, Essebsi saw to it that the constitutional assembly guidelines prescribed proportional representation designed to benefit smaller parties – many of them the remnants of the CDR. This made it very difficult for the opposition – led by Ennahda, an Islamic political party allied with secularists – to control the constituent assembly without receiving an overwhelming majority of the popular vote.

Moreover, the regime also ensured that items to be passed within the constituent assembly had to garner supermajority support. This meant that opposition groups were unable to muster the votes needed to ban elites of the former ruling party from the political system. The proximate result was that the constituent assembly exhibited a power-sharing arrangement, the so-called Troika, that distributed leadership roles between the opposition and holdovers from the Ben Ali regime. The ultimate result was that a center-right party, Nidaa Tounes, composed of holdovers from the authoritarian regime, rose as the main opposition to Ennahda. In 2014, the party's standard bearer, none other than Essebsi himself, won Tunisia's first freely and fairly held presidential election, marking the end of the transition to democracy.

The opposition, however, is not completely powerless during the constitution making process. To the contrary, the opposition will often attempt to mobilize support via popular protests or general strikes to try to get a better bargain (as occurred in Peru in 1979, for example). But it can also be co-opted. What is the incentive for the opposition leadership and their supporters to play by the autocratic regime's rules, rather than attempt to upend a process stacked against them? Having a seat at the table, even with a flawed constitution, is better than being excluded completely. Moreover, the constitution is then typically put to a popular vote via a plebiscite or referendum.

The process by which a constitution is crafted and adopted can give political elites an upper hand on the eve of democratic transition, allowing them to secure a series of guarantees that their interests will be credibly upheld in the long term. This requires that elites pay considerable attention to institutional design, as well as the content of constitutional provisions. In terms of institutional design, what matters is how power is distributed, both in terms of geography and in terms of different social groups and organizations and the rules that convert

TABLE 3.1. *Elites' Constitutional Strategies for Enduring Influence*

Constitutional Measures to Ensure Elite Dominance	Practical Manifestations
a) Vote aggregation rules	Electoral system design; malapportionment; gerrymandering; indirect elections
b) Military integrity	Military vetoes; appointed military senators; parallel judicial organs for military
c) Defanging the opposition	Selective party bans; lack of voter protections; lack of protection for unions; selective restrictions on the franchise
d) Protection of former regime elements from prosecution	Prohibition on retroactive criminal punishment
e) Safeguarding assets and rents	Constitutional guarantees to private property; allow committee system to have input from special interests
f) Constitutional stability	Federalism; bicameralism; prohibition on citizen-led legislation via referenda; supermajority thresholds for constitutional change

numbers into political representation and authority. In terms of content, what matters are provisions that protect political elites' lives and livelihoods and vouchsafe the property rights and rents of incumbent economic elites. Other measures that are salient are those that weaken the opposition, whether it consists of outsider economic elites or other groups that are threatening to both political and incumbent economic elites, such as extreme left-wing parties.

Table 3.1 displays the constitutional means authoritarian elites can pursue to ensure their dominance over the longer term, as well as the practical institutional designs and constitutional provisions this entails. It is important to underscore that not all of these are necessarily used by elites in the context of any given democratic transition; elites can tailor-make the design to fit the circumstances. Nonetheless, these are the most common constitutional means to achieving their interests.

The left column outlines the principal constitutional means to ensure elite dominance: vote aggregation rules and measures that govern military integrity, govern constitutional stability, weaken the opposition, protect political incumbents from the outgoing regime from criminal prosecution, and protect the property rights and rents of both incumbents and their economic allies. The right column outlines examples for each of these categories. While we expand upon each of these lists further and provide examples from actual constitutions inherited by democracies from previous authoritarian periods in later sections, here we briefly define some of the terms included in Table 3.1.

Let us begin with vote aggregation rules. Perhaps the most important element in authoritarian elites' strategy for gaining overrepresentation in the legislature or executive branch is to choose an electoral system design that maps votes to seats in a way that allows them to gain strong entry into the legislature, senate, or cabinet. This can include systems of proportional representation or outright quotas if elites fear they will be wiped out under majoritarianism. Alternative tools that can yield the same end – or exacerbate the distortions of the electoral system to overrepresent elites – include malapportionment (a distortion in the translation of votes to legislative seats), gerrymandering to create political districts in which elites are overrepresented compared to the general population, or even indirect elections (e.g., election of the executive by an elite-led senate) rather than direct elections.

For many outgoing authoritarian regimes, especially those composed of generals or other elements of the military or their allies, it is also important to protect the military's political, organizational, and economic interests. This enables the military to maintain leverage well after any individual dictator leaves office. Sometimes this means allowing the military to veto legislation that pertains to its interests (e.g., national security), or in extreme cases allowing it to intervene in national politics when "the national interest" is threatened, such as annulling elections. Furthermore, the military will often push for a parallel military judicial branch not subsumed under the civilian judicial system that is charged with adjudicating and punishing wrongdoing within the military. This ensures that military figures do not play by civilian rules and can provide cover for illicit military activity, whether cracking down indiscriminately on the opposition or cutting side deals with foreign investors in state-owned enterprises run by the military. Somewhat more innocuously, military vetoes can also connote the ability of the military to choose and remove its own leaders and have power over its own budgets.

In terms of weakening the opposition under democracy, outgoing elites can seek to undermine measures that protect the integrity of the vote, making it harder for non-elites to exercise their political voice and thus watering down the franchise and the accountability of citizens' elected representatives. One way to do this historically was by forestalling the introduction of the secret ballot, thus allowing employers or other powerful actors to intimidate non-elites into voting for political parties that do not represent their economic interests. Another mechanism with a historical pedigree is the implementation of restrictions on the franchise based on ethnicity, literacy, property, or social class. In modern times, voting restrictions have more to do with voter registration requirements, whether citizens get time off work to vote, and whether there are restrictions, such as prohibiting absentee balloting.

Table 3.1 also outlines other important constitutional measures to ensure elite dominance via a constitution, such as protecting former regime elements from prosecution, safeguarding elite assets and rents, and ensuring constitutional stability. The practical manifestations of these measures are perhaps more self-evident than the others. We return to all of these design features again in depth later in this chapter.

Enforcing Elite-Biased Constitutions under Democracy

Outgoing authoritarian elites go to significant lengths to design constitutions that will benefit them once democracy is set in motion. But why would a democracy that inherits such a constitution maintain it? This credible commitment problem that authoritarian elites face in the handover of power is at the core of democratic transition.

Many constitutional bargains, although sometimes patently one-sided, endure in the long run. There are several reasons such constitutions are self-enforcing. First and foremost, these constitutions contain the seeds of their own perpetuation. Many autocratic constitutions create a host of crisscrossing checks and balances that steeply raises the transaction and collective action costs required to cobble together a broad coalition for change. Furthermore, they often incorporate provisions that require supermajority vote thresholds for constitutional change. Some of these are quite onerous; for instance, requiring two-thirds of both houses of congress to support amending the constitution. Therefore, while it might be easy to oppose specific elements of a constitution, it is far more difficult to agree on what to replace it with and even more difficult to marshal the support to effectuate that change.

Second, if a democratic government selectively enforces laws it opposes, it risks undermining its own authority and legitimacy. Ignoring proscriptions against punishing former elites, even if it would prove politically popular, raises the specter that other laws unrelated to immunity clauses for former elites can be transgressed down the line – a precedent that could risk backlash from a range of different groups in society who fear that they might be the next targets.

Third, former autocratic elites can prevent constitutional safeguards from being eroded under democracy by steadfastly exploiting the power afforded by the constitution to further cement their political advantages. For example, they can gerrymander electoral districts to split opposition votes in a way that grants them more seats in the legislature. Alternatively, they can redraw districts, create or eliminate districts, or reassign the number of seats in each district to amplify the electoral voice of favored political allies.

Also, former autocratic elites can push early on for public policies that widen inequality, giving them an advantage in terms of collective action, resources, and de facto power over the less well off. They can then gain favorable policies either via legal means, such as lobbying and financing campaigns, or illegally, via corruption. Moreover, if these elites can finance and support political parties and social actors such as the media, they can mobilize coalitions around issues that benefit them economically and politically.

Moreover, the constitution is a focal point that the military or other former autocratic elites can use to coordinate to oppose any threats to their interests and to forestall any attempts at punishing their misdeeds under dictatorship. Attempts by elected politicians under democracy to weaken or rescind elite-friendly measures left behind by autocratic political elites and their economic allies risk galvanizing those elites and inducing them to launch a coup. The ability of elites to coordinate such a collective response, triggered by a violation of the constitution, is an "off the path" threat that deters elected politicians from making radical political changes.

Finally, former authoritarian elites can even reduce the likelihood that a country becomes a signatory to the International Criminal Court – for instance, by incorporating constitutional provisions emphasizing national judicial sovereignty. In doing so, they can head off attempts by subsequent leaders to draw in the international community to prosecute abuses under dictatorship.

MEASURING POLITICAL REGIMES AND CONSTITUTIONAL ORIGINS

The previous section makes the case that constitution making and constitutional design are at the heart of the political context surrounding democratic transitions. When political incumbents and their economic allies are exiting an authoritarian regime and replacing it with a democratic one, constitutions can formalize the extrication negotiation and set up a friendly political ecosystem that will endure well beyond the first free and fair election. If elites are relatively strong on the eve of transition, they should be able to impose constitutions that were created under autocracy and protect their interests after transition. If elites are relatively weak on the eve of transition, then they should not be able to impose a constitution before free and fair elections. Instead, democracies that adopt new constitutions can create new rules for the political game more favorable to the majority.

How can we measure this phenomenon in a valid and reliable way? Doing so entails defining and operationalizing both regime types and constitution making across a wide range of countries and time periods.

We follow Przeworski et al. (2000)'s groundbreaking work and define democracy as a regime in which the executive and legislature are elected, there is more than one political party, and control of the executive alternates between parties (i.e., the incumbent party does not always win). We use post-WWII data from Cheibub et al. (2010), who employ this coding scheme and update the data as close as possible to the present. For the 1800–1945 period, we rely on data from Boix et al. (2013), who also adhere to this coding scheme. This is a popular, mainstream way of measuring electoral democracy in the literature and the approach we have taken in prior work on this topic (Albertus and Menaldo 2013; 2014).

In terms of measuring constitutional engineering by outgoing authoritarian regimes that hand over power to a democracy, we identify the type of constitution that a democracy operates under. We consider a country as inheriting an autocratic constitution if it operates with a constitution created under dictatorship. Conversely, a country is identified as having a democratic constitution if it creates a new constitution upon transition, operates according to a prior democratic constitution that was in place before the previous period of dictatorship, or passes a new constitution sometime after democratization. Data on the origins of constitutions are taken from the Comparative Constitutions Project, which codes the formal characteristics of written constitutions for nearly all independent states since 1789 (see Elkins et al. 2010).

It is important to highlight that we attempt to be conservative in our coding of what counts as an autocratic or a democratic constitution in an effort to bias against the hypotheses we test in this book. We only code autocratic constitutions as those that are drafted and adopted in years of entirely authoritarian rule. This implies that there are some circumstances in which constitutions that are promulgated in the first calendar year of a new democratic regime are in part drafted with the involvement of the outgoing authoritarian regime (in some cases, under a transitional arrangement) and embed provisions in part favored by those actors. Coding these constitutions as democratic constitutions – since they are designed to institute and guide democracy in the very year democracy takes root, and often with the participation of representatives of popular sectors – *biases against us* in that it underweights the authoritarian influence embedded in these constitutions. This makes it more difficult to uncover the authoritarian or, more likely, mixed effects of these somewhat hybrid constitutions.

One illustrative example is Portugal, for which we code the constitution guiding the transition as a democratic constitution, despite some elements that suggest it was contaminated by authoritarian elite biases. The military's ouster of the longstanding president Antonio Salazar in April 1974 ushered in two years of political turmoil. A constituent assembly was formed to guide a democratic transition and included a mix of representatives of the military, selected economic elites, and popular sectors (especially from the left). The constitution was drafted and largely completed in 1975 under military rule, even while it was unclear whether the military would ultimately allow the constitution to guide a popular transition. Yet, while it swept aside the formal vestiges of Salazar's fascist-leaning regime, it enshrined a military-led Revolution Council that served as an advisor to the president and de facto constitutional court. Changes to the constitution were prohibited for a minimum of five years.

Nonetheless, the constitution was fundamentally shaped by popular forces for the purposes of democracy and provided for a dual presidential-parliamentary system, political parties, regular elections, and an independent judiciary. The constitution was promulgated on April 2, 1976. Legislative elections took place on April 25, 1976, and a presidential election followed in short order on June 27, 1976.

Relatedly, there is the issue of legacies from colonial rule or foreign occupying powers. Democratic constitutions subsume two distinct types of regimes: those that operate with constitutions that they write themselves upon transition and those that are democratic from their inception as independent nations. Some of the latter set of countries split from democratic forebears. These are straightforward cases to which our theory can clearly be extended: new democracies that split from a former democracy typically inherit a democratic legacy from

their forbearer. Many countries that win independence as democracies, however, remain subject to the influences or dictates of their former colonial occupier. While these influences can be limited in some cases, in others, they mimic
forms of elite-biased democracy. These latter countries that begin as democracies inherit colonial legacies from their forbearers that introduce institutional
distortions biased in favor of colonial-era elites. We revisit this issue in detail
in Chapter 8.

Finally, there is the issue of whether democratic constitutions authored by
outsider economic elites and the masses are able to obviate all extraconstitutional elite biases that might endure after the fall of the authoritarian regime.
In scenarios in which popular democracies are being crafted by outsider and
economic elites and the masses, political incumbents and their economic partners do not control the terms of the transition and might not have a seat at the
table during the negotiation of the democracy's founding constitution. It can
appear, therefore, that they are entirely cut out of the new political deal and
have no role in shaping the country's new institutions and economic order. Yet
even in these circumstances, sources of de facto power (e.g., high-profile roles
in the military and high levels of asset inequality) can allow former political
or economic incumbents to have an outsized influence on a transition and the
ensuing democracy. In short, despite their inability to affect changes to formal
institutions, elites from the previous regime might be able to game the system
by controlling major cultural institutions, the media, and political parties that
can compete and even win under democracy (Riedl 2014; Slater and Wong
2013; Ziblatt 2017).

The bottom line is this: all of these issues – the coding dilemma that Portugal
illustrates, our decision to code former colonies and formerly occupied countries as inheriting "democratic constitutions," and the sources of de facto power
such as political parties that give outgoing elites advantages and are not captured in a democracy's new constitution – bias against our empirical analysis. It
makes it harder for us to detect a systematic relationship between elite-biased
democracies, which do not include this subset of countries, and the outcomes
we hypothesize to occur in the wake of an elite-biased democratic transition.

GLOBAL TRENDS IN POLITICAL REGIMES AND AUTOCRATIC CONSTITUTIONS

We now identify and document the trends in elite bias under democracy since
1800 across the world using the data on constitutions outlined in the former
section. The main takeaway is that elite-biased democracy is commonplace. It
is not relegated to the pre–Cold War era of franchise restrictions and indirect
elections. To the contrary, elite-biased democracy is more common after World
War II. Although democracies that inherit constitutions from their autocratic
predecessors can rewrite the deal by annulling their constitutions or amending
them, this is a relatively rarer occurrence, yet one that became more prevalent

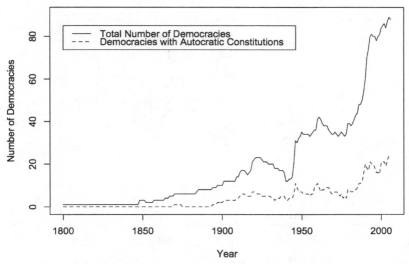

FIGURE 3.1. Trends in democracy and autocratic constitutions since 1800.

in the post–World War II era. The bottom line, however, is that many democracies start out biased by elites. In fact, a substantial majority inherit their constitutions from a previous period of dictatorship.

Figure 3.1 displays the number of democracies in the world. It also shows the number of democracies over time that operate under autocratic constitutions. The figure clearly depicts the three broad "waves" of democracy that have been previously documented (Huntington 1991). The first wave began in the late 1800s. Interestingly, most of the world's first democracies prior to 1900 were instituted either with no constitution (the United Kingdom) or under a constitution drafted at the coterminous founding of both representative government and the nation itself (e.g., Greece, New Zealand, Norway, Switzerland, and the United States). These precocious democracies are geographically clustered in Europe. Starting in the interwar period, more countries became democratic under the aegis of autocratic constitutions. The number of democracies with autocratic constitutions again climbed, though not as steeply, in the wake of World War II. It skyrocketed throughout the 1990s and into the early 2000s as the number of democracies mushroomed globally. In other words, while democracy has spread broadly in the last several decades, former authoritarian regime elements have maintained beachheads in ostensibly free countries and cast an enduring shadow on how much of the world's free people live.

Figure 3.2 displays the ratio of democracies operating under an autocratic constitution versus those operating under a democratic constitution. This figures allows us to draw attention to several additional, interesting trends that are not as easily garnered from Figure 3.1. With the exception of France, which

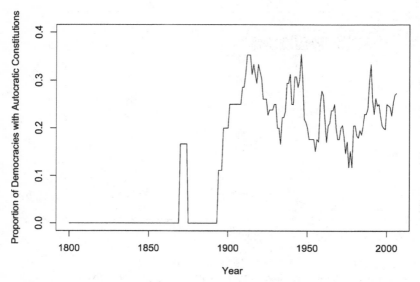

FIGURE 3.2. Proportion of democracies with autocratic constitutions since 1800.

operated under an autocratic constitution from 1870 to 1875, it was nearly unheard of for a democracy's social contract to have blatant authoritarian authorship prior to 1900. Beginning around 1900, however, this pattern shifted definitively. Between 15 percent and 35 percent of the world's democracies have operated with autocratic constitutions since 1900. The number reached nearly 40 percent on the eve of World War I, as democratic regimes in countries such as Argentina, Chile, Denmark, and Sweden were burdened with constitutions penned under prior authoritarian regimes. This tendency decreased in the interwar period, only to spike again in the wake of World War II, largely on the back of Latin American countries such as Costa Rica, Panama, and Venezuela, though not exclusively (e.g., Italy).

During the Cold War era and beyond, democracy was again a volatile affair. The proportion of democracies with autocratic constitutions declined throughout the 1960s and 1970s. Yet since 1980, the proportion of democracies with autocratic constitutions has grown. To be sure, as the pace of democratization slowed after 1990, many consolidating democracies began to shed the constitutions they had inherited from their autocratic predecessors in favor of new constitutions that more closely reflected the popular will. This coincided with the rise of the so-called New Left in democracies that had reached maturity (Debs and Helmke 2010). But this was not enough to stave off a new batch of democracies with autocratic constitutions in the early 2000s.

Table 3.2 shines further light on the phenomenon of elite-biased democracy. This table lists all democratic transitions from 1800 to 2006 and identifies whether they inherited elite-biased constitutions from their autocratic

TABLE 3.2. *Cases of Democratic Transition by Autocratic Constitutional Legacy*

Country	Transition Year	Autocratic Constitution (Annul)*	Country	Transition Year	Autocratic Constitution (Annul)*
Albania	1991	–	Kenya	1998	A
Argentina	1912	A	Korea, South	1960	A
Argentina	1946	A	Korea, South	1988	A
Argentina	1958	A	Kyrgyzstan	2005	A (2006)
Argentina	1963	A	Lebanon	1946	–
Argentina	1973	A	Liberia	2006	A
Argentina	1983	–	Madagascar	1993	A (1998)
Bangladesh	1986	–	Malawi	1994	–
Belgium	1894	A	Mali	1992	–
Benin	1991	A	Mauritania	2007	–
Bhutan	2007	–	Mexico	2000	A
Bolivia	1979	A	Mongolia	1990	–
Bolivia	1982	A	Myanmar	1960	–
Brazil	1946	–	Nepal	1990	–
Brazil	1985	A (1988)	Nepal	2008	–
Bulgaria	1990	A (1991)	Netherlands	1897	A
Burundi	1993	A	Nicaragua	1984	–
Burundi	2005	A	Niger	1993	A
Cen. African Rep.	1993	A (1994)	Niger	2000	A
Chile	1909	A	Nigeria	1979	A
Chile	1934	A	Nigeria	1999	–
Chile	1990	A	Norway	1884	–
Colombia	1937	A	Pakistan	1972	A (1973)
Colombia	1958	A (1991)	Pakistan	1988	A
Comoros	1990	A (1992)	Pakistan	2008	–
Comoros	2004	A	Panama	1949	A
Congo	1992	–	Panama	1952	A
Costa Rica	1946	A	Panama	1989	A
Costa Rica	1949	–	Paraguay	1989	A (1992)
Cuba	1909	–	Peru	1946	A
Cuba	1940	–	Peru	1956	A
Cyprus	1983	A	Peru	1963	A
Czechoslovakia	1989	A	Peru	1980	A
Denmark	1901	A (1915)	Peru	2001	A
Dominican Rep.	1966	–	Philippines	1946	–
Ecuador	1946	–	Philippines	1986	–
Ecuador	1948	–	Poland	1989	A (1992)
Ecuador	1979	A (1984)	Portugal	1976	–
Ecuador	2002	–	Romania	1990	A (1991)
El Salvador	1984	A	Senegal	2000	A (2001)
Fiji	1992	A (1997)	Serbia	2000	A (2003)

(*continued*)

TABLE 3.2 *(continued)*

Country	Transition Year	Autocratic Constitution (Annul)*	Country	Transition Year	Autocratic Constitution (Annul)*
France	1848	–	Sierra Leone	1996	–
France	1870	A (1875)	Sierra Leone	1998	–
Georgia	2004	A	Spain	1931	–
Ghana	1969	–	Spain	1977	A (1978)
Ghana	1979	–	Sri Lanka	1989	A
Ghana	1993	A	Sudan	1965	A
Greece	1926	–	Sudan	1986	A
Greece	1974	–	Sweden	1911	A (1974)
Guatemala	1945	–	Taiwan	1996	–
Guatemala	1958	A	Thailand	1975	A
Guatemala	1966	A	Thailand	1979	A (1981)
Guatemala	1986	A	Thailand	1992	A (1997)
Guinea-Bissau	2000	A	Thailand	2008	–
Guinea-Bissau	2004	A	Turkey	1961	–
Honduras	1957	–	Turkey	1983	A
Honduras	1971	A	Uganda	1980	–
Honduras	1982	–	Uruguay	1919	A (1933)
Hungary	1990	A	Uruguay	1942	A (1952)
Indonesia	1999	A	Uruguay	1985	–
Ireland	1922	–	United Kingdom	1885	–
Italy	1919	A	Venezuela	1946	A (1947)
Italy	1946	A (1947)	Venezuela	1959	A (1961)
Jamaica	1962				

Note: Table 3.2 includes all cases of democratic transition from 1800 to 2008 as coded by Cheibub, Gandhi, and Vreeland (2010).

* A: Autocratic constitution adopted prior to democratic transition. Year of annulment following transition, if any, in parentheses.

Data on constitutions as coded by Elkins et al. (2010) end in 2006. This table does not include countries that were occupied and in the course of occupation their regime changed (e.g., Germany and Finland).

predecessors and whether they subsequently annulled these constitutions. The table does not include countries that have been democratic since their founding (e.g., Canada, Finland, and the United States) or countries whose regime type changed during an interregnum marked by foreign occupation (e.g., Germany). There were a total of 122 democratic transitions during this time period.

Figure 3.3 graphically displays how these transitions elapsed over time, breaking them down into those in which the new democracy inherits an autocratic constitution or instead adopted one of their own after transition. Eighty

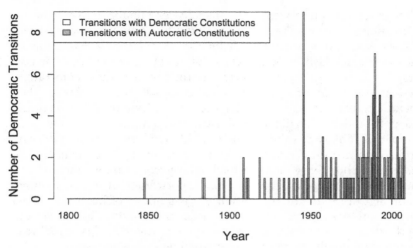

FIGURE 3.3. Transitions with and without autocratic constitutions, 1800–2006.

of these democracies (66 percent) inherited a constitution from their autocratic predecessors. This includes countries now considered strong liberal democracies, such as France (1870) and Denmark (1901). This figure is considerably higher than the proportion of *all democracies* that have historically operated under an autocratic constitution.

There are two reasons for this. First, out of those elite-biased democracies, twenty-six annulled their inherited constitutions at some point during democracy (see Table 3.2) – including both France and Denmark. Second, there are a host of countries that became democratic upon independence and therefore never experienced a transition from dictatorship to democracy (Canada, Finland, and the United States are again illustrative examples).

As Table 3.2 and Figure 3.3 illustrate, and as has been documented elsewhere (Huntington 1991), there was a dearth of democratic transitions before 1950. There were only thirty-three separate democratizations before this date, and this includes some countries that transitioned to democracy twice (i.e., from dictatorship to democracy, then back to dictatorship and back again to democracy), such as Argentina and France. Out of those thirty-three transitions, about half of them (eighteen) were characterized by an elite-biased process in which an autocratic constitution was adopted before the first bout of free and fair elections. Interestingly, while the Netherlands, Belgium, and Norway all inherited constitutions from their autocratic predecessors (monarchs), the United Kingdom and Ireland did not.

The predominance of elite-biased democracy becomes amplified after 1950. Seventy percent of new democracies during this period adopted constitutions that had been created under autocracy. In some cases, during this period, as in the pre–World War II period, autocratic constitutions that were adopted on the eve of democratic transition were later amended or annulled after democratization, creating provisions that rein in the power of outgoing elites in favor of the masses. A total of 6 percent of all country years from 1950 to 2006 are democracies with amended autocratic constitutions (15.4 percent of all democracy years). Furthermore, a total of nineteen of the countries that democratized with elite-biased constitutions during this period subsequently shed their inherited autocratic constitutions for new social contracts. Countries such as Brazil, Madagascar, Poland, and Thailand are illustrative examples.

In contrast to Table 3.2, Table 3.3 takes a different approach and displays information on former dictators who were in power on the eve of democratization, while again containing the data for holdover constitutions inherited by democracies from autocracies. Table 3.3 also reports the year in which outgoing dictators left office, the total duration of their rule in office, and whether they were transitional leaders. Transitional leaders come to power in various contexts: the death of a longstanding dictator, consensus bargains in the wake of civil conflict, or simply the retraction of a regime.

The table considers all leaders who held power within one year of the transition to democracy and were not democratically elected. We draw data on leaders from the Archigos dataset, which codes every country's leaders over the 1875–2004 period. We also adjust the country-year data on political regime type and constitutional status to the leader-year level. The first nondemocratic leader we observe on the eve of democratization is Gladstone from the United Kingdom in 1885. The last nondemocratic leader is observed in 2004 (Burjanadze, from Georgia). There were 149 leaders who were in power under dictatorship within one year of democratic transition in this time period.

Some interesting patterns stand out. While the average number of days in power across all leaders is 1,640, there is a marked difference between leaders who exit dictatorship under an autocratic constitution, imposed before the first free and fair elections, and those who do not. While the average number of days in office for dictators who manage to impose a constitution before democratization is 1,777 days, for those without an elite-biased constitution it is only 1,431 days. Furthermore, the majority of leaders who exit dictatorship – 90 out of 149 (60 percent) – do so under the aegis of an authoritarian constitution.[2]

CONSTITUTIONAL ENGINEERING CASE BY CASE

Table 3.4 displays all the instances of democracies that inherited constitutions from previous authoritarian regimes since 1800, along with the most important constitutional impediments to popular rule associated with these elite-biased

[2] In one case, Betancourt in Venezuela, we code the constitutional circumstances of the leader's exit (see Table 3.3) differently than the circumstances of the country's transition to democracy (see Table 3.2). Betancourt presided over a transition to democracy via an autocratic constitution but then promulgated a new democratic constitution later in his term.

TABLE 3.3. *Outgoing Autocrats upon Democratization, 1875–2004*

Country	Leader	Year of Exit	Days in Office	Transitional	Autocratic Constitution
Albania	Alia	1990	2089	No	No
Argentina	R. S. Peña	1911	446	No	Yes
Argentina	Bignone	1983	528	No	No
Argentina	Farrell	1946	817	No	Yes
Argentina	Aramburu	1958	901	No	Yes
Argentina	Guido	1963	563	No	Yes
Argentina	Lanusse	1973	793	No	Yes
Bangladesh	Ershad	1985	1376	No	No
Belgium	Beernaert	1894	3439	No	Yes
Benin	Kérékou	1991	6734	No	Yes
Bolivia	Pereda Asbun	1978	127	No	No
Bolivia	Padilla Aranciba	1979	258	No	Yes
Bolivia	Guevara Arze	1979	86	No	Yes
Bolivia	Natusch Busch	1979	16	No	Yes
Bolivia	Torrelio Villa	1982	349	No	Yes
Bolivia	Vildoso Calderón	1982	82	Yes	Yes
Brazil	Vargas	1945	5485	No	No
Brazil	Linhares	1946	94	Yes	No
Brazil	Figueiredo	1985	2199	No	Yes
Bulgaria	Lukanov	1990	155	No	Yes
Burundi	Buyoya	1993	2138	No	Yes
Burundi	Ngueze	1993	7	No	Yes
Central African Rep.	Kolingba	1993	4435	No	Yes
Chile	P. Montt	1908	836	No	Yes
Chile	Alessandri y Palma	1933	372	No	Yes
Chile	Pinochet	1990	6026	No	Yes
Colombia	López Pumarejo	1936	878	No	Yes
Colombia	Paris	1958	455	No	Yes
Comoros	Bob Denard	1989	4238	No	Yes
Comoros	Azali Assoumani	2003	584	No	Yes
Congo	Nguesso	1992	4943	No	No
Costa Rica	Picado Michalski	1945	603	No	Yes
Costa Rica	León Herrera	1949	384	No	No
Cuba	Palma	1906	1593	No	No
Cuba	Laredo Bru	1940	1383	No	No
Cyprus	Kyprianou	1982	1977	No	Yes
Czechoslovakia	Husak	1989	7782	No	Yes
Denmark	Sehested	1901	457	No	Yes
Dominican Republic	Berreras	1965	116	No	No

(continued)

TABLE 3.3 *(continued)*

Country	Leader	Year of Exit	Days in Office	Transitional	Autocratic Constitution
Dominican Republic	Godoy	1966	302	Yes	No
Ecuador	Velasco Ibarra	1945	580	No	No
Ecuador	Mancheno	1947	11	No	No
Ecuador	Suárez	1947	15	Yes	No
Ecuador	Arosemena Tola	1948	340	Yes	No
Ecuador	Gustavo Noboa	2002	1075	No	No
Ecuador	Poveda Burbano	1979	1308	No	Yes
El Salvador	Magaña Borja	1984	762	No	Yes
Fiji	Mara	1992	1642	No	Yes
Georgia	Shevardnadze	2003	4276	No	No
Georgia	Burjanadze	2004	64	Yes	Yes
Ghana	Afrifa	1969	154	Yes	No
Ghana	Akuffo	1979	335	No	No
Ghana	Rawlings	1979	112	Yes	No
Ghana	Rawlings	1992	4019	No	Yes
Greece	Pangalos	1926	423	No	No
Greece	Kondylis	1926	104	Yes	No
Greece	Ionannides	1974	242	No	No
Guatemala	Ubico Castañeda	1944	4886	No	No
Guatemala	Ponce Valdez	1944	113	No	No
Guatemala	Árbenz Guzmán	1945	146	Yes	No
Guatemala	Castillo Armas	1957	1109	No	Yes
Guatemala	Mendoza Azurdia	1957	4	No	Yes
Guatemala	Flores Avendano	1958	126	Yes	Yes
Guatemala	Peralta Azurdia	1966	1189	No	Yes
Guatemala	Mejia Victores	1986	891	No	Yes
Guinea-Bissau	Vieira	1999	6749	No	No
Guinea-Bissau	Mane	1999	8	Yes	No
Guinea-Bissau	Correia Seabra	2003	15	Yes	No
Guinea-Bissau	Henrique Rosa	2003	95	Yes	No
Guinea-Bissau	Sanha	2000	280	Yes	Yes
Honduras	Héctor Caraccioli	1957	427	No	No
Honduras	Paz García	1982	1270	No	No
Honduras	López Arellano	1971	2804	No	Yes
Hungary	Grosz	1989	504	No	No
Hungary	Szuros	1990	197	Yes	Yes
Indonesia	Habibie	1999	518	No	Yes
Ireland	de Valera	1921	980	No	No
Ireland	Griffith	1922	215	No	No
Ireland	Collins	1922	11	Yes	No
Italy	Bonomi	1945	377	Yes	Yes
Italy	Parri	1945	160	Yes	Yes

TABLE 3.3 *(continued)*

Country	Leader	Year of Exit	Days in Office	Transitional	Autocratic Constitution
Italy	Orlando	1919	598	No	Yes
Kenya	Moi	1997	7072	No	Yes
Lebanon	El Khoury	1945	771	No	No
Madagascar	Ratsiraka	1993	6496	No	Yes
Malawi	Banda	1994	10912	No	No
Mali	Amadou Touré	1992	439	No	No
Mexico	Zedillo	2000	2192	No	Yes
Mongolia	Batmonh	1990	2028	No	No
Myanmar	Ne Win	1960	504	No	No
Nepal	Birendra	1990	6858	No	No
Netherlands	Roell	1897	1176	No	Yes
Nicaragua	Ortega	1983	1628	No	No
Niger	Wanke	1999	256	Yes	Yes
Niger	Seibou	1993	1985	No	Yes
Nigeria	Abubakar	1999	355	Yes	No
Nigeria	Obasanjo	1979	1327	No	Yes
Pakistan	Yahya Khan	1971	995	No	Yes
Pakistan	Zia	1988	4062	No	Yes
Pakistan	Ishaq Khan	1988	108	Yes	Yes
Panama	Noriega	1988	1966	No	Yes
Panama	Díaz Arosemena	1949	301	No	Yes
Panama	Arosemena	1952	511	No	Yes
Paraguay	Stroessner	1989	12627	No	Yes
Peru	Ugarteche	1945	2060	No	Yes
Peru	Fujimori	2000	3771	No	Yes
Peru	Odría	1956	2193	No	Yes
Peru	Pérez Godoy	1963	228	No	Yes
Peru	Lindley López	1963	148	Yes	Yes
Peru	Morales-Bermúdez	1980	1795	No	Yes
Peru	Valentín Paniagua	2001	248	Yes	Yes
Philippines	Marcos	1986	7363	No	No
Poland	Jaruzelski	1988	2632	No	Yes
Portugal	Costa Gomes	1976	663	No	No
Romania	Ceaușescu	1989	9045	No	Yes
Senegal	Diouf	2000	7031	No	Yes
Serbia	Milošević	2000	4164	No	Yes
Sierra Leone	Strasser	1996	1357	No	No
Sierra Leone	Bio	1996	73	Yes	No
Sierra Leone	Koroma	1998	264	Yes	No
South Korea	Rhee	1960	4274	No	Yes
South Korea	Ho Chong	1960	108	Yes	Yes
South Korea	Chun Doo Hwan	1988	2739	No	Yes

(continued)

TABLE 3.3 *(continued)*

Country	Leader	Year of Exit	Days in Office	Transitional	Autocratic Constitution
Spain	Berenguer	1931	381	No	No
Spain	Arias Navarro	1976	236	No	Yes
Spain	Suárez González	1976	184	Yes	Yes
Sri Lanka	Jayewardene	1989	4363	No	Yes
Sudan	Abboud	1964	2176	No	No
Sudan	al-Khalifa	1965	226	Yes	Yes
Sudan	Swar al-Dahab	1986	396	No	Yes
Sweden	Lindman	1911	1951	No	Yes
Taiwan	Lee Teng-Hui	1995	2910	No	No
Thailand	Kriangsak	1978	415	No	Yes
Thailand	Sanya	1975	496	No	Yes
Thailand	Panyarachun	1992	395	No	Yes
Thailand	Kraprayoon	1992	50	No	Yes
Thailand	Panyarachun	1992	106	Yes	Yes
Turkey	Gürsel	1961	533	No	No
Turkey	Evren	1983	1160	No	Yes
Uganda	Banaisa	1980	328	No	No
Uganda	Paulo Muwanga	1980	214	Yes	No
United Kingdom	Gladstone	1885	1869	No	No
Uruguay	Baldomir	1941	1292	No	Yes
Uruguay	Álvarez Armalino	1985	1278	No	No
Uruguay	Feliciano Viera	1919	1462	No	Yes
Venezuela	Medina Angarita	1945	1628	No	Yes
Venezuela	Betancourt	1945	75	Yes	No
Venezuela	Larrazábal	1958	296	Yes	Yes
Venezuela	Sanabria	1959	92	Yes	Yes

Note: Data on leaders, tenure in office, and manner of exit are from Archigos (Goemans et al. 2009). Constitutions are coded by Elkins et al. (2010) and adjusted to leader years by the authors.

charters. Broadly speaking, this table recalls the elements of constitutional engineering by elites on the eve of democratization identified in Table 3.1. We now identify case by case how authoritarian elites bring to life their strategy to dominate politics under the ensuing democracy through vote aggregation rules and measures that govern military integrity, constitutional stability, weakening the opposition, protecting political incumbents from the outgoing regime from criminal prosecution, and protecting the property rights and rents of both outgoing political elites and their economic allies.

Specifically, Table 3.4 identifies whether the constitution incorporates or is accompanied by federalism, bicameralism, proportional representation, or the banning of left-wing parties. It also identifies whether legislation can

TABLE 3.4. *Features of Elite Bias in Autocratic Constitutions*

Country	Year	Federal/ Unitary	Bicameralism	Electoral System	Leftist Extremist Party Ban	Popular Initiation of Legislation	Prohibits Ex Post Punishment	Property Rights Protection	Miscellaneous
Argentina	1912	Federal	Bicameral	Majoritarian		No	Yes	Yes	Indirect elections for senate, restrictions on the franchise, no secret ballot
Argentina	1946	Federal	Bicameral	Majoritarian	Banned	No	Yes	Yes	Indirect elections for senate
Argentina	1958	Federal	Bicameral	Majoritarian	Banned	No	Yes	Yes	Indirect elections for senate, military veto
Argentina	1963	Federal	Bicameral	Proportional	Banned	No	Yes	Yes	Indirect elections for senate
Argentina	1973	Federal	Bicameral	Proportional	Banned	No	Yes	Yes	Malapportionment
Belgium	1894	Unitary	Bicameral	Proportional		No	No	Yes	Indirect elections for senate, supermajority amend., restrictions on the franchise
Benin	1991	Unitary	Unicameral	Proportional	No ban	No	Yes	Yes	Supermajority amend.
Bolivia	1979	Unitary	Bicameral	Proportional	Banned	No			Malapportionment, military veto
Bolivia	1982	Unitary	Bicameral	Proportional	Banned	No			Malapportionment
Brazil	1985	Federal	Bicameral	Proportional	Banned	No	Yes	Yes	Supermajority amend., malapportionment
Bulgaria	1990	Unitary	Unicameral	Mixed	No ban	No	Yes	Yes	Supermajority amend.
Burundi	1993	Unitary	Unicameral	Proportional	Banned	No	Yes	Yes	Supermajority amend.
Burundi	2005	Unitary	Bicameral	Proportional	Banned	No	Yes	Yes	Indirect elections for senate, supermajority amend.
Central African Rep.	1993	Unitary	Unicameral	Majoritarian	Banned				

(continued)

TABLE 3.4 (continued)

Country	Year	Federal/ Unitary	Bicameralism	Electoral System	Leftist Extremist Party Ban	Popular Initiation of Legislation	Prohibits Ex Post Punishment	Property Rights Protection	Miscellaneous
Chile	1909	Unitary	Bicameral	Majoritarian	Banned	No	Yes	Yes	Supermajority amend., restrcitions on the franchise, no secret ballot
Chile	1934	Unitary	Bicameral	Majoritarian	Banned	No	Yes	Yes	Restrictions on the franchise, no secret ballot
Chile	1990	Unitary	Bicameral	Binomial	Banned	No	Yes	Yes	Appointed senators, supermajority amend., constitutional court can ban parties, malapportionment
Colombia	1937	Unitary	Bicameral	Proportional	Banned				
Colombia	1958	Unitary	Bicameral	Proportional	Banned				
Comoros	1990	Unitary	Unicameral	Majoritarian	No ban				
Comoros	2004	Unitary	Unicameral	Majoritarian	No ban	No	No	Yes	Supermajority amend.
Costa Rica	1946	Unitary	Unicameral	Proportional	Banned	No	Yes	Yes	Supermajority amend.
Cyprus	1983	Unitary	Unicameral	Proportional	Banned	No	Yes	Yes	Supermajority amend.
Czechoslovakia	1989	Federal	Bicameral	Proportional	Banned				
Denmark	1901	Unitary	Bicameral	Majoritarian	Banned	No	No	Yes	Malapportionment, restrictions on the franchise
Ecuador	1979	Unitary	Unicameral	Proportional	Banned	Yes	Yes	Yes	Supermajority amend., malapportionment
El Salvador	1984	Unitary	Unicameral	PR 3-seat districts under quota-remainders	Banned	No	Yes	Yes	Supermajority amend., military veto
Fiji	1992	Unitary	Bicameral	Majoritarian	Banned	No	Yes	Yes	

Country	Year								Notes
France	1870	Unitary	Unicameral		No ban	No			No secret ballot
Georgia	2004	Unitary	Unicameral	Mixed	Banned	No	Yes	Yes	Supermajority amend., constitutional court can ban parties, malapportionment
Ghana	1993	Unitary	Unicameral	Majoritarian	Banned	No	Yes	Yes	Supermajority amend., malapportionment
Guatemala	1958	Unitary	Unicameral	Proportional	Banned	No	Yes	Yes	Military veto
Guatemala	1966	Unitary	Unicameral	Proportional	Banned	No	Yes	Yes	Malapportionment, military veto
Guatemala	1986	Unitary	Unicameral	Proportional	Banned	No	Yes	Yes	
Guinea-Bissau	2000	Unitary	Unicameral	Proportional	Banned	No	Yes	Yes	
Guinea-Bissau	2004	Unitary	Unicameral	Proportional	Banned	No	Yes	Yes	Supermajority amend., indirect elections for executive, military veto
Honduras	1971	Unitary	Unicameral	Proportional	Banned	No	Yes	Yes	Supermajority amend., military veto
Hungary	1990	Unitary	Unicameral	Mixed	No ban	No	No	No	
Indonesia	1999	Unitary	Unicameral	Proportional	Banned	No	No	No	Supermajority amend., military veto
Italy	1919	Unitary	Bicameral	Proportional	Banned	No	Yes	Yes	Supermajority amend., malapportionment
Italy	1946	Unitary	Bicameral	Proportional	Banned	No	Yes	Yes	
Kenya	1998	Unitary	Unicameral	Majoritarian	No ban	No	Yes	Yes	
Korea, South	1960	Unitary	Bicameral	Majoritarian	Banned	No	Yes	Yes	Supermajority amend., constitutional court can ban parties, malapportionment
Korea, South	1988	Unitary	Unicameral	Mixed	Banned	No	Yes	Yes	Supermajority amend., malapportionment
Kyrgyzstan	2005	Unitary	Unicameral	Mixed	Banned	Yes	Yes	Yes	Supermajority amend., constitutional court can ban parties

TABLE 3.4 (continued)

Country	Year	Federal/Unitary	Bicameralism	Electoral System	Leftist Extremist Party Ban	Popular Initiation of Legislation	Prohibits Ex Post Punishment	Property Rights Protection	Miscellaneous
Liberia	2006	Unitary	Bicameral	Majoritarian		No	Yes	Yes	
Madagascar	1993	Unitary	Bicameral	Proportional	Banned	No	Yes	Yes	Supermajority amend.
Mexico	2000	Federal	Bicameral	Mixed	Banned	No	Yes	Yes	Supermajority amend.
Netherlands	1897	Federal	Unicameral						
Niger	1993	Unitary	Unicameral	Mixed	No ban	No	Yes	Yes	Supermajority amend.
Niger	2000	Unitary	Unicameral	Proportional	No ban	No	Yes	Yes	Supermajority amend.
Nigeria	1979	Federal	Bicameral	Majoritarian	Banned				
Pakistan	1972	Federal	Bicameral	Majoritarian	Banned				
Pakistan	1988	Federal	Bicameral	Majoritarian	Banned				
Panama	1949	Unitary	Unicameral	Majoritarian		Yes	Yes	Yes	Supermajority amend.
Panama	1952	Unitary	Unicameral	Proportional	No ban	Yes	Yes	Yes	Supermajority amend.
Panama	1989	Unitary	Unicameral	Mixed	Banned	No	Yes	Yes	Supermajority amend., malapportionment
Paraguay	1989	Unitary	Bicameral	Mixed	Banned				Appointed senators
Peru	1946	Unitary	Bicameral	Mixed	Banned				Restrictions on the franchise, military veto
Peru	1956	Unitary	Bicameral	Proportional	Banned				Restrictions on the franchise
Peru	1963	Unitary	Bicameral	Proportional	Banned				Restrictions on the franchise
Peru	1980	Unitary	Bicameral	Proportional	No ban	No	Yes	Yes	Appointed senators, supermajority amend.
Peru	2001	Unitary	Unicameral	Proportional	No ban				
Poland	1989	Unitary	Bicameral	Majoritarian	Banned				
Romania	1990	Unitary	Bicameral	Proportional	Banned				
Senegal	2000	Unitary	Bicameral	Proportional	No ban				
Serbia RB	2000	Federal	Unicameral	Proportional	No ban				
Spain	1977	Federal	Bicameral	Proportional	No ban				Military veto

Sri Lanka	1989	Unitary	Unicameral	Proportional	Banned	No	Yes	Yes	Supermajority amend.
Sudan	1965	Unitary	Unicameral	Majoritarian	Banned	No	Yes	Yes	Supermajority amend.
Sudan	1986	Unitary	Unicameral	Majoritarian	Banned	No	No	No	Restrictions on the franchise, indirect elections for the senate, supermajority amend.
Sweden	1911	Unitary	Bicameral	Proportional	Banned	No	No		
Thailand	1975	Unitary	Bicameral	Majoritarian	Banned				
Thailand	1979	Unitary	Bicameral	Majoritarian	Banned				
Thailand	1992	Unitary	Unicameral	Majoritarian	Banned				
Turkey	1983	Unitary	Unicameral	Proportional	Banned	No	Yes	Yes	Constitutional court can ban parties, malapportionment, military veto
Uruguay	1919	Unitary	Bicameral	Proportional	Banned	Yes	No	Yes	Indirect elections for senate, supermajority amend.
Uruguay	1942	Unitary	Bicameral	Proportional	No ban				
Venezuela	1946	Federal	Bicameral	Proportional	Banned	No	Yes	Yes	Indirect elections for executive, restrictions on the franchise, military veto, no secret ballot
Venezuela	1959	Federal	Bicameral	Proportional	Banned				Indirect elections for executive

Notes: There are several cases of mixed systems; we code systems as PR if they have any elements of PR. Malapportionment is indicated at values above 0.05, with data from Samuels and Snyder (2001) and country-specific sources; historical data are missing for numerous countries. In the miscellaneous category, we include interesting or particularly salient characteristics of the constitution. Failure to report a characteristic for any given constitution in the miscellaneous category could mean either that this feature is absent or that data are not available to determine its presence. Failure to report a characteristic in the other categories indicates that data are missing for that feature.

Sources: Database of Political Institutions; Elkins et al. (2010); V-Dem; Mainwaring and Pérez-Liñán (2014); Bakke and Wibbels (2006); Henisz (2002); Gerring, Thacker, and Moreno (2005); Engerman and Sokoloff (2000); and country-specific sources.

be initiated by popular referendum, whether the constitution prohibits punishment retroactively, and whether there are protections for property rights enshrined in the constitution. Finally, the table also includes a miscellaneous category incorporating other, more idiosyncratic forms of elite bias such as military vetoes over critical policy domains, supermajority thresholds for constitutional amendment, severe malapportionment, and indirect elections.

We note that there are some democracies in the table that are not heavily gamed by elites to begin with, and shortly after the democratic transition, the constitution is abandoned or strongly reformed to make it more democratic. Two of these cases – Poland and Romania – are Eastern European transitions that occurred in the late 1980s and early 1990s, around the fall of the Berlin Wall. Another case is Italy, which democratized in 1946 after the United States and its allies defeated Mussolini and the Axis Powers and occupied the country. Shortly thereafter, in 1947, the constitution was replaced with a new, more popular charter. The same is true after Senegal's 2000 democratic transition; the constitution inherited from the autocratic period was annulled the year after free and fair elections.

In the sections that follow, we flesh out each of the most pervasive elements (expressed in the columns of Table 3.4) used by authoritarian elites to protect their interests on the eve of democratization. We start with structural elements such as federalism, bicameralism, and the electoral system. We then turn to banning of left-wing parties, prohibiting retroactive criminal punishment, forestalling popular initiation of legislation, and protecting property rights, and lastly to additional elite-biased features such as malapportionment and restrictions on the franchise.

Federalism

Table 3.4 documents sixteen cases of federalism, including countries such as Argentina, Brazil, Netherlands, Nigeria, Pakistan, Spain, and Venezuela.[3] Federalism can buttress the privilege of both former authoritarian political elites and incumbent economic elites by allowing elites who reside in the periphery to win power, set their own policies, and keep any national-level policies that challenge their influence at bay. These elites want an insurance policy in case the tide of national-level politics turns against them. Federalism provides such insurance by building in another check against the broad popular will.

Take the United States – a nation that was democratic since inception and is therefore not included in Table 3.4. It began its life with several onerous elite biases, many of which were centered on federalism and some of which still endure. For instance, segregationist policies were enshrined at the state

---

[3] Of course, federalism is also more likely to bind in larger countries with more heterogeneous populations.

level during the Jim Crow era, despite national-level legislation that ostensibly granted equal rights to citizens of all races.

Political sovereignty at the provincial level can also be used to curb taxation and redistribution or to adopt regulations that are friendly to regional businesses. Returning to the US example: Southern oligarchs made states' rights a cornerstone of the federal bargain in order to ensure local control over their economies – and especially to build a bulwark against Northern abolitionists that sought to end slavery.

South Africa's 1994 transition exemplifies the importance of federalism.[4] The 1993 constitution defined a transitional power-sharing agreement from 1994 to 1999 and set up the institutional architecture that would guide South African democracy during and beyond this period. Crucially, provinces were allowed to adopt their own constitutions. Minority groups were awarded a veto in local governments over policies that affected them. In essence, the federal structure created a "hostage" game between elite-run provinces such as the Western Cape and the majority-controlled government that enabled elites to block redistribution (Inman and Rubinfeld 2005).

Bicameralism

Table 3.4 displays forty-three cases of bicameralism in countries as diverse as Belgium, Madagascar, Thailand, and Uruguay. The presence of two legislative chambers can be useful to former authoritarian political and their economic allies to safeguard their interests on the eve of democratization. Many upper chambers were historically composed of indirectly elected or appointed legislators, who often sided with elites – indeed, they were often themselves elites or were appointed by elites – when crafting tax and regulatory legislation.

More prosaically, an upper chamber can act as an additional veto point, making it much harder to change the status quo. If the status quo upon transition leaves a legacy of policies and institutions that favor authoritarian interests and their economic elite allies, this should make it harder to adopt redistributive policies that can hurt the interests of former incumbent economic elites. For example, it is much harder for opposition parties to use the legislature to challenge a conservative-leaning executive when there are two houses and both are required to censure or impeach the president.

Finally, a second chamber can exercise political power by delaying legislation that is unfriendly to elite interests or by significantly amending bills that are crafted in more populist lower houses – for instance, by watering down

---

[4] Although most regime-type measures consider South Africa as democratic since 1994, it is not included in this table because, on technical grounds, it does not yet qualify as a democracy according to the coding rules we explained above: there has been no alteration in the executive branch between different political parties.

provisions that call for higher taxes on politically influential citizens and businesses (see Tsebelis and Money 1997).

We revisit all these points ahead in our case studies of Sweden (Chapter 6) and Chile (Chapter 7). In these countries, bicameralism has been an important tool used by former authoritarian elites to both protect their interests and sustain elite-biased systems in general.

Favorable Electoral Systems

Elite-biased constitutions can usher in electoral systems that will translate votes to seats in a way that is favorable to elites. The most common example is the adoption of proportional representation (PR), in which elites seek to make it more likely that small conservative parties will gain a political foothold and induce gridlock. Table 3.4 indicates forty-eight cases of PR, the latter including mixed electoral systems in which at least some seats are elected through PR.

As research on the strategic choice of electoral rules has argued (e.g., Rokkan 1970; Boix 1999), PR is a heads-I-win, tails-you-lose bet for minority parties. In the best-case scenario, candidates with preferences close to that of the former dictator win and are able to implement their preferred policy agendas and shelve harmful outcomes such as the possibility of punishment for past crimes. In the worst-case scenario, former regime elements and sympathizers will at least gain a toehold in government that likely affords them veto power over major issues.

Bulgaria after Communist rule exemplifies this. When the former dictator, Andrey Lukanov, was charged with corruption under democracy, the minority Communists in parliament (the Bulgarian Socialist Party) were able to successfully push the government to drop the charges against him, despite the fact that they only controlled 44 percent of the seats.

In Chapter 6, we consider the case of Sweden, in which political incumbents adopted PR on the eve of its transition to full democracy with the blessing of their economic allies. There we recount how elites protected a host of biases, including an indirectly elected senate that overrepresented them, by strategically replacing their first-past-the-post electoral system with PR in a bid to retain seats in both parliamentary chambers after they broadened suffrage. This helped them cling to power long after they had lost a majority of political support among an enlarged set of voters.

We also note that other sui generis electoral systems have also been introduced by elites on the eve of democratization. In El Salvador, a military junta aligned with conservative parties supported permissive electoral rules that contained elements of PR, including outright quotas, during a transitional constitutional convention to bolster the representation of right-wing parties.

In Chile, there was a binomial electoral system – the only one of its kind in the world. As we will discuss in detail in Chapter 7, Chile's binomial electoral system established two-member districts that long militated in favor of left–right parity, despite a numerical disadvantage for the conservatives. Requiring coalitions to capture two-thirds of the vote in order to win both seats in a district, the binomial electoral system favored the creation of umbrella coalitions that incentivized the left to partner with centrist political parties, leading to the adulteration of their egalitarian political agenda. This system was tailor-made to bolster conservatives – who typically polled above one-third but less than one-half of electoral support – on the basis of Pinochet's 1988 plebiscite.

Banning of Left-Wing Parties

Table 3.4 also documents the banning of left-wing parties. This table contains a total of fifty-six cases in which left-wing parties were banned either directly by the constitution or indirectly through a constitutional court. Quite often, constitutions introduce constitutional courts and endow them with the capacity to proscribe selected political parties. In the case of left-wing parties, several charters heavily restrict the ability of communist or other extreme left parties to operate or run for office, and some explicitly ban them.

Examples of left-wing party bans include countries as wide-ranging as Denmark, Indonesia, Chile, Ghana, Burundi, South Korea, Madagascar, Sri Lanka, Turkey, and Nigeria. A notorious example is Guatemala's 1956 constitution, which banned socialist and communist parties after a bloody coup overthrew populist president Jacobo Árbenz in 1954. Similarly, in Chile, the Constitutional Tribunal formed prior to the 1989 transition was authorized to declare parties that threatened democracy unconstitutional. Behind the scenes, former authoritarian elites had a say in this process because the military-dominated National Security Council was allowed to appoint two judges to this seven-judge court under the auspices of the 1980 constitution. Similarly, in Turkey, the 1982 constitution that guided the transition to democracy created a constitutional court with the ability to ban political parties while stripping the authority of the legislature to make court appointments and instead vesting it in institutions such as the presidency that were heavily influenced by the outgoing military.

Prohibiting Retroactive Criminal Punishment

In the case of prohibiting retroactive punishment, several constitutions in Table 3.4 make it easier for dictators and regime insiders who committed human rights abuses and indulged in corruption and other crimes to skirt punishment after democratization. This is especially salient for outgoing elites because the opposition that negotiates the transition might face strong political incentives ex post to renege on the terms of the deal that ushers in democracy. Also, democracy can empower new actors that did not participate in the transition pact itself and have an even weaker incentive to abide by the original pact. With the transition episode receding into the backdrop, it is these actors especially who would face the strongest incentives to prosecute former regime officials.

There are at least thirty-eight cases in which we can identify that retroactive punishment was prohibited by the constitution. The examples run the gamut, including Argentina, Brazil, Venezuela, Mexico, El Salvador, Fiji, Benin, Ghana, Kenya, Liberia, Sudan, Bulgaria, South Korea, Kyrgyzstan, Madagascar, and Niger. Moreover, this potentially does not capture additional constitutions for which we could not ascertain whether punishments could or could not be applied retroactively.

Turkey is an excellent, and egregious, example of how elites can use a constitution to limit punishment after democratization. In the 1982 constitution, the top military brass and their collaborators made sure there was a series of clauses and articles that granted them immunity from prosecution for any crimes during the period they held power. The most important of these was Provisional Article 15, which was finally abolished in 2010. It stated, "No allegation of criminal, financial or legal responsibility shall be made, nor shall an application be filed with a court for this purpose in respect of any decisions or measures whatsoever taken by the Council of National Security."

Popular Initiation of Legislation

Numerous charters in Table 3.4 fail to provide for or explicitly prohibit the popular initiation of legislation. Some examples include Belgium, Burundi, Cyprus, Kenya, and South Korea. These are sometimes naked efforts by former authoritarian elites to avoid losing control over policy once they formally step down from power. Elites from the former authoritarian order can find themselves vulnerable to the masses or outsider elites when individuals can legally gather signatures and force ballot initiatives that have policy bite. They might therefore constitutionally prohibit the popular initiation of legislation to avoid an end run around their legislative influence and, most importantly, as a way of keeping their elite-biased charter intact.

Protections for Property Rights

We identify at least forty-two cases where the sanctity of property rights is enshrined in the constitution. These include Denmark, Chile, Argentina, Ghana, Brazil, Guatemala, Panama, Turkey, Kenya, Georgia, Uruguay, and Belgium. Outgoing elites are often keen to make property rights sacrosanct in the constitution before exiting dictatorship to lock in the status quo distribution of resources, even if their property and the profits connected to it were secured in an unlawful or unjust fashion. In fact, especially if that is the case.

Outside of the explicit constitutional protection of property rights, many elite-biased constitutions empower actors to block threats to the property rights of authoritarian-era incumbent economic elites. Consider Ecuador. Citing the

1946 and 1967 constitutions, the Ecuadorian Supreme Court and Congress repeatedly blocked legislation initiated by "populist" presidents Arosemena (1961–1963) and Velasco (1968–1973) that was unfriendly towards elites, including higher corporate taxes and agrarian reform (Isaacs 1993). Also consider Colombia. The country's 1961 Agrarian Reform Act gave landowners decision-making authority over agrarian reform zones, allowing them to block legislation that was unfriendly to their economic interests (Albertus and Kaplan 2013).

In turn, provisions of this ilk might make it harder to expropriate property under democracy in general, even under the auspices of eminent domain, and deter aggressive redistribution through regulations, taxation, and public spending. The reason is that making property rights inviolate – even if only for a minority – helps establish a focal point that can galvanize opposition by any group against any state trespass, whether real or perceived (Weingast 1997).

Additional Elite Bias Features

The miscellaneous category in Table 3.4 outlines additional, notable measures of elite bias on a constitution-by-constitution basis. These include restrictions on the franchise, the lack of a secret ballot, the requirement of legislative supermajorities to amend the constitution, and malapportionment. They also include whether the constitution prescribes executive elections through indirect means (electoral colleges or legislative vote) or legislative elections through indirect means. Yet another measure of elite bias is the appointment, rather than election, of legislators, especially those connected to the former authoritarian regime. This typically occurs in the upper chamber.

Among the pervasive measures to advance incumbent elite interests is malapportionment that overrepresents rural power brokers and especially large landowners. Argentina's democratic experiments have always included two chambers that are considerably malapportioned, especially the upper house – a pattern typified by the short-lived introduction of three senators for each region in 1972, one of whom represented wealthy constituents. New districts have also been created in sparsely populated areas.

Towards the same end, a different tactic was pursued in Brazil: the military regime in the 1970s placed limits on the number of seats that could be allocated to each multimember district – even in those that were highly populated. This blunted the relative weight of the urban vote (Snyder and Samuels 2004). The military then split the conservative state of Mato Grosso in two, creating the new state of Mato Grosso do Sul and increasing representation to this electorally favorable region. On the eve of democratization, it again followed up by increasing the number of seats per district, further advantaging rural, already overrepresented states. The ensuing democracy then inherited this formula.

Other Latin American examples stand out for reasons other than malapportionment. Chile's revived democracy in 1990 inherited a host of appointed senators – top military brass from the Pinochet regime – in a bid to limit the power of ascendant, leftist political parties, a point we will revisit in Chapter 7. Bolivia's 1967 constitution is an egregious example of a mix of constitutional engineering to limit populist policies. Colonel René Barrientos Ortuño spearheaded a coup against a civilian government in 1964 and, three years later, under the aegis of a new constitution, he dismantled the mine workers' union, suppressed strikes, exiled union leaders, and granted private investors preferential treatment. In turn, the 1967 constitution served Barrientos's economic allies well in the lead up to Bolivia's transitions to democracy in 1979 and 1981 and beyond.

Literacy requirements on exercising the franchise were also a mainstay of Latin American constitutions under democratic rule. In Brazil, they were only rescinded in 1985. In Peru and Ecuador, they were rescinded in 1980.

Finally, Latin American constitutions are also replete with military veto points. For instance, in the Honduran constitution of 1957, Articles 318 through 330 stipulate that the chief of the armed forces would be selected by the military, that his command over the military would supersede the president's, and that he could deny presidential oversight of the military budget. In Chapter 7, we will outline a series of similar political prerogatives that the Chilean military carved out for itself in the 1980 constitution it foisted upon the ensuing democracy.

A host of historical examples from Europe are also worth remarking on. Denmark's 1901 constitution enshrined malapportionment and restrictions on the franchise to exclude groups such as impoverished adults and those that declared bankruptcy from voting. Belgium's 1894 constitution called for indirect elections for the senate, required a supermajority to amend the constitution, and ushered in restrictions on the franchise. Sweden's autocratic constitution also ushered in restrictions on the franchise, a point that we will revisit in Chapter 6. In France, the 1870 constitution did not provide for the secret ballot, despite the adoption of the secret ballot by several neighboring countries, enabling early elections under democracy to take place under the influence of vote buying and clientelism.

Finally, even recent examples from the Arab Spring embody the attempt by elites to craft a transition deal that will protect them after elections using, among other devices, military vetoes. While Egypt did not complete its initial steps toward democracy, what is very clear is that leading generals and other insiders from the Hosni Mubarak era spent considerable time and energy ensuring that they could save their skins under a new regime. After ousting Mubarak, Egypt's powerful military apparatus wrote explicit provisions into a new constitution to protect their autonomy and strength and to insulate them from prosecution. Article 198 of the constitution states, "The Military

Judiciary is an independent judiciary that adjudicates exclusively in all crimes related to the Armed Forces, its officers and personnel." Furthermore, this military judiciary was declared autonomous and cannot be dismantled. It is therefore not at all surprising that when Muhammad Morsi was elected president in the immediate aftermath of the Arab Spring, after Mubarak was ousted, and sought to annul the constitution, he was quickly ousted by the military.

CONCLUSION

This chapter lays out the preponderant, most effective method of forging democracy from above: through authoritarian constitutions that explicitly favor outgoing elites. These constitutions are drafted under authoritarian rule but subsequently foisted upon new democracies in an effort to define the rules of the game and protect elements of the old authoritarian order. Such constitutions are exceedingly common. Indeed, almost 70 percent of countries that transitioned to democracy after WWII have done so under authoritarian constitutions. Furthermore, roughly a third of the world's democracies today operate under authoritarian constitutions.

Outgoing dictators and their allies often invest substantial resources and effort in crafting these documents. These are often pitched and protracted political battles that are tied to the negotiations that extricate a dictator from power. They might backfire or fail. But these fights are worth it to authoritarian elites. Authoritarian constitutions often specifically include provisions to protect outgoing incumbents from prosecution, to enshrine the military's autonomy, and to vouchsafe the property and rents of oligarchs. Authoritarian elites therefore seek to make these provisions nonnegotiable and irrevocable.

Given the elitist features prevalent in these constitutions, can it really be said that those democracies that operate under them are actually democratic? Is this not the continuation of authoritarianism by a different name? If by democracy we mean free and fair elections with political alternation, the answer is an unequivocal "yes": these are real democracies. Paragons of democracy such as the Netherlands operated for decades under elite-biased constitutions.

Democracies can experience a wide range of elite bias and operate under a range of institutions that vary in terms of which social groups they tend to favor and by how much. While these biases do not undermine democracy per se, they give democratic leaders less wiggle room. And while these biases impinge on public policies that have everyday impacts on citizens, it does not rob citizens of freedom of expression and assembly or the right to vote and participate politically in other ways. Furthermore, elite-biased constitutions cannot forestall all change. Nimble political entrepreneurs, even within conservative parties, can pop up from time to time and find a way to better represent average citizens – a point we take up in Chapter 5.

In short, the history of democracy in many cases has been, unbeknownst to most research on this topic, severely constrained from inception. Recognizing this fact helps reconcile one of the enduring puzzles in contemporary political economy: free and fair elections do not necessarily translate into policies that benefit the majority of the population and level the playing field. Rather, democracy is often less egalitarian than many authoritarian episodes. The next chapter turns to the origins and effects of these constitutions to shine light on this puzzle.

4

Evidence on the Causes and Consequences of Democracy

Democracy has its discontents. When measured against its lofty ideals, democratic practice often fails to live up to the expectations of its citizens: the representation of marginalized groups is lackluster, it is less pluralistic than one would expect from free-ranging competition between political parties, and it falls short of inclusivity in the sense that the groups who make it into office or have their voices heard are only rarely representative of their constituents in terms of income, education, and social status. Democracy is also less egalitarian than is often presumed. The policies that are adopted by freely and fairly elected officials often diverge from the self-reported preferences of the majority of citizens, and the poor and middle-income earners usually get the short end of the stick. Karl Marx went so far as to label democracy a charade – a set of rules and norms that benefits the bourgeoisie at the expense of the proletariat.

Democracy's critics, however, cannot gainsay the vast fruits it has delivered in selected countries. Citizens in Scandinavia, Canada, New Zealand, and Australia are among the happiest and most fulfilled in the world. Part of the reason is that they live in generous welfare states that offer cradle to grave social insurance and benefits. Democratic governance has solved age-old human miseries such as famines. It has brought millions of people out of poverty. It led to a Europe that, for the first time in centuries, is absent of war, and whose countries embarked on an ambitious political project to unify its diverse and ever-wealthier citizens.

Previous scholars have had trouble identifying, ex ante, exactly which democracies fail to live up to democracy's promise for greater representation, pluralism, inclusiveness, and egalitarianism, and which do not. Clearly, not all democracies merely perpetuate the oligarchic practices of their authoritarian predecessors; not all of them leave large swaths of citizens on the sidelines or adopt policies that hurt the poor, let alone the middle class. Not all of them disappoint.

This chapter makes an original empirical contribution to the study of the causes and consequences of democracy. It spells out how holdover elites from the previous autocratic regime can use tailor-made democracy as a Trojan horse to perpetuate their political and economic hegemony at the expense of other elites and regular citizens. We outline and test hypotheses that spell out, ex ante, which democracies will look more like their autocratic predecessors and continue to benefit a select few politicians and special interest groups while nonetheless staging regular free and fair elections, allowing for a free media and protecting basic citizen rights. We also spell out which democracies experience real change after democratization and become more representative, pluralistic, inclusive, and egalitarian than both their autocratic predecessors and democratic peers.

To do so, we take several steps. We begin by outlining and testing hypotheses about the birth of these starkly different regimes, explicating why some dictatorships end and become democracies that are biased by the elites who ruled the previous regime while others end abruptly and radically, becoming a popular version of democracy that hues more faithfully to the preferences of all of its citizens. We continue by systematically explaining the variation in governance patterns as well as fiscal and material outcomes observed under democracy. Finally, we also explain why some new democracies mete out justice against former dictators to punish them for their crimes under authoritarianism while others allow them to enjoy comfortable lifestyles and live long and prosperous lives. In short, this chapter helps us understand why some democracies disappoint the majority of their citizens and even outside observers while others approximate the political and economic potential often attributed to them by democracy's staunchest defenders.

GETTING TO DEMOCRACY

We start by testing the theoretical predictions about transitions to democracy that stem from our theoretical framework in Chapter 2. Recall that the key to explaining democratic transition in a way that encompasses the varieties of democratic experience in the world is to make three distinctions that have not been previously made in the literature. First, we distinguish between different types of democratic transitions: from dictatorship to elite-biased democracy and from dictatorship to popular democracy. Second, we distinguish between different actors in dictatorship: political incumbents, incumbent economic elites, outsider economic elites, and the masses. By extension, we identify the actors who want to exit dictatorship and their opportunities for a favorable exit. Third, we distinguish between the broader "structural" forces behind democratic transition and the proximate events, or "triggers," that precipitate a democratization at a discrete point in time.

Our main theoretical predictions regarding regime outcomes, encapsulated in Table 2.1, in Chapter 2, identify four outcomes of interest: elite-biased democracy, popular democracy, consolidated dictatorship, and volatile dictatorship. These outcomes are driven by a combination of structural underpinnings that support dictatorship (state strength and autocratic legislatures) and proximate factors that destabilize dictatorship (e.g., revolution or economic crisis).

As we argued in Chapter 2, when structural underpinnings are present but proximate factors pose a threat to incumbent political and economic elites under dictatorship, shared uncertainty about their fate creates focal points for coordination between these actors. These ruling elites will band together, lest they sink alone. They therefore leverage the structural underpinnings available to them, such as a legislature or substantial administrative and infrastructural capacity, and then exit the dictatorship under the aegis of a favorable constitutional arrangement.

By contrast, the absence of proximate factors that can destabilize dictatorship give an upper hand to incumbent elites. Meanwhile, outsider economic elites might be gathering or losing strength, depending on the vagaries of the economy. Yet the presence of structural underpinnings can enable incumbent economic elites to coordinate with political incumbents to repress outsider economic elites and the masses under a stable dictatorship. These ruling partners should be able to consolidate their rule and perpetuate an authoritarian regime in which both benefit from mutual cooperation.

When proximate factors are active in the absence of structural underpinnings, then incumbent economic and political elites will again be relatively weakened. Consequently, there is a clear window of opportunity for democracy. Coordination between outsider economic elites and the masses becomes possible. Together they can instigate a revolution and push for a transition to popular democracy, displacing dictators and their economic allies in the process.

Finally, when proximate factors and structural underpinnings are absent, there is again an indeterminate effect on the strength of both incumbent and outsider economic elites. Dictatorship will prevail, but incumbent economic elites and outsider economic elites will struggle with one another. The result is volatility. Incumbent economic elites might push their political elite partners to attack and expropriate outsider economic elites in order to improve their own position and gain a credible commitment from political elites to support them. Burning bridges in this manner can, for example, signal the political elite's dependence on incumbent economic elites. However, leader cycling could shift the ruling coalition and renew competition among economic elite groups, precipitating another round of volatile dictatorship.

Hypotheses about Democratization

We seek to explore several hypotheses about the causes of democracy implied by our theory. First, there should be a strong, positive relationship between state capacity and a transition to an elite-biased democracy. Second, there should also be a strong, positive relationship between the presence of a legislature under dictatorship and a transition to an elite-biased democracy. Third, natural disasters should precipitate these transitions – that is, the interaction of autocratic legislatures and natural disasters should be positively associated with transitions to elite-biased democracy. Fourth, shocks such as economic growth collapses, currency crises, and revolutions should make popular democracy more likely. However, this should be conditioned by whether the incumbent elites can offset ensuing popular mobilizations by availing a legislature. If they can do so, this should blunt the impact of these shocks. In other words, the interaction of autocratic legislatures and these "negative shocks" should be negatively associated with transitions to popular democracy.

Case Evidence

Before undertaking a systematic statistical evaluation of the hypotheses outlined in the previous section, we first offer a host of examples that corroborate these hypotheses. First, consider a few examples of the importance of state capacity in allowing incumbent elites to exit a dictatorship on favorable terms and obtain an elite-biased democracy. South Africa on the eve of transition was by far the richest country in sub-Saharan Africa. The state was quite strong; it implemented and enforced an apartheid system in which a tiny white elite segregated, repressed, extracted from, and systematically humiliated a black majority numbering in the millions, cordoning them off into ghettos and depriving them of economic opportunity. During its heyday, the white oligarchy used deep surveillance to monitor the movements and thwart the plans of the opposition, imprison both insurgents and civilians by the thousands, and mount sophisticated operations abroad to deter a challenge to their rule. They also raised substantial taxes and trained a highly professional bureaucracy to implement this repressive system.

It is therefore no surprise that the apartheid regime had the capacity to orchestrate a favorable transition on the back of a new constitution. South Africa's 1993 constitution defined a transitional power-sharing agreement from 1994 to 1999, called the Government of National Unity, in which the opposition African National Congress (ANC) agreed that the National Party (NP), the ruling party, would be part of the government during this period (Wood 2000, 187). Moreover, provinces were allowed to adopt their own constitutions, enabling elites in particularly affluent provinces to tailor-make provisions protecting their interests. Cabinets were to make consensus decisions. Minority groups were awarded a veto in local governments over policies that affected them. A sunset clause protected military, police, and civil service members from replacement once the new government was in power.

The NP understood that "negotiating a transition always means that it is a very different process than revolution; you retain a veto over the form of the new society" (Sisk 1995, 84). The result was that "ownership and control of the commanding heights of the economy, the repressive apparatuses of the state...the judiciary, the top echelons of the civil service, of tertiary education and strategic research and development, have remained substantially in the same hands as during the heyday of Apartheid" (Alexander 2002b, 64).

Next, consider an example of a dictatorship that held the reins of a weaker state and floundered when attempting to impose a constitution to guide a potential transition. In 1952 Venezuela, a military junta that had been in power for three years held elections for a constituent assembly that was charged with drafting a new constitution and choosing a provisional president. Lacking the ability to identify and co-opt the opposition via a legislature, the military assassinated dissident army officers and others opposed to military rule. Two million votes were cast in the presidential election that followed, and it was won by the leader of an opposition party, Jóvito Villalba Gutiérrez of the Unión Republicana Democrática.

The result was unexpected and proved intolerable to the regime. The head of the junta, Marcos Pérez Jiménez, ignored the results of the election and proclaimed himself president. He then banned opposition parties. Although the constituent assembly finally met in 1953 and ultimately ratified Jiménez's presidency, it was unable to agree on a stable succession mechanism that could protect the military elite beyond the medium term. Jiménez remained in power another six turbulent years before being ousted in a coup.

To consider the importance that autocratic legislatures have in allowing incumbent autocratic elites to exit the dictatorship and impose an elite-biased democracy, take the example of Mexico under the Partido Revolucionario Institucional (PRI; Institutional Revolutionary Party). The country was ruled by a single-party dictatorship between 1929 and 2000 under the aegis of the 1917 constitution. This charter helped institutionalize the ruling group that went on to form the PRI – including the political elites who rose from the ashes of the Mexican Revolution and their economic allies. It also erected the modern Mexican legislature.

The legislature served as an active forum for policy making under the PRI regime. On the one hand, it helped usher in a plethora of economic pathologies: a highly regressive tax structure, a concentrated banking system that led to severe credit rationing, parallel private and communal property rights regimes in the countryside, and protectionist tariffs that propped up woefully inefficient industrial conglomerates. On the other hand, the legislature was not always a simple rubber stamp or a venue to host the regime's insiders and place them on the state payroll.

However, the legislature did serve as a major forum for ensuring political continuity. This was even the case through democratization. It was a political beachhead for the leadership of the PRI after the party lost the executive branch for the first time in 2000. Not only did PRI members continue to be elected to the legislature (indeed, they recaptured the executive as well in

2012), but they also used that body to guide the transition and ensure that the labyrinthine political and economic institutions created under dictatorship would not simply go up in smoke after democratic transition. Regime officials also leaned on the legislature to avoid prosecution for the graft, corruption, and human rights violations they perpetrated under single-party rule.

How does a structural underpinning, such as a legislature, interact with a proximate factor, such as a natural disaster, to bring about a transition to elite-biased democracy? Mexico is again an illustrative case. In September 1985, the country – which, at that point, had been ruled by the PRI for fifty-six years – suffered an earthquake of historic proportions. The temblor jolted central Mexico and particularly affected Mexico City, the country's political and economic capital. Registering 8.1 on the Richter scale, the earthquake destroyed hundreds of buildings – including several government facilities and scores of public housing projects, highways, and other infrastructure – and felled telecommunications for several weeks. Tens of thousands died. Hundreds of thousands were rendered homeless.

Government officials responded by protecting key state assets, including the presidential palace and the legislature, and repressing disgruntled citizens who were left to fend largely for themselves to rescue victims and survive. Popular protests and movements sprung up with alacrity, and the regime hunkered down rather than face these grievances head on. The government also barred foreign assistance and aid from entering the country in a bid to save face and keep the world in the dark about the extent of the damage.

In many ways, this was the beginning of the end for the Mexican dictatorship. After succumbing to popular pressure engendered in part by the 1985 earthquake and the regime's botched response, the Miguel de la Madrid administration introduced an electoral reform law in 1986 that increased opportunities for opposition parties to gain greater political representation. He also adopted public financing for elections. The 1986 Electoral Reform Law enlarged the lower house from 400 to 500 seats; it also increased the number of congressional seats filled by proportional representation by a factor of two. The ruling party went on to lose several seats in both the upper and lower houses of congress. It also began to lose state elections for governorships – starting with several large and influential states in the north of the country, such as Chihuahua – and state-level legislatures at an increasing rate.

However, it would be a full decade before the PRI lost control of the legislature to opposition parties and fifteen years until it lost control of the executive branch. Furthermore, as outlined previously, when Mexico ultimately transitioned to democracy, it did so under the auspices of the 1917 constitution, which meant that outgoing authoritarian elites were well protected even after they lost control of the executive branch.

Another example of how a natural disaster that occurred in the presence of a legislature spurred democratic opening is Myanmar. In early May 2008, a powerful hurricane – the costliest cyclone ever to hit the Indian

Ocean – struck the country and killed 140,000 people. The storm surge hit the most densely settled part of the country, displaced more than 1 million people, ruined crops and eroded arable land, and fostered widespread disease. The military junta that ruled Myanmar at the time was negligent in three important ways: it did not properly alert citizens living in the river delta most affected by the storm surge, it did not coordinate a comprehensive rescue effort, and it limited the entry of foreigners who pledged to assist in the rescue and recovery efforts. This disaster galvanized the military to circle the wagons, and did not shake its resolve to conduct a public referendum previously scheduled for May 10, 2008 on a new constitution that heavily favored the military regime. The 2008 constitution served as the legal framework for the country's later political liberalization and popular elections, and reserved a quarter of the legislature's seats and many of its most important positions for the military.

How do proximate factors drive transitions to popular democracy rather than, as in the Mexico and Myanmar examples, to elite-biased democracy? As we have discussed, revolution is a proximate factor that can induce a transition to popular democracy. Guatemala's 1945 democratic transition is one example. Mass protests and popular pressure ousted General Jorge Ubico Castañeda from office in 1944 and set the stage for democratic elections, which were won by Juan José Arévalo. A new popular constitution was adopted in 1945, stipulating, among other progressive measures, that land must fill a social function. This was a paramount change, given that the majority of the population worked in the agricultural sector. It allowed for expropriation of uncultivated *latifundios* while simultaneously providing protection of productive land as well as municipal and communal land. This legal infrastructure reduced legislative and bureaucratic barriers and set the stage for a more comprehensive land reform under Arévalo's successor, Jacobo Árbenz.

A final proximate factor that can spur a transition to popular democracy is an economic crisis, especially if accompanied by a currency or debt crisis. Argentina is a notorious case. During the tenure of a military dictatorship in the 1970s, the country was hit by two currency crises and a sovereign debt crisis. The first currency crisis occurred in 1975, followed by a second in 1981. A sovereign debt crisis hit in 1982.

These crises had their origins in the 1970s, when a decline in the availability of international financing led the government to rely on monetary policy and restrictive bank regulations. The deterioration of the fiscal situation spurred several bouts of capital flight, precipitating two currency crises. While the government eventually eased up on financial repression, the real exchange rate appreciated and the current account deficit increased. This led to both high inflation and a serious output shock.

The timing of these crises themselves was largely determined outside of Argentina's borders, however, especially in regards to the sovereign debt crisis.

Higher world interest rates were quickly and unexpectedly ushered in by the chairman of the US Federal Reserve Paul Volcker on the eve of Argentina's 1982 crisis in a bid to tamp down historically high levels of inflation in the United States.

Once this occurred, Argentina's military government was no longer able to finance its foreign debt denominated in dollars and defaulted on ballooning interest payments. This, along with the fact that the military junta gambled for resurrection by goading Great Britain into the Falklands War in 1982 and then lost in humiliating fashion, catalyzed the generals to exit the regime before they had a chance to extricate themselves on friendly terms. Argentina then adopted a new democratic constitution after free and fair elections.

We next evaluate statistical evidence that suggests that these are not isolated examples, but instead reflect underlying trends in democratization across both space and time. Furthermore, Chapters 7 and 8 will offer more fine-grained evidence to support these hypotheses, undertaking an evaluation of the mechanisms behind them in the cases of Sweden and Chile, respectively.

MEASUREMENT

To test whether the aforementioned cases are reflective of a broader, generalizable relationship, we first need to measure the key variables in the theory in a way that is valid and reliable. We start by doing so for democratic transitions.

Measuring Democratic Transition

The key dependent variable in the analyses that follow is regime transition. Consistent with Chapters 2 and 3 and our above discussion, we argue that there are two principal types of democracy. The first is the elite-biased variety, in which a new democracy inherits its constitution and system of government from the outgoing political incumbents and their economic allies before they exit dictatorship. The second is the popular variety, in which a new democracy codifies a constitution and constructs its system of government after the first set of free and fair elections.

To be able to differentiate between these two types of democratic regime types, we avail the variables used in Chapter 3. Transition to elite-biased democracy, which we operationalize as a new democracy that inherits a constitution from a previous period of autocratic rule, proxies for a transition to democracy biased by former incumbents and their economic allies. This is a binary variable coded as a "1" the year of transition to this type of democracy and "0" otherwise. We also operationalize transition to popular democracy in a similar manner. A country has a transition with a democratic constitution if it creates a new constitution upon transition or operates according to a prior democratic constitution that was in place before the previous period of dictatorship. This is also a binary variable coded as a "1" the year of transition to this type of democracy and "o" otherwise. The sources we use to create these variables follow from the previous chapter.

Measuring Elite Coordination Potential

To understand why some countries transition to elite-biased democracy burdened with the authoritarian legacy of the past while others are characterized by a blank slate in which a new group of political incumbents reset the rules of the game after free and fair elections, we also need to operationalize the structural and proximate factors that encourage democratization as outlined above.

Incumbent Political and Economic Elites

In terms of structural factors, there are two variables that capture the conditions that make a transition to an elite bias more likely. Those are state capacity and the existence of a legislature under autocracy.

To measure state capacity, we leverage the fact that countries with longer legacies as sovereign states have had a greater chance to develop state capacity tied to the development of intensive agriculture, urbanization, and the use of money. In other words, the longer a state has existed as an organized and coherent political unit, the greater its ability to penetrate the hinterlands, establish a monopoly on violence, and tax and regulate the economy. We therefore follow Menaldo (2016) and measure state capacity as the number of years a country has been a sovereign nation (logged, after adding 1) to proxy for the longevity of a state's infrastructure and bureaucratic culture. This variable is coded beginning the first year of independence for countries that were either colonized or seceded from another country. Those that became independent prior to 1800 are coded as sovereign since 1800.

The mean value for the unlogged version of this variable is 41.1 years. It ranges from 0 to 206 years. Coding this variable starting in 1800 biases against our hypotheses because many countries that transitioned to elite-biased democracy, such as France, Denmark, Hungary, Sweden, and Belgium, were sovereign nations long before 1800.

To measure the existence of a legislature, we take the variable legislature from Henisz (2000), with data updated to 2006. Legislature is a dummy variable coded as a "1" when there is a legislature that is "constitutionally effective": it has power to make laws, is meaningfully autonomous from the executive, and exercises veto power in some policy domains. A total of 38 percent of the authoritarian regime years in our sample have a legislature. We choose this measure of legislative efficacy over others, such as Gandhi (2008), because it is coded since the nineteenth century. It therefore provides the most coverage.

In terms of proximate factors that precipitate a transition from dictatorship to elite-biased democracy, we first examine natural disasters. Natural disasters have the benefit of being exogenous events (i.e., they are not influenced by political machinations surrounding potential regime transitions). This reduces the likelihood that any relationship between the onset and aftermath of the natural disaster and a regime transition is spurious. To operationalize natural disasters, we measure the presence and intensity of earthquakes using earthquake impact.

We focus on earthquakes over other natural disasters for several reasons. First, they are more ubiquitous than natural disasters such as floods that are based in part on idiosyncratic climate patterns. Second, earthquakes are not man made: while many famines, floods, and fires break out naturally, others are the result of government policies or lack of governance. For example, floods are often a result of poor infrastructure in coastal or riverine areas, such as a lack of levees and drainage. Some fires are the result of poor fire management. Finally, it is easy to measure earthquakes because of their geological nature, and scientists have now tracked them systematically for decades. By contrast, natural disasters such as floods, along with their human impact, are hard to identify historically, especially in poorer regions, where the development of effective media has been slow.

We operationalize earthquakes as earthquake impact from Keefer, et al. (2011). To capture magnitude, the authors use the (base-10 logarithmic) Richter scale, in which marginal increases on the scale imply sizable magnitude increases. The authors transform the Richter scale magnitude according to the formula 10exp(magnitude-5) to measure the much larger effect of earthquakes with a larger Richter score. This transformation also drops all minor earthquakes below magnitude 5.0, which are unlikely to cause major damage, let alone to kill people. They weight each transformed quake magnitude value by the average population density within fifteen kilometers of the earthquake's epicenter. This takes into account that earthquakes in more densely populated areas kill more people, all else equal. Finally, they sum up all of the population density-weighted transformed quakes in a country year. This variable ranges from 0 to 148.58 with a mean of 0.68 and a standard deviation of 5.38.

In the regressions in which we evaluate the effect of earthquakes on transitions, we also control for earthquake propensity, which we again take from Keefer, et al. (2011). This helps account for the fact that some countries are simply more earthquake prone than others and therefore are more at risk of suffering from intense earthquakes. It is measured as the sum of earthquake strengths of quakes above magnitude 6.0 over the period 1960 to 2006, transformed in the same manner as we have outlined.

Outsider Economic Elites and the Masses
We also identify several proximate factors that tilt in favor of the establishment of popular democracy. The first is revolution. Outsider economic elites can use mass discontent to help foment popular action that can usher in popular democracy. As discussed in Chapter 2, even attempted but failed revolutions can force authoritarian incumbents to rush into a transition bargain more quickly

than they would have otherwise done, decreasing their ability to manipulate the transition process to safeguard their interests after democratization.

Our measure of revolution is from Banks (2009: 12), which he defines as "any attempted or successful forced change in the top governmental elite or any armed rebellion whose aim is independence from the central government." We capture the presence of a revolution using a dummy variable that is coded "1" when a revolution occurs and "0" otherwise. The data on revolution dates back to 1919. A total of 20.9 percent of the authoritarian regime years in our sample exhibit revolutionary activity.

A second proximate factor that can encourage democratization is a dramatic slowdown in economic growth. We code economic growth collapse as a "1" when economic growth in a given country year is more than one negative standard deviation from the country's mean growth rate (dating back to either 1800 or, if the country was established after 1800, its year of independence). It is otherwise coded "0." This measure captures the fact that mean country growth rates differ substantially, for a variety of reasons, and a relatively low growth rate for one country can be a relatively high growth rate for another. A growth crisis occurs in 11.3 percent of the authoritarian regime years in our sample.

We also hypothesize that currency and debt crises matter for precipitating popular democracy. To measure currency and debt crises, we code whether there was one or both of these two types of crises in any given year using the variables conceptualized and coded by Laeven and Valencia (2008). According to the authors, a currency crisis is "a nominal depreciation of the currency of at least 30 percent that is also at least a 10 percent increase in the rate of depreciation compared to the year before" (6). In order to identify exchange rate depreciations, the authors use the percent change of the end-of-period official nominal bilateral dollar exchange rate. For countries that satisfy this criterion for several years in a row, they use the first year of each five-year window as the crisis year. To measure sovereign debt crises, they identify episodes of sovereign debt default and debt restructuring. We have coverage for this variable between 1970 and 2006 for the entire world. Currency or debt crises occur in 4.7 percent of the authoritarian regime years in our sample.

It is worth underscoring that although we measure changes in the balance of power between allied economic elites and outsider economic elites in ways that capture exogenous sources of this change, there can of course be endogenous sources of change as well. One notable source of endogenous change that Kuznets (1955) famously focused on is industrialization, stressing the rise of an urban working class and the relative decline of the traditional agricultural sector. Another example is autochthonous innovation (rather than technology that transfers uniformly across the globe). These endogenous sources of change can empower outsider economic elites, raising the potential threat they pose to political incumbents and their allies.

One implication is that our empirical analyses might actually undercount episodes in which incumbent political elites and their economic allies have incentives and opportunities to exit the regime on propitious terms. By the same token, we might also undercount episodes in which outsider economic elites and the masses institute popular democracy. This should make it harder to find systematic evidence in favor of our hypotheses. On the other hand, since these endogenous sources of economic change tend to be a product of political institutions and policies, omitting them from our measures of proximate factors that precipitate regime change is advantageous from the perspective of sound causal inference.

Controls

We also control for several possible confounders across our models. These are all lagged by one period. As in prior work on the determinants of democratization, we control for log(per capita income) and log(total natural resource income per capita). The former captures the idea that wealthier and more modern societies should be more likely to transition to democracy. The latter measures income generated from the production of all hydrocarbons and industrial metals and captures the notion that countries that are reliant on natural resources might be more, or less, likely to democratize. We take both variables from Haber and Menaldo (2011) because they have coverage starting in 1800. Per capita income in log terms varies from 5.45 to 11.85 with a mean of 7.80. The unlogged mean is $2,435 per capita. Natural resource income varies from –4.61 to 4.40 with a mean of –2.72 and a standard deviation of 1.94.

We also follow Albertus and Menaldo (2012b) and measure coercive capacity as military size. There we argue that by virtue of its ability to deploy an internal security force and project the regime's power, a larger, more powerful military will be able to protract autocratic rule. We measure military size per 100 inhabitants and log it after adding .01 to address the zero values in the dataset. This measure ranges from –4.61 to 2.50 with a mean of –0.82 and a standard deviation of 1.14.

STATISTICAL STRATEGY FOR ESTIMATING DEMOCRATIC TRANSITIONS

We now turn to a statistical analysis that estimates the probability that an autocratic regime will transition to an elite-biased democracy versus a popular one as a function of the variables outlined in the previous sections. As depicted in Table 3.2 of Chapter 3, there are 122 transitions to democracy from 1800 to 2006. During this period, we observe 204 authoritarian regime spells across 139 countries (some countries, of course, witness multiple spells of authoritarianism as they transition from dictatorship to democracy and back to dictatorship). Out of the 122 transitions, 80 led to elite-biased democracy, in which a new democratic regime inherits a constitution from its autocratic predecessors. The rest culminated in popular democracy, whereby a new democratic regime crafts its own constitution after free and fair elections. That leaves 82 right-censored authoritarian regime spells; these are countries with authoritarian regimes that were still in power as of 2006.

In order to test our hypotheses about the determinants of either elite-biased or popular democracy, we estimate a series of hazard models that calculate a dictatorship's risk of succumbing to democracy as a function of the independent variables. In particular, we use competing-risks regression models based on the method of Fine and Gray (1999), which builds on the Cox proportional hazards approach.[1] In a typical survival analysis, one measures the time to failure as a function of some observed or experimental factors (e.g., the time from initial cancer treatment to relapse as a function of smoking, exercise, etc.). In a competing-risks framework, however, an alternative outcome could obtain that impedes the occurrence of the event of interest (e.g., death due to a reason other than cancer).

For our purposes, we seek to examine the time it takes for an authoritarian regime episode to "fail" into either an elite-biased democracy or a popular democracy. If an authoritarian regime transitions into an elite-biased democracy, then this new condition prevents that same authoritarian regime from transitioning into a popular democracy. Likewise, an authoritarian regime that transitions into a popular democracy prevents that same regime from transitioning into an elite-biased democracy.

Competing-risks models also account for right-censoring in a manner similar to other survival models. This is important because, as we have pointed out, some authoritarian regime spells in our data are ongoing. These authoritarian regimes could transition into elite-biased democracies or popular democracies in the future but had not done so as of the end of our sample period.

To estimate these models, we pool the data, allowing us to exploit both between and within variation. Robust standard errors clustered by country address heteroskedasticity and any intragroup correlation within countries. We note that we include linear, quadratic, and cubic terms for time to rule out the possibility that some of our independent variables are merely proxying for secular trends (e.g., years of sovereignty might be correlated with a heightened risk of democratization at the global level). Furthermore, the results are robust to adding region fixed effects to control for time-invariant and region-specific unobserved heterogeneity that might impact the likelihood that a country transitions to democracy of a specific form. Finally, the results are similar if the models that follow are instead estimated with the standard errors clustered by year to address contemporaneous/spatial correlation.

---

[1] We conducted tests of the proportional subhazards based on the Schoenfeld residuals to justify the proportional hazards assumption. The results are robust to estimating simpler Cox proportional hazard models or multinomial logit models.

STATISTICAL RESULTS

Table 4.1 displays the results of these survival models. We report the raw coefficients from the regressions rather than the hazard ratios. Columns 1 through 3 examine the determinants of transition to elite-biased democracy. Columns 1 through 2 test the hypotheses about structural factors that are conducive to transitions to elite-biased democracy. In Column 1, the key independent variable is log(sovereignty), which proxies for state capacity. The coefficient is, as expected, positive, statistically significant at the .05 level, and represents a fairly strong substantive effect. Increasing the number of years a country has been sovereign by twenty years above the mean while all other variables are held constant increases the estimated rate of failure to an elite-biased democracy by 17.8 percent.

In Column 2, the key independent variable is legislature. Legislature also performs according to our expectations: it is positive and statistically significant at the .05 level. Moving from the absence of an effective legislature to the presence of a legislature yields a hazard ratio equal to 1.83. Therefore, the estimated rate of failure to an elite-biased democracy is increased by 83 percent with the presence of a legislature.

Figure 4.1 graphically displays the cumulative incidence function for transitions to elite-biased democracy as a function of whether an authoritarian regime has an effective operating legislature. Authoritarian regimes of all ages that have a legislature are more likely to transition to elite-biased democracy. This difference becomes especially pronounced after roughly two decades of authoritarian duration. By this time, authoritarian regimes have typically established stable distributional arrangements and institutions. Consistent with our theory, those regimes with effective legislatures that can be used to craft a favorable democratic arrangement are more likely to lead to elite-biased democracy.

Column 3 tests the "sufficiency hypothesis" we outlined earlier: while the accumulation of state capacity or presence of a legislature might predispose an autocratic regime toward experiencing a transition to elite-biased democracy, these factors do not, on their own, explain the timing of transition. Column 3 examines how natural disasters in the form of earthquakes impacting more densely settled populations influence transition timing. While the coefficient on legislature (in the absence of an earthquake) is again positive, as expected, if there is an earthquake in an autocracy that lacks a legislature, it is less likely that there will be a transition to elite-biased democracy. This supports our theoretical priors. The absence of a forum that would otherwise allow incumbent authoritarian elites to coordinate prevents these actors from transitioning to their preferred regime outcome in what amounts to extenuating circumstances that strengthen the hand of the opposition.

The interaction terms of legislature and earthquake reveal that as earthquakes increase in intensity, they can make a transition to elite-biased

TABLE 4.1. *Transitions to Elite-Biased Democracy and Popular Democracy,*
1816–2006

Dependent Variable	Elite-Biased Democracy			Popular Democracy		
	Model 1	Model 2	Model 3	Model 4	Model 5	Model 6
log(years of sovereignty)	0.412** (0.187)					
Legislature		0.603** (0.240)	0.579** (0.280)	−0.369 (0.645)	−0.391 (0.571)	−1.189* (0.652)
Earthquake impact			−0.331* (0.194)			
Earthquake impact*legislature			0.329* (0.191)			
Revolution				1.107** (0.518)		
Revolution*legislature				−1.485* (0.901)		
Economic growth collapse					0.960** (0.430)	
Economic growth collapse*legislature					−15.644*** (0.972)	
Currency or debt crisis						1.324** (0.626)
Currency or debt crisis*legislature						†
log(GDP per capita)	0.434** (0.186)	0.489*** (0.186)	0.449** (0.202)	0.318 (0.325)	0.127 (0.267)	0.438 (0.303)
log(military personnel per 100)	−0.274* (0.166)	−0.226 (0.152)	−0.130 (0.177)	−0.165 (0.203)	−0.192 (0.198)	−0.193 (0.277)
log(resource income per cap)	−0.148 (0.096)	−0.126 (0.097)	−0.220** (0.099)	−0.189 (0.156)	−0.149 (0.145)	−0.223 (0.155)
Earthquake propensity			0.003*** (0.001)			
Time trends	Yes	Yes	Yes	Yes	Yes	Yes
Observations	4,939	4,992	3,604	4,598	4,914	3,054

* $p < 0.10$; ** $p < 0.05$; *** $p < 0.01$ (two-tailed).
Notes: All models are competing risks regressions. Raw coefficients rather than subhazard ratios are reported. Standard errors clustered by country are in parentheses. Constants and time dummies are not shown. All independent variables are lagged one period.
† This variable is dropped from Model 6, since no transitions to popular democracy occur in the presence of a legislature and a currency or debt crisis.

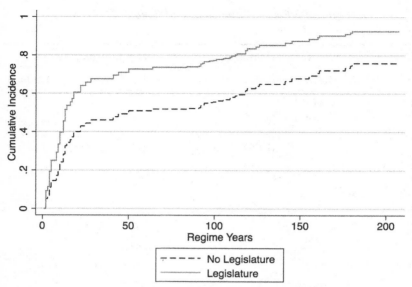

FIGURE 4.1. Rate of dictatorship death and replacement by elite-biased democracy.

Notes: Figure 4.1 graphically displays the cumulative incidence function for transitions to elite-biased democracy as a function of whether an authoritarian regime has an effective operating legislature. This graph is produced by calculating hazard predictions from the regression depicted in Table 4.1, Column 2. We hold all other variables at their means.

democracy *more* likely in the presence of a legislature. When a disaster strikes, the presence of a forum that enables incumbent authoritarian elites to coordinate strengthens their ability to ride out the disaster to a transition to their preferred regime outcome when the power of outsider economic elites and the masses increases. Therefore, while a legislature is necessary for incumbent authoritarian elites to flee the regime on favorable terms, the timing of a transition to elite-biased democracy is precipitated by an exogenous shock that incentivizes these incumbents to head for the exits while they are still relatively strong.

Columns 4 through 6 evaluate the determinants of transitions to popular democracy. Transitions to elite-biased democracy are now modeled as a competing risk in these models. As we outlined, a popular democracy should be more likely in the presence of shocks. However, in some cases, this phenomenon is conditioned by whether the incumbent political elites can offset ensuing popular mobilizations by availing a legislature.

Column 4 demonstrates that a revolution that occurs in the absence of a legislature (the uninteracted term for revolution) makes a transition to popular democracy much more likely. The hazard ratio in this case jumps to 3.03,

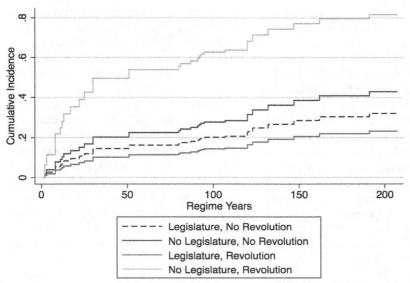

FIGURE 4.2. Rate of dictatorship death and replacement by popular democracy.
Notes: Figure 4.2 graphs the cumulative incidence function for transitions to popular democracy as a function of whether an authoritarian regime has an effective legislature and whether the regime experiences a revolution. This graph is produced by calculating hazard predictions from the regression depicted in Table 4.1, Column 4. We hold all other variables at their means.

indicating a threefold increase in the estimated rate of failure to a popular democracy. By contrast, a revolution that occurs in the presence of a legislature makes a transition to popular democracy less likely. The hazard ratio drops to 0.33, indicating that the rate of failure to popular democracy is decreased by 67 percent.

Figure 4.2 graphs the cumulative incidence function for transitions to popular democracy as a function of whether an authoritarian regime has an effective legislature and whether the regime experiences a revolution. This figure further clarifies the Model 4 predictions. Relative to the baseline omitted category of no legislature and no revolution, an authoritarian regime without a legislature that experiences a revolution is much more likely to transition to popular democracy at any regime age, and by quite sizeable margins. A legislature tamps down the likelihood of transition to a popular democracy across the range of regime years. Importantly, a legislature can even help elites coordinate to forestall the effects of a revolution on the likelihood of a popular transition. In short, legislatures make revolutionary movements a mere bump in the road for sitting autocrats (in other words, we fail to reject the hypothesis that legislature and revolution*legislature are statistically significantly different with a p-value = 0.40).

Similarly, Column 5 demonstrates that while a growth collapse that occurs in the absence of a legislature (the uninteracted term for growth collapse) makes a transition to popular democracy more likely, a growth collapse that occurs in the presence of a legislature makes a transition to popular democracy much less likely. Indeed, a legislature essentially wipes out any chance that a growth collapse will translate into popular democracy.

Finally, Column 6 demonstrates that a currency and/or sovereign debt crisis absent a legislature (the coefficient on currency or debt crisis) makes a transition to popular democracy more likely. As previously, legislature is negatively tied to transitions to popular democracy. This model does not include the interaction between a currency or debt crisis and a legislature, however, because there are simply no cases in our dataset in which popular transitions occur when both of these factors are operative. Therefore, we cannot estimate such a regression. We note that this is consistent with our theory. A legislature makes it easier for political incumbents to deal with such crises without forcing an authoritarian regime to fold under the weight of popular discontent.

OUTCOMES UNDER ELITE-BIASED DEMOCRACY

Whereas the previous section tests the determinants of authoritarian regimes transitioning to either elite-biased democracy or popular democracy, we next move on to testing our hypotheses about the consequences of constitutions inherited from previous autocratic regimes after democratization. As outlined in Chapter 2, we expect popular democracies to differ fundamentally from their elite-biased counterparts. In terms of governance, they should be more representative, pluralistic, and inclusive. In terms of fiscal, monetary, and material outcomes, they should be more redistributive. We therefore test several hypotheses that link a democracy's constitutional origins to governance and material outcomes under democratic rule. We also compare these outcomes to those that obtain under dictatorship. Our sample thus includes both democracies and dictatorships.

Measurement Strategy for Explaining Outcomes under Democracy

We divide the description of our dependent variables according to their historical coverage and sources. The first set of hypotheses we test are a mix between the type of governance we expect under different types of democracy and some of the material outcomes we expect. What these share is that we have coverage for the variables that operationalize these outcomes starting in 1900. The second set of hypotheses, by contrast, are a mix between fiscal and monetary outcomes, centered on redistribution and macroeconomic policy. What these share is that we have coverage on these variables in the post–Cold War era; moreover, for all of them but one, this coverage begins in the 1970s.

We first examine five variables that capture governance and material out-comes. Data for each of these variables are taken from the V-Dem dataset. The first variable is range of consultation. This variable captures the range of consultation at the elite level regarding important policy changes. The unscaled version varies from 0, in which the leader or a very small group makes authoritative decisions on their own, to 5, in which consultation engages elites from "essentially all parts of the political spectrum and all politically relevant sectors of society and business" (Lindberg et al. 2013: 26). V-Dem then converts the ordinal scale to interval using a Bayesian item response theory measurement model. For our sample, range of consultation varies between –3.07 and 3.85 with a mean of 0.19 and a standard deviation of 1.45.

The second variable is the percentage of the population with suffrage. This variable captures the percentage of adult citizens (as defined by statute) that has the legal right to vote in national elections. It does not take into consideration restrictions related to having been convicted for a crime or to being legally incompetent. Furthermore, it covers legal restrictions rather than those that are de facto operative. In our sample, this variable ranges from 0 to 100 with a mean of 88.70 and a standard deviation of 24.55.

The third variable capturing governance and material outcomes is egalitarian democracy. This variable captures the extent to which the ideal of egalitarian democracy is achieved, or to the contrary, whether "material and immaterial inequalities inhibit the exercise of formal rights and liberties, and diminish the ability of citizens from all social groups to participate" (Lindberg et al. 2013: 7). Egalitarian democracy is operative when the rights and freedoms of individuals are protected equally across all social groups and resources are also distributed equally across social groups. This variable is an interval index that ranges from 0.04 to 0.99 in our sample with a mean of 0.54 and a standard deviation of 0.25. Higher values indicate more egalitarian outcomes.

The fourth variable is equal distribution of resources. This variable captures the extent to which both tangible and intangible resources are distributed in society. It is an index formed by taking the point estimates from a Bayesian factor analysis model of the indicators for the provision of particularistic or public goods, means tested versus universalistic welfare policies, educational equality, health equality, power distributed by socioeconomic position, power distributed by social group, and power distributed by gender. Equal distribution of resources ranges between 0.02 and 0.99 in our sample with a mean of 0.53 and a standard deviation of 0.28. Again, higher values indicate a more equal distribution of resources.

The fifth and final variable capturing governance and material outcomes is representation of disadvantaged groups. This variable specifically taps socioeconomically disadvantaged groups whose members have an average income significantly below the median national income and measures how well disadvantaged social groups in a country are represented in the national legislature. The ordinal version of this variable ranges from 1 and 2 at the low end, when disadvantaged groups have no representation at all or are highly under-represented relative to their proportion of the general population, respectively, to 5 at the high end, when disadvantaged groups are overrepresented relative to their proportion of the general population. V-Dem converts the ordinal scale to interval using a Bayesian item response theory measurement model. The interval measure ranges from −3.21 to 3.30 in our sample with a mean of −0.46 and a standard deviation of 1.07.

Redistribution from rich to poor can take many forms and ranges from income redistribution to the provision of means tested social insurance to asset redistribution. We expect to find across places and time periods that elite-biased democracies will have smaller governments in general; allocate less public money to education, healthcare, and housing; and have more regressive tax structures.

We begin with the most general and crude measure of redistribution, the total size of the government. To be sure, this measure is a noisy way of capturing redistribution because it contains elements that are not strictly redistributive, such as spending on public goods and services or the financing of government operations. However, the size of government, as measured by the Penn World Table's government consumption variable (as a percentage of GDP), has coverage starting in 1950.[2] Conceivably, this should allow us to obtain greater statistical power because we have more than two decades' worth of observations before globalization began to intensify. Government consumption has a mean of 18.53 percent and a standard deviation of 10.16 percent.

We also measure redistribution via progressive spending. Our first measure of redistributive spending is social spending as a percentage of GDP. This consists of government expenditures on education, health, and housing. This spending is progressive because it involves (1) the transfer of social resources to alter inequality induced by market outcomes and (2) the attempt to equalize the life chances of poorer individuals via investments in human capital. Increased social spending narrows market inequality by boosting the income and life chances of the poor majority. It is therefore redistributive in nature (see Lindert 2004). The source for these variables is Albertus and Menaldo (2014a), who use several primary and secondary sources and follow the guidelines and coding rules set forth in the International Monetary Fund's (IMF) *Government Finance Statistics Yearbook*. Social spending is nearly normally distributed with a mean of 6.00 percent of GDP, a standard deviation of 3.39 percent, a minimum value of 0 percent, and a maximum of 22.46 percent of GDP.

The third way in which we measure redistribution is taxes on income, profits and capital gains (as a percentage of GDP; henceforth, progressive taxation). This variable addresses the potential shortcoming that public expenditures on

---

[2] This variable excludes income transfers and public investment and is weighted by the relative prices that prevail in the world economy via adjustments for purchasing power parity.

social spending or social protection are not always tantamount to redistribution from the rich to the poor. If there is a regressive tax structure in place, then the poor majority bears the brunt of the fiscal burden and are "getting what they paid for" if the government orients spending toward education, health, housing, welfare, and insurance.

Income taxation serves as a proxy for the progressivity of the tax structure because tax rates on these sources either increase with income or tend to be levied on citizens at the upper end of the income distribution. Increasing marginal rates are the norm across both developing and developed countries and ensure that, at least from a de jure perspective, income taxation is progressive. Even nominally flat income tax rates can be progressive; both developing and developed countries tend to offer generous deductions and exemptions for taxpayers below the median income. Finally, rampant evasion of direct taxes by the poor in developing countries means that the wealthy are often the only group of citizens that effectively pays any income taxes. Capital gains taxes levied at flat rates also tend to be progressive: relatively wealthier citizens disproportionately tend to earn interest, dividends, and profits on capital investments.

The source for this variable is Albertus and Menaldo (2014a), who use several primary and secondary sources and follow the guidelines and coding rules set forth in the IMF's *Government Finance Statistics Yearbook*. Progressive taxation has a mean of 6.68 percent with a standard deviation of 5.90 percent and ranges from 0 percent to 34.62 percent.

While we will corroborate our intuition that popular democracies should have more progressive tax structures than elite-biased ones in later sections, the difference is not huge. Furthermore, as Figure 4.3 clearly shows, the gap between redistributive spending and redistributive taxation is large during this period and has steadily increased over time. Recall that in the post–Bretton Woods era, popular democracies should have less progressive tax systems than might be expected given the advent of financial globalization. We theorize that this is because governments have increasingly availed off-balance-sheet instruments to pay for social spending.

Commensurate with our explanation in Chapter 2 of how exchange rate policy can be part and parcel of a strategy of off-balance-sheet redistribution using monetary policy during the post–Bretton Woods era, we measure the flexibility of the exchange rate as de facto exchange rate fixity from Levy-Yeyati and Sturzenegger (2005). To grasp the wisdom in using this measurement strategy, consider Cristina Kirchner, who served as Argentina's president between 2008 and 2015, and her late husband, Nestor Kirchner, who served the previous term, between 2003 and 2007. The Kirchners steadfastly courted the political support of national labor unions by attempting to return labor to its preeminent role in Argentine politics, and redistributive macroeconomic policies were used aggressively by the Kirchners to advance this goal. This included raiding pension funds to paper over budget deficits and using exchange rate

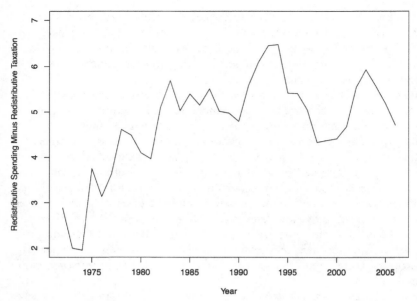

FIGURE 4.3. Gap between redistributive spending and redistributive taxation since 1972.

Notes: Redistributive spending is total spending on education, health, housing, welfare, and social insurance as a percentage of GDP. Welfare and social insurance include both on kind and in cash transfers. Redistributive taxation is direct, progressive taxation on income, profits, and capital gains as a percentage of GDP. Taxes on income, profits, and capital gains capture the progressivity of the tax structure because tax rates on these sources either increase with income or tend to be levied on citizens at the upper end of the income distribution. See measurement discussion in the text for further information on sources and methods.

and monetary policy to stoke a consumption boom that was accompanied by inflation in the double digits.[3]

De facto exchange rate fixity captures the actual exchange rate, rather than just the de jure exchange rate. It is based on the nominal exchange rate, the volatility of the exchange rate, and the volatility of international reserves. This ordinal variable ranges from 2, which is a fully flexible rate, to 5, which is fully fixed. Exchange fixity has a mean of 4.09 and a standard deviation of 1.23.

Measuring Regime Type
The key set of independent variables in the analysis of governance and material outcomes pertains to a country's regime type. Building on Chapter 3 and the

---

[3] Their strategy also included defaulting on billions of dollars in sovereign debt and the expropriation of foreign multinationals, with the most prominent case being the takeover of Repsol, a Spanish owned oil company.

analyses conducted earlier in this chapter, we focus on three types of regimes. The first is elite-biased democracy. Elite Biased Democracy are country years of democratic rule when the democracy operates under a constitution from a previous period of autocratic rule. The second is popular democracy. This pertains to country years of democratic rule if the democracy operates under a new constitution that it forged upon transition or if it operates according to a prior democratic constitution. It also pertains to country years of democratic rule that follow the annulment of an autocratic constitution and its replacement with a democratic constitution. The third is autocracy. This pertains to every country year of autocratic rule.

Controls

We also control for several variables whose omission might potentially confound the results. We lag all of these controls by one period. We add the log of real per capita income because increases in wealth are expected to boost demand for public spending. This variable ranges from 5.45 to 11.85 with a mean of 8.15 and standard deviation of 1.03. We also include log population, from the Correlates of War 3.0, because the scope of government regulation and spending can be characterized by economies of scale. Log population ranges from 11.71 to 20.99 with a mean of 16.00 and a standard deviation of 1.45. Total resources income per capita (in thousands) is included because corporate taxes on the profits earned by oil, gas, and mining firms can boost government spending and/or inflate the total income tax receipts collected by the government. The logged version of this measure has a mean of −2.77 and a standard deviation of 1.68 and ranges from −4.61 to 4.40. The source for these three variables is Haber and Menaldo (2011).

We also control for the growth rate of real per capita income in order to ensure that transitionary political periods are not unduly proxying for economic crises. A transition to democracy and the early stages of a new regime can be associated with this phenomenon, as we reported in Table 4.1; this could also impact public spending. The economic growth rate variable has a mean of 1.7 percent and a standard deviation of 7.7 percent.

We also introduce three additional controls for the post-WWII analyses of fiscal and monetary policy. Trade openness, measured as exports plus imports as a share of GDP (percent) from the Penn World Tables 6.2, is included because it can influence redistributive transfers either positively or negatively. This variable has a mean of 72.41 and a standard deviation of 46.20. Manufacturing value added (as percentage of GDP), taken from the World Bank's (2012) World Development Indicators (WBDI), is included because increases in the manufacturing sector represent greater taxable capacity and ease of tax collection. This variable has a mean of 15.10 percent and a standard deviation of 7.64 percent, with a minimum of 0.16 percent and a maximum of 43.35 percent. The old age ratio, from the WBDI, is the percent of the population above sixty-five years of age. This variable captures the extent of demand for intergenerational transfers. It ranges from 1.06 percent to 20.42 percent with a mean of 5.58 percent and a standard deviation of 4.15 percent.

STATISTICAL STRATEGY FOR EXPLAINING OUTCOMES UNDER REGIMES

Across each of the dependent variables we outlined, we estimate a series of static, country fixed effects models that also include year fixed effects. These were estimated using ordinary least squares (OLS). The inclusion of country fixed effects in the regressions controls for country-specific and time-invariant heterogeneity (for example, geography) that might jointly influence a country's propensity to experience a democratic transition under conditions of elite weakness and its governance structures and degree of redistribution.[4] Furthermore, as we will describe, it allows us to interpret the results from the perspective of a difference-in-differences analysis. The inclusion of year fixed effects controls for time period–specific and time-varying heterogeneity (for example, shocks to the global economy) that might also be correlated with governance structures and redistribution. We estimate Driscoll-Kraay standard errors to address heteroskedasticity, serially correlated errors, and spatial correlation.

We always include two main independent variables in the statistical models. The first is a dummy variable capturing democracy with an autocratic constitution. The second is a dummy variable capturing all democracies. Each enters the regression equations in levels.

Given this approach, the coefficients reported in the table are calculated and labeled as follows. The raw coefficient on democracy with autocratic constitution, elite-biased democracy (relative to popular democracy), is the difference in outcomes between countries that transitioned to democracy with an autocratic constitution and those that democratized with their own, new constitution (i.e., popular democracies). In other words, this coefficient captures the difference in the differences. Moreover, the raw coefficient on the dummy variable capturing all democracies can be interpreted as the difference in outcomes between popular democracy and autocracy, or popular democracy (relative to autocracy).

We also report changes in the outcomes induced by a transition to elite-biased democracy vis-à-vis autocracy. This last set of coefficients is calculated directly from the estimated coefficients on elite-biased democracy (relative to popular democracy) and popular democracy (relative to autocracy). Specifically, it is calculated by adding these coefficients. In other words, it does not itself enter the regression models as an additional variable. To ensure that the standard

---

[4] Unlike in the Table 4.1 models, where we estimate the determinants of democratization using survival analysis, the dependent variables in Tables 4.2 and 4.3 have much greater within-country variation, which enables us to include country fixed effects without dropping substantial data.

errors and p-values obtained from this transformation are valid, we use the delta method to obtain these calculations.

We note that the coefficient for popular democracy (relative to autocracy) represents a lower bound on the changes in public policies we should expect after this type of democratization. The reason is that popular democracy includes both democracies that write their own constitution after free and fair elections and those that, although they do not inherit constitutions from autocratic forbearers per se, do not necessarily start life with a constitution of their own making. First, there are countries that are democratic upon independence from a colonial occupier but that do not subsequently pass their own constitution under democracy (e.g., India, Sri Lanka, and Cuba from 1909 to 1915). There are also a handful of country-year observations in which a given country operates under no constitution but instead has a suspended document and might operate under emergency rule (e.g., Uruguay, 1933; Nicaragua, 1984–1986). By default, these are coded as popular democracies because they do not operate under an autocratic constitution. Finally, there are countries that gain independence after splitting from a larger federation (e.g., Slovakia starting in 1993). Because independence usually dramatically redraws the lines of political battle, we do not attribute former constitutions to individual successor states. We discuss these issues, and the implications for democracy associated with colonial and predecessor state legacies, in depth in Chapter 8.

We also note that while changes from autocracy to popular democracy should definitely lead to palpable changes in governance, it is not clear ex ante that changes from autocracy to popular democracy should yield large changes in redistribution. The reason is that while some autocracies are status-quo oriented, others are quite progressive and engage in policies that systematically weaken existing economic elites through redistribution (Albertus 2015; Albertus and Menaldo 2012a; Menaldo 2016).

What about our predictions in the context of changes from autocracy to elite-biased democracy? These transitions should lead to changes toward more democratic governance, yet hardly as democratic as their popular democracy counterparts. At the same time, in terms of redistribution, former autocratic elites should generally do at least as well under elite-biased democracy as they did under dictatorship. However, while political incumbents and their economic allies might flee an autocracy for greener pastures, this does not always mean that, once they get to democracy, they will be able to reduce the level of redistribution vis-à-vis dictatorship. Even when former autocratic elites can manipulate the rules of the game under democracy, governing coalitions might become somewhat more inclusive after the transition, and therefore, redistribution might increase along some dimensions. Yet this should be the exception, and its magnitude should not pose a fundamental threat to former authoritarian elites.

Building from Chapter 2, we focus the bulk of our attention across each of the models on elite-biased democracy (relative to popular democracy). Our

hypotheses for this variable are clear, as this coefficient most closely opera-
tionalizes the counterfactual of interest: if we observe a change from autocracy
to elite-biased democracy, what would public policy have been like had the
change instead been from autocracy to popular democracy?

EMPIRICAL RESULTS FOR GOVERNANCE AND MATERIAL
OUTCOMES

Table 4.2 reports the results of the outcomes of interest related to governance
and material well-being. Elite-biased democracies have a smaller range of consultation than popular democracies (Column 1). They also exhibit a smaller
percentage of the population with suffrage (Column 2), are less egalitarian
across social groups (Column 3), and have a more unequal distribution of
resources across members of society (Column 4). Moreover, they are less
likely to represent disadvantaged groups (Column 5). In each case, except for
Column 5, the coefficient on elite-biased democracy is statistically significant
at the .01 level; in Column 5, it is significant at the .05 level. Moreover, across
all the models, the results also turn out as expected in terms of the change from
autocracy to elite-biased democracy (the coefficients are positive and statistically significant at the .01 level) and from autocracy to popular democracy
(the coefficients are positive, greater in magnitude than those that represent the
change from autocracy to elite-biased democracy, and statistically significant at
the .01 level). In short, during the twentieth century and beyond, democracies
biased by elites have been less pluralistic, inclusive, representative, and egalitarian than their popular counterparts.

In terms of the magnitude of these effects, consider the substantive significance of perhaps the most intuitive result reported above, the percentage of
the adult population with suffrage. Relative to autocracies, popular democracies have a seven-point boost in adult suffrage. This is hardly surprising;
after all, democracies are much more likely to grant their citizens the franchise. However, adult suffrage is an estimated 3.56 percent lower in elite-biased
democracies than in popular democracies. Elite-biased democracies, therefore,
hover between autocracies and popular democracies in terms of the franchise,
and the effect is substantively large. To be sure, suffrage in contemporary
democracies is near universal, so the gap between elite-biased democracy and
popular democracy is no longer consequential. But historically, tweaking suffrage rules to disenfranchise crucial voting blocs that can make a difference
to the results of an election (e.g., minority groups and/or the poor) has been
a tried and true method of overrepresenting conservative parties in the legislature or even the executive branch. One illustrative example is the US South
during the Jim Crow era.

Columns 6 through 10 now include autocratic regime types and other
characteristics of the dictatorship on the eve of democratization as control
variables. These variables capture several autocratic legacies that can have a

TABLE 4.2. *Autocratic Constitutions and Participation in Decision-Making*

Dependent Variable	Range of Consultation	Percent Pop. with Suffrage	Egalitarian Democracy	Equal Distribution of Resources	Representation of Disadvant. Groups	Range of Consultation	Percent Pop. with Suffrage	Egalitarian Democracy	Equal Distribution of Resources	Representation of Disadvant. Groups
	Model 1	Model 2	Model 3	Model 4	Model 5	Model 6	Model 7	Model 8	Model 9	Model 10
Elite-biased Democracy (Relative to popular dem.)	-0.319***	-3.559***	-0.053***	-0.047***	-0.076**	-0.203***	-3.156***	-0.075***	-0.066***	-0.125***
	(0.058)	(0.969)	(0.006)	(0.008)	(0.031)	(0.068)	(0.879)	(0.007)	(0.008)	(0.027)
Popular democracy (Relative to autocracy)	1.526***	7.020***	0.128***	0.110***	0.328***	1.648***	4.816***	0.115***	0.084***	0.259***
	(0.057)	(0.943)	(0.004)	(0.005)	(0.040)	(0.150)	(1.457)	(0.012)	(0.016)	(0.069)
Economic growth rate	0.002	0.937	-0.012	-0.012	-0.123	-0.021	-0.103	-0.018	-0.022	-0.166*
	(0.130)	(1.982)	(0.017)	(0.019)	(0.096)	(0.131)	(1.804)	(0.016)	(0.017)	(0.087)
log(GDP per capita)	0.301***	-1.178	0.028***	0.045***	0.221***	0.305***	-2.591***	0.041***	0.056***	0.227***
	(0.053)	(0.867)	(0.005)	(0.007)	(0.035)	(0.057)	(0.689)	(0.005)	(0.006)	(0.036)
log(resource income per capita)	-0.068***	-1.005**	-0.003**	-0.003**	-0.010	-0.068***	-0.857***	-0.010***	-0.009**	-0.020
	(0.013)	(0.420)	(0.001)	(0.001)	(0.021)	(0.012)	(0.425)	(0.001)	(0.002)	(0.021)
log(population)	-0.308***	14.583***	0.003	0.027*	0.535***	-0.370***	13.383***	0.009	0.025*	0.536***
	(0.052)	(1.394)	(0.010)	(0.014)	(0.061)	(0.053)	(1.605)	(0.007)	(0.011)	(0.062)
Multiple-parties legacy						-0.113*	0.954	0.002	0.011	0.027
						(0.064)	(0.541)	(0.005)	(0.007)	(0.028)
Personalist legacy						-0.236***	0.213	-0.036***	-0.059***	-0.187***
						(0.073)	(0.891)	(0.008)	(0.011)	(0.054)
Military legacy						0.255***	5.464***	0.050***	0.050***	0.136***
						(0.075)	(0.829)	(0.009)	(0.010)	(0.050)
Single-party legacy						-0.200**	-5.222***	0.021**	0.020	0.361***
						(0.081)	(0.938)	(0.009)	(0.013)	(0.062)

(*continued*)

TABLE 4.2 (*continued*)

Dependent Variable	Range of Consultation	Percent Pop. with Suffrage	Egalitarian Democracy	Equal Distribution of Resources	Representation of Disadvant. Groups	Range of Consultation	Percent Pop. with Suffrage	Egalitarian Democracy	Equal Distribution of Resources	Representation of Disadvant. Groups
	Model 1	Model 2	Model 3	Model 4	Model 5	Model 6	Model 7	Model 8	Model 9	Model 10
Oligarchy legacy						-0.360**	1.529	0.047***	0.053***	-0.128
						(0.171)	(2.485)	(0.014)	(0.019)	(0.095)
Transitional legacy						0.058	-5.012***	0.035***	0.062***	0.144**
						(0.087)	(1.640)	(0.013)	(0.015)	(0.072)
Elite-biased democracy (Relative to autocracy)	1.207***	3.461***	0.075***	0.062***	0.252***	1.445***	1.661	0.040***	0.018	0.134*
	(0.051)	(0.976)	(0.005)	(0.006)	(0.033)	(0.152)	(1.512)	(0.012)	(0.016)	(0.074)
Year fixed effects	Yes	Yes	Yes	Yes	Yes	Yes	Yes	Yes	Yes	Yes
Country fixed effects	Yes	Yes	Yes	Yes	Yes	Yes	Yes	Yes	Yes	Yes
Countries	156	156	156	156	156	153	153	153	153	153
Observations	8,489	8,489	8,489	8,489	7,756	7,685	7,685	7,685	7,685	6,982

* $p < 0.10$; ** $p < 0.05$; *** $p < 0.01$ (two-tailed)
Driscoll-Kraay standard errors in parentheses. Country fixed effects are controlled for via a within transformation. Constants and time dummies are not shown. All independent variables are lagged one period.

lingering impact under democracy and can constitute substitutes or comple-ments to elite-biased constitutions. As we outlined in Chapter 3, this can take the form of strong militaries (Przeworski 1991), hegemonic parties (Ziblatt 2017; Slater and Wong 2013), or preexisting political structures (Grzymala-Busse 2002). This helps us neutralize the concern that democracies that inherit autocratic constitutions might merely be unduly proxying for other attributes of how former regime insiders exercised power that continue to matter after democratization.

First, we include variables for whether the regime evidences elements of sin-gle party, military, personalist, or "oligarchic" rule. Several autocratic regimes in the pre-World War II era (e.g., the United Kingdom prior to 1885) are char-acterized by multiparty competition among civilian politicians amid restricted franchise. These cases do not fit neatly into the authoritarian regime typology that we embrace in this series of regressions (see Geddes 1999). We therefore code these cases as "oligarchy" and note that the results are not sensitive to recoding these observations as single-party or personalist regimes. The baseline category of comparison for these authoritarian regime types is countries that have been democratic since independence.

We also control for the number of de facto parties on the eve of democrati-zation, an alternative way to operationalize the power of former regime insid-ers. This variable is coded "0" when there are no de facto parties, "1" when there is one de facto party, and "2" when there are multiple de facto parties. We code countries that are democratic since independence as having the maximum number of de facto parties on the eve of democratization.

Finally, we also control for whether the democracy follows a transitional leader – a nondemocratic leader who came to power with the stated purpose of calling democratic elections and lasted less than one year in office – because it should be less likely that these types of authoritarian regimes will have a lasting influence that endures after democratization. Transitional leaders typi-cally take the helm once the old order begins to crumble, meaning that the previous order is less likely to exert its own independent legacy on the subse-quent regime.

While some of the results ratify the idea that the political and institu-tional features of the previous autocracy might have an enduring effect after democratization, controlling for these legacies does not materially affect our main results. In fact, they are strengthened. Consistent with others authors' insights, if regimes were previously personalist, they are, on balance, less representative, inclusive, and egalitarian. The opposite is true if a democracy follows a military regime – perhaps because these regimes tend to retrench completely from mainstream politics when they retreat to the barracks. Single-party legacies, as well as an oligarchical heritage, are a mixed bag. On the other hand, if regimes were oligarchic, they appear to be, on balance, more egalitarian.

Fiscal and Monetary Outcomes in the Post–World War II Era

Table 4.3 reports the results of fiscal and monetary outcomes of interest for which we have coverage in the post–World War II period. As outlined previously, this includes data between 1950 and 2006 for total government spending and data between the 1970s and 2006 for our more specific measures of redistribution and the type of exchange rate regime. These results are also consistent with our theoretical expectations. Elite-biased democracies have smaller governments than popular democracies by an estimated 1.78 percentage points of GDP (Column 1). Column 2 demonstrates that they also exhibit less social spending (a reduction of 0.51 percentage points of GDP) and have more regressive tax systems (a reduction of 0.58 percentage points of GDP). Finally, they are more likely to have fixed exchange rates (Column 4).

Furthermore, the magnitudes of the effects are substantial. Consider the first three columns. The within-country standard deviation in size of government is 4.03 percent of GDP. It is 1.62 percent of GDP for social spending and 2.48 percent of GDP for progressive taxation. The estimated effect of a transition to elite-biased democracy therefore shifts the size of government by half a standard deviation and social spending by a third of a standard deviation. Over time, these effects cumulate into substantial differences in the role of government in society and the size and scope of the welfare state. As outlined previously, the effect on progressive taxation is more muted due to the constraints posed by globalization.

As expected, the results regarding the change from autocracy to popular democracy are mixed. The sign on each of the regressions is as anticipated: popular democracies tend to have larger governments, more social spending, more progressive tax structures, and less rigid exchange rates than their autocratic predecessors. However, only social spending (Column 1) and exchange rate (Column 4) are statistically significant at conventional levels. Consistent with what we explained earlier about the limits of progressive taxation under democracy in the era of globalization, the results obtained in Column 3 are underwhelming. They are not statistically significant and, even if they were, the magnitude of the effect is small. A change to popular democracy from autocracy only yields an increase of 0.22 percentage points in taxes obtained from income, profits, and capital gains (percent of GDP). This is roughly one-fourth of the change in total government spending obtained in Column 1 and appreciably less than the 0.28 percentage point increase in social spending obtained in Column 2.

Finally, and again as expected, the results on the change from autocracy to elite-biased democracy roughly track those for elite-biased democracy relative to popular democracy. While a transition to an elite-biased democracy reduces total government spending relative to autocracy, we cannot say with a high degree of statistical certainty that it does the same for social spending (although the coefficient is negative). We can say, however, that a transition to

TABLE 4.3. *Autocratic Constitutions and Fiscal and Macroeconomic Outcomes*

Dependent Variable	Size of Government	Social Spending	Progressive Taxation	Exchange Rate Fixity	Size of Government	Social Spending	Progressive Taxation	Exchange Rate Fixity
	Model 1	Model 2	Model 3	Model 4	Model 5	Model 6	Model 7	Model 8
Elite-biased democracy (Relative to popular dem.)	-1.780***	-0.507**	-0.583***	0.189*	-1.563***	-0.799***	-0.520***	0.258**
	(0.302)	(0.226)	(0.172)	(0.110)	(0.265)	(0.199)	(0.141)	(0.125)
Popular democracy (Relative to autocracy)	0.879**	0.284	0.220	-0.374***	4.914***	0.181	0.911*	0.093
	(0.338)	(0.231)	(0.246)	(0.102)	(0.703)	(0.839)	(0.526)	(0.205)
Economic growth rate	-5.065**	-1.376	-1.048	0.352	-5.479***	-1.063	-1.246	0.170
	(1.894)	(0.938)	(1.545)	(0.247)	(1.867)	(0.906)	(1.570)	(0.252)
log(GDP per capita)	0.123	2.060***	3.773***	0.156	0.421	1.929***	3.941***	0.195
	(0.477)	(0.284)	(0.628)	(0.146)	(0.573)	(0.250)	(0.752)	(0.156)
log(resource income per capita)	-0.411**	0.003	0.579***	0.017	-0.275	0.057	0.601***	0.007
	(0.173)	(0.123)	(0.123)	(0.031)	(0.178)	(0.128)	(0.149)	(0.036)
log(population)	-2.551***	2.946***	-2.527	0.120	-1.099	3.235***	-2.032	0.101
	(0.883)	(0.658)	(1.639)	(0.211)	(0.863)	(0.831)	(2.052)	(0.169)
Manufacturing value added	0.073*	-0.047**	-0.069***	-0.015*	0.068**	-0.043*	-0.062***	-0.011*
	(0.031)	(0.020)	(0.020)	(0.008)	(0.030)	(0.022)	(0.019)	(0.006)
Trade openness	0.002	-0.007	0.006	0.001	0.008	-0.007	0.007*	0.002
	(0.007)	(0.005)	(0.004)	(0.002)	(0.008)	(0.006)	(0.004)	(0.002)
Old age ratio	-0.482***	-0.350***	-0.583***	0.062	-0.749***	-0.307***	-0.719***	-0.006
	(0.164)	(0.094)	(0.119)	(0.044)	(0.205)	(0.122)	(0.233)	(0.071)
Multiple-parties legacy					-0.531**	-0.074	0.377**	-0.011
					(0.235)	(0.478)	(0.181)	(0.096)
Personalist legacy					-2.938***	-0.353	-0.464	-0.315*
					(0.525)	(0.346)	(0.280)	(0.158)
Military legacy					-3.732***	0.506	-1.504***	-0.128
					(0.490)	(0.505)	(0.355)	(0.141)
Single-party legacy					0.214	0.369	-1.588***	-0.787***
					(0.499)	(0.551)	(0.467)	(0.221)

(*continued*)

TABLE 4.3 (continued)

Dependent Variable	Size of Government Model 1	Social Spending Model 2	Progressive Taxation Model 3	Exchange Rate Fixity Model 4	Size of Government Model 5	Social Spending Model 6	Progressive Taxation Model 7	Exchange Rate Fixity Model 8
Oligarchy legacy					-2.171**	3.244*	1.080	0.841***
					(0.906)	(1.731)	(1.111)	(0.278)
Transitional legacy					-2.861***	1.231	-0.521	-0.718***
					(0.913)	(0.741)	(0.429)	(0.260)
Elite-biased democracy	-0.901***	-0.229	-0.364***	0.185**	3.351***	-0.618	0.390	0.350
(Relative to autocracy)	(0.308)	(0.202)	(0.126)	(0.077)	(0.646)	(0.814)	(0.454)	(0.245)
Year fixed effects	Yes	Yes	Yes	Yes	Yes	Yes	Yes	Yes
Country fixed effects	Yes	Yes	Yes	Yes	Yes	Yes	Yes	Yes
Countries	151	124	135	144	145	118	129	138
Observations	4,080	2,197	2,668	2,697	3,886	2,077	2,520	2,575

* $p < 0.10$; ** $p < 0.05$; *** $p < 0.01$ (two-tailed)
Driscoll-Kraay standard errors in parentheses. Country fixed effects are controlled for via a within transformation. Constants and time dummies are not shown. All independent variables are lagged one period.

an elite-biased democracy makes the tax system more regressive and that it makes it more likely that a country will adopt a more rigid exchange rate. In short, the coefficients on elite-biased democracy relative to autocracy suggests that outgoing authoritarian leaders and their economic allies are getting what they want out of democracy: a deal that is at least as good, if not better, for them as dictatorship.

As in Table 4.2, Columns 5 through 8 of Table 4.3 now include autocratic regime types on the eve of democratization as control variables. These variables tap the bargaining power of outgoing regimes before transition. We again include variables for whether the regime evidences signs of single-party, military, personalist, or oligarchic rule. The baseline category is again countries that have been democratic since independence. We also control for the number of de facto parties on the eve of democratization. Finally, as before, we also control for whether the democracy follows a transitional leader.

As with Table 4.2, while some of the results ratify the idea that the previous autocracies' political and institutional features can have an enduring effect after democratization, controlling for these legacies does not strongly impact the main results. In fact, those results are, as before, strengthened.[5] Consistent with others authors' insights, if regimes were previously personalist, they are, on balance, less redistributive under democracy. The same is the case if they were military dictatorships. On the other hand, if regimes were oligarchic, they appear to be, on balance, somewhat more redistributive under democracy.

THE FATE OF FORMER DICTATORS

The conventional wisdom is that dictatorships end badly for dictators. Hitler famously committed suicide. Ceauşescu was summarily executed by a firing squad in the midst of a popular revolution. Gaddafi was tortured by a mob and then shot dead during the 2011 Arab Spring uprisings; his corpse was dragged through the streets of his hometown, Sirte, as mobs cheered and jeered at his mutilated remains.

Other dictators have escaped death but end up experiencing isolated and pitiful lives in exile. There are several infamous examples from Africa. The Democratic Republic of Congo's Mobutu and Uganda's Idi Amin come to mind. Perhaps Valentine Strasser is not a household name, but he is a stark reminder about the perils of dictators who lose power on terms that are not of their own choosing. Today, he barely ekes out a living as a poor farmer on the outskirts of Freetown, Sierra Leone – not too far from the presidential palace he used to call home. In Sudan, another former dictator, Abdel Rahman Swar

---

[5] The results are not as strong when evaluating the effects of elite-biased democracy relative to autocracy. However, aside from size of government (which flips to a positive sign), the statistically insignificant coefficients suggest that outgoing authoritarian elites get roughly an equivalent deal under elite-biased democracy compared to dictatorship.

al-Dahab, runs the Islamic Dawa Organization, a Sudanese nongovernmental organization with ties to the global Muslim Brotherhood. On paper, this might seem like a somewhat attractive fate, but he is far away from the opulence he was accustomed to during his reign. His organization has also been targeted by Western governments for having ties to terrorist entities.

There is another group of former dictators who fare quite well after they leave office, however. One of the most illustrative cases in that of Chun Doo-hwan, the last South Korean military dictator who became notorious for high-level graft. Although found guilty of mutiny, insurrection, and bribery in the 1990s and sentenced to death in 1996, his sentence was commuted in 1997. A supreme court ruling then ordered him to repay some $200 million in bribes. Yet twenty years later, he lives in a lavish mansion in Seoul and is occasionally seen golfing at exclusive clubs. He has paid back a mere quarter of the money he was ordered to return by the supreme court. This is despite the fact that his family members have been linked to secret offshore companies and that prosecutors themselves found a heap of his money stuffed in apple boxes in a cement warehouse.

Although data on the fate of former dictators is far more readily available than for other top authoritarian elites, there is reason to believe that many of these other top elites also meet a happy ending. Take the case of several key elites that were members of Brazil's last military government under João Figueiredo. After democratization, Figueiredo's foreign minister became ambassador to Italy and then joined the International Monetary Fund (IMF); his industry and commerce minister was elected mayor of Minas Novas and became president of the Development Bank of Minas Gerais; his communications minister became vice president of Standard Electrica; his development minister was elected twice as a senator and served as minister of justice under President Fernando Collor.

Can we say anything systematic about the fate of former dictators? Are there conditions under which they can escape the dire fates we outlined previously and instead live out their lives in relative comfort or even luxury, as exemplified in the case of Chun Doo-hwan? In Chapter 2, we argued that political incumbents who are relatively strong on the eve of democratic transition should be able to impose constitutions created under autocracy that protect their rights and interests after transition. Earlier in this chapter, we demonstrated that this means less representation for non-elites under democracy, as well as less pluralism, less inclusiveness, and less redistribution. We now explore whether that also means a decreased propensity to punish outgoing dictators. In Chapter 2, we hypothesized that this is indeed the case.

Consider again the case of South Korea. Chun Doo-hwan drafted a new, authoritarian constitution in 1981 and gave an impassioned speech in defense of the constitution in April 1987. He then anointed a top general from inside his Democratic Justice Party, Roh Tae-woo, as his successor. Popular uproar in reaction led to a more open election, but Roh still won the day. Chun skated free during Roh's term in office and only faced legal troubles when Roh was replaced – yet as mentioned, his ultimate outcome has been whiling away his days at golf clubs and in his mansion while sheltering money abroad.

MEASUREMENT STRATEGY FOR EXPLAINING FORMER DICTATORS' FATES

To test the hypothesis that an autocratic constitution can help shelter former dictators from punishment, we construct a global cross-section of dictators who were in power before democratic transitions and who were eligible to be punished under democracy after the transition. Table 3.3 in Chapter 3 lists all of these dictators and whether the ensuing democratic regime inherited a constitution from the previous autocratic regime. The first dictator in the data set is observed as far back as 1885 (Gladstone, from the United Kingdom), and the last nondemocratic leader is observed in 2004 (Burjanadze, from Georgia).

The first dependent variable measures whether a leader is punished upon relinquishing office, with data taken from Archigos (Goemans et al. 2009). This source has coverage on this variable between 1875 and 2004. Following the logic outlined by Goemans (2008), the post-exit fate of leaders is only recorded up to one year after they lost office to obviate the possibility that the leader's behavior after losing office is responsible for any type of punishment instead of his or her behavior in office. The original version of this variable records three different punishments: exile, imprisonment, and death. Given the sparseness of data in some categories (e.g., death), we collapse these into a binary variable.

The last outgoing leaders prior to democracy were severely punished in a total of 19 of 113 cases, or 17 percent. If we consider all dictators who held power within one year of the transition to democracy, a total of 34 of 145 leaders (23 percent) were punished.[6] If instead we exclude transitional leaders who served in office less than one year and managed a transition to democracy, 33 of 111 leaders (30 percent) were punished.

The second dependent variable is the number of years a dictator survived after giving up office. We use both Archigos and secondary sources to code the lifespans of dictators who exited power between 1875 and 2004. We track their lifespans up until 2016. This variable is right-censored in that former dictators who are still alive in 2016 are dropped from the analysis. Among all dictators who held power within one year of the transition to democracy and have since died, average lifespan was 17.18 years, with a standard deviation of 11.5 years, a minimum of 0 years, and a maximum of 50 years.

Similar to the previous round of regressions on governance, fiscal, and material outcomes under democracy, the key independent variable in the ensuing

---

[6] In three cases, the leader died of natural causes during office. In one case, punishment outcomes are missing.

analyses is elite-biased democracy. As before, this is a dummy variable that captures the type of constitution a democracy has upon transition. As in the previous analyses, we follow Cheibub et al. (2010) and define democracy if the chief executive and legislature is elected, there is more than one political party, and alternation in power occurs. Also as before, we use the regime type data from Boix et al. (2013) for the 1800–1945 period and the data from Cheibub et al. (2010) for the post–World War II period. Unlike in the previous analyses, however, we adjust the country-year regime data to the leader-year level to measure what former dictators' post-tenure fates are after democratization. We do so using information on the timing of the first set of free and fair elections in the year a country becomes democratic. Those leaders who were in power prior to the elections are coded as nondemocratic; those who were elected under the first set of free and fair elections are coded as democratic. Therefore, we relegate attention to the postdemocratization, post-tenure fate of the first set of former incumbents.

We also include several control variables that might also affect the likelihood of leader punishment. The first set comprises former dictators' individual characteristics. The second set comprises country-level covariates observed on the eve of democratic transition.

We control for a host of leader-specific characteristics taken from Archigos. These include the manner of leader entry – regular, irregular, or via foreign imposition – since leaders who force their way into power through coups and conflict might be more likely to face punishment upon democratization than leaders who are elected through regular, albeit illegitimate, elections. We also control for the log of leader tenure because it is possible that long-lived dictators with a stronger reputation for iron-fisted rule will be more likely to face retribution than short-lived leaders. In addition, we include a variable for the number of previous times in office, since dictators who come and go from office might be perceived as a greater threat to democracy and therefore elicit punishment. We also control for a leader's age upon entry into office, since older leaders might be perceived as weaker or more easily punished because their contemporaries are less likely to hold the reins of critical coercive institutions such as the military.

Finally, we control for whether leaders were tasked with shepherding the transition process. We code the dummy variable transitional leader as a "1" if two conditions are met: (1) the former dictator lasted in power less than one year and (2) the former dictator's stated goal was to call elections and step aside once this task was completed. We identify twenty-nine of those leaders, seventeen of whom were involved in a transition process guided by an autocratic constitution.

We also control for several country-level factors, all taken from Haber and Menaldo (2011). We include a variable for the log of per capita income, since wealthier countries might have a greater capacity to punish former leaders. We control for the economic growth rate (of per capita income) because outgoing autocrats who deliver more desirable public policies such as economic growth might face a lower incidence of post-transition punishment. We also control for the presence of civil war and the log of population size. These two factors might also influence the odds that a former dictator is brought to account. Finally, we control for variables that operationalize leaders' experience with international conflict and war from the International Crisis Behavior Project version 7. Following Debs and Goemans (2010), these controls capture whether during ongoing crises and war the leader was a challenger, a defender, or inherits a conflict from a previous leader, and whether a leader won, lost, or suffered a draw in a crisis or a war.

STATISTICAL STRATEGY FOR EXPLAINING DICTATOR FATES

We conduct two types of statistical analyses on our sample of former dictators observed during the first year of democracy. The first set of regressions is centered on explaining the relationship between democracies with autocratic constitutions and the probability that former dictators will be punished upon democratization. We therefore estimate a series of probit regressions. The second set of regressions is centered on explaining the relationship between democracies with autocratic constitutions and outgoing dictators' mortality under democratization – that is, how long they live after they hand over power. We estimate OLS models in these regressions, although the results are robust to negative binomial specifications as well. Across the models, we cluster the standard errors by country to address the fact that the residuals might be correlated in systematic ways within countries.

We also note that the results reported in Table 4.4 are robust to different experiments that we do not report. The results are robust to controlling for region fixed effects. They are also robust to dropping leaders who came to power under dictatorship but were subsequently elected and became democratic leaders. These include cases such as Betancourt in Venezuela, Velasco Ibarra in Ecuador, and Ershad in Bangladesh.

Empirical Results for Dictator Fates

In Table 4.4, Column 1, the regression is estimated on the subsample of last outgoing dictators prior to democracy, our most basic sample of former dictators. We include all of the controls outlined previously. As expected, elite-biased democracy is negative. Moreover, the coefficient represents a strong effect, both substantively and statistically. Holding the continuous variables at their means and setting civil war and transitional leader to zero, a democracy that inherits a constitution from its autocratic predecessor is 25 percent less likely to punish the dictator in office on the eve of transition. Also as expected, transitional leaders are less likely to be punished upon democratization than nontransitional leaders at a high level of statistical significance.

TABLE 4.4. *Autocratic Constitutions and the Fate of Outgoing Dictators*

Dependent Variable	Punishment: Exile, Imprisonment, or Death				Post-tenure Lifespan	
Sample:	Only Last Dictator In Power	All Within One Year	Only Last Dictator In Power	All Within One Year	Only Last Dictator In Power	Only Last Dictator In Power
	Model 1	Model 2	Model 3	Model 4	Model 5	Model 6
Elite-biased democracy	-0.828**	-0.614**	-0.806*	-0.619*	0.512**	0.509**
	(0.357)	(0.297)	(0.457)	(0.342)	(0.217)	(0.236)
Manner of entry	-0.021	-0.124	0.053	0.054	0.261	0.172
	(0.349)	(0.279)	(0.464)	(0.363)	(0.237)	(0.240)
log(time in office)	-0.097	-0.052	-0.614***	-0.298***	-0.095	-0.028
	(0.191)	(0.098)	(0.216)	(0.091)	(0.148)	(0.161)
Age at entry into office	-0.019	-0.014	0.002	-0.010	-0.017	-0.019
	(0.022)	(0.018)	(0.022)	(0.019)	(0.016)	(0.016)
Previous times in office	0.533	0.196	-0.134	-0.096	0.389	0.428
	(0.514)	(0.465)	(0.687)	(0.616)	(0.240)	(0.285)
Civil war	0.887*	0.324	0.405	0.354	-0.374	-0.235
	(0.480)	(0.473)	(0.680)	(0.477)	(0.478)	(0.417)
Economic growth rate	2.171	1.439	7.621**	2.876	-0.213	-0.372
	(2.438)	(1.860)	(3.475)	(2.035)	(0.973)	(1.018)
log(per capita income)	0.352	0.022	0.793***	0.281	-0.133	-0.112
	(0.223)	(0.201)	(0.247)	(0.209)	(0.183)	(0.181)
log(population)	-0.178	-0.170	-0.158	-0.155	0.181**	0.167*
	(0.128)	(0.109)	(0.141)	(0.119)	(0.085)	(0.094)

	(1)	(2)	(3)	(4)	(5)	(6)
Transitional leader	-1.680***	-1.966***	-2.264***	-2.173***	-0.205	-0.064
	(0.622)	(0.511)	(0.839)	(0.580)	(0.351)	(0.324)
Military regime			-0.579	-0.506		0.220
			(0.487)	(0.399)		(0.236)
Single-party regime			0.902	0.122		-0.358
			(0.584)	(0.484)		(0.453)
Personalist regime			2.508***	1.621***		-0.256
			(0.608)	(0.351)		(0.300)
Conflict participation controls	Yes	Yes	Yes	Yes	Yes	Yes
Observations	102	133	102	133	76	76

* $p < 0.10$; ** $p < 0.05$; *** $p < 0.01$ (two-tailed)
Standard errors clustered by country in parentheses. Models 1–4 are probit models. Models 5–6 are OLS models.
Constants and time dummies are not shown.

In Column 2, we widen the window of time before democratization and include all dictators who were in power at some point during one full year before democratic transition. This allows us to include multiple dictators who ruled in a country during the same year leading up to the regime change.

This addresses two issues. First, in some countries, such as the Dominican Republic in the aftermath of the assassination of Trujillo in 1961, the democratization process was quite volatile and characterized by several leaders who replaced each other before yielding to democracy. Second, in some countries, there were long-lived dictators who could be subject to punishment upon democratization but were replaced shortly before the transition. This model includes these leaders despite the fact that they were not technically the last dictator who held office. By contrast, in Column 1 such dictators are excluded because they were not the last dictator observed before democratic transition. While including all leaders who held power in the run-up to democracy boosts the observations by 30 percent, the results are largely unchanged.

In Columns 3 and 4, we now include autocratic regime types on the eve of democratization as control variables. As in Tables 4.2 and 4.3, the inclusion of these variables is intended to capture the bargaining power of outgoing regimes before transition. We include variables for whether the leader was at the helm of a single-party, military, personalist, or oligarchic regime. Oligarchy is the omitted baseline category in these models. The results confirm those in Columns 1 and 2: an autocratic constitution significantly reduces the likelihood that an outgoing dictator will suffer punishment. We note that the results are also robust to dropping autocratic regime types and instead including the number of de facto political parties on the eve of democratization.[7]

In Columns 5 and 6, we respecify the dependent variable as the number of years a dictator survived after giving up office. We log this variable after adding one to address zero values and estimate OLS regressions. Because we drop right-censored data on outgoing dictators who were still alive when the dataset ends, these models contain fewer observations than those across Columns 1–4.

In Column 5, we include the basic set of control variables. The results are consistent with expectations: previous dictators who live in democracies that inherited a constitution from their autocratic predecessor live 5.1 percent longer than those who do not. In Column 6, we introduce autocratic regime type legacies. The main results are materially identical.

In conclusion, we find that regardless of the control variables we introduce, how we define entry into the set of former dictators who could be conceivably punished upon democratization, or how we specify the dependent variable, former dictators have much better outcomes under new democracies when they inherit their constitutions from autocratic regimes.

---

[7] This variable, however, is only available at the country-year rather than the leader-year level. Consequently, we estimated this model on the sample of the last dictators in power who lasted more than one year.

CONCLUSION

This chapter explores the determinants of transitions to democracy and the consequences of democratization in groundbreaking fashion. Take the causes of democracy first. This chapter is the first to empirically model the democratic transition process by unpacking democratizations into two distinct types: those that are elite biased, because they inherit a constitution from their autocratic predecessor, and those that are more popular, because freely and fairly elected leaders write their own democratic constitutions. This chapter also presents one of the first tests for novel hypotheses about the causes of democratization rooted in structural factors erected under the previous autocratic regime: high levels of state capacity and the presence of a legislature under autocracy are more likely to culminate in transitions to elite-biased democracy. Finally, this chapter shows that the interaction of structural factors and precipitating factors, such as natural disasters, revolutions, and economic crises, is crucial for comprehending why some regimes transition to elite-biased democracy versus popular democracy, as well as explaining the timing of those transitions.

This chapter therefore offers new insights into the causes of democracy. We now know when, where, and why some autocracies end their lives only to continue as gamed democracies with similar features, whereas others fundamentally transform themselves into more representative, pluralistic, inclusive, and egalitarian regimes.

This chapter also tackles an enduring puzzle in political economy on the consequences of democracy. Even though median voter–inspired theories of democracy argue that democracies should be more redistributive than dictatorships, evidence for this claim has proven elusive. In this chapter, we identify the scope conditions under which democratization induces greater representation, pluralism, inclusiveness, and redistribution. Political incumbents and their economic allies might actually prefer democracy to autocratic rule if they can impose roadblocks to redistribution under democracy ex ante.

Consistent with this claim, this chapter presents evidence that there is a relationship between democracy and more egalitarian political and economic outcomes, but only if elites are politically weak during a transition, as operationalized by their inability to impose a constitution on the new democracy before exiting power. In short, the political and economic promise of democracy for greater equality is indeed possible, but only if a democratic regime can create a new constitution that redefines the political game. This finding holds across a host of measures of democratic governance and fiscal, monetary, and material outcomes.

Finally, this chapter also examines how the circumstances of democratic transition affect the consequences of losing office for outgoing dictators. We find that outgoing dictators who are able to impose a holdover constitution during democratization and beyond are less likely to face severe punishment upon relinquishing their rule. They also live longer. Our findings suggest that for dictators who fear their ousting in the face of domestic unrest or potential instability, democracy can provide a plausible avenue for protecting their most basic interests – but only if it has been previously engineered to do their bidding.

How does our story differ from competing theories that try to account for why democracy is often less egalitarian than anticipated, or even less egalitarian than dictatorship? Among these alternative stories are other notions about the legacies of the previous authoritarian regime. Most of these competing theories either point to the de facto power of outgoing elites and the shadow of that power under democracy (Acemoglu and Robinson 2008) or incorporate the notion that civil society and citizen organization and association was quashed under dictatorship and cannot recover under democracy (Bernhard and Karakoç 2007). Some authors, for example, argue that a lingering coup threat, unalloyed to any constitutionally derived military veto or inflated military power, cows democrats from pursuing policies that might hurt oligarchs and former dictators (Acemoglu and Robinson 2001). Other authors argue that the seeds of a clientelistic democracy lie with previous dictators' divide-and-rule tactics or that they reflect the legacy of ethnically based patronage politics under patrimonial rule (Keefer 2007).

Our story, by contrast, is about the actual workings of democracy. Democracies often inherit elite-biased institutions from the previous regime that define the de jure rules of the game during democratic rule. These institutions shape public policy under democracy and the material outcomes tied to those policies. In other words, our mechanism differs from others in that inequality and other outcomes that deviate from conventional expectations about democracy are the result of freely and fairly elected politicians playing by the rules of the game imposed on them by their autocratic predecessors.

5

Unraveling the Deal

Constitutional Annulments and Amendments under Elite-Biased Democracy

The previous two chapters demonstrate how and why outgoing authoritarian elites spend their dear political capital, time, and resources to ink constitutions that they then foist on new, elected regimes. They craft these democracy founding documents prior to the inaugural elections sometimes years, if not decades, before the actual transition. Chapter 3 illustrates how outgoing elites tip the scales of the democratic game in their favor to protect their most vital interests. And by showcasing that across a host of institutional, policy, and material outcomes democracies that inherit constitutions from their autocratic predecessors favor elites instead of the median voter, Chapter 4 demonstrates that this is an effective strategy.

In those chapters, we argue that authoritarian elites who seek to protect their hides and their broader interests under democracy are all too aware of the possibility that newly elected leaders under democracy might rewrite the rules. They therefore lean on various measures to prevent this from happening. They attempt to design constitutions in a way that creates a firewall that protects erstwhile political incumbents and their economic allies. Specifically, constitutional engineers combine elements such as favorable electoral rules or malapportionment along with obstacles to constitutional change such as requiring large supermajorities to scrap the constitution. This allows outgoing authoritarian elites to replicate their de facto strength in new ways that derive explicitly from de jure protections. Yet this strategy is not always foolproof and, in some cases, it contains the seeds of its own destruction.

Democracies sometimes escape the constitutional straitjacket they inherit from their autocratic predecessors. Some eventually annul their "founding" constitutions and replace them with entirely new documents. Others considerably amend their inherited autocratic constitutions over time, eliminating the most egregious forms of elite bias.

In this chapter, we address several questions that are salient to both researchers and policy makers. What are the important changes that take place when authoritarian documents are annulled or amended under democracy? What clauses are struck, and what is the new content that emerges? And when and how can those groups that are marginalized under an elite-biased democracy empower themselves to modify the rules of the game to improve their position?

To address these questions, this chapter explores several facets of constitutional change under elite-biased democracy. First, we examine the details of their annulments and amendments. Second, we look at the factors that explain why some elite-biased democracies with constitutions inherited from their authoritarian past discard those documents at some point down the line, whereas other democracies retain these charters. Third, we evaluate the effect that changes to elite-biased constitutions have on governance, fiscal, and material outcomes. Therefore, this chapter parallels Chapter 4 in many ways, except that we are now looking at the causes and consequences of reforms that make democracies more popular, rather than the causes and consequences of democratization with autocratic characteristics.

As we demonstrate in Chapters 3 and 4, elite-biased democracies are very dissimilar from their popular counterparts. In many respects, they are more like autocracies than proponents of democracy would like to admit: their political, social, and economic outcomes are less inclusive, pluralistic, and egalitarian than popular democracies.

However, these differences are not necessarily permanent. An elite-biased democracy can be significantly reformed and its institutions transformed. Indeed, these changes can come quickly and can occur unexpectedly.

Of course, as expected, this chapter finds that brazen attempts by newly elected politicians to immediately rewrite the terms of democratic transition dominated by outgoing elites are relatively rare phenomenona. This speaks to the enduring power of authoritarian constitution making as a device to vouchsafe continuity across regime transition. When they do occur, however, changes to an elite-biased democracy's institutional design tend to gut explicit and implicit provisions that protect elites. For example, elected representatives might rescind protections to former authoritarian elites' property rights and safeguards against prosecution for crimes they perpetrated under the previous regime. Indeed, most of the annulments of constitutions inherited by democracies from previous autocratic regimes, or amendments that seriously change the rules of the game, center on these issues.

This chapter also finds that major reforms to elite-biased democracy that make these systems more pluralistic, inclusive, and egalitarian typically occur after the original authoritarian stakeholders have died. In most cases, meaningful changes to the constitutions imposed by outgoing dictators only occur after the most powerful members of the last authoritarian regime have expired. As coordination by remaining members of the former authoritarian regime and their successors becomes more difficult, major constitutional change is more likely.

Moreover, we also find that once serious constitutional change such as this occurs, real social, political, and economic changes ensue. Reforms can have a big, positive impact on the welfare of the majority under democracy. Pluralism, inclusiveness, and egalitarianism blossom. In turn, fiscal and monetary policies become more popular and begin to benefit the median voter more than the oligarchy. The wellbeing of regular people can therefore be drastically improved.

THE POLITICS AND PROCESS OF REFORMING ELITE-BIASED CONSTITUTIONS

What is the process by which elite-biased constitutions are amended or replaced altogether? Usually the constitution itself spells out the rules guiding its own reform process in great detail. Sometimes amendments are proposed by referenda. Other times they are crafted in the legislative branch. Still other times expert commissions are created.

A famous example is Spain in 1978, when a seven-member panel monikered "the Fathers of the Constitution" was selected from the elected members of a restored parliament that also served as a constituent assembly. They were commissioned to pen a new constitutional draft, which was subsequently submitted to parliament for approval. Still other times, new constitutional assemblies are convoked from scratch, as was the case in Colombia in 1991.

It is also worth noting that decisions about this process can be very tendentious. Different factions will have stakes in supporting different processes. Unsurprisingly, their support is often linked to their expectations of whether the proposed amendments will benefit them politically or hurt them. An illustrative example of this phenomenon is Indonesia. Amendments were proposed by smaller parties to Indonesia's 1999 constitution, unleashing an epic fight over how these amendments would be drafted and discussed. While some parties favored a referenda process, others lobbied for the establishment of an expert commission.

Our theoretical framework can help make sense of the major actors who participate in constitutional struggles under elite-biased democracies, as well as their motives for doing so and the strategies they pursue. Consider Myanmar in 2016. The country's first elected government in almost five decades took power early that year after winning elections in November 2015. The National League for Democracy (NLD), the country's main opposition party, enjoyed a sweeping victory, displacing the military-dominated ruling party, which lost the majority of its seats in parliament and the presidency. A major partner allied with the NLD in this effort was the small business sector. Long in the wilderness under the military regime, these businesses faced onerously high borrowing rates, due in part to poor trade financing facilities, formidable transaction costs, and punishing taxes. Meanwhile, military-connected businesses were coddled with barriers to entry and generous subsidies.

Almost immediately, the leader of the newly anointed governing party, Aung San Suu Kyi, sought to overturn a constitutional ban that barred her from becoming president – ostensibly because her children are British citizens. Suu Kyi also declared that she will behave as the real leader of Myanmar – "be above the [elected] president" – and control him from behind the scenes, a stratagem made easier by the fact that he is a loyalist handpicked by Suu Kyi before the 2015 elections. Moreover, the NLD's parliamentary majority proposed a law that carves out a new political office for her, formalizing the de facto subordination of Myanmar's constitutionally designated president. Suu Kyi has also attempted to push through numerous economic reforms aimed at enervating the military-connected oligarchs and bolstering the economic fortunes of small businesses.

The military and its proxies in the Burmese parliament have not taken this threat to their power lying down. They have pushed back forcefully. They argue that Suu Kyi's recalcitrance and ad hoc proposals violate the constitution, a document they authored and subsequently used to structure the democratic transition. They have therefore been keen to defend its prerogatives by, inter alia, monopolizing the 25 percent of the seats needed to ratify a constitutional amendment. So far, they have kept the line.

CONSTITUTIONAL ANNULMENTS AND AMENDMENTS

Before we systematically examine the causes and consequences of reforms to elite-biased democracies, we outline the frequency and content of these constitutional changes across place and time. Table 5.1 reports major changes to autocratic constitutions under democracy between 1800 and 2006. It identifies the full set of annulments to these charters. There are twenty-six cases of constitutions that are annulled at some point after democratization.

Table 5.1 also records whether a major amendment to an elite-biased constitution occurred and whether that amendment was popular in nature – in terms of eliminating elite-biased measures – or instead accentuated elite biases. Specifically, it contains details of the first set of major amendments to authoritarian constitutions observed under democracy during this period.[1] There are only twelve major amendments to constitutions that made them more popular.

---

[1] We focus on the first set of major amendments because they represent the initial, successful, and consequential challenge by democratically elected representatives to the social contract imposed by outgoing authoritarian elites. Of course, some of these constitutions continue to be amended repeatedly – in some cases, hundreds of times. Later amendments tend to build on initial, opening progress, however, a point that we will return to later and in the cases of Sweden (Chapter 6) and Chile (Chapter 7).

There are thirty-six cases of democracies operating with autocratic constitutions that were never amended at all after democratization.

The bottom line is that elite-biased constitutions tend to be enduring deals between the political forces that were dominant before democratization and the opposition: they are rarely changed in ways that hurt the previous political incumbents and their economic allies, and when they are, this tends to happen years, if not decades, after the constitution is inherited by the new democracy.[2] Moreover, some changes to elite-biased constitutions actually reinforce elite advantages. Many of these changes, whether they are connected to annulments or amendments of constitutions, help solidify the political power of former autocratic incumbents. These include, for example, the introduction of bicameralism, as well as the adoption of proportional electoral rules.

Of course, not all elements of constitutional reform serve to undermine elite interests, or have any effect, for that matter. The reason is that these changes are about issues that are orthogonal to issues that relate to elite bias versus populism. For example, aspirational statements can be added to constitutions without transforming who wields power and who benefits from constitutional change. Amendments can also involve changes to the voting age, issues of multilingualism and multiculturalism (such as enshrining an indigenous language as an official language), issues involving religion and the separation of church and state, and foreign policy.

We omit these types of constitutional reforms from the table. A host of cases illustrate the logic behind this decision. Consider Ghana. The only amendment to Ghana's 1992 constitution, which served as a framework for its democratic transition in 1993, occurred in 1996 and primarily dealt with procedural provisions concerning the legislature, provisions concerning dual citizenship, and stipulations guiding the hiring of civil servants.

Table 5.1 also contains a series of columns that highlight the features of constitutional change. If the autocratic constitution was annulled, it outlines elements of the constitution that replaced it. If the autocratic constitution was instead amended, it highlights the main structural changes and its new features.

Annulments of Elite-Biased Constitutions

Consider first the annulments in Table 5.1 – changes that scrap elite-biased constitutions and replace them with more popular charters. Perhaps most prominent are annulments that swept through Eastern Europe after the fall of Communism. Countries such as Bulgaria, Poland, and Romania scrapped the

---

[2] In some exceptional cases, a struggle between former authoritarian elements and reformers begins almost immediately upon democratization. This is especially true if the opposition wins the new regime's inaugural elections and can therefore appeal to a popular mandate to legitimize a precocious attempt to reform the constitution.

TABLE 5.1. *Major Changes to Autocratic Constitutions under Democracy*

Country	Year	Annulment Year	Major Political Changes Linked to Annulments	First Set of Major Popular Amendments	Major Political Changes Linked to Amendments
Argentina	1912			No amendments	
Argentina	1946			1949	Popular changes: rescinds indirect elections and replaces them with plurality formula
Argentina	1958			No amendments	
Argentina	1963			No amendments	
Argentina	1973			No amendments	
Belgium	1894			1921	Popular changes: universal male suffrage
Benin	1991			No amendments	
Bolivia	1979			No amendments	
Bolivia	1982			No major popular amendments	Elite-biased changes: introduction of steeper supermajority requirements for constitutional change (1993, 1994)
Brazil	1985	1988	Popular changes: allows for popular referenda; ban on leftist parties lifted; made it easier to amend constitution	No major popular amendments	
Bulgaria	1990	1991	Elite-biased changes: adopts proportional electoral system; strengthens protection of property rights	No major popular amendments	

Country					
Burundi	1993			No amendments	
Burundi	2005			No amendments	
Central African Republic	1993	1994	Popular changes: civilian control over military increased; unicameralism adopted	No amendments	
Chile	1909			No major popular amendments	Elite-biased changes: empowerment of the military in executive politics (1924)
Chile	1934			1963, 1967, 1970	Popular changes: gives government broader powers to expropriate land (1963); nationalization of mines (1967); allow illiterates to vote (1970)
					Elite-biased changes: limits parliamentary initiatives on public expenditures (1943)
Chile	1990			2005	Popular changes: reduction of military role in politics; elimination of appointed senators; opens door for electoral reform away from overrepresenting conservative parties
Colombia	1937			No major popular amendments	
Colombia	1958	1991	Popular changes: party ban lifted	1968	Popular changes: lifts bans on electoral competition; abolishes two-thirds majority requirement to pass legislation

(continued)

TABLE 5.1 (*continued*)

Country	Year	Annulment Year	Major Political Changes Linked to Annulments	First Set of Major Popular Amendments	Major Political Changes Linked to Amendments
Comoros	1990	1992	Elite-biased changes: bicameralism adopted	No amendments	
Comoros	2004			No amendments	
Costa Rica	1946			No amendments	
Cyprus	1983			No major popular amendments	
Czechoslovakia	1989			No major popular amendments	
Denmark	1901	1915	Elite-biased changes: move to proportional electoral system	No amendments	
			Popular changes: universal suffrage extended		
Ecuador	1979	1984	Popular changes: prohibits ex post punishment	No major popular amendments	
El Salvador	1984			1992	Popular changes: civilian control over military increased
Fiji	1992	1997	Popular changes: ethnic Fijians give up guaranteed legislative minority in lower house	No amendments	
			Elite-biased changes: protects landholdings of powerful ethnic Fijians		

Country	Year		Changes
France	1870	1875	Elite-biased changes: adopts indirectly elected senate
Georgia	2004		No major popular amendments
Ghana	1993		No major popular amendments
Guatemala	1958		No amendments
Guatemala	1966		No amendments
Guatemala	1986		No major popular amendments
Guinea-Bissau	2000		No amendments
Guinea-Bissau	2004		No amendments
Honduras	1971		No major popular amendments
Hungary	1990		No major popular amendments
Indonesia	1999		No major popular amendments
Italy	1919		No amendments
Italy	1946	1947	Elite-biased changes: quasi federalism adopted; stronger property rights protection. Popular changes: party ban lifted; right to form trade unions; universal suffrage

(*continued*)

TABLE 5.1 (*continued*)

Country	Year	Annulment Year	Major Political Changes Linked to Annulments	First Set of Major Popular Amendments	Major Political Changes Linked to Amendments
Kenya	1998			No major popular amendments	Elite-biased changes: gives parliament the ability to do constitutional change rather than civil society (1999)
Korea, South	1960			No major popular amendments	
Korea, South	1988			No amendments	
Kyrgyzstan	2005	2006		No amendments	
Liberia	2006			No amendments	
Madagascar	1993	1998	Elite-biased changes: federalism adopted	No major popular amendments	
Mexico	2000			No major popular amendments	
Netherlands	1897			1917	Elite-biased changes: proportional representation introduced Popular changes: universal suffrage and corporatist bargaining
Niger	1993			No amendments	
Niger	2000			No amendments	
Nigeria	1979			No amendments	
Pakistan	1972	1973	Elite-biased changes: federal form of government adopted; two-thirds majorities and assent of president required for constitutional amendment	No amendments	

Country	Year	Amendments	Changes
Pakistan	1988	No major popular amendments	
Panama	1949	No amendments	
Panama	1952	No major popular amendments	
Panama	1989	1994	Popular changes: standing armed forces abolished
Paraguay	1989 1992	No amendments	Elite-biased changes: former presidents allowed to serve in senate for life; active duty members of the military banned from political participation
Peru	1946	No amendments	
Peru	1956	No major popular amendments	
Peru	1963	1964	Popular changes: facilitates land reform
Peru	1980	No major popular amendments	
Peru	2001	2004	Elite-biased changes: 2002 decentralization of government structure. Elite-biased changes: 2002 decentralization of structure of government (national, regional, municipal). Popular changes: popular initiation of legislation introduced, including popular recalls

(continued)

TABLE 5.1 (*continued*)

Country	Year	Annulment Year	Major Political Changes Linked to Annulments	First Set of Major Popular Amendments	Major Political Changes Linked to Amendments
Poland	1989	1992	Popular changes: easier to reject amendments to legislation made by senate	No major popular amendments	
Romania	1990	1991	Elite-biased changes: party ban introduced	No amendments	
Senegal	2000	2001		No amendments	
Serbia RB	2000	2003	Elite-biased changes: introduces bicameralism	No major popular amendments	
Spain	1977	1978	Elite-biased changes: introduces bicameralism; devolves power to local governments; property rights strengthened Popular changes: party ban dropped	No amendments	
Sri Lanka	1989			No major popular amendments	
Sudan	1965			No major popular amendments	
Sudan	1986			No major popular amendments	

Country					
Sweden	1911	1974			Popular changes: universal suffrage extended at local followed by national level
Thailand	1975			No major popular amendments	
Thailand	1979	1981	Constitution suspended	No amendments	
			Elite-biased changes: bicameralism enacted; proportional representation adopted	No major popular amendments	
Thailand	1992	1997	Popular changes: direct elections in both houses of congress		
Turkey	1983			1987	Popular changes: party ban lifted
Uruguay	1919	1933	Constitution suspended	No major popular amendments	
Uruguay	1942	1952		No major popular amendments	
Venezuela	1946	1947	Popular changes: direct elections for the executive; expands workers' rights; introduces secret ballot	No amendments	
Venezuela	1959	1961	Popular changes: popular initiation of legislation allowed	No amendments	

Sources: V-Dem Dataset, Comparative Constitutions Project, Database of Political Institutions, Gerring, Thacker & Moreno (2005), Bakke and Wibbels (2006), Henisz (2000), Mainwaring and Perez-Linan (2013), and country-specific sources.

communist constitutions that had guided their political systems and replaced them with charters that invoked multiparty competition and free and fair elections.

To be sure, former communist apparatchiks did not simply vanish into thin air. Instead, communists and their sympathizers often attempted to reinvent themselves or hide their pasts and recapture political office (Nalepa 2010; Grzymala-Busse 2002). In some cases, they were successful in ensuring institutional provisions such as proportional representation that would ensure they would not be wiped off the political landscape.

Annulments transcend Eastern Europe, of course. In Fiji, the annulment of the 1992 constitution in 1997 withdrew the guaranteed legislative minority in the lower house enjoyed by ethnic Fijians, who represent the majority of the country's landowners. In the Central African Republic, the 1993 constitution was repealed and replaced in 1994. This made the constitution more popular by, among other things, abolishing the upper chamber and also weakening the political power of the military.

Popular Amendments to Elite-Biased Constitutions

Next consider amendments to elite-biased constitutions. Several historical examples from Europe stand out. In Belgium, Sweden, and the Netherlands, suffrage was extended to all males in 1921, 1919, and 1917, respectively – but not before elites won some protections to their electoral fortunes by adopting proportional representation, a point that we will return to below and in Chapter 6 in the case of Sweden.

Chile is also a representative example of changes to an elite-biased charter that created a more popular political framework. The first major amendment to the 1934 constitution, in 1943, took one step backward, limiting the parliament's power of the purse. Subsequent amendments in the 1960s and 1970s made politics more pluralistic and egalitarian. The government was given broader powers to expropriate land, mines were nationalized, and illiterate citizens were allowed to vote. Then in 2005, amendments were made to Pinochet's authoritarian 1980 constitution that made it more popular as well. These included curtailing the military's role in politics, the elimination of appointed senators, and opening the door for electoral reform in a way that would reduce the overrepresentation of conservative parties. We discuss these changes in greater depth in Chapter 7.

There are also notable cases of popular amendments outside of Europe and Latin America. For example, in 1987 a major amendment to Turkey's 1983 constitution lifted a ban on some opposition parties that were outlawed. This paved the way for the later rise of new parties such as the Justice and Development Party, which, since the early 2000s, has dominated Turkish politics and managed to rescind several of the guarantees that shielded top military leaders from prosecution.

Further Elite Entrenchment under Elite-Biased Constitutions

In contrast to these popular constitutional reforms, elite-biased constitutions can also be made even more biased in favor of former authoritarian elites after democratic transition. An illustrative example is Kenya. The ruling Kenya African National Union (KANU) presided over democratization in 1998. As part of the transition, the powers to introduce and guide constitutional change were granted to civil society. KANU, however, quickly began backpedaling when they realized that they could lose control over the process. KANU, which dominated the parliament, revested the power to introduce constitutional change with the parliament.

A similar scenario played out in Bolivia, which transitioned to democracy in 1982 under an authoritarian constitution. Concerned with snowballing popular pressures for change, the parliament introduced constitutional amendments in 1993 and 1994 requiring larger supermajorities in both houses of congress in order to amend or replace the constitution.

Finally, even in cases in which there are changes made to an elite-biased constitution that make it more popular, there can simultaneously be elements that cut against that grain and introduce elite-biased elements. In terms of annulments of elite-biased constitutions, consider Thailand in 1997. While popular changes made to the 1992 constitution included adopting direct elections in both houses of congress, this charter was also modified in a manner that enhanced the power of elites: bicameralism was enacted and proportional representation was adopted.

THE CAUSES OF CONSTITUTIONAL ANNULMENT AND AMENDMENTS

What explains the adoption of major reforms to elite-biased democracy in the form of constitutional annulments and amendments? As we argue in Chapter 2, the key to understanding this phenomenon is to identify the actors who want to modify the rules of the game under democracy, their opportunities for a favorable change to those rules, and the catalyst that ultimately pushes them to it. We take up all three of these factors in order to spell out concrete hypotheses about the causes of reform to elite-biased constitutions under democracy.

Whereas those who benefit from an elite-biased democracy are the former political incumbents from the previous autocratic period and their economic elite allies, it is outsider economic elites and the masses who are slated to benefit from a fundamental change to the rules of the game. Their ultimate goal is to make sure the country remains democratic, but they seek to transform it into a more popular democracy by reforming its elite-biased elements. Practically speaking, they can accomplish this objective by forcing a timetable for constitutional reform upon the government. This can include convoking a new constituent assembly and calling new elections, preferably culminating in a constitution that is more pluralistic, inclusive, and egalitarian. Alternatively, they can build broad support for consequential amendments to a country's political charter and then craft a plan to ensure that those amendments are realized.

What are the opportunities available to outsider economic elites and the masses to make this happen? First and foremost, they must be able to coordinate to agitate for political change. That means that the outsider economic elites who are the losers from the extant system of property rights, economic policies, and regulations must be able to organize citizens and civil society organizations to rally around the cause of constitutional reform. Outsider economic elites can start this process by stoking a debate about the merits and justice of the current charter. They can spearhead outreach campaigns and espouse pro-reform propaganda. They can also stimulate media coverage that increases interest in their cause or pushes opposition parties to adopt constitutional reform as an item in their political platforms. Importantly, due to their economic status, outsider economic elites have the financial wherewithal to bankroll these campaigns.

What might allow outsider economic elites to pull off such an ambitious agenda? After all, this agenda threatens the rights and interests of the erstwhile authoritarian elements that hold disproportionate sway over the democracy and benefit from its biases. The most important permissive condition is the death of the previous dictator – or, similarly, the death of key insiders in the previous regime.[3]

Recall from Chapter 3 that autocratic constitutions foisted on new democracies and designed by outgoing autocratic regimes often embed provisions that are explicitly intended to cover the lifespan of former autocratic elites. Most straightforwardly, many autocratic constitutions grant congressional posts to the most powerful members of the former authoritarian regime. These posts often entail immunity from prosecution and expire along with the deaths of the key members who inhabit them.

Other constitutional provisions that advantage outgoing authoritarian elites besides explicit protections can also weaken after the deaths of former authoritarian insiders. Take electoral system design. As indicated in Chapter 3, by constructing favorable vote aggregation rules, outgoing autocratic elites enhance the likelihood that they will be reelected to political office. This affords them the ability to forestall constitutional revisions. Yet electoral systems, while much stickier than ad hoc political posts created for outgoing autocratic elites, could nonetheless be more fragile when their original designers are no longer alive and no longer need them as shields. Furthermore, as the next generation

---

[3] This does not require that every member from the old guard who ruled under authoritarianism dies. A few holdover elites might even be willing to sell their former economic allies down the river when a crisis hits in exchange for guarantees to their own parochial and personal political advantages that last a while longer.

of politicians comes on the scene, these new political players might find tweaks to the electoral system to be to their advantage.

Because former political leaders under dictatorship face the most severe potential threats under democracy, they attempt to construct airtight institutional elements that will endure – at least until they pass from the scene. These elements do not endure, however, if former incumbent elites find it harder to coordinate to block changes to the constitution. Posts linked to the lifespans of the former elites are one such focal point. Once these expire, their absence makes it harder for remaining elites tied to the old regime – and their successors – to coordinate to block constitutional changes. This capacity to coordinate to support key elements of a holdover constitution is eroded further when the democracy's institutions become occupied by political successors for which the stakes of change are lower. The next generation of politicians, for instance, is not subject to being punished for misdeeds committed under the dictatorship.

To be sure, holdover constitutions do not always unwind as soon as the previous dictator dies. The capacity to coordinate on the part of the heirs of the former authoritarian regime might erode, but it certainly does not vanish. In many cases, coordination capacity remains formidable. Reform must therefore be won by an organized opposition that seeks constitutional change. And that requires a nudge.

There are a host of precipitating factors that can facilitate the coordination of outsider economic elites and the masses – the two main actors who stand to benefit the most from fundamental changes to the rules of the game. Some of these factors – such as major political scandals or bungled foreign wars – differ by country and time period and therefore are idiosyncratic in nature. Others, however, are more likely to yield predictable shifts in the balance of power between incumbent elites on the one hand and outsider economic elites and the masses on the other hand.

Sustained negative shocks to economic growth are one proximate factor that can provide the final trigger for outsider economic elites and the masses to coordinate and organize for constitutional change. Economic crises can set in motion two simultaneous dynamics that can catch incumbent elites flat-footed. First, a crisis can make it much easier for outsider economic elites to make the case to the masses that the economic status quo is fragile, unstable, and threatening to their basic livelihoods. Stimulating broad-based collective action against the status quo should therefore be considerably easier in such circumstances. Second, negative economic shocks can temporarily weaken incumbent economic elites, the major beneficiaries of the economic status quo. This again opens up an opportunity for outsider economic elites and the masses to push for change.

Consider an example from Indonesia's attempts to amend its autocratic constitution in 2000, as the Asian flu hit its economy. As one politician pushing for change argued to other amendment drafters, "If we do not amend the constitution at this time, there will be no amendment at all, even if the condition is more stable. The lessons from other countries show that, the amendment of constitutions may only be carried out during political upheaval, as is happening now" (Indrayana 2008, 189).

A second proximate factor that can trigger the outsider economic elites and the masses to coordinate and organize for constitutional change is a sharp shift in a country's economic openness. It is well documented that rapid shifts in economic openness can redefine the winners and losers in an economy (Rogowski 1989) and lead to substantial short-term economic dislocation. This again generates two dynamics that tilt in favor of the opposition winning changes to the constitutional status quo. First, outsider economic elites can convince those groups who lose ground during a changing economy – in this case, those who lose their jobs once tariff barriers come down – that the system is rigged against them. The newly unemployed, as well as those who take a hit to their economic bottom line, should be easier to recruit during an organizational drive to topple the political status quo.

Second, rapid shifts in economic openness can in some circumstances weaken incumbent economic elites or strengthen outsider economic elites. This shift in the balance of economic power can be translated to the political realm as outsider economic elites pour funding into opposition parties that espouse constitutional reform. Outsider economic elites can also use their relatively greater resources to lobby politicians to support reform in exchange for side benefits.

Empirical Predictions

There are several empirical implications that we can deduce from this discussion of constitutional change under elite-biased democracy. There should be a strong, positive relationship between the death of the previous dictator and the ability to change a holdover autocratic constitution. The reason for this "reduced-form" prediction is that, although we cannot pin down all of the possible precipitating factors that galvanize the outsider economic elite and the masses to act together to overturn the status quo, we can say with considerable confidence that, whatever the ultimate catalyst, when the day comes these political outsiders will be more likely to coordinate and upend the status quo when the old autocratic guard is dead and gone. By this time, the constitution will have already fulfilled its most important goals.

There are, however, at least two common amplifying factors that tend to weaken incumbent economic elites who were powerful in the previous authoritarian regime and any remaining former autocratic political elites. One is a prolonged economic crisis. Another is a major shift in economic openness that reconfigures the winners and losers in an economy. When such proximate circumstances transpire after the former old guard has died off, they are likely to precipitate consequential redesigns in the constitutional status quo that yield a reformed social contract – one that makes democracy more popular.

MEASUREMENT STRATEGY FOR EXPLAINING CONSTITUTIONAL
CHANGE

This section outlines our measurement strategy for testing the hypotheses laid
out in the previous section.

Measuring Constitutional Change

The key dependent variable in the analyses that follow is the annulment or
amendment of an autocratic constitution. This is a binary variable that is coded
as a "1" in the year an autocratic constitution is annulled or amended under
democracy and "0" otherwise.[4] As in the previous chapter, data on the origins of
constitutions as well as constitutional changes are taken from the Comparative
Constitutions Project. Data on regime type are again from Cheibub et al. (2010)
for 1946–2006 and Boix et al. (2013) for the 1800–1945 period.

Measuring Coordination Potential between Outsider Economic
Elites and the Masses

To understand why some countries reform elite-biased constitutions under
democracy while others do not, we also need to operationalize and measure
the structural and proximate factors that encourage constitutional reform as
previously outlined.

In terms of structural factors, the key variable that helps operationalize
the conditions that make constitutional change more likely is the death of the
key players of the former authoritarian regime. Practically speaking, we cannot identify and measure all focal points used by former authoritarian elites
to coordinate in order to block constitutional changes. For example, one of
these focal points might be the posts reserved for former dictators, as outlined
earlier. What we can do is to proxy for the expiration of these focal points.
Because former dictators are potentially key focal points and lightning rods of
the authoritarian era, we proxy for the expiration of these focal points with the
former dictator's death.

We therefore identify the previous ruling dictator using data from Archigos
(Goemans et al. 2009) and then track the year of the former dictator's death.
Country years following the death of the former dictator are coded "1,"

---

[4] As Table 5.1 indicates, there are far fewer major constitutional changes. We note that coding the
dependent variable in this more inclusive manner biases against us, however, because it introduces noise: we are including both major and minor amendments in this measure, and some
minor amendments are orthogonal to the interests of outgoing authoritarian elites or only affect
their interests in minor ways. Using major amendments produces similar, though somewhat
weaker, results, given that the number of amendments that are coded in this way is reduced
significantly.

whereas those in which the dictator remains alive are coded "o." In 40 percent of all country years of democracy with an autocratic constitution in our data, the previous dictator has already passed away.

In terms of proximate factors, we operationalize the aforementioned concepts in the following manner. To operationalize dramatic slowdowns in economic growth, we code economic growth shock as the number of country years in a five-year lagged window when economic growth is more than one negative standard deviation from the country's mean growth rate (dating back to either 1800 or, if the country was established after 1800, its year of independence). This measure is advantageous in that mean country growth rates differ substantially for structural reasons, and a relatively low growth rate for one country could be a relatively high growth rate for another. We use a window because it can take time for the opposition to organize and successfully push for change once an economic growth crisis hits. The mean of this variable is 0.38 across all country years of democracy with an autocratic constitution in our data; the standard deviation is 0.71.

To measure rapid changes in economic openness that can empower outsider economic elites, we code trade openness shock as the first difference in exports plus imports as a share of GDP (percent) over a five-year period. Data on trade openness are from the Penn World Tables 6.2. We have coverage on trade openness between 1950 and 2006 for the entire world. The mean five-year first difference in trade openness is 3.33, and the standard deviation is 11.81. We note that the results are robust to measuring trade shocks in different ways.

Controls

We also control for several possible confounders across our models. These are all lagged by one period. We control for log(per capita income) and log(total natural resource income per capita). The former captures the idea that more prosperous and modern societies might be more likely to overturn elite-biased constitutions, in part because outsider economic elites and the masses are likely to be wealthier and therefore more likely to marshal the resources to solve the collective action problem than in poorer countries. The latter measures income generated from the production of all hydrocarbons and industrial metals and captures the notion that countries that are reliant on natural resources might be less – or perhaps more (see Menaldo 2016) – likely to become more democratic. We take both variables from Haber and Menaldo (2011) because they have coverage starting in 1800.

We also follow Albertus and Menaldo (2012b) and measure coercive capacity as military size. Elite-biased democracies that have a greater ability to deploy an internal security force and project the regime's power via a larger, more powerful military might be better able to forestall popular efforts to reform existing institutions, especially if these efforts play out in unorganized street demonstrations. We measure military size per 100 inhabitants and log it after adding .01 to address the zero values in the dataset.

EMPIRICAL STRATEGY FOR EXPLAINING CONSTITUTIONAL CHANGE

We now turn to a statistical analysis that estimates the probability that a democratic regime will annul or amend an autocratic constitution as a function of the variables outlined in earlier sections. Because we focus on changes to elite-biased constitutions, the analysis is limited to the set of country years in which democracies operate under an autocratic constitution. During the 1800–2006 period, we observe eighty spells of elite-biased democracy in which a new democratic regime inherits a constitution from its autocratic predecessors. These episodes span forty-nine countries. Of these episodes, autocratic constitutions were amended in some way in fifty cases. In another eight cases, democracy gave way to dictatorship prior to any amendment or annulment of an autocratic constitution. That leaves twenty-two right-censored regime spells of elite-biased democracy; these are democratic countries with unamended autocratic constitutions that were still in operation as of 2006.

In order to test our hypotheses about the determinants of constitutional change, we estimate a series of hazard models that calculate a country's risk of succumbing to constitutional change as a function of the independent variables we have outlined. In particular, and similar to the analysis of democratic transitions in Chapter 4, we use competing-risks regression models.

For our purposes, we examine the time it takes for an elite-biased democratic regime episode to "fail" into a more popular democracy. If an elite-biased democracy transitions back to dictatorship, then this new condition prevents that same regime from transitioning into a more popular democracy. Importantly, competing-risks models also account for right-censoring in a manner similar to other survival models. This is important because some regime spells of elite-biased democracy in our data are ongoing. These regimes could become more popular in the future but had not done so as of the end of our sample period.

To estimate these models, we pool the data, allowing us to exploit both its between and within variation. Robust standard errors clustered by country address heteroskedasticity and any intragroup correlation within countries. Furthermore, the results are robust to adding region fixed effects to control for time-invariant and region-specific unobserved heterogeneity that might impact the likelihood that a country transitions to a more popular form of democracy. We include linear, quadratic, and cubic terms for time to rule out the possibility that some of our independent variables are merely proxying for secular trends. Finally, the results are similar if the models that follow are instead estimated with the standard errors clustered by year to address contemporaneous/spatial correlation.

TABLE 5.2. *Annulments and Amendments of Autocratic Constitutions under Democracy*

Dependent Variable	Annulment/Amendment of Autocratic Constitution			
	Model 1	Model 2	Model 3	Model 4
Previous dictator dead	0.942**		0.527	0.514
	(0.383)		(0.539)	(0.369)
Previous transitional leader dead		−0.210		
		(0.654)		
Economic growth shock			−0.271	
			(0.197)	
Previous dictator dead* Economic growth shock			0.801**	
			(0.370)	
Trade openness shock				0.015
				(0.011)
Previous dictator dead* Trade openness shock				0.108***
				(0.037)
log(GDP per capita)	0.602***	0.600***	0.570**	0.673***
	(0.228)	(0.225)	(0.253)	(0.203)
log(military personnel per 100)	−0.249*	−0.235*	−0.309**	−0.528***
	(0.135)	(0.139)	(0.149)	(0.152)
log(resource income per capita)	0.213**	0.193**	0.196**	0.255**
	(0.088)	(0.090)	(0.090)	(0.106)
Time trends	Yes	Yes	Yes	Yes
Observations	347	347	346	221

* $p < 0.10$; ** $p < 0.05$; *** $p < 0.01$ (two-tailed)
All models are competing risks regressions. Raw coefficients rather than subhazard ratios are reported. Standard errors clustered by country are in parentheses. Constants and time dummies are not shown. All independent variables except the status of the former dictator are lagged one period. Sample is restricted to democratic country years with autocratic constitutions.

Empirical Results

Table 5.2 displays the results of these regressions. We report the raw coefficients from the regressions rather than the hazard ratios. Columns 1–2 test the hypotheses about structural factors that are conducive to reforms to elite-biased democracy. In Column 1, the key independent variable is whether the dictator from the previous episode of authoritarian rule is dead. The coefficient is, as expected, positive, statistically significant at the .05 level, and represents a fairly strong substantive effect. When all other variables are held constant, if the former dictator has died, this increases the estimated rate of failure (experiencing constitutional change) by 156 percent.

As a "placebo test," in Column 2 we examine the effect of the death of transitional leaders on constitutional change. These are leaders who came to power on the eve of transition with the explicit intent of calling free and fair elections

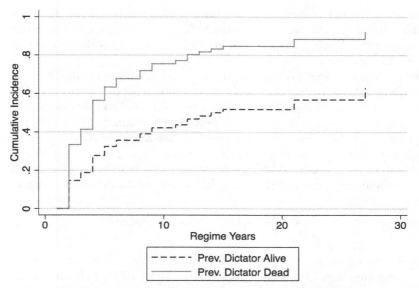

FIGURE 5.1. Rate of constitutional amendment or annulment by former dictator death. *Notes:* Figure 5.1 graphically displays the cumulative incidence function for constitutional change under elite-biased democracy as a function of whether the dictator from the previous authoritarian regime has died. This graph is produced by calculating hazard predictions from the regression depicted in Table 5.2, Column 1. We hold all other variables at their means.

and who held office for less than one year. These leaders are unimportant when it comes to generating focal points or permissive conditions for scrapping or amending autocratic constitutions. As anticipated, the death of transitional leaders has no statistically distinguishable impact on constitutional change.

Figure 5.1 graphically displays the cumulative incidence function for constitutional change in elite-biased democracy as a function of whether the previous dictator has died. Elite-biased democracies of all ages are more likely to amend or annul their constitutions following the death of the former dictator. This difference becomes especially pronounced toward the middle and end of the first decade of elite-biased democracy.

While the death of a former dictator and his consequent absence from the political scene might predispose an elite-biased democracy toward experiencing constitutional change, it does not explain the precise timing of change. Column 3 demonstrates that economic growth shocks following the death of the previous dictator make constitutional change much more likely. The hazard ratio for the interaction between the death of the previous dictator and economic growth shocks translates into a 123 percent increase in the estimated rate of failure (that is, experiencing constitutional change). By contrast, an economic growth shock that occurs when the previous dictator is still alive has no distinguishable impact on constitutional change. Similarly, constitutional change is not more likely following the death of the previous dictator when economic times are good.

Column 4 demonstrates a similar finding for trade openness shocks. A trade openness shock following the death of the previous dictator increases the likelihood of constitutional change. The hazard ratio connected to this interaction term is 1.11, indicating an 11 percent increase in the estimated rate of "failure". In contrast, a trade openness shock that occurs when the previous dictator is still alive has no statistically distinguishable impact on constitutional change. Similarly, constitutional change is not more likely following the death of the previous dictator absent a trade shock, though the coefficient is positive.

OUTCOMES FOLLOWING AMENDMENTS TO ELITE-BIASED DEMOCRACY

Whereas the previous section tests the determinants of elite-biased democracies experiencing constitutional change in the form of entirely new constitutions or amendments to autocratic constitutions, we now examine the consequences of constitutional amendments. The analysis therefore parallels what we did in Chapter 4: we now examine a set of hypotheses about governance under democracy (this time with an amended autocratic constitution), another set about material outcomes, and a final set about macroeconomic policies.

In terms of governance under democracies that amend constitutions from their autocratic predecessors, we expect that these regimes will be more pluralistic, inclusive, and representative than elite-biased democracies. Indeed, they should behave more like popular democracies that are founded with their own constitutions because reforms to an autocratic constitution under democracy should empower the median voter. In other words, previous political incumbents and their economic allies who carved out entire policy domains for themselves via autocratic constitutions should get the short end of the stick following constitutional amendments. This is because, as indicated in several cases in Table 5.1, amendments to autocratic constitutions can sometimes rewrite vote aggregation rules that overrepresent parties sympathetic to holdover regime insiders, eliminate appointed congressional positions that are occupied by former authoritarian regime elites, assert greater civilian control over military affairs while stripping the latter of vetoes over key policy domains, open up competition to political parties that were previously banned, or rewrite the rules governing property rights protection.

In terms of the fiscal and material outcomes under elite-biased democracies that experience a constitutional amendment, we expect an increase in redistribution relative to elite-biased democracies whose constitutions remain entirely intact since democratic transition. Democracy should become more redistributive following constitutional amendments to elite-biased democracy as it should more faithfully represent the preferences of the median voter. By contrast, when elites can avoid constitutional change after democratization, the elite-biased regime should be less redistributive than it would have been under either popular democracy or an elite-biased democracy that amends its constitution.

Tracking the outcomes from Chapter 4, we expect to find that elite-biased democracies that amend their constitutions will have larger governments in general, allocate more public money to education, healthcare, and housing, and have more progressive tax structures. Of course, in line with the discussion in Chapter 4, globalization has complicated the ability to use key redistributive tools, such as the regulation of labor markets and progressive taxation, to their full extent. Consequently, democracies that amend their autocratic constitutions should also avail macroeconomic policies that have the potential to redistribute in favor of the median voter. In particular, they should be more likely to adopt flexible exchange rates that give them monetary autonomy. By contrast, democracies in which outgoing autocratic elites have imposed the rules of the game via an autocratic constitution, and successfully defended them by forestalling constitutional change, are more likely to have fixed exchange rates.

MEASUREMENT STRATEGY FOR EXPLAINING OUTCOMES UNDER DEMOCRACY

We employ a range of measures of governance and material outcomes to examine the impact of constitutional amendments on consequential policy change. These outcomes track those in Chapter 4. The first set of outcomes is therefore again the range of consultation, the percentage of the population with suffrage, egalitarian democracy, equal distribution of resources, and representation of disadvantaged groups. The second set of outcomes is again the size of government, social spending, progressive taxation, and exchange rate fixity. All of these variables are described in detail in Chapter 4. The control variables in our analyses are the same as those employed in Chapter 4 for governance and material outcomes.

Measuring Regime Type

The key independent variables in the analysis are, similar to Chapter 4, associated with a country's regime type. We compare the outcomes associated with governance and material outcomes under the full sweep of regimes and constitutional circumstances. This includes dictatorship, popular democracies that operate with their own constitutions, elite-biased democracies that operate with autocratic constitutions that have not undergone any changes, and elite-biased democracies whose autocratic constitutions have been amended under democracy. Our sample thus includes both democracies and dictatorships.

Our coding also mirrors the previous chapter. Popular democracy and autocracy are coded in the same way. Elite-biased democracy is now coded as a "1" for every country year of democratic rule if the democracy operates under an autocratic constitution that has not been amended. Democracy amends auto-cratic constitution is coded as a "1" in country years of democratic rule that follow the amendment – but not the annulment – of an autocratic constitution. As in Chapter 4, we code democracies that entirely annul their autocratic constitutions and pass new democratic constitutions as popular democracies.

EMPIRICAL STRATEGY FOR EXPLAINING OUTCOMES UNDER REGIMES

Across each of the dependent variables outlined in the previous section, we estimate a series of static country fixed effects models that also include year fixed effects in a similar fashion to Chapter 4. These models are estimated using ordinary least squares (OLS).

The inclusion of country fixed effects in the regressions controls for country-specific and time-invariant heterogeneity (e.g., geography) that might jointly influence a country's propensity to experience a democratic transition under conditions of elite weakness – or to amend its autocratic constitution – and its governance structures and degree of redistribution. It also allows us to inter-pret the results from the perspective of a difference-in-differences analysis.

The inclusion of year fixed effects controls for time period–specific and time-varying heterogeneity (e.g., shocks to the global economy) that might also be correlated with governance structures and redistribution. We estimate Driscoll-Kraay standard errors to addresses heteroskedasticity, serially corre-lated errors, and spatial correlation.

We always include three main independent variables: a dummy variable capturing all democracies, a dummy variable capturing democracy with an autocratic constitution, and a dummy variable capturing democracy with an amended autocratic constitution. Each enters the regression equations in levels. Given this approach, the raw coefficient on democracy with autocratic consti-tution, elite-biased democracy (relative to popular democracy), is the differ-ence in outcomes between countries that transitioned to democracy with an autocratic constitution and those that democratized with their own, new con-stitution (i.e., popular democracies). In other words, this coefficient captures the difference in the differences. The raw coefficient on the variable captur-ing amended autocratic constitutions, democracy amends autocratic constitu-tion (relative to elite-biased democracy), is the difference in outcomes between countries that operate with an amended autocratic constitution and those that operate with an autocratic constitution that is unchanged from the time of democratic transition. The raw coefficient on the all democracies variable can be interpreted as the difference in outcomes between popular democracy and autocracy. We refer to this as popular democracy (relative to autocracy).

As in Chapter 4, the coefficient for popular democracy (relative to autocracy) represents a lower bound on the changes in public policies we should expect after this type of democratization. The reason is that popular democracy includes both democracies that write their own constitutions after free and fair elections and those that, although they do not inherit constitutions from autocratic forbearers per se, do not necessarily start life with a constitution of their own making (e.g., if they are democratic upon independence from a colonial occupier).

While changes from autocracy to popular democracy should definitely lead to palpable changes in governance, it is not clear ex ante that changes from autocracy to popular democracy should yield big changes in redistribution because, as Chapter 4 lays out, there is substantial heterogeneity under autocracy when it comes to redistribution.

Our predictions for elite-biased democracy (relative to popular democracy) track those in Chapter 4. Elite-biased democracies should be associated with more restricted participation in decision-making than their popular counterparts. They should also be tied to lower rates of redistribution.

In line with the focus of this chapter, however, we focus our attention across each of the models on democracy amends autocratic constitution (relative to elite-biased democracy). Our hypothesis for this variable is clear: changes to autocratic constitutions under democracy should yield shifts toward more democratic governance and greater redistribution.

Empirical Results for Governance and Material Outcomes

Table 5.3 reports the results of the outcomes of interest related to governance and material well-being. Democracies that amend their autocratic constitutions have a broader range of consultation than elite-biased democracies that retain all elements of the constitutions they inherit upon democratization (Column 1). Democracies that amend their autocratic constitutions also exhibit a larger percentage of the population with suffrage (Column 2) and are more egalitarian across social groups (Column 3). Moreover, they have a more equal distribution of resources across members of society (Column 4) and are more likely to represent disadvantaged groups (Column 5). Furthermore, across all the models, the results also turn out as expected in terms of the change from autocracy to popular democracy (the coefficients are positive and statistically significant) and in terms of the difference between elite-biased democracies with unamended constitutions and popular democracies (the coefficients are negative and statistically significant).

In terms of the magnitude of these effects, democracies with amended autocratic constitutions tend to have outcomes that hover around those for popular democracies and, in some cases, are even more progressive. Consider the percentage of the adult population with suffrage. Relative to autocracies, popular democracies have a seven-point boost in adult suffrage. Adult suffrage is an estimated seven points lower in elite-biased democracies with unamended constitutions than in popular democracies. Democracies with amended autocratic constitutions, however, have an estimated thirteen-point boost in adult suffrage over elite-biased democracies that retain all elements of the constitutions they

TABLE 5.3. *The Effects of Amending Autocratic Constitutions on Participation in Decision-Making*

Dependent Variable	Range of Consultation	Percent Pop. with Suffrage	Egalitarian Democracy	Equal Distribution of Resources
	Model 1	Model 2	Model 3	Model 4
Elite-biased democracy	−0.548***	−7.203***	−0.063***	−0.048***
(Relative to popular dem.)	(0.059)	(1.327)	(0.007)	(0.008)
Popular democracy	1.538***	7.201***	0.129***	0.110***
(Relative to autocracy)	(0.057)	(0.965)	(0.004)	(0.005)
Democracy amends aut. const.	0.944***	13.499***	0.081***	0.050***
(Relative to elite-biased dem.)	(0.089)	(2.369)	(0.121)	(0.133)
Economic growth rate	−0.006	0.822	−0.012	−0.012
	(0.130)	(2.014)	(0.017)	(0.019)
log(GDP per capita)	0.308***	−1.073	0.028***	0.045***
	(0.054)	(0.859)	(0.005)	(0.007)
log(resource income per capita)	−0.072***	−1.071**	−0.003**	−0.003**
	(0.013)	(0.416)	(0.001)	(0.001)
log(population)	−0.309***	14.571***	0.003	0.027*
	(0.052)	(1.350)	(0.010)	(0.014)
Multiple-parties legacy				
Personalist legacy				
Military legacy				
Single-party legacy				
Oligarchy legacy				
Transitional legacy				
Year fixed effects	Yes	Yes	Yes	Yes
Country fixed effects	Yes	Yes	Yes	Yes
Countries	156	156	156	156
Observations	8,489	8,489	8,489	8,489

* $p < 0.10$; ** $p < 0.05$; *** $p < 0.01$ (two-tailed)
Driscoll-Kraay standard errors in parentheses. Country fixed effects are controlled for via a within transformation. Constants and time dummies are not shown. All independent variables are lagged one period.

Representation of Disadvant. Groups	Range of Consultation	Percent Pop. with Suffrage	Egalitarian Democracy	Equal Distribution of Resources	Representation of Disadvant. Groups
Model 5	Model 6	Model 7	Model 8	Model 9	Model 10
-0.226^{***}	-0.455^{***}	-7.951^{***}	-0.087^{***}	-0.073^{***}	-0.284^{***}
(0.053)	(0.066)	(1.390)	(0.008)	(0.009)	(0.045)
0.336^{***}	1.628^{***}	4.444^{***}	0.114^{***}	0.084^{***}	0.247^{***}
(0.040)	(0.147)	(1.444)	(0.012)	(0.016)	(0.065)
0.485^{***}	0.890^{***}	16.232^{***}	0.108^{***}	0.086^{***}	0.559^{***}
(0.122)	(0.100)	(2.623)	(0.014)	(0.016)	(0.115)
-0.126	-0.028	-0.250	-0.019	-0.022	-0.169^{*}
(0.096)	(0.131)	(1.838)	(0.016)	(0.017)	(0.086)
0.227^{***}	0.307^{***}	-2.552^{***}	0.041^{***}	0.056^{***}	0.229^{***}
(0.035)	(0.059)	(0.666)	(0.005)	(0.006)	(0.035)
-0.013	-0.073^{***}	-0.947^{**}	-0.010^{***}	-0.010^{***}	-0.023
(0.020)	(0.012)	(0.415)	(0.001)	(0.001)	(0.021)
0.533^{***}	-0.379^{***}	13.223^{***}	0.008	0.025^{**}	0.529^{***}
(0.061)	(0.054)	(1.525)	(0.007)	(0.010)	(0.062)
	-0.096	1.278^{**}	0.003	0.011^{*}	0.037
	(0.062)	(0.533)	(0.005)	(0.007)	(0.028)
	-0.238^{***}	0.174	-0.036^{***}	-0.059^{***}	-0.185^{***}
	(0.072)	(1.026)	(0.008)	(0.011)	(0.057)
	0.276^{***}	5.865^{***}	0.051^{***}	0.051^{***}	0.149^{***}
	(0.074)	(0.811)	(0.009)	(0.010)	(0.049)
	-0.241^{***}	-6.012^{***}	0.019^{*}	0.019	0.333^{***}
	(0.091)	(1.046)	(0.009)	(0.013)	(0.071)
	-0.298^{*}	2.717	0.050^{***}	0.055^{***}	-0.080
	(0.169)	(2.575)	(0.014)	(0.019)	(0.091)
	0.066	-4.850^{***}	0.035^{***}	0.062^{***}	0.150^{**}
	(0.087)	(1.641)	(0.013)	(0.015)	(0.071)
Yes	Yes	Yes	Yes	Yes	Yes
Yes	Yes	Yes	Yes	Yes	Yes
156	153	153	153	153	153
7756	7,685	7,685	7,685	7,685	6,982

inherit upon democratization. This is a consequential shift, especially historically, when suffrage restrictions were more common.

That elite-biased democracies with amended autocratic constitutions have
an even greater boost to suffrage than popular democracies in this case might
be due to the fact that amending an autocratic constitution typically takes both
time and considerable organizational effort. When these barriers are overcome,
groups pushing for reform appear to be quite successful in changing the status
quo and can leapfrog popular democracies. This supports the notion that a
democracy that inherits an elite-biased constitution from its predecessor is not
necessarily doomed for eternity: these constitutions, although usually quite difficult to amend, are not destiny.

In short, during the twentieth century and beyond, democracies that amend
their autocratic constitutions have been more pluralistic, inclusive, representative, and egalitarian than their elite-biased counterparts that operate with
exactly the same constitutions they inherit upon democratic transition.

As in Chapter 4 (Table 4.2), Columns 6 through 10 of Table 5.3 now control
for autocratic regime types, transitional leaders, and the number of de facto
parties on the eve of democratization. These variables again serve to capture
the bargaining clout of outgoing regime insiders before democratic transition.
The baseline category for the autocratic regime type variables is countries
that have been democratic since independence. While some of these variables
are correlated with our outcomes of interest, the main results hold across the
board, remaining similar in both statistical and substantive terms.

Fiscal and Monetary Outcomes in the Post–World War II Era

Table 5.4 reports the results of fiscal and monetary outcomes for which we
have coverage following World War II. This includes data on total government
spending between 1950 and 2006, as well as and data starting in the 1970s
for social spending, progressive taxation, and the type of exchange rate regime.
The results again conform to our theoretical expectations, and the magnitudes
of the effects are substantial. Elite-biased democracies that amend their autocratic constitutions have larger governments than those that do not change
their constitutions by an estimated 3.27 percentage points of GDP (Column
1). Column 2 demonstrates that they also engage in more social spending (an
increase of 3.80 percentage points of GDP) and have more progressive tax
systems (an increase of 2.19 percentage points of GDP). Finally, they are less
likely to have fixed exchange rates (Column 4).

As expected, the results regarding the differences between elite-biased
democracy and popular democracy for these outcomes are the opposite of those
discussed earlier, and the results are strong across the board. This is consistent
with the findings in Chapter 4. Lastly, and again consistent with our expectations and the findings in Chapter 4, the results regarding the change from
autocracy to popular democracy are mixed. The sign on each of the regressions is as anticipated: popular democracies tend to have larger governments

TABLE 5.4. *The Effects of Amending Autocratic Constitutions on Fiscal and Macroeconomic Outcomes*

Dependent Variable	Size of Government Model 1	Social Spending Model 2	Progressive Taxation Model 3	Exchange Rate Fixity Model 4	Size of Government Model 5	Social Spending Model 6	Progressive Taxation Model 7	Exchange Rate Fixity Model 8
Elite-biased democracy	−2.333***	−1.740***	−1.220***	0.297*	−1.782***	−2.068***	−1.116***	0.332**
(Relative to popular dem.)	(0.418)	(0.328)	(0.330)	(0.150)	(0.369)	(0.354)	(0.327)	(0.148)
Popular democracy	0.933***	0.403*	0.288	−0.387***	4.894***	0.322	0.912*	0.095
(Relative to autocracy)	(0.337)	(0.210)	(0.252)	(0.102)	(0.696)	(0.820)	(0.537)	(0.209)
Democracy amends aut. const.	3.266***	3.799***	2.187***	−0.480*	2.162***	4.151***	2.028***	−0.460*
(Relative to elite-biased dem.)	(0.733)	(0.857)	(0.597)	(0.261)	(0.648)	(0.904)	(0.638)	(0.247)
Economic growth rate	−5.064**	−1.406	−1.066	0.352	−5.477***	−1.112	−1.254	0.170
	(1.888)	(0.925)	(1.563)	(0.246)	(1.863)	(0.898)	(1.581)	(0.252)
log(GDP per capita)	0.129	2.137***	3.823***	0.150	0.422	1.988***	3.969***	0.192
	(0.479)	(0.295)	(0.643)	(0.148)	(0.573)	(0.259)	(0.765)	(0.157)
log(resource income per capita)	−0.425**	−0.068	0.548***	0.019	−0.282	−0.025	0.567***	0.008
	(0.173)	(0.115)	(0.126)	(0.032)	(0.180)	(0.118)	(0.153)	(0.037)
log(population)	−2.563***	2.710***	−2.589	0.107	−1.112	2.864***	−2.174	0.094
	(0.880)	(0.670)	(1.649)	(0.210)	(0.867)	(0.821)	(2.068)	(0.168)
Manufacturing value added	0.072**	−0.049*	−0.070***	−0.015*	0.068**	−0.044*	−0.063***	−0.011*
	(0.031)	(0.021)	(0.020)	(0.008)	(0.030)	(0.022)	(0.019)	(0.006)
Trade openness	0.002	−0.007	0.006	0.001	0.008	−0.006	0.007*	0.002
	(0.007)	(0.005)	(0.004)	(0.002)	(0.008)	(0.005)	(0.004)	(0.002)
Old age ratio	−0.483***	−0.348***	−0.584***	0.062	−0.751***	−0.310**	−0.728***	−0.005
	(0.163)	(0.095)	(0.121)	(0.044)	(0.205)	(0.125)	(0.237)	(0.071)
Multiple-parties legacy					−0.512**	−0.044	0.407**	−0.017
					(0.231)	(0.477)	(0.183)	(0.097)
Personalist legacy					−2.943***	−0.527	−0.493	−0.308*
					(0.530)	(0.376)	(0.294)	(0.158)

(*continued*)

TABLE 5.4 (continued)

Dependent Variable	Size of Government	Social Spending	Progressive Taxation	Exchange Rate Fixity	Size of Government	Social Spending	Progressive Taxation	Exchange Rate Fixity
	Model 1	Model 2	Model 3	Model 4	Model 5	Model 6	Model 7	Model 8
Military legacy					-3.696***	0.676	-1.404***	-0.135
					(0.482)	(0.518)	(0.352)	(0.140)
Single-party legacy					0.174	0.368	-1.662***	-0.777***
					(0.519)	(0.654)	(0.486)	(0.220)
Oligarchy legacy					-2.203**	3.047*	1.069	0.897***
					(0.915)	(1.635)	(1.096)	(0.273)
Transitional legacy					-2.870***	0.867	-0.598	-0.719**
					(0.913)	(0.762)	(0.436)	(0.267)
Year-fixed effects	Yes	Yes	Yes	Yes	Yes	Yes	Yes	Yes
Country-fixed effects	Yes	Yes	Yes	Yes	Yes	Yes	Yes	Yes
Countries	151	124	135	144	145	118	129	138
Observations	4080	2197	2668	2697	3886	2077	2520	2575

* $p < 0.10$; ** $p < 0.05$; *** $p < 0.01$ (two-tailed)
Driscoll-Kraay standard errors in parentheses. Country fixed effects are controlled for via a within transformation. Constants and time dummies are not shown. All independent variables are lagged one period.

than their autocratic predecessors, more social spending, more progressive tax structures, and less rigid exchange rates. However, the coefficient on progressive taxation falls short of statistical significance at conventional levels, and its magnitude is also small. This is consistent with the Chapter 4 discussion of progressive taxation under democracy in the era of globalization: genuinely redistributive taxation is a very difficult feat to pull off during this time period, even in the most popular of democracies.

As in Table 5.3, Columns 5–8 of Table 5.4 now include autocratic regime types on the eve of democratization as control variables. These variables tap the bargaining power of outgoing regimes before transition. We also control for the number of de facto parties on the eve of democratization and for whether the democracy follows a transitional leader. As with Table 5.3, while some of the results suggest that the previous autocracies' political and institutional features might have an enduring effect after democratization, the main results are all similar when controlling for these legacies. In other words, the rules of the game matter, not only de facto power that lingers after democratization.

CONCLUSION

For citizens in democracies that inherit their constitutions from an autocratic predecessor, democracy might disappoint. Public policies and representation are likely to be tilted in favor of elites. But all is not lost. Although it is far from easy, democracies can reinvent themselves and renovate the social contract periodically. This chapter demonstrates the conditions under which this occurs and the consequences that transpire. It also explores the types of consequential changes that have actually occurred to the autocratic constitutions that most new democracies are saddled with.

The biggest takeaway is that elite-biased constitutions are much more likely to be overturned once the old guard from the former authoritarian regime is dead and gone. This is not simply because former dictators can intervene in politics to forestall change; instead, autocratic constitutions are often constructed with half-lives: the most important institutional elements are designed to endure until generational change presents the opportunity for a new dawn.

But this new dawn is not automatic. It must be won by an organized opposition that seizes on economic crisis or a shift in the balance of power. New actors that arise on the political scene are often critical in this process. The upshot is that while it is politically difficult to break the shackles of an authoritarian constitution, once this is accomplished there are often substantial shifts in the policies observed under democracy that bring fiscal and monetary outcomes closer to the median voter's preferences.

For anxious democrats in new democracies that are hobbled by their authoritarian pasts, the lesson is clear: bide your time and then seize on opportunity once it presents itself. Patience is the key; consequential change is more likely to be successful once the old authoritarian guard has been lowered into the grave.

6

Sweden

From Agrarian Oligarchy to Progressive Democracy

Sweden is one of the world's most egalitarian countries. On some counts, it is the most egalitarian. Its major political parties agree on the importance and goals of its welfare state, which is one of the most generous in the world. In Sweden, there is broad consensus that the state should help secure an individual's rights to a job, a place to live, and an education. Aggressive redistribution is the warp and woof of this system. It is based on social spending and direct transfers such as old-age pensions, family allowances, health insurance, and housing subsidies.

Some international comparisons can help throw Swedish exceptionalism into high relief.[1] Between 2000 and 2010, the top decile's share of total income in Sweden was less than 30 percent. In the United States, by contrast, the top decile's share was between 45 and 50 percent. Other relatively egalitarian countries besides Sweden include France and Germany, where the top decile's share of total income was around 35 percent.[2]

In terms of the Gini coefficient calculated after taxes and transfers, in 2013 Sweden had one of the lowest scores, 28.1. While countries with middling levels of inequality include Canada, Estonia, Greece, Ireland, Israel, Japan, and Italy, countries with the highest scores include the United States, Mexico, Brazil, and China. Unsurprisingly, Sweden is one of the most redistributive countries in the world: in 2013, the difference between its market income inequality and post-tax and transfer inequality was 16 points, implying that the country's strong social safety net is responsible for a large share of its egalitarian profile.

The middle class also fares relatively well in Sweden.[3] In 2010, median disposable income was $15,000 (US dollars) – by way of comparison, median per

---

[1] These figures are from Piketty (2014, 230).

[2] The figures in the following two paragraphs are from Wang and Caminada (2011).

[3] These figures are from Leonhardt and Quealy (2014), who draw on the latest LIS. They are in 2014 dollars and are adjusted for purchasing power parity.

capita income was $18,700 in the United States that year. More importantly, Sweden has recently recorded greater improvements for the middle class than other Organization for Economic Cooperation and Development (OECD) countries on the back of respectable growth rates: "Even with a large welfare state in Sweden, per capita GDP there has grown more quickly than in the United States over almost any extended recent period – a decade, 20 years, or 30 years. Sharp increases in the number of college graduates in Sweden, allowing for the growth of high-skill jobs, has played an important role" (Leonhardt and Q. Qealy 2014).

Finally, Sweden is an upwardly mobile society. The country's intergenerational correlation of education and earned incomes, a way of measuring the reproduction of skill hierarchy over time, is exceedingly low, noticeably lower than in France and Germany (Piketty 2014, 339). This is in large part due to a very progressive education system and generous vocational training (Thelen 2014, 174). Meanwhile, the United States' intergenerational correlation coefficient is two-thirds greater than Sweden's.

Swedish exceptionalism is impressive. What explains it? Conventional wisdom states that Sweden is egalitarian today because it has always been egalitarian. Some variants of this explanation stress the uniqueness of its rural structure (Tilly 1992). Others stress the fact that employers and employees have a long history of harmony and consensus building and have tended to agree on the need to invest in strong vocational education and social insurance to create a productive workforce centered on high value–added exports (Iversen and Soskice 2006).

But a host of key facts belie the idea that Sweden has always been equal.[4] Between 1900 and 1910, the concentration of wealth in Sweden equaled that of France and Britain. Indeed, Sweden's wealth concentration was higher than the concentration of wealth in the United States around this time. And even when the concentration of wealth in Sweden among the top 10 percent began to diminish after World War I, the benefits accrued mostly to the middle 40 percent of the wealth distribution. The same can be said about income inequality during the 1900–1910 period. Sweden was more unequal than several European countries around this time. For example, the share of total income held by the top centile was 25 percent and exceeded that observed in Britain and Germany – hardly egalitarian societies at the time.

If Sweden has not always been exceptionally equal, then what social and political structures account for its prior inegalitarianism? As late as the mid-nineteenth century, Sweden had a relatively feudal political structure: a monarchy presided over a parliament in which four estates – which permanently represented the nobility, merchants, peasants, and the church – codified a stratified economic and social order. Large landowners often ruled in an alliance with the crown. While Sweden became more "constitutional" and less "feudal"

[4] The following facts are from Piketty (2014, 245–246, 418–425).

over time, old and new elements of the upper class allied themselves with the king and found ways to secure political supremacy. They gained overrepresentation in the parliament and imposed restrictions on the franchise. Despite the impressive march of liberalism and socialism in Sweden on the heels of industrialization, urbanization, and modernization, holdover political institutions endowed the gentry and inefficient oligopolists with greater influence than meets the eye. They maintained disproportional sway over Swedish politics for several decades into the twentieth century.

At a formal, institutional level, the country transitioned to democracy in 1911 – shortly after widely broadening male suffrage in 1909. Yet this chapter demonstrates that important elite biases remained, principally in the form of important restrictions on the franchise, and voting and representation weighted by wealth in the upper chamber, which remained indirectly elected.

Eventually, however, incumbent economic elites' hegemony weakened. Popular democracy made gradual inroads. Adult suffrage was again broadened in 1921, and wealth-weighted voting for the senate was also eliminated that year. Wealth requirements for serving in the senate were dropped in 1933, and exceptionally long terms were reduced, making it easier to eliminate holdover representatives from the immediate post-transition period. A series of piecemeal additional changes occurred in ensuing decades, culminating in the elimination of the senate entirely in 1970, which accompanied a new constitution. Later changes, such as the extension of the franchise to immigrants in municipal elections, cemented in a broad movement toward more popular democracy and, concomitantly, more progressive social policies.

In large part, because it inherited a constitution from its authoritarian predecessor, egalitarianism in Sweden was delayed after its democratic transition, and the full potential of its unique welfare state model remained unrealized. Indeed, popular protests arose in the post–World War I period after democracy failed to deliver better opportunities for most Swedish citizens. Consequential political change began to take root in the decades after transition, but only gradually. The upshot is that specific institutional reforms yielded the broad contours of a social safety net in Sweden, especially for wage earners participating in large firms that were part of a tripartite corporatist arrangement, but hardly into what we know as Sweden's exceptionally progressive welfare state. The later set of political reforms outlined previously culminated in massive and broad-based social spending coupled with an enhanced social safety even further down the line.

Therefore, the full carapace of the Swedish welfare state ultimately took decades to develop. Slightly more than two decades after Sweden's transition to democracy, it made some progress in shaking off its most acute elite biases. Consequently, Sweden became more progressive beginning in the 1940s. The Social Democrats came to represent the middle and lower classes in both the city and countryside, presiding over the Golden Age of prosperity after the Great Depression. Labor unions were incorporated into the highest echelons of policy-making by the 1940s, and centralized wage bargaining became institutionalized. This pattern consolidated in the late 1970s and 1980s, as the Social Democrats delivered on promises for a more robust welfare state and equitable society.

The chief goal of this chapter, therefore, is to present a systematic, novel, and detailed explanation of these events and their consequences rooted in our theoretical framework. This explanation helps better understand the important nuances in the development of the Swedish welfare state than accounts rooted in the assumption that Sweden has always been exceptional. We now turn to telling this story in detail – to describe and explain why and how Sweden transitioned from an elite-biased democracy to a more popular version.

INCUMBENT ECONOMIC ELITES UNDER DICTATORSHIP

Sweden originated as a small kingdom in the fourteen century, the byproduct of the merger of several smaller kingdoms. Through imperial acquisition, it grew much larger in the centuries that followed. The country reached its territorial peak in the seventeenth century, growing to encompass lands in Germany, Poland, the Baltics, Finland, Norway, and Russia. It later shrunk considerably after losing several wars.

Sweden was a constitutional monarchy that veered between parliamentary parity and absolutism between the seventeenth and nineteenth centuries. During that time, the monarchy was allied with two ostensibly distinct sets of economic elites.

The first was the landed nobility. They were formally represented in the royal council that advised the king and had a permanent presence in the parliament as one of four estates. The landed nobility was the largest and strongest group in Sweden's so-called feudal parliament. By the middle of the 1600s, they owned two-thirds of the farmland in Sweden and Finland (Metcalf 1987, 103), as Finland was part of Sweden at the time. Over the ensuing centuries, they remained a powerful group in Swedish society, partially because "primogeniture was in force until the end of the nineteenth century, and some entails on large dynastic fortunes in Sweden persist to this day" (Piketty 2014, 420n27). During the nineteenth century, large landowners supported tariffs on imported grain. They favored protectionism and nationalism. They decried the emigration of farmers from Sweden to the United States and to urban cities, which they blamed on free trade.[5]

---

[5] Eventually, this group allied with the Farmers' Party, which also represented smaller farmers and grew to oppose free trade because imports from Russia and North America had led to a drastic plummeting of prices for Swedish farm products. Along with landed aristocrats, the Farmers' Party sought to prevent full enfranchisement because it was slated to adulterate the political power of landholders from rural districts (Congleton 2011, 397).

The second group of incumbent economic elites were government-granted and enforced monopolies, including guilds, and a nascent manufacturing sector that was protected by tariffs and other subsidies (Congleton 2011, 383). Some of these privileged industrial firms came into existence as early as the 1600s. Others emerged in the 1700s, represented most prominently by the Swedish East India Company in 1731, which was awarded a monopoly on trade with the Far East that was accompanied by government subsidies for the manufacturers of luxuries such as porcelain and silk. The Swedish parliament, the Riksdag, was able to prop up these incumbent economic elites by directing credit to nascent industries through its influence over the Bank of Sweden. Most of the bankrollers of these new, government-coddled ventures were themselves nobles, so that nominally distinct incumbent economic elites – the landed nobility versus industrialists – were often one in the same (Metcalf 1987, 111).

Finally, and tied to this latter group, incumbent economic elites also included industries that had at first favored liberal reforms in the nineteenth century, often including free trade, but came to rely on government support: "Antiliberal arguments were taken up by many industrialists who had previously favored the liberal reform agenda but profited from protectionist measures in the late nineteenth and early twentieth centuries. For example, Swedish cartels in sugar, milling, and oleomargarine were able to obtain significant (and profitable) protective tariffs in the early 20th Century" (Congleton 2011, 396 citing Heckscher 1954, 263).

As anticipated by our theoretical framework in Chapter 2, the relationship between the Swedish monarchs and their incumbent economic elites was not always rock solid. For example, in the late 1600s, Karl XI struck against many noble families and expropriated their lands and stripped them of their noble titles. The king also elevated new nobles into positions of greater authority (e.g., awarding seats in the noble chamber of parliament) from the ranks of the military and bureaucracy. This inflation of titles devalued the political and economic status of extant landholders. Eventually, in the late eighteenth century, due to a strong fiscal crisis precipitated by Sweden's participation in international wars, the nobility was heavily taxed for the first time in Swedish history via a tax on estates. In 1789, the king abolished noble privileges without the consent of the noble chamber in parliament. Later, in the early twentieth century, progressive taxes on income, wealth, and inheritance would be introduced to help defray the costs of increases in defense spending in the wake of World War I.

The Swedish nobility also had to contend with a rapidly industrializing and urbanizing country. The rise of the gentry, the upper strata of the merchant class, and the growing numbers of influential non-nobles who were not in the Riksdag eventually represented a threat to the nobility's vested interests. This was coupled with agitation from all corners of society for liberalization and greater democracy.

Incumbent Economic Elites Use Parliament to Protect Their Interests

The early kingdom of Sweden, Finland, and Norway had parliaments (*tins*) that met at regular intervals to address judicial and legislative issues and select their ruler. The kingdom had a Magna Carta–like event in 1319, in which the Swedish elite attempted to constrain the powers of the monarch. This was followed by the establishment of a permanent royal council composed of nobles. Assemblies were subsequently called on a frequent basis to settle matters of taxation and royal succession. Eventually, the parliament began to meet more regularly as formal gatherings of four estates: the nobles, burghers (town leaders), clerics, and peasants (non-noble landlords).

Over time, parliament became more powerful, allowing the elites to defend their interests by constraining the monarchs. In 1617, the Riksdag Act circumscribed the king's powers and gave greater authority to parliament over taxes and war making; in the 1650s and 1660s, parliament became more independent, met more regularly, and secured veto power over new laws. During the so-called Age of Liberty, which lasted until 1770, Sweden's parliament exercised dominance over the king.[6]

Throughout the consolidation of Sweden's constitutional monarchy, the incumbent economic elites solidified their status as on par with the crown despite the fact that the nobility was composed of only 0.5 percent of the population (Metcalf 1987, 110). While the nobles had the largest and most influential parliamentary chamber, voting for the Riksdag's other three chambers was indirect and heavily weighted by wealth.[7] Moreover, the Conservative Party faithfully represented landowners and other business interests and successfully fought back many attempts to curtail the power of the nobility and the system of privileges that gave large landowners a lock on Swedish civil, military, and economic affairs. Therefore, during most of the authoritarian period, the landed nobility was able to minimize its tax burden, despite Sweden's participation in several wars.

This is not to say that the crown was the perfect agent of the economic elite. The country's constitutional monarchy nurtured and processed several political struggles.[8] Estates were pitted against each other on issues that included

---

[6] The monarch retained formal executive control and exercised leverage over parliament by controlling the bureaucracy, however (Congleton 2011, 377). Indeed, many historians contend that Sweden's monarchy was absolutist between the late 1600s and 1720, when the Riksdag was considerably weakened. Indeed, the so-called Age of Liberty can be considered an interregnum: between 1770 and 1810, Sweden again veered toward absolutism in conjunction with its participation in several international wars.

[7] The burgher chamber was selected by town councils (resident burghers who paid taxes with voting weighted by their tax contributions), and most often, their elected representatives were the town mayors. The peasant chamber representatives were appointed by local county governments (members of which owned land and were independent, with votes weighted by land holdings).

[8] In 1772, under King Gustav III, a new constitution was foisted on the parliament and backed by the threat of force. It renewed the king's power to call and dismiss parliament and the ability

"the structure of the Riksdag, the distribution of power among the branches of government, the freedom of the press, education, public insight into the state administration, and the liberalization of the economy" (Metcalf 1987, 182).

Liberal ideology and administrative, civil, and economic reforms continued apace during the nineteenth century, leading to Sweden's modernization, and putting it on par with other European countries. Most importantly, an enclosure movement ushered in a uniform property rights system, Swedish laborers gained the right to work wherever they pleased, and a national railroad system and deregulation helped create a common national market.

The incumbent economic elites in this period were able to use their political might to steer new policies in directions that benefited them.[9] Indeed, even when conservative forces suffered political losses, they later recuperated and strengthened their grip on policy. A good example of this, which we will return to ahead, is the advent of free trade in the 1850s. Free trade proved to be a short-lived experiment; important agriculturalists and industrialists, especially textile manufacturers, were able to reimpose tariffs during the 1880s.

The relative success of the incumbent economic elites under Sweden's autocracy is readily apparent in the numbers on capital and income inequality during the 1900–1910 decade.[10] The richest 10 percent controlled most of the country's wealth – roughly 90 percent. Indeed, while the wealthiest 1 percent controlled more than 50 percent of Sweden's assets, the poorest 50 percent held less than 5 percent. In terms of income inequality, the top decile's proportion was more than 45 percent of total income, compared with 40 percent in the United States at the time. And the top centile's proportion of total income exceeded 20 percent.

THE RISE OF OUTSIDER ECONOMIC ELITES

During the 1850s and 1860s, rapid industrialization occurred in Sweden. This coincided with the rise of liberal ideology and the political strengthening of liberal forces, who gradually became organized as disciplined political parties and movements. Copper and iron industries grew more rapidly as industrial applications developed, especially the steel industry. Other fledgling industries included more modern timber and banking sectors, as well as railroads, paper, explosives, matches, chemicals, and telephones. None of these industries relied on explicit government support or subsidies.

---

to appoint members of the council of state. Gustav then rammed through other constitutional reforms that bequeathed him with even greater power at the expense of the parliament, including the nobility.

[9] This sometimes meant that monarchs sided with liberal causes. A representative example is Oscar I, who ruled from 1844 to 1859 (Metcalf 1987, 184–188).

[10] All of the figures that follow are from Piketty (2014).

The owners of the firms operating in these new sectors did not have representation in the Riksdag. Therefore, these segments of the rising outsider economic elite, as well as senior civil servants, created their own political organizations, including the National Economic Society in 1877 (Heckscher 1954, 263). At the same time, the middle class and working class were gaining economic power and organizing politically and often fought alongside commercial interests for free trade and other liberal causes.

Consistent with our theoretical framework in Chapter 2, the rise of Sweden's outsider economic elite and their eventual political marriage with segments of the masses was the result of multiple forces. It was partially exogenous – a by-product of technological changes, the diffusion of liberal ideology, and the emergence of modern warfare demanding mass mobilization and conscription. The rise of the outsider economic elites was also partially endogenous. Consider that

the liberal and labor movements advanced middle-class and working-class interests, two subpopulations that were rapidly expanding as a consequence of industrialization and increased commerce. The latter was partly a consequence of previous reforms, insofar as liberal economic reforms in the first half of the nineteenth-century Sweden (and elsewhere) had increased economic growth and development. Reducing economic privileges from the medieval period allowed new technologies to be adopted more rapidly and specialization to increase, which raised average income as predicted by most economic theories...These developments...reduced support for many long-standing medieval institutions. A variety of politically active groups inside and outside of government pressed for suffrage expansion and trade liberalization. (Congleton 2011, 394)

Figure 6.1 graphs the evolution of the change in the relative importance of non-agricultural capital over recent Swedish history. It evinces that private wealth held as financial assets, defined as currency, deposits, bonds and loans (as a percentage of GDP) exploded in the run-up to democratization in 1911.

Changing technology helps explain in large part the huge gulf that opened up between the incumbent economic elites and the outsider economic elites, who benefited from the reduction in transportation costs associated with the advent of steamships and who could now exploit Swedish comparative advantages in mining, timber, and some manufactured products. The outsider elites sought to trade freely with the rest of the world on the heels of the repeal of trade tariffs during the mid-nineteenth century. They came to include businesses and upper-middle class liberals. Indeed, besides free trade, they favored deregulation to increase market competition.[11]

There were two broad-based political parties that separately took up the mantle of reform. The Liberal Coalition Party, led by Karl Staaff, was formed in the late nineteenth century and began to spearhead concrete reforms to

---

[11] Reforms sought by liberals also included educational liberalization, a free press, due process, and a separation of powers.

FIGURE 6.1. Private wealth held as financial assets in Sweden (percent GDP).
Source: The World Wealth and Income Database (2016)

advance their progressive agenda. The Liberals introduced bills broadening the franchise on an annual basis between 1890 and 1896.[12] The Social Democrats, founded in 1889 and led by Hjalmar Branting, teamed up with the Swedish labor movement, which was able to galvanize public opinion behind social causes and democracy and pressured the government by organizing strikes and public demonstrations. Besides universal suffrage, the Social Democrats favored limited work weeks, social insurance, and increased safety regulations.

Reaction to Liberalization by Incumbent Economic Elites

The history of Sweden's liberalization is tied to the battle over trade. The advent of free trade in nineteenth-century Sweden was detrimental to the incumbent economic elite. While agriculturalists were hurt by rising cereal imports from Russia and the United States, many domestic manufacturers could not compete with a flood of imported goods. The conservative cause therefore grew to

---

[12] A formidable Swedish suffrage movement began in the 1760s on the back of the spread of Enlightenment ideology (Congleton 2011, 381; Metcalf 1987, 144). Later on, the New Liberal Society (founded by Adolf Hedin) advocated for full enfranchisement. Some of the arguments these parties made in favor of broadening the franchise was to engender a more egalitarian social order. They also argued that it was the right thing to do in light of increased conscription of men as a means for upgrading and modernizing the country's armed forces. The slogan coined by the Social Democratic Party, "One man, one vote, one rifle," embodied this sentiment (Lewin 1988, 67).

encompass monopolists and cartels that had been created in the wake of indus-trialization (Congleton 2011, 395). Specifically, government-supported domes-tic industries that had been invited by the burgher estate to join the Riksdag in 1830 made common political cause with members of the nobility and wealthy farmers. These groups joined forces and directly lobbied the crown for help.

As before, these insider economic elites could not always count on the mon-archy to defend their interests, however. During the nineteenth century, Swedish monarchs sometimes sided with the ascendant outsider economic elites – new industries in rising, export-oriented economic sectors. Indeed, by the middle of the nineteenth century, advocates of free trade secured the full political support of the king. In the ensuing years, outsider economic elites' political patrons, the Liberals and Social Democrats, were able to successfully fend off many legisla-tive attempts at protectionism in the Riksdag.

The incumbent economic elites patiently waited to exact their revenge. By the 1880s, agriculturalists and several industries allied with the crown clawed back free trade policies. In the late 1800s, tariffs pushed by landed elites, farm-ers, and some industrialists were imposed on wheat and rye, other foodstuffs, and industrial products. The monarchy switched its previous position and sided with protectionist forces, in part because tariffs turned out to be a lucra-tive source of revenues that could help defray the mounting costs of military expenditures – a reaction against the increasing "Russification" of Finland.

Figure 6.2 supports the notion that this strategy was successful. It graphs the value of private wealth held as agricultural land as a percentage of GDP. Despite industrialization, the economic prowess of landed interests and associ-ated agricultural activity intensified over the middle of the nineteenth century.

In addition, political liberalization movements were met by counterreac-tions by economic elites and other conservative forces who sought to increase the requirements for membership in the parliament and to overrepresent elite interests: "Thanks to the tariff issue, the protectionist agrarians were suspi-cious of any expansion of the suffrage, since it was generally thought that any such expansion would benefit the free traders. The free traders, on the other hand, had a direct interest in lowering the threshold of requirements for vot-ing" (Metcalf 1987, 212).

During the nineteenth century, incumbent political and economic elites therefore attempted to steer increased political and economic liberalization, and eventually democracy, in a direction more propitious to themselves. They accomplished this feat through a century-long bout of constitutional engineer-ing that ultimately culminated in a more representative and inclusive gov-ernment that nonetheless favored incumbent elites in a manner that allowed them to punch above their weight. Numerous elite biases were responsible for Sweden's inveterate inability to keep up with its European neighbors in the quest for both democracy and egalitarianism: "In international terms, suf-frage reform came relatively late to Sweden, and it was tied to rather strong conservative guarantees, including a minimum voting age of 24, proportional

FIGURE 6.2. Private wealth held as agricultural land in Sweden (percent GDP).
Source: The World Wealth and Income Database (2016)

representation, and the requirement that voters have paid taxes both to the
state and the municipality. Not only did Sweden lag behind Denmark and
Norway, but it also lagged behind Finland, where universal suffrage for men
and women was established in 1906" (Metcalf 1987, 215).

LATE NINETEENTH- AND EARLY TWENTIETH-CENTURY CONSTITUTIONAL ENGINEERING

This section explores the tools and techniques used by Sweden's incumbent
political elites and their economic allies to counteract rising challenges to their
political and economic power over the nineteenth and early twentieth centuries. This enabled them to arrive at a democratic outcome on favorable terms.
We explore the long-neglected bout of constitutional engineering that benefited elite forces, which occurred under the aegis of the 1809 Instrument of
Government. This bout of constitutional engineering was so insidious that it
took decades of tweaking and piecemeal dismantling to finally obtain popular
democracy. It proceeded gradually, a project concocted by elites in order to
benefit themselves that grew more sophisticated over time.

The 1809 constitution was crucial to the incumbent economic elites and their
political patrons for two reasons. First, it reestablished the political preeminence
of the incumbent economic elites, returning them to equal footing with the monarchy, and slowed the rise of the outsider economic elites, protecting the political

and economic interests of the incumbent economic elites in the face of major changes wrought by industrialization, urbanization, and modernization. Second, the constitution set the stage for several follow-up episodes of constitutional engineering over the nineteenth century that blunted the impact of increased popular participation and demands for full suffrage. The most important was the creation of a bicameral legislature with significant elite biases and the adoption of proportional representation (PR) on the eve of franchise extension.

The 1809 charter reestablished a constitutional monarchy after an absolutist interlude. It was foisted on Sweden's new monarch, Karl XIII, after a coup launched by the nobility and key military and civil officials against Gustav Adolf IV in protest against his absolutism and insistence on retaking Finland from the Russians (Metcalf 1987, 170). The constitution was the product of a constitutional convention that was headed by a committee of fifteen members: six nobles, three clergymen, three burghers, and three peasants. After two weeks of deliberations, it was approved by the four estates and was adopted the same day that King Karl XIII ascended to the throne.

The constitution returned to a balance of power that again put the Swedish parliament on equal footing with the crown and, by implication, ushered in a system that again favored the incumbent economic elites.[13] The parliament continued to be based on the estate system and therefore contained the four traditional chambers: noble, clerical, town, and country. The 1809 charter introduced a system of royal succession and endowed parliament with veto authority over taxation and public budgets. Other constraints against the monarch included an obligation for the king to consult his cabinet and greater powers granted to legislators, including their ability to censure members of the king's cabinet. Harkening back to the "Age of Liberty," the 1809 charter also enjoined regular parliamentary meetings. Moreover, any amendments to the 1809 Constitution required approval over two successive Riksdag sessions and majorities across all four estates.

Subsequent changes made the parliament even more powerful vis-à-vis the monarch. The Cabinet Act of 1840 gave ministers taken from the legislature formal authority over different aspects of government policy, explicitly demarcating them as forming part of the cabinet. The Riksdag Act of 1866 gave the parliament greater authority over taxation and public budgets.

While the battle between absolutism and parliamentary supremacy raged, these forces were nonetheless aligned when it came to defending their interests against outsider economic elites. And they used the 1809 constitution to defend these interests. Four main institutional tools were sharpened by monarchs and conservative politicians over the ensuing century to advantage incumbent political and economic elites and to stage-manage a democratic transition that would guarantee their continued influence thereafter.

---

[13] Indeed, a key reason for the constitution was to prevent Gustav's heirs from serving as future monarchs in order to hinder yet another return of absolutism.

The first was the bicameral legislature. The second was elaborate restrictions on the franchise. The third was PR. The fourth was muscular political decentralization.

Bicameralism

The Swedish Senate (first chamber) was the brainchild of Louis De Geer, the minister of justice and chancellor of the Riksdag. De Geer was a nobleman who was the son of a landowner with a foot in the world of heavy industry. The two-chamber legislature replaced the four-chamber "medieval" legislature in 1866 via the Riksdag Act promulgated that year. While national electoral law replaced local-level laws, the voting system continued to be weighted by wealth. The logic of the senate was "to prevent narrow and hasty decisions and was to serve as a conservative check on the Second Chamber by providing stability and continuity" (Metcalf 1987, 233). Indeed, while "he [De Geer] himself said that he wanted to put power 'in the hands of the middle classes'... in reality he favored the aristocracy and wealthy groups, on the one hand, and the farmers, on the other" (Metcalf 1987, 191).

The impetus behind the bicameral legislature was to reform the basis of representation away from the estate system – based on fixed terms of office – on terms that were more felicitous to the incumbent economic elites. Eligibility for membership in the senate was now based purely on wealth, rather than family heritage (nobility). These changes received wide support from the nobles, wealthy burghers, and non-noble industrialists, who could now obtain seats in parliament (Congleton 2011, 390).

The rules were as follows. The senate had 120 members who had to be older than thirty-five and had to possess real estate with an assessed value of at least 80,000 riksdaler or receive an annual income subject to taxes of at least 4,000 riksdaler. This meant that only a tiny fraction of Swedish citizens were ultimately eligible for seats in the senate. Indirect elections were held for the upper chamber: the senate was elected by the county councils and city councils of Sweden's largest cities, and these councils were populated by well-to-do landowners and businessmen. Moreover, local voting rights were weighted by income and wealth. Specifically, the votes for the provincial councils were heavily weighted according to the amount of taxes they paid. Finally, while members served nine-year terms, a system of successive elections meant that only one-sixth of the senate's members were elected in any given cycle. The senate's low turnover prevented sharp changes of direction.

Taken together, these measures heavily constrained pluralism and inclusiveness. Restrictions on membership and voting protected the voice of the wealthy and educated: "The weighted-voting system often allowed local elections to be determined by a handful of wealthy men or women. In 10 percent of the districts, the weighted votes of just three or four voters could be decisive" (Congleton 2011, 388, citing Verney 1957, 91).

In describing the political ramifications, Lewin (1988) writes, "The 1866 rules gave the franchise to 5.5 percent of the Swedish population, or roughly 21 percent of all legally competent men. Only a few new people gained the right to vote during the next few decades due to inflation and rising salaries and wages...The First Chamber became even more dominated by high-born aristocrats and plutocrats than the Estate of Nobility before 1866" (55).

The senate was crowded with businessmen, industrialists, county governors, and general directors of state agencies. These individuals tended to be more educated than the population as a whole and were from larger cities. In short, the senate continued, if not exacerbated, the system of acute political privileges enjoyed by incumbent economic elites during the preceding estate system.

The conservative bias introduced by Sweden's two-chamber parliament is brought into sharp relief when compared to other European experiences. Metcalf (1987) explains that, "One year before the North German Federation and Great Britain gave industrial workers the right to vote, and seventeen years after Denmark had adopted the principle of universal male suffrage, Sweden's landowning classes were given a level of political influence that no longer fully corresponded to their relative position in the realities of Sweden's social and economic life" (193).

Ultimately, the creation of the senate worked to align the interests of the aforementioned older elite, noblemen whose status and wealth was based on landed estates, and industrialists who produced for the domestic market. It is therefore not surprising that the senate repeatedly blocked reforms aimed at extending the franchise that emanated in the lower house. As Lewin (1988) writes, "No matter what arguments the Left resorted to, it was unable to overcome the Right's resistance to broader suffrage, not even after the Left had formed a government. A solid Conservative majority in the First Chamber resisted every reform proposal, 'wisely slow in action but firm and strong in opposition.' These words from the 1809 constitutional committee described a reality that leftist demands for suffrage reform were unable to overcome for decades" (69).

The senate's endurance beyond democratization, and all the elite biases this entailed, proved to be unsurprisingly contentious. The Social Democrats vociferously criticized it in the 1920s and 1930s, often targeting their ire at the successive system of elections because it favored nonsocialists and especially the Conservative Party. Several prime ministers, cabinet members, and party leaders were members of the senate, especially during the 1920s (Metcalf 1987, 236), which attests to the fact that Sweden's upper chamber was not merely a ceremonial vestige.

Restrictions on the Franchise over the Nineteenth Century

The 1866 reforms to the 1809 constitution also contained measures that, in conjunction with indirect elections for the senate, overrepresented the interests of incumbent economic elites. A supermajority was needed to pass major policy decisions. The voting age for elections to county councils and electoral colleges was twenty-seven years. Most importantly, the lower house was also constructed with an eye toward protecting elite interests.

Although the creation of the lower house (the so-called second chamber) in 1866 was a concession to upper-middle class farmers, burghers, and liberals who favored broader suffrage and a reduced role for the nobility in the government, it also contained features friendly to conservative interests. While the elections for the lower house were to be direct, voter eligibility was restricted on the basis of wealth and income: the electorate consequently consisted of successful farmers, bureaucrats, small businessmen, doctors, and lawyers (Congleton 2011, 389). Practically speaking, only around 20 percent of adult males had the right to vote for members of the lower house.

Large landowners represented in the lower house were against extending suffrage. They did not want their position in that body to shrink. They made arguments that they were a counterweight to anarchism, communism, and socialism (Lewin 1988, 56). Most importantly, they controlled the constitutional committee in the lower house that was charged with considering suffrage extensions and repeatedly blocked attempts throughout the late nineteenth and early twentieth centuries to extend suffrage further.

Proportional Representation

Despite the formidable obstacles to popular representation outlined previously, by the turn of the twentieth century progressive political ideas had clawed their way into the mainstream, and many proposals for extending the franchise and electoral reform began to circulate in the lower house. By 1905, the Liberals and the Social Democrats held a majority of the seats in the lower house; their political success was largely propelled by the improving economic fortunes of the urban merchant class, on the back of rising manufactured exports. Conservative forces were squarely on the defensive.

Conservatives headed by Salomon Lindman took power in 1907 after the resignation of the Liberal Party. The Liberals had failed to pass progressive reforms, including increased suffrage.[14] But Conservatives estimated that they would not be able to block suffrage reform forever. Consequently, Lindman decided to get ahead of the curve and crafted a plan for increased suffrage that would simultaneously broaden the Conservative Party's appeal and bring more supporters into the fold as a way to blunt the rise of Liberals and Social Democrats.

The 1909 franchise extension was accomplished by eliminating property requirements for voting. This doubled the franchise from 500,000 to 1 million voters and was tantamount to nearly universal male suffrage. There remained

---

[14] Lindman (1862–1935) was a successful industrialist before becoming a legislator. He served on the board of directors of several iron ore mining companies (Congleton 2003, 27n22).

consequential caveats, however: The completion of military service and tax payment remained requirements for voting. Also, individuals in bankruptcy or on poor relief could not vote. In short, some of the most disadvantaged members of Swedish society remained disenfranchised.

Lindman also sought to reduce the distortionary effects of the weighted voting scheme for selecting members of the senate. Specifically, the maximum weighting of votes was reduced from 5,000 to 40. Moreover, the senate's office term was reduced from nine to six years, and wealth requirements for seats in the first chamber were reduced from 80,000 to 50,000 krona. But as we will discuss in detail in the sections that follow, a host of elite biases that favored conservatives remained. Some of the most prominent were the persistence of weighted voting, wealth requirements for membership in the chamber, and indirect elections.

Lindman simultaneously proposed changing the electoral rules used to select district representatives in both legislative chambers: he imposed PR to protect conservatives and minority parties who would not have fared well under winner-take-all rules in single-member districts under increased suffrage. In some districts, the Liberals had become exceedingly popular; the same was true for the Social Democrats in other districts (Congleton 2011, 400; Rodden 2011, 50).[15]

Lewin (1988) eloquently emphasizes this logic:

It could not be assumed that demands for universal manhood suffrage would continue to be defeated in Parliament. There were now too many people who supported such a reform. Sweden would soon be the only country in Europe that did not allow all adult men to vote. No, the introduction of universal manhood suffrage was certainly unavoidable. But could this process take place in a way less harmful to the Conservatives than by embracing the suffrage ideas of the Left? If such a solution could be found, it was better to act now, while the Conservatives were in government and could direct the political game...Democracy was on the doorstep. Even the Conservatives had to accept universal manhood suffrage. But the question was whether the country – confronted by a militant Left that denied the throne, the sword, and the altar – should continue to elect its M.P.'s by a majority method...Given the new situation that had arisen in Sweden, there was good reason to ensure the minority some protection by switching to a proportional representation system of elections. This change would at least guarantee the country's conservative elements an influence equivalent to their strength in the electorate. (70–71)

PR would also enable conservatives to retain control of the senate and therefore continue to block populist reforms. In order to accomplish this objective, PR would be used to elect the provincial councils, which would in turn elect representatives to the senate. In other words, indirect elections to the upper house were retained, and because these were vested in the municipal level, they

---

[15] A large literature has corroborated the insight that conservative parties strategically favored PR during transitions to democracy across Europe, both as a reaction against socialism and to ward off electoral extinction (Colomer 2004, 187; Rokkan 1970; Boix 1999).

gave incumbent business interests outsized influence, as explained previously.[16] Yet the Conservatives feared that PR might also fragment the opposition to the Left. So they tried to strike a balance by adopting the D'Hondt method for translating votes into seats, which favored them, given their larger party size at the time.

Incumbent economic elites had an obvious interest in securing their rights under a manipulated democracy through constitutional engineering, but what about their political patrons? In this book, we also stress the important role played by political elites in orchestrating strategic democratization. Similar to their economic allies, they are also keen to protect their interests during and after such a transition – especially their personal security and finances. In the Swedish case, this role was embodied by the monarch, King Gustav V, who threw his support behind these suffrage and electoral "reforms" because they were accompanied by a 25 percent increase in his budget and because his powers would not be reduced by them, including his ability to name cabinet members, the prime minister among them (Congleton 2011, 401).[17]

In short, the PR electoral system was adopted in parallel to universal manhood suffrage to protect the Conservative Party and prevent the parliament from being dominated by the Left. Although the Social Democrats grew to become Sweden's biggest and most important party after democratization and the Liberals became a shell of their former selves, the Conservatives exploited the favorable rules that had been created for them by shrewd constitutional engineers during Sweden's long transition. For several decades after the 1911 shift, they and allies such as the Centrist Party were overrepresented in both chambers.

Moreover, PR not only created scores of safe seats for the Right in the Riksdag but enduringly altered the Left's electoral strategy: "In the long term, too, Lindman's strategy of dividing the Left bore fruit: To lure back the right-wing Liberals who had supported the [Conservatives'] suffrage reform, Staaff [the Liberals' leader] partially shifted Liberal policy toward the right" (Lewin 1988, 78–79).

This was in part a consequence of the centrifugal tendencies introduced by PR: elements of the Far Left broke off from the Social Democrats after democratization, with the Communists being the most prominent example. Eventually, splinter parties occupied their own political enclave in the lower house. For example, by 1918, the Left Socialists had 11 out of 230 seats in the

---

[16] However, the property requirements for senate membership were reduced, and a forty-grade scale of income weighting scheme for provincial council voters replaced the tax rate–based scale; nevertheless, the new scheme gave voters electoral influence that was roughly proportional to their wealth, and the councils themselves continued to geographically overrepresent wealthy enclaves.

[17] This would change shortly, however, as the monarch ceded more powers to the parliament after democratization and by and large remained above the political fray as the twentieth century progressed.

lower house (Metcalf 1987, 217). This balkanization complicated matters for the Social Democrats in a way that tended to benefit conservatives and traditional business interests.

Decentralization

Besides the national-level elite biases we discussed earlier, a strong current of political decentralization was inherited from the institutions bequeathed by outgoing authoritarian elites. This decentralization strengthened the political hand of local aristocrats, particularly in the countryside, where landowners remained quite powerful. Indeed, Hinnerich and Petterson-Lidbom (2014) conclude on the basis of a rigorous analysis of forms of local government – which operated either through direct or representative democracy, determined in part by a population threshold – that elite de facto power strongly persisted until at least the late 1930s. These authors find that more sparsely populated locales that more frequently operated under direct democracy were more likely to be captured by local elites who marshaled agenda power and divide-and-rule tactics to repress spending on public welfare to the tune of 40–60 percent vis-à-vis locales with multiparty competition. Because education, health care, and poor relief were provided by local governments and largely financed by them as well, this mattered greatly for the distribution of income and opportunities and access to social insurance.

SWEDEN'S TWENTIETH-CENTURY ELITE-BIASED DEMOCRACY AND FIRST STEPS TOWARD POPULAR DEMOCRACY

According to the coding rules we discuss in Chapters 3 and 5, Sweden's popular democratic experience began in 1974. The reason is that, in 1974, a popular constitution was introduced, decades after Sweden's ruling Conservatives in the Riksdag had extended the franchise coupled with the adoption of PR. The most momentous institutional change, which preceded the 1974 constitution, was the elimination of the upper chamber. This was followed in short order by complementary changes that further entrenched the popular nature of Sweden's democracy: all legislative decisions were to be made by majority vote, the terms of legislators were reduced to three years, the voting age was lowered to eighteen, a direct popular veto of proposed constitutional reforms via referendum was introduced, and the franchise was extended to immigrants in municipal elections.

In this book, we have argued that there are good reasons for why one should look at constitutions and constitutional change when deciding whether a regime type qualifies as a popular democracy versus an elite-biased democracy. In Chapter 3, we showed that elite-biased measures are almost always a byproduct of constitutional engineering in which outgoing elites from the previous regime encode political advantages into the ensuing democratic political system that distorts political representation in their favor. In Chapter 5, we argued that this scenario can surely change, but the mechanics by which it changes again underscore the importance of constitutions: major changes that level the political playing field for the masses are usually enshrined in the revocation of an inherited autocratic constitution or through constitutional amendments that rescind elite-biased measures.

This is palpable in the case of Sweden on the following grounds: as we have demonstrated, the country's initial democratic transition on the back of the 1909 franchise extension was littered with barriers to popular participation. These measures were built atop the 1809 constitution, which was imposed by a small coterie of oligarchs at the height of monarchical reign and was inherited by Sweden's democracy. After the democratic transition, which was completed in 1911, the franchise remained limited to men and restricted on the basis of military service, the payment of taxes, and solvency. Voting for the senate was weighted by wealth, there were stringent wealth restrictions on who could serve in the senate, and supermajority support was needed for important legislative items, including certain fiscal issues.

But elite-biased institutions – as well as changes to them – do not always occur in the context of constitutions. Indeed, in some cases, legal and political changes that fall short of constitutional reform can strip away and adulterate elite-biased rules. This is especially true in older democracies (e.g., the United Kingdom) that have gradually transitioned from monarchy to constitutional monarchy and then to liberal democracy. There, the major reforms to the political arena making it more competitive and egalitarian have occurred through statutory change.

Similarly, in Sweden, and in a way that stands out from the vantage of our framework, a host of important elite-biased rules encoded in its democratic transition were eliminated via extraconstitutional reforms in the decades after its 1911 democratic transition and before major constitutional change in 1974. Indeed, because of this, one could comfortably argue that the country's popular democracy actually begins much earlier than 1974. Most prominent – and discussed in detail in the following section – are the series of liberalizing reforms in 1921, and then again in the 1930s. These reforms were aimed at eradicating barriers to voting based on wealth that violated the one-person-one-vote principle and at broadening participation in the senate.

While in this book we prefer to defer to our formal coding rules in order to prevent post hoc rationalizations from influencing our descriptive statistics and quantitative models, we acknowledge that some of these coding decisions might be noisy approximations of the actual political equilibria; in Sweden between 1911 and 1974, one could argue that this is the case.

The Initial Decade of Elite-Biased Institutions

Sweden had become a full-fledged industrial country by the time the franchise was extended in 1909, helping the Social Democrats monopolize the electoral support of the mass of the population: urban laborers. Beginning in 1914, they held more seats in the lower house than the Liberals. Yet democracy in Sweden was carefully stage-managed in such a way that these rising actors were hemmed in.

The first major test of the effectiveness of Sweden's elite biases after suffrage extension was pension reform. Various politicians had called for worker pensions beginning in 1895, though early proposals focused on industrial laborers to the exclusion of the countryside. Unsurprisingly, agrarian interests blocked these early reform attempts. The 1909 franchise changed this equation, but not without necessitating compromise. A seemingly progressive pension reform was finally adopted in 1913, making old-age insurance universal. Yet the rural-based coalition that backed the Conservatives, which included large landholders, were able to win critical concessions: the inclusion of rural laborers and the requirement that individuals make pension contributions as opposed to employer-based contributions, albeit with income-tested supplements for those with inadequate earnings-related benefits (Anderson 2009, 227).

Notwithstanding pension reform, political contestation in the first decade following Sweden's democratization revolved largely around preparation for and consequences of World War I. The dynamics again revealed the outsized influence of elites from the pre-democratic era, as their political and economic interests dominated the debate over Sweden's role in the Great War.

The prime minister in the immediate lead-up to the war was Karl Staaff, a fiscal conservative (from the Liberal Party) who wanted to limit increases in defense spending. King Gustav V, who had succeeded Oscar II, spoke out against Staaff's delays in funding defense. Conservatives wanted a longer training program for infantry in preparation for World War I, with many in the Liberal Party (the so-called defense enthusiasts) siding with the Conservatives. The conflict over defense culminated in 1914 with a farmers' demonstration in Stockholm. There were 30,000 participants who marched to the royal palace, most of them farmers allied with the Conservative Party. Gustav V received the demonstrators and roundly disavowed both the government and the Riksdag. Staaff resigned in protest.

In 1914, Hjalmar Hammarskjöld became prime minister after new special parliamentary elections, which gave the Conservatives a plurality in the lower house. His government was conservative in nature but not tied to any established party. The party platform was defense heavy, espousing a strident monarchical and nationalist message; indeed, its motto was "Defense First: With God for King and Fatherland." Parties on the left appealed to constitutionalism and opposition to heavy defense spending. The Conservatives – with the strong, overt support of the monarch – were able to push through a big increase in defense spending in the immediate aftermath of the special elections, principally due to the outbreak of World War I in August 1914.

The regularly scheduled elections at the end of 1914 delivered a plurality to the Social Democrats in the lower house for the first time. By this point, the Liberals had lost much of their support among industrial workers, and farmers and burghers had defected to the Right (Carlsson 1987, 219). This was fueled, in part, by the fact that both Liberals and Social Democrats continued to support free-trade policies and thus the grain imports that undercut the rents of landowners and incomes of farmers. This made good political sense, as the parties on the left represented consumers and urban wage laborers, who benefited from free trade by virtue of cheap food imports on the one hand and higher wages on the other hand, as Sweden was a labor-abundant country at the time.[18]

Despite its initial efforts to remain neutral in World War I, Sweden was greatly influenced by the machinations of outside powers. The Conservatives continued, as they had for decades, to support some limits to trade – especially imported grain – during the war. At the same time, however, Sweden sought to export timber, iron ore, (re-exported) copper, and animal products to both the Entente and Central Powers, while importing large amounts of coal and limited amounts of grain from Great Britain. In 1915–1916, Sweden was progressively pressured by a tightening blockade by Great Britain, which attempted to prohibit the re-export of traded products to Germany and otherwise restrict Swedish trade.

The contours of Sweden's war and trade posture mirrors the political struggles we outlined previously. Hammarskjöld effectively undermined imports of grain by disallowing Britain from inspecting Swedish ships, which suited the economic interests of his political coalition – that is, this decision was part and parcel of a mercantilist approach to trade in which unfettered Swedish exports of minerals and timber were coupled with limits on grain imports that could harm the land rents of large landholders and the incomes of middle-class farmers. The Left during this period was united against Hammarskjöld, accusing him of fostering a "hunger regime," which was also consistent with the material interests of their political coalition. In short, the economic incumbents who benefited under Swedish authoritarianism and subsequently under the country's elite-biased democracy were pitted against the rising economic elites, who struggled for greater power and influence over economic policy after democratization and who could now use external pressure from the Allied Powers as leverage to orient the country's trade policies closer to its preferences.

Britain used its trade relationships with individual Swedish firms to attempt to tilt Sweden toward the Entente and keep it open to the transit of goods between Britain and Russia.[19] The balance between Great Britain and Sweden shifted dramatically, however, with the Bolshevik Revolution in Russia in February 1917 and the United States' entry into the war. The transit issue became less important once Russia was no longer a major player in the war on the heels of the revolution. At the same time, Sweden became increasingly dependent on British grain due to shortages. Sweden's bargaining position vis-à-vis the

---

[18] This is consistent with the preferences of these groups anticipated by Heckscher-Ohlin trade theory.

[19] This paragraph closely draws on Salmon (1997).

British was dramatically weakened. Moreover, Sweden's two chambers under-funded Hammarskjöld's defense appropriations request in March 1917, dividing the government against itself and leading Hammarskjöld to resign early.

Sweden was therefore exceptionally vulnerable to a major change in its economic equilibrium and social and political upheaval. After Hammarskjöld stepped down, a faction of moderate Conservatives were tasked to form a new government, paving the way for greater opposition influence. Tobacco manufacturer Carl Swartz became the prime minister. While trying to increase access to grain supplies from Britain to alleviate a grain shortage, his already weakened government was quickly faced with national food riots in April 1917 and coterminous demonstrations in Stockholm supporting the Bolshevik Revolution (Tilton 1974, 567). This was coupled with the forced inventorying of farmers' food holdings and the expropriation of potatoes. The unrest then spread to military units.

Campaigning for regularly scheduled elections at the end of 1917 got under way in the summer. On September 8, in the middle of the election, a major political scandal erupted. The United States published the Luxburg papers, exposing Swedish diplomatic collusion with the Germans. This discredited the Conservative government's rhetoric of attempted neutrality and contributed to their sound electoral defeat, although the 1917 elections were largely dominated by economic issues having to do with food prices and constitutional issues.

Conservatives went from eighty-six to fifty-seven seats in the lower chamber, behind the Social Democrats and Liberals, respectively. A coalition of Liberals and Social Democrats took over the cabinet and Nils Edén, the head of the Liberal Party, became the prime minister. One of the Edén government's most momentous achievements was securing a major agreement with the United States, Great Britain, France, and Italy. The terms of this agreement crucially included improved access to imported grain (Carlsson 1987, 220). This was a boon to the political coalition represented by the Social Democrats, who had become the champions of consumers and urban laborers, both of whom directly benefited from cheaper food. Conversely, it was a blow to large land-holders and thus the Conservative Party.

Initial Reforms to Elite-Biased Democracy

The stage was set for a series of reforms to the elite-biased nature of Sweden's democracy. Hjalmar Branting, head of the Social Democrats who had served in the Edén cabinet, became the next prime minister. He was able to push through key liberalizing reforms. These were to mirror three popular demands for change. First, that the weighting for votes in the senate tilted toward wealthy landowners be abolished. Second, that suffrage be strengthened by reducing requirements for voters to have paid state and municipal taxes. Third, that the franchise be extended to women. These reforms were approved by the lower house, which was now squarely in the hands of the Social Democrats. The senate, however, still overrepresented with the agents of economic elites, vetoed these proposed changes in 1918.

Yet Conservative intransigence would not last. Local revolutionaries and radicals were strengthened by major political revolts in Germany in November 1918 at the conclusion of World War I, which were catalyzed with the seizure of key ports and the fleeing of the Kaiser from Berlin. These radicals demanded the abolition of the monarchy, along with the upper chamber, and called for an end to universal military service. They also pushed for universal suffrage.

With revolution knocking on the door, the Conservatives decided to compromise. A set of reforms were implemented in late 1918–1919 and 1921, drawing a distinction between local and national elections. At the local level, in municipal and county assembly elections, women were granted the right to vote, and the requirement that taxes be paid to exercise suffrage was loosened to having paid taxes at least once in the three years prior to an election. To counterbalance these reforms somewhat, the voting age for these elections was increased. The national-level reforms in 1921 went further, however. Tax-payment requirements for voting were dropped, suffrage was extended to women, and the voting age was reduced from twenty-four to twenty-three. The 1921 reforms also eliminated the weights tied to wealth when voting for the senate and allowed the introduction of direct elections to the senate based on PR instead of via a slate of electors. Finally, in 1922, voting restrictions based on lack of military service were eliminated. Taken as a whole, this meant that adult suffrage was broadened dramatically: the share of the adult population that was eligible to vote more than doubled.

In summary, the heyday of a one-sided, thoroughly elite-biased democracy in Sweden was relatively short: it only lasted about a decade. The key reason that this "honeymoon" was short lived, however, was because of the pressure and aftermath of a largely exogenous event, World War I. Conservatives could have hardly predicted the assassination of Archduke Franz Ferdinand and its concomitant consequences and reactions.

Yet given that the Great War did happen, elite-biased democracy in Sweden took the first steps toward unraveling in ways that are consistent with our theoretical framework. First, although the monarchy in Sweden was not first eliminated, the gravity and import of the office was critically drained by the expulsion, execution, and exile of monarchs across the European continent in the context of World War I. Monarchs were run out of countries such as Germany, Austria-Hungary, Finland, and Greece. The Russian czar and his family were executed. A weakened respect for monarchy created permissive conditions for reform.

Shocks to the balance of trade and a political scandal tied to the Conservatives' handling of Sweden's wartime neutrality were the straws that broke the camel's back. Conservatives' affinity with landowners, and their protectionism vis-à-vis domestic grain production at the expense of consumers, decimated their popular support when the British blockade caused bread rationing in 1917. Riots and demonstrations ensued (Tilton 1974, 567). Knocked back on their heels, Conservatives quickly suffered another devastating blow as their secret diplomatic relations with the Germans were publicly exposed. Finally, Sweden was at the cusp of being swept up in revolutionary fervor as radicalism was ignited in Germany in the aftermath of the armistice and Kaiser Wilhelm II's abdication. Within the course of a year, Social Democrats and the Left strengthened dramatically and used popular unrest to push Conservatives as far as they would go toward reform.

Consistent with our framework, the opposition seized on the ability to coordinate to effectuate real popular changes, including demanding the overthrow of the monarchy, the abolition of the senate, the abolition of military service, and unrestricted suffrage. But that is not the whole story, however, as elements of elite bias remained: the constitutional engineering ushered in by the early 1900s would continue to cast a long shadow, constraining the Social Democrats and their allies.

Growing Social Democratic Hegemony

Between 1920 and 1932, Sweden was characterized by unstable minority governments. In the aftermath of the major political reforms adopted in the 1920s, the main political cleavage was along the lines of socialism versus nonsocialism. Furthermore, two new parties entered the system with a stable base of support: the Agrarian Union and the Communists. The Agrarian Union centered on farmers distinct from the large landowners who were foundational to Conservatives; they nonetheless shared interests in protectionist policies shielding the rural sector. The Agrarian Union and Communists exploited the fact that liberals were weakened by the Liberal Party split in 1923 over the prohibition of alcohol, only to reunite in 1934. The upshot is that nonsocialist parties held roughly two-thirds of the seats in the first chamber in the 1920s and early 1930s.

Yet the Conservatives and their allies were weakened by a series of setbacks, many of which were beyond their control. At the end of the 1920s, the agricultural sector was flagging due to increased global competition and falling considerably behind the manufacturing sector. Lindman, the Conservative prime minister who had minority support in the parliament, resigned in the wake of the two parliamentary chambers upholding a commission's recommendation to eschew tariffs on grain, despite pleas for relief by farmers and other affected parties in the countryside (Stjernquist 1987, 259).

These trends were exacerbated by the Great Depression. A deep economic crisis unleashed historically high unemployment, sparking widespread strikes. In 1931, the military shot five demonstrators dead at Lunde, fanning widespread discontent. To address the economic crisis in the countryside, the Swedish government granted price protections to grain and dairy farmers.

In 1932, Prime Minister Gustaf Ekman, who had led the committee against raising tariffs on grain and was now the head of the Liberal People's Party, was forced to resign after a major political scandal involving campaign finances. This paved the way for the Social Democrats to increase their electoral representation in both legislative chambers.

Furthermore, 1932 marked the beginning of a strategic and unprecedented alliance between workers and farmers that would constitute the political underpinning of Social Democratic rule beginning in the 1930s and lasting well into the post–World War II period. Under the (second) prime ministership of Hjalmar Branting, the Social Democrats struck an agreement with the Agrarian Union and relied on their support (in what was known pejoratively as the "horse trade") to pass legislation. They then engaged in a quid pro quo with the Agrarian Union in which they exchanged this crucial support for limited protectionist trade policies and agricultural price supports (Stjernquist 1987, 263).[20] This was the start of a new political coalition centered on mutual class interests between rural and urban laborers, rather than the sectoral concerns that predominated during the heyday of elite-biased democracy before the 1920s reforms.[21]

The effect that this "red-green alliance" had on social democracy in Sweden beginning in the 1930s outstripped the more minor, formal institutional changes that occurred simultaneously: the elimination of wealth requirements for eligibility in the senate[22] and the reduction in the length of terms for that chamber.[23] Effectively, outsider economic elites exchanged increased redistribution for favorable economic policies. This new political arrangement enabled Social Democrats to consolidate a new class-based coalition that transcended the old rural/urban divide that had riven urban workers and farmers, with the latter siding with the Conservatives in favor of protectionism. This coalition was further strengthened by the fact that it presided over the return to prosperity following the Great Depression.

[20] This alliance sparked considerable controversy among rural interests. Indeed, Olof Olsson, one of the pioneers of the farmers' political movement and the leader of the Agrarian Union in 1932, opposed the alliance and resigned his position in protest. The negotiations for the alliance occurred behind his back. "Sköld's smorgasbord" was not to be enjoyed by Olof.

[21] The genesis of this alliance can perhaps be dated to 1888, when livestock farmers split from grain producers and joined the Liberals in opposing tariffs on agricultural imports (see Ansell and Samuels 2014, 55).

[22] The material impact of this reform was not that pronounced, however, as wealth requirements had already been significantly reduced and high rates of inflation associated with World War I had eroded their real value. The 1909 reform that reduced wealth requirements lowered the required real estate wealth for serving in the senate from $539,200 (80,000 kr.) in real estate wealth in 2014 dollars to $337,000 (50,000 kr.). The 1909 reform also reduced the income requirement to $20,200 in 2014 dollars (from 4,000 kr. to 3,000 kr.). After factoring in inflation, the wealth requirement effectively became $138,400 by the end of World War I and the income requirement was effectively reduced to $8,100.

[23] Moreover, in 1937, the voting age was lowered in the senate from twenty-seven to twenty-three.

The consolidation of this class-based coalition ushered in ensuing reforms that softened further restrictions on the franchise in the 1940s: the voting age was lowered to twenty-one in the senate in 1941, the franchise was extended in national elections in 1944 to citizens on poor relief or in bankruptcy, the voting age was lowered to twenty-one in the lower chamber in 1945, and also in 1945, the franchise was extended in municipal elections even to those citizens who do not pay taxes. Given social policy reforms in the intervening years, which we will outline further in the following sections, these reforms only effectively extended the franchise by a small percent of the adult population.

THE DAWN OF SWEDEN'S GOLDEN AGE OF
PROGRESSIVE POLICY

Group-based conflict is mediated by institutions, and different institutions often protect different groups. In the case of Sweden beginning in the 1930s, the groups who were protected by powerful national legislative institutions increasingly came to encompass portions of the lower class in key sectors of the Swedish economy, due in part to the alliance between the Social Democrats and the Agrarian Union. Therefore, economic policy began to reflect their interests in ways that afforded them higher wages and protection in the way of social insurance. These policies were further underpinned by modest additional institutional changes and changes to the franchise that empowered them politically. Finally, increased income leveling further reinforced their de jure power.

The crown jewel of income leveling was an informal institution pioneered in the late 1930s: centralized wage bargaining. While this system was colored by certain elite biases that we will explicate later on, it nevertheless contributed to income leveling among organized wage laborers in both export and non-export sectors. This was primarily achieved by putting them in charge of Sweden's unemployment insurance system, which gave workers a strong incentive to join unions. The Swedish National Employers' Federation (SAF) and the Union Confederation (LO) institutionalized centralized wage bargaining with the Saltsjöbaden Agreement in 1938, a watershed deal to manage labor disputes at the confederal level. Beginning in 1953, the SAF and LO bargained in a centralized fashion. While wages were set according to "solidaristic pay," in which equal wages were paid for equal work, differentials between employees at different levels of an organization were reduced (see Thelen 2014, 177).

Rapid economic growth with a relatively egalitarian distribution of income sped up after the end of World War II (see Piketty 2014). This era saw great progress made on the social insurance front. In 1943, a comprehensive child care system was created. In 1946, pension reforms were launched, uncoupling the level of pension benefits from contributions. In addition, pensions became standardized and centralized (Kaufmann 2013, 125). In 1947, a bill was introduced that provided support for families with children. Comprehensive health insurance ensued in 1955, making health insurance obligatory. As late

FIGURE 6.3. Income share held by Sweden's richest 10 percent.
Notes: Missing values for selected years early in the time series are linearly interpolated.
Source: The World Wealth and Income Database (2016).

of 1930, only 20 percent of the adult population was insured. In 1945, after state subsidies were raised, the insurance rate among citizens rose from 20 percent to 48 percent. By 1955, of course, 100 percent of Swedes were insured (Kaufmann 2013, 134). Then in 1957, the Social Assistance Act was passed, centralizing welfare provision, which was previously administered and largely financed by local governments in a somewhat regressive manner. Finally, the Social Democrats also began to make considerable investments in public education, provided housing assistance to lower-income citizens, and financed job retraining.

Taken together, these policies ushered in a drastic reduction in inequality in the post–World War II period. As Figure 6.3 evinces, while in 1935 the income accruing to the top 10 percent was 36 percent, by 1954 it was 29 percent. Poverty was also markedly reduced.

LONG SHADOW OF ELITE BIASES

While Sweden made unprecedented progress toward a more popular democracy between the end of World War I and World War II, lingering political distortions moderated the equalizing effect of the Swedish corporatist system and reduced the scope and generosity of fiscal transfers. These distortions were both formal, primarily due to electoral rules, and informal in nature.

Despite the fact that their star rose precipitously in the decades after the 1921 institutional reforms, PR continued to hobble the Social Democrats' ability to vanquish their political foes. On the one hand, they were rarely able to win a majority of seats in the lower house due to party fractionalization. Indeed, for the nineteen general elections starting in 1911, the Social Democrats were only able to achieve the majority of seats twice, with the first occasion occurring in 1941. This meant that, in the vast majority of occasions, they either headed minority governments or teamed up with the Agrarian Union and other parliamentary parties in coalition cabinets. Therefore, the Social Democrats were often forced to rely on coalitions to pass bills in both houses.

Moreover, even when the Liberals surpassed the Conservatives as the largest opposition force, this did not prove catastrophic for landowners or incumbent firms, as Liberal members of parliament (MPs) began to side with conservatives on economic matters. The Liberal Party had become much more moderate over time – since at least 1948, it had been supported increasingly by white-collar workers.

On the other hand, conservative elements remained important competitors to the Social Democrats, enabling them to check their power. This is true even after the important 1921 reforms that dramatically broadened the franchise and eliminated weighted voting on the basis of wealth. The electoral rules for the first chamber implied that Conservatives were overrepresented in that chamber vis-à-vis the second chamber in every election pairing from the 1920s until the 1950s. The Social Democrats, by contrast, were underrepresented in the upper house relative to their lower house seat share from the early 1920s until the immediate post–World War II period.[24]

This discrepancy was induced by several factors. First, as mentioned previously, there were wealth limits on eligibility to run for the upper house prior to 1933. Second, members of the upper chamber were indirectly elected by county councils. Although the weighting of votes by wealth for these elections was dropped in 1921, the effects of this reform were only felt with a considerable lag. That is because the sequence was as follows: county councilors were elected first, and they would then elect members of the upper chamber (i.e., they could elect these members up to four years after they themselves were elected); the upper-chamber members in turn served eight-year terms (Immergut 2002, 238).[25] Furthermore, upper-chamber representatives were elected on a rolling basis, with one-eighth of the body elected each year.

---

[24] For instance, Conservatives won 25 percent of seats in the lower house in 1932 but 33 percent in the upper house in 1933 and 19 percent of seats in the lower house in 1936 but 30 percent in the upper house in 1937. By contrast, Social Democrats won 45 percent of seats in the lower house in 1932 but 39 percent of seats in the upper house in 1933 and 49 percent of seats in the lower house in 1936 but 44 percent in the upper house in 1937.

[25] These county council elections occurred concurrently with elections for local rural governments, which themselves were heavily influenced by the de facto power of local landowners (Hinnerich and Pettersson-Lidbom 2014).

Finally, politicians who served in the county councils often simultaneously served in the senate. While this was sometimes true of the second chamber as well, it was a more typical occurrence in the first chamber. The effect was that the economic interests of localities were aggressively represented at the national level, and by extension, rural matters sometimes had an outsized influence in the senate given the configuration of county councils.[26] Indeed, "the tendency of these members toward sympathetic understanding of the problems of local governments and a degree of cohesiveness in support of them is reflected in the fact that they are at times referred to as the 'fifth party' in the Riksdag" (Sandalow 1971, 767).

In sum, significant political distortions remained despite Sweden's progress toward a more popular form of democracy. These distortions, in turn, had important economic consequences: although social insurance blossomed and greatly benefited urban formal workers during this period, lingering political distortions moderated the equalizing effect of the Swedish corporatist system and mitigated the full promise of the welfare state.

Several of the most notable consequences are as follows. The advent of Swedish welfare state was accomplished along with strong constraints on wage increases and restrained monetary and fiscal policies. Business interests successfully mobilized resources to fight against economic planning and defeated the Postwar Program of the Swedish Labor Movement (Lewin 1988, 31). Labor unions remained subservient to the state, which augured well for business interests. The Unemployment Commission, created in 1914, first brought employers and unions together to hammer out wage negotiations through so-called policy concertation – with the government as "mediator." By 1926, however, labor unions had withdrawn from this body in protest against the "free market" views held by both employers and state officials. Indeed, in 1928, it was made illegal for workers to strike during wage negotiations, sharply reducing their bargaining leverage.

The Swedish welfare state also did not involve overly generous fiscal transfers (Upchurch, Taylor, and Mathers 2016, 38). During the 1960s, government spending was not that much higher than in other OECD countries (Freeman, Topel, and Sweedenborg 1997, 8). Moreover, although Sweden became a "high-tax country" in the 1960s, it was really on the back of a nationwide sales tax that was regressive in nature, one that was eventually replaced by a value added tax (Lodin 2011, 36). Indeed, during the 1960s, Sweden's share of consumption taxes (as a percentage of GDP) was noticeably higher than the average of the fifteen European OECD members.

Finally, it should be noted that although fiscal policy in the immediate aftermath of World War II was progressive, in the sense that high wealth and

---

[26] This was further exacerbated by the fact that there were a minimum number of seats assigned per county council, inducing some disproportionality in favor of smaller (and more rural) councils.

estate taxes passed to help finance the war remained on the books, it was not very progressive in the sense that income taxes were only moderately high, at least by Swedish standards (Lodin 2011, 29). For example, even at the highest income brackets, both average and marginal tax rates in 1948 are comparable to those in 2008, after considerable reductions during the late 1990s and early 2000s. Moreover, wealth and estate taxes in 1948 were less progressive than in the 2000s. This helps explain why Sweden's level of income inequality remained relatively stagnant during the 1950s and 1960s: between 1950 and 1969, the income accruing to the top 10 percent was stuck at 30 percent (see Figure 6.3).

THE ADVENT OF POPULAR DEMOCRACY

The Riksdag Act of 1970 eliminated the indirectly elected senate, the last major vestige of overt elite bias in the Swedish political system. This was the culmination of several reforms throughout the preceding decades that sought to make the senate more inclusive. For example, higher voting ages for county council elections had already been repealed; the same is true of the relatively older age required to be elected to the senate.

The change to unicameralism was made in a relatively straightforward manner. The upper house was simply merged with the lower house. This meant that the new unicameral parliament had 350 total seats: the 120 seats in the first chamber plus the 230 seats in the second chamber.[27] The terms of office for each legislator was reduced to three years.

The parliament's structure and modus operandi were also made quite basic: all legislative decisions were to be made through majority vote. Of the 350 seats, 40 became adjustment seats to be distributed among the constituencies and parties having the largest number of excess votes in each constituency after the first 310 seats had been distributed. This ensured even greater proportionality.

On a superficial level, there were several changes to the workings and constitution of the Swedish parliament after the advent of unicameralism. One was the professionalization of the legislature, which meant fewer representatives from private spheres of Swedish life, including agricultural and industry. For example, the number of farmers in the unicameral version of Riksdag fell precipitously compared to the old second chamber, as did the prevalence of business leaders and other figures from civil society (Metcalf 1987, 233).

More far-reaching and impactful changes occurred as well. First and foremost, smaller majorities could form to pass legislation more quickly and with less debate. This change had a synergistic interaction with previous efforts to liberalize Swedish politics, especially the erosion of the norm of approving

---

[27] The size of the chamber was later changed to 349 seats.

major legislation through supermajorities. Consider that "the weakening of the supermajority norm for major programs, together with the formal reform of the parliament, clearly reduced the size of the majority required to pass large-scale and durable legislation, whereas the shift to unicameral governance simplified the task of constructing such majority coalitions. After 1970 new policies formally required only a single majority in a single chamber. Together the constitutional changes significantly reduced the cost of passing new legislation" (Congleton 2003, 160).

The final farewell to elite bias was the annulment of the 1809 constitution in 1974. On the one hand, this amounted to a formality: the new constitution merely elevated PR, the elimination of the senate, and parliamentary supremacy over the king to the constitutional level.[28] On the other hand, Sweden's democracy became even more popular, as the new constitution introduced a provision that created a direct popular veto, via referendum, of any proposed constitutional amendments.

Proximate Reasons behind the 1970s Reforms

In terms of policy and law, the roots of the change to unicameralism go back to a constitutional commission appointed by the government in 1954. This commission suggested scrapping the 1809 constitution in order to codify changes to Sweden's constitutional monarchy. The top two objectives were to endow parliament with greater power and to replace the bicameral system. In 1966, all relevant parties agreed, in practice, to dissolving the second chamber. In 1967, the constitutional commission presented a final proposal, which called for the elimination of the senate. This was adopted into law in 1969 and went into effect in 1970.

The politics behind the decision were not without irony. During the 1960s, the nonsocialist parties controlled the lower house of parliament but not the upper house, which was dominated by the Social Democrats. Consequently, the nonsocialist parties had the most to gain from dissolving the senate – at least in the short term. The Social Democrats had exercised control of the senate since 1941.

Yet ultimately, and as to be expected, it was the Social Democrats who pushed for eliminating the senate. The heavy electoral losses they suffered in 1966 convinced them that gutting the first chamber was in their best interest in the long run. It would further dilute the already muted overrepresentation of conservative elements. Eliminating the upper house would both consolidate the socialists' hold on power over the long haul and give them greater authority and flexibility (Holmberg and Stjernquist 1996, 16). This would allow the Social Democrats to indulge in the more populist policies preferred by their constituents.

---

[28] The king was no longer in charge of the formation of new governments. The king was also written out of any role involving votes of no confidence.

Our theoretical framework can shine light on these "bookending" institutional changes in the 1970s. As we outlined in Chapter 5, structural change is often a key precipitant of liberalizing reforms to elite-biased constitutions. Sweden certainly exhibits this dynamic. The Swedish economy and society had drastically changed, especially after World War II. It shifted from an agriculturally focused political economy, based in the countryside and complemented by basic industries, to a manufacturing powerhouse powered by a dense concentration of skilled urban laborers who churned out high value–added products destined for foreign markets. Figures 6.1 and 6.2 clearly adduce this change. In turn, a huge gulf in productivity between the agricultural and manufacturing sectors opened up. The result was that, over time, conservative forces had lost political clout as their electoral bases had dramatically weakened.

Swedish democracy had also gradually unleashed the masses. They had grown bolder under the political hegemony of the Social Democrats. This came to a head during the 1960s. In 1968 especially, there was heavy popular unrest in the form of repeated strikes and protests that consistently brought thousands to the street. Worker dissatisfaction with the distributional consequences of centralized wage bargaining was at the forefront of mass frustration.

Effects of Popular Democracy

What were the changes wrought by Sweden's definitive turn to popular democracy? Politics took a sharp left turn. Unicameralism, both directly and indirectly, precipitated an explosion in government spending that strengthened the welfare state considerably.[29] And as we shall see shortly, the Swedish political economy model's top heaviness contributed to a serious economic crisis that precipitated important market oriented reforms. Consider that

Swedish outlays on government programs, which were reasonably 'normal' until the 1970s, have increased more rapidly than in other OECD countries. Government expenditures averaged 35 percent of GDP in the 1960s. After that, they increased more rapidly than in other OECD countries, reaching an average of 63 percent in the 1980s, much higher than in other OECD countries. The 1990s crisis pushed government expenditures to about 70 percent of GDP. (Freeman, Topel, and Swedenborg 1997, 8)

The Social Democrats paid for their more aggressive social transfers with progressive taxation. Swedish income taxes rose precipitously in the 1970s, especially after the formal annulment of the 1809 constitution in 1974. Tax

---

[29] Increases in progressivity occurred at both national and subnational levels. An extension of the suffrage to noncitizens occurred at the municipal level in 1976 in the close aftermath of the 1974 constitutional reform, leading to a substantial additional increase in municipal social spending. This is because noncitizens represented an important new segment (13 percent in 1976) of the electorate (see Vernby 2013).

reforms launched in 1971 and 1974 increased both marginal taxes and the total tax owed by the highest brackets. Most importantly, the rationale behind these reforms was to accelerate redistribution; for this reason, tax rates on poorer households were reduced (Lodin 2011, 41).

Other salient reforms after 1970 centered on the Swedish corporatist model and were designed to benefit labor. For example, wage earner funds intended to democratize capital ownership were conceived in the 1970s and implemented in the early 1980s. The transition to decentralized wage bargaining, away from the solidaristic model that had served to restrain wages, began in 1983, when industrial unions defected from peak-level bargaining agreements and began to negotiate their own deals with employers (Iversen 1996). Once this split happened, negotiations began to be concluded at the sectoral or industry level. The upshot was an explosion in both union density and the number of employees governed by wage-bargaining agreements.

The onset of unicameralism and associated populist reforms in the 1970s also fed an increased preoccupation with maximizing employment despite adverse effects on inflation, which unsurprisingly rose in tandem with these efforts. Not only was hiring workers stepped up, but firing was made more difficult, and the Swedish state became an employer of last resort. Finally, the Swedish state more heavily regulated the labor market and macroeconomy to produce greater equality.

CHALLENGES TO THE WELFARE STATE AND THE RESILIENCE OF POPULAR DEMOCRACY

In the wake of increased trade and capital mobility, the state's post-1970 muscular intervention in labor markets, its loose monetary policy, and its high levels of spending became unsustainable. However, rather than a turn to full-fledged neoliberalism, Sweden addressed a painful economic downturn induced by macroeconomic imbalances with a measured approach that did not sacrifice egalitarianism and social insurance. The reason is that, by the 1990s, Sweden's popular democracy had been well cemented.

As we discussed in Chapter 2, free capital mobility between countries tied to floating exchange rates was unleashed beginning in the early 1970s, and an increased push for freer trade in the 1980s reached a crescendo in the late 1990s. To foreshadow the deep crisis that this portended, consider that between 1980 and 1990, Sweden experienced an outward flow of investment capital of over fortyfold (Iversen 1996, 417).

Due to looser monetary policy and a very aggressive campaign to boost public employment, as well as more generous spending on social insurance and income transfers, inflation became a major problem during the late 1970s. This ushered in several currency devaluations and paralleled the death of the centralized, "inflation moderating" wage-setting regime that had come of age under corporatism (Freeman, Topel, and Swedenborg 1997, 8).

Sweden was beset with other economic problems as well.[30] Heightened government regulation and high taxes slowed Swedish productivity, leading to sluggish growth. In the process, Sweden's international competitiveness suffered greatly, and as a result, capital headed for the exits and exports declined.

The result was a huge economic contraction and fiscal crisis. Between 1990 and 1993, Sweden suffered a major recession: a cumulative output drop of around 5 percent associated with a steep decline in both industrial production and services. This was accompanied by a long decline in gross capital formation and, eventually, a cratering of employment. Unsurprisingly, as tax revenues imploded and Sweden's generous safety net kicked in, its fiscal situation worsened considerably: in 1993, the deficit was an astonishing 13 percent of GDP.

In order to rectify the situation, and to ward off growing discontent from both laborers and capitalists, a host of reforms were adopted by Social Democratic governments in the 1990s.[31] These were centered on decentralization, deregulation, and a reduction in Sweden's marginal tax rates. In terms of decentralization, the government eased up on public-sector employment and wage increases to tamp down inflation, privatized many state-run firms, and allowed for bonuses and other market mechanisms to incentivize private investment and productivity. In terms of deregulation, the government liberalized the banking, insurance, and retail sectors, often by harmonizing laws and regulations to satisfy EU directives. In terms of fiscal reform, a reduction in marginal income tax rates was accompanied by a greater reliance on value-added taxes (VATs).

The Swedish Welfare State Today

The reforms begun in the 1990s eventually turned the Swedish ship around. The country's competitiveness recovered, private investment firmed up, and fiscal deficits shrunk. Economic growth returned on the back of notable productivity growth.

Most impressively, Sweden's social safety net did not really retrench in a significant way, although the modes and methods used by the Social Democrats to fund and run the welfare state did change drastically. The fiscal system became much less progressive and VATs began to pay for much of the country's still generous social insurance programs (Wang and Caminada 2011).

Indeed, while the tax system became less progressive, social spending became even more progressive. The programs financed by the state now include sickness benefits, occupational injury and disease benefits, disability benefits, old-age and survivor benefits, child/family benefits, unemployment compensation, maternity and other family leave, military veteran benefits, and social-assistance cash benefits. Swedish governments continue to readily invest

[30] This section draws on Freeman, Topel, and Swedenborg (1997).
[31] This paragraph closely draws on Iversen (1996).

in education, health, and job training. Spending on higher education in Sweden ranks amongst the highest in the world, approaching 3 percent GDP, and university tuition fees are amongst the lowest (Piketty 2014, 340, 430). Finally, Sweden has virtually eliminated poverty. Therefore, despite important changes, Sweden remains quite egalitarian (see Figure 6.3).

CONCLUSION

This chapter argues that a big reason for Sweden's exceptionalism in recent decades is that it became a popular democracy. This victory was hard fought and protracted and culminated in the abolition of the indirectly elected upper house in 1970. Despite setbacks to the welfare state associated with a severe economic crisis during the late 1980s and early 1990s, calculated reforms steered things in a more balanced and sustainable direction. Indeed, in the Swedish case, it could even be said that the Social Democrats grew too strong for their own good after finally slinking off the last vestiges of elite bias that had weighed down Sweden's democracy. Yet the country found a way to strike a bargain between the demands of one of the world's most generous welfare states and the need for increased competitiveness and productivity in the face of globalization – allowing for the coexistence of a high standard of living alongside a strong social safety net and egalitarianism.

One of the major contributions of this chapter is to show that Sweden was not always exceptional. Similar to most of the world's other democracies, both old and new, Sweden's experiment in popular rule was flawed from conception and only improved after a messy and prolonged process. Sweden therefore represents the paragon of democracy's potential. If one of the world's most celebrated advanced democracies shed its autocratic legacy so resoundingly and successfully – albeit belatedly – perhaps other countries burdened with elite biases can yet do the same.

7

Chile

From Authoritarian Legacies to a New Dawn?

Chile, much like Sweden, is an exceptional country in many ways. It is extremely heterogeneous in terms of geography and climate, stretching from arid and almost barren deserts in the north to blistering cold in the pristine mountain passes that stretch toward Antarctica in the Earth's southernmost sea. It is the world's number-one producer of copper, and its wine, fruits, and vegetables are consumed across the world year round. It is a country of immigrants, especially from Europe; the descendants of Germans, French, and especially English men and women helped forge a modern nation that, in many ways, was the most politically stable and most "republican" country in Latin America during the nineteenth century. It was also among the first in the continent to industrialize and witness the blossoming of a strident labor union.

Its political history is likewise exceptional in certain aspects. By the middle of the twentieth century, even though Chile had begun its life as an oligarchy with a laissez faire economy, which was linked by free trade with the rest of the world and hosted free banking, the country was transformed into a popular democracy.[1] By the 1930s, it was characterized by staunch protectionism and a closed capital account, anchoring a strong labor movement and egalitarian social policies – indeed, Chileans elected an avowed communist as president in 1970.

By then, unlike most of its Latin American brethren, it had largely escaped the parade of coups and revolutions that ripped those countries asunder since their independence from Spain in the early 1800s. But by the end of the twentieth century, Chile had experienced a brutal military dictatorship that lasted almost two decades and managed to upend its precocious welfare state – only to return to democracy at the close of the twentieth century. At the

---

[1] By free banking we mean that wildcat financiers could take deposits without a license and emit their own bills.

beginning of the twenty-first century, Chile's economy grew so quickly that it is now rightfully considered Latin America's most vibrant economy, if not its most successful democracy. This reputation, however, masks the return of economic and social stratification and political polarization after the authoritarian interlude.

This chapter tells the story of a tumultuous and insightful political cycle. Chile transited from a republican oligarchy to a popular democracy in the mid-twentieth century. This was followed by a ruthless military dictatorship, which after a managed political transition culminated in an elite-biased civilian government.

While there is no doubt that Chile is a democracy today, if we scratch under the surface the legacy of its autocratic predecessor is quickly revealed. Consider that the net Gini coefficient under President Augusto Pinochet hovered between forty-eight and fifty, but that more than a decade after democratization the Gini was still stuck at fifty. Only in 2010 did it fall to forty-seven, a higher level of inequality than Chile experienced at any point under popular democracy in the twentieth century and a higher level than most of its South American neighbors.

How did this happen? The broad details of the story as is commonly told by lay people and researchers alike are well known. After displacing the first freely elected Communist in the western hemisphere with the tacit consent of the CIA, Pinochet presided over a right-wing military dictatorship that pursued capitalist economic principles based on strict monetarism and fiscal austerity under the guidance of economists from the University of Chicago. This supposedly ushered in a capitalist revolution in which economic growth was secured through private investment and international trade. Moreover, after democratization, growth was favored over equity: the results of Pinochet's neoliberal experiment were so patently successful that the Chilean people abandoned militant leftism in favor of centrism and prosperity.

In this chapter, we tell a much different story. The Pinochet regime was not a blind adherent to neoliberal scripture; its economic program was often ideologically inconsistent, if not purposely vague, because its goals were preeminently political. During the early days of the regime, key members of the military and the lawyers tasked with legitimizing the regime through decrees and the writing of a new constitution flirted with fascist ideology and valorized the Franco dictatorship in Spain and its "corporatist ideology." Yet they abandoned that approach when it was clear that their economic program would benefit from a restricted democratic framework and that the opposition would not countenance indefinite authoritarianism. The regime's primary task was, instead, to revive a defunct coalition that had died during the Great Depression and was buried under popular democracy.

Because that erstwhile coalition included the mineral sector, large landowners, banking, and private enterprise, this led Pinochet to adopt a mishmash of disparate policies that were only nominally neoliberal. While there is no doubt that the dictatorship tended to favor free trade and the market allocation of resources, key economic policies were adjusted over time, sometimes radically, especially when it came time to bail out the regime's allies in times of stress – most prominently after the 1982 financial crisis – and to weaken the regime's enemies in order to impose a new political equilibrium.

Ahead we will spell out how the outgoing Pinochet regime imposed institutional constraints that deliberately hamstrung the capacity of subsequent democratic administrations to engage in market distortions and promote egalitarianism. This was not because the dictatorship had a strong preference against regulation and redistribution rooted in economic theory; rather, it was a cudgel used to cripple the coalition that had ascended during popular democracy. Protected domestic manufacturers and organized labor had dominated Chilean politics since the Great Depression.

The 1980 constitution, married to Pinochet's self-styled neoliberal policies, sought to destroy that alliance. The constitution created a congress populated by a host of unelected senators. It also gave rise to a unique binomial electoral system that militated in favor of left-right parity despite a numerical disadvantage for the conservatives. Twenty-five years after the democratic transition, the Chilean Left is only now starting to make headway on undoing this elite-biased institutional legacy.

This chapter also makes other contributions. It is often assumed that military juntas tend to intervene in democratic politics for the sake of the national interest when democracy has gone off the rails because of an excess of populism and demagoguery or the infiltration of radicals and terrorists. In this vein, some analysts have taken Latin American militaries at their word when they say that the purpose of their coups is to save democracy from itself and restore the constitution (see, e.g., Stepan 1973). And even if overtly political and self-serving intentions are ascribed to military officers who orchestrate coups that interrupt democracy and subsequently take over power, it is usually assumed that the generals want to return to the barracks as quickly as possible and will do so as soon as they secure the interests of the military as an organization (Geddes 1999, 2003; Wright 2008).

We depart from these views. This book, and this chapter in particular, holds that military officers, like all other autocrats, intervene in civilian politics to help themselves and their economic allies. If that can be done quickly, fine; if it takes time, so be it. Rather than acting as dispassionate stewards of the military as an organization, coup perpetrators who originate in the armed forces are usually wont to game the political system through constitutional engineering and then exit on favorable terms. Indeed, because they directly control the state's most coercive apparatus, they are uniquely positioned to erect an elite-biased democracy that they can then manipulate behind the scenes after they return to the barracks.

CHILE DURING THE NINETEENTH CENTURY: A "REPUBLICAN"
OLIGARCHY

Chile stands out vis-à-vis other Latin American countries in that after it achieved
independence from Spain in 1818 it experienced relative political stability,
which allowed for the nascent state to consolidate in short order. Rather than
experience frequent coups, rebellions, and civil wars, as did Latin America's
other republics during the nineteenth century, Chile was characterized by a
republican system of government controlled by the country's oligarchy.

Extensive land ownership was a cornerstone of this oligarchy. Large estates
predominated in Chile at the end of the nineteenth century and into the early
twentieth century as a result of the enormous land grants (*mercedes*) and trusts
(*encomiendas*) bequeathed to conquistadors and other Spanish families by the
crown (Thome 1989, 218). *Encomenderos* were allowed to use the labor of
the population in their jurisdiction. By the early 1800s, most of these consolidated estates were used for cattle ranching, but new export markets opening
in the mid-late 1800s brought a shift to wheat, which required more labor.
Landowners established large resident work forces on their property, spurring
inquilinaje, a "quasi-feudal patron-client institution that was a central feature
of Chile's agrarian structure for nearly a century" (Thome 1989, 218).[2] These
inquilinos formed a growing rural middle class, and while they began as rent-
ers, displacing day laborers (peons and slaves) who became temporary and
migrant workers, the *inquilinos* gradually lost their relative independence and
became laborers.

In 1928, a mere 2.5 percent of landowners held 78 percent of arable land
(Thiesenhusen 1995, 89–90). And with the exception of mine owners, large
landowners had the highest per capita income of any social group in Chile
in the late nineteenth century (Rodríguez Weber 2009). Increased agricultural
demand from expanding international trade, growing domestic commercial
centers, and burgeoning mining centers in northern Chile led to a doubling
of the acreage used for agriculture and a tripling of acreage that was irrigated
between 1875 and 1930 (Thiesenhusen 1995, 90). Colonizers occupied untilled
land, and the farming frontier expanded until the early twentieth century.

There were other important segments of the oligarchy – many of which
evolved over time and were gradually incorporated into the halls of political
power. First were the mining firms. During the better part of the nineteenth
century, copper, silver, and coal mines were owned and operated by Chileans
or foreign transplants. As Chile's exports of these commodities intensified over
the nineteenth century, many self-made mining barons became fabulously
wealthy and either married into the families who owned large haciendas or

---

[2] For an in-depth treatment of how labor-dependent agriculture impacts democratic development,
see Albertus (2017).

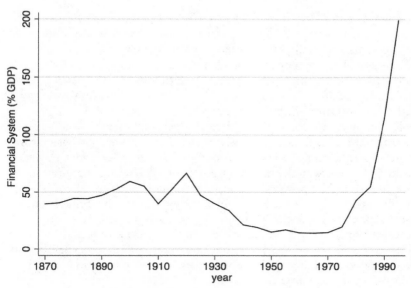

FIGURE 7.1. History of Chile's financial system.

Notes: The financial system is the sum of the market value in 1995 Chilean pesos (percent of GDP) of the Chilean stock market, mortgages, domestic government bonds, and bank deposits.

Source: Braun et al. (2000).

bought large tracts of land themselves. Therefore, there grew to be considerable overlap between large landowners and mining interests (Rueschemeyer, Stephens, and Stephens 1992, 176). By the turn of the twentieth century, mining had become Chile's most important source of foreign exchange and the government's most important source of public revenues (Marfán 1984, 91).

Two other groups also became ascendant over time. Merchants emigrated to Chile from European countries and, for the most part, settled on the coast (primarily in Valparaíso) and helped broker long-distance trade. In addition, bankers accrued mass fortunes by financing the landowners, miners, and merchants and eventually broadened their allocation of capital to a burgeoning middle class by bankrolling a fledgling mortgage market. Figure 7.1 reveals that by 1900 the financial system was more than 50 percent of GDP. Similar to the owners of mines, these financiers entered the ranks of the established aristocracy via kinship ties or the ownership of haciendas. Eventually there was considerable overlap between bankers, landowners, and mining interests (Rueschmeyer, Stephens, and Stephens 1992, 182).

While on the surface political conflict was muted, institutionalized, and conducted in a seemingly plural fashion through contestation in the Chilean parliament, the political system was rigged to benefit the landowning, mining, and bank-owning elite. They dominated the Chilean parliament and extracted policies that greatly benefited them at the expense of consumers and wage laborers. This was especially true in terms of monetary and exchange rate policies. Frequent currency devaluations benefited exporters, who could price their commodities more competitively in international markets yet pay their employees in depreciated Chilean pesos. These employees were also hurt by price inflation due to the rising cost of imports.

Large landowners coordinated to defend their power and landholdings through organizations such as the powerful Sociedad Nacional de Agricultura. This organization helped the oligarchy propel several presidents into power. It persisted until the 1960s with the stated intent of "defending the interests of agriculture against public powers and popular opinion."

The result was, for lack of a better term, a republican oligarchy. McBride (1936) provides a stark picture of Chile in the early twentieth century: "A twentieth-century people still preserving a feudal society; a republic based on the equality of man, yet with a blueblood aristocracy and a servile class as distinctly separated as in any of the monarchies of the Old World" (14). This entrenched political economic order would soon end, however – and quite abruptly.

CHILE'S EXPERIMENT WITH POPULAR DEMOCRACY

According to the coding rules we discuss in Chapters 3 and 5, Chile's popular democratic experiment lasted from 1963 to 1973. In 1963, an autocratic constitution, originally promulgated in 1925 and inherited in 1934 by a newly minted democracy from the previous dictatorship, was amended. The consequences were immediate and consequential. That year, the government was given broad powers to expropriate land. Other amendments that further "popularized" Chilean democracy followed in 1967, when the constitution sanctioned the nationalization of mines, and in 1970, when the franchise was extended to illiterates.

However, in some ways, it might be more accurate to argue that, despite the fact that the Chilean democracy inherited a constitution from an autocracy in 1934, the country's popular democracy actually began in 1934, not 1963. The military regime that assumed political control in 1924 after an unprecedented coup explicitly sought to strengthen the Chilean presidency and usher in democracy.

On paper, Chile's republican oligarchy was a parliamentary regime before that coup. While this was made official in 1891, Chilean presidents had lost their power gradually over decades, which came to a head in 1890, when a civil war broke out between the navy, which sided with the congress, and the army, which sided with the president, over the executive's budgeting authority. While the navy prevailed in that conflict, the army had the last laugh. It was behind the 1924 coup and 1925 constitution and expressly intended to replace the semiparliamentary system of government to end the gridlock and passivity that had plunged the nation into repeated crises.

In the process, the coup toppled a regime in which oligarchic parties monopolized the congress. Under the previous system, legislators could dismiss individual cabinet members and exercise supremacy over the executive branch. A small group of rich families had brutally repressed labor movements and blocked any group other than the traditional aristocracy from having its voice heard (Drake 2009, 141). Meanwhile, the political parties exercising power in the Chilean Congress before 1925 engaged in corruption and clientelism and relied on the armed forces to enforce their political will. Electoral fraud was the norm.

The 1925 constitution promulgated by the army replaced the oligarchic republican regime that explicitly benefited the incumbent economic elite. It not only sought to make the executive stronger than the congress; it also made the government more accountable to the people, shifting the balance of power toward citizens. While the president was directly elected, national plebiscites could be called to adjudicate disputes between the executive and parliament over constitutional amendments. Furthermore, the constitution was drafted with the help of a consultative assembly composed of citizens and public servants.

Why did the military feel compelled to intervene to change a political equilibrium that benefited the oligarchy? They sought to address festering economic and social problems aggravated by the fact that there was extreme turnover in the cabinet and political instability in general fomented by the republican oligarchy (see Drake 2009, 140). The military justified the new constitution and its content on the grounds that it better represented popular sectors and the country's youth and would help the government make progress on important social problems, which had been allowed to fester under the ostensibly parliamentary regime.

Faundez (1997) states it eloquently when he writes,

In the 1920s, the objective of both President Arturo Alessandri Palma (1920–25) and General Ibáñez (1927–31) was to design an institutional framework to channel the new social forces that, though apparent in society, did not as yet have adequate political representation. The legislative package that Alessandri could not persuade the Congress to approve and that Ibáñez – relying on the threat of military intervention succeeded in getting through in a matter of hours – was meant to resolve urgent social issues that the Congress had shown little or no interest in resolving. It is interesting that, despite their ideological differences, both Alessandri and Ibáñez regarded the restoration of presidentialism as indispensable to the resolution of the political and economic crisis. (305)

We can conceptualize the 1925 constitution and subsequent transition to a presidential democracy as the military junta's attempt to throw the incumbent economic elite – domestic owners of mines, landed aristocrats, and their financiers – under the bus. As we explored in earlier chapters, a betrayal of this sort is a lingering danger to economic elites who reluctantly hitch their wagons to political patrons under autocracy. These patrons are potentially capricious and, as we outlined in the previous chapter when discussing nineteenth-century Sweden, can always threaten to switch their loyalties to an ascendant economic elite.

As the Chilean political economy fundamentally changed in the early and middle decades of the twentieth century, the country's oligarchic past was coming to a close. A new set of economic elites was ascendant – centered on manufacturing finished products for a domestic market and incorporating important groups from the urbanized labor force. While the consolidation of this new coalition was the by-product of concerted government action, its advent was rooted in an "exogenous shock" of sorts: World War I.

In the case of Chile, the Great War had created a cleavage between politicians and established economic elites that only widened in the 1920s. During the war, Chileans had been unable to import the goods from Europe and the United States that they had grown accustomed to consuming. Yet Chilean exports, including nitrates, copper, and wheat, were in record demand as the war's belligerents stepped up their purchases of these commodities to fuel their war efforts. This created the possibility for homegrown Chilean manufacturers, who had already been on the rise since the late nineteenth century, to grab an increasing slice of market share on the back of domestic consumers' increased purchasing power.[3] Amazingly, during the conflict's four years, Chilean manufacturing increased by more than 50 percent (Palma 1984, 64).

This changing of the guard was consolidated after the end of hostilities. The rise of synthetic nitrates at the tail end of World War I, which greatly accelerated after the Great War, considerably weakened Chilean nitrate producers. Similarly, a sharp reduction in the international demand for Chilean wheat after the end of hostilities knocked large landholders on their heels. Figure 7.2 showcases the spectacular increase in the country's manufacturing sector during the 1920s.

As they became more sophisticated and grew wealthier, industrialists lobbied government officials for strategic protectionism and for cheaper credit. Chilean politicians were increasingly receptive to a new and quickly rising coalition of domestic manufacturers and wage laborers. These actors were able to easily organize in urban areas – especially in Santiago, the capital, and Valparaíso, the country's most important port and an important commercial center – and lobby bureaucrats and elected representatives to obtain favorable policies more directly and with greater haste. This included the introduction of an income and corporate tax in 1923, a slew of laws that improved collective bargaining and working conditions, and generous social insurance funds. It helped that the Chilean organized labor movement was particularly precocious

---

[3] The Chilean government had adopted a few protective tariffs in the late nineteenth century and also nurtured a domestic steel industry (see Hurtado 1984, 43).

FIGURE 7.2. The rise and fall of Chilean manufacturing.
Source: Astorga, Bergés, and FitzGerald (2011).

by Latin American standards. It cut its teeth in copper, nitrate, and coal mines during the late nineteenth century and had affiliated with international anarchist and socialist patrons in the early twentieth century (Palma 1984, 62–63).

For their part, political incumbents could benefit from the stream of rents associated with protectionist policies and directed credit to industry. This was either in the form of greater tax revenues or kickbacks and lucrative positions on the board of directors of industrial companies or the union halls of newly empowered labor syndicates. They could also tax a gaggle of new firms serving the domestic market.

The Great Depression Cements a New Coalition

While World War I helped give birth to a fledgling coalition between nascent manufacturers and urban laborers, the Great Depression consolidated this unlikely marriage, to the chagrin of incumbent economic elites. Chile was hit extremely hard by the economic downturn. In terms of lost investment, exports, and economic growth, the Chilean economy was the hardest hit in the entire world – and it did not fully recover until the early 1980s.

Rapid urbanization, which coincided with the Great Depression, further weakened traditional oligarchs and strengthened the hand of nascent industrialists. Yearly growth in agricultural demand was nearly double that of growth in agricultural output for the 1930–1964 period (Kay 2002, 466). After the

1930s, the agricultural trade balance became increasingly negative, making Chile a net importer. The contribution of agriculture to GDP declined from 15 percent in 1930 to 10 percent in 1964, and out-migration from the agricultural sector drove down wages in other sectors of the economy and led to agricultural labor force comprising only 20 percent of the total labor force in 1964, down from 35 percent in 1930 (466).

Explicit government policies hastened the changing of the guard. In a bid to counteract the severe economic contraction and deflation ushered in by the Great Depression, Chile's government turned to increasingly muscular policies. While at first Chilean authorities attempted to address the depression in an orthodox manner, by remaining on the Gold Standard and turning to fiscal austerity despite crippling deflation and unemployment, the government eventually succumbed to mounting social pressures and experimented with heterodox measures. This included abandoning the Gold Standard, adopting stringent currency controls, and indulging in aggressive monetary and fiscal stimulus. Monetary policy was considerably loosened and budget deficit spending exploded (Palma 1984, 78). Chile also defaulted on its foreign debt and adopted capital controls. A currency devaluation of more than 70 percent acted as a protective shield for Chile's homegrown manufacturers.

These policies further weakened erstwhile oligarchs who had made their fortunes in the mining and agricultural sector, as well as banks that helped finance these firms. Figure 7.1 reveals the strong reversal in the financial sector's economic importance; by 1950, it had contracted by more than half.

In the aftermath of the Great Depression, successive Chilean governments sought to accelerate import-substituting industrialization (ISI; see Bulmer-Thomas 2003). This included adopting astronomically high tariffs on competing imports across most finished goods and subsidies for the inputs associated with industrial production through a cascading tariff structure and preferential import exchange rates for industrial raw materials, fuels, and intermediate goods. Complementary incentives encouraged ever heavier manufacturing applications. This included using the Instituto de Crédito Industrial, founded in 1928, as a piggy bank to direct credit to favored industrial projects with loans that carried negative real interest rates at the expense of savers who were on the losing end of this trade (Diaz Alejandro 1985, 7).

The economic rationale given by government officials for protectionist policies was Keynesian; however, the political logic that drove these policies was rooted in the ascendancy of the industrial-wage laborer coalition outlined previously. While it is true that the export market for Chilean copper and agricultural commodities had collapsed during the Great Depression, and the state seemed like the natural candidate to cultivate internal demand as a last resort, the government's increased involvement in the supply side of economy through protectionism and overt credit direction was deepened beyond any recognizable attempt to jumpstart a Keynesian multiplier.

During the Radical era, in which three presidents from this party held power in succession between 1938 and 1951, ISI became politically institutionalized. Successive Chilean governments erected a baroque maze of bureaucracies dedicated to tweaking tariffs and dialing up import quotas and licenses; managing multiple exchange rates; setting wages, prices, and interest rates; managing monopsonies for "strategic" imports, and doling out cheap credit to heavy industry at a frenetic pace. Increasingly, unprofitable firms were propped up through protectionism and direct subsidies. As Figure 7.2 makes clear, this strategy was quite successful: by the 1950s, Chile was a thoroughly industrialized country and, not coincidentally, trade openness declined drastically between 1930 and 1980 (Braun et al. 2000, 7).

Many authors have described this political-economic equilibrium as one rooted primarily in the distribution of benefits to core groups. This is consistent with our theoretical framework, in that popular democracy was enshrined to benefit a nascent coalition of political incumbents allied with rising economic elites who were at loggerheads with, and sought to destroy, the previous generation of economic elites. For example, Hurtado (1984) claims that the state essentially took over – or at least directed – productive functions to benefit and protect its urban constituents (59).

The rising economic elites and key segments of the masses made out like bandits. Despite the elevated prices they faced for domestically made goods, Chilean consumers benefited from price controls and subsidies. Public-sector employees benefited from good pay and benefits. Organized labor likewise benefited from generous compensation and guaranteed jobs. New businesses in manufacturing, construction, and services flourished, often on the back of fiscal incentives. Those at the bottom of the ladder benefited from generous welfare spending on education, housing, and health care. Finally, urban dwellers benefited from the cheap food bankrolled by the suppression of rural wages engendered by the repressive control landlords exercised over peasants, at least until 1958 (Przeworski 1991, 83; Baland and Robinson 2008).

How Popular Was Chile's Democracy before the 1960s?

The cleavage between incumbent political elites and landowners was nascent rather than complete in 1925 and took years to really reach fruition. Large landowners suffocated political change through high-level capture and a dense web of valuable political alliances. It is not surprising, therefore, that the 1925 constitution took up the land issue modestly, stipulating that property ownership had to be consistent with "the need to maintain and improve social order" (Lapp 2004, 66). Article 10 provided that "the state will promote the convenient division of land into private property."

At the same time, however, it declared the "inviolability of all property," interpreted to mean that expropriated land had to be paid for in cash at the market value at sale, for which the government had few resources (Thiesenhusen 1995, 96). The amount of compensation had to be determined by the courts and was to be paid before the state could obtain possession of the property (Thome 1989, 193). In late 1925, the Dirección General de Tierras, Colonización e Inmigración was created by Decree Law 601 to give definitive title to colonizers who had obtained possession of their land before January 1, 1921 (Garrido 1988, 54). The Caja de Colonización Agrícola (CCA) was created by Law 4496 in 1928, charged with forming colonies intended to organize and intensify production, providing loans to rural smallholders, subdividing latifundios in the central zone to found new colonies, and amending property titles in the southern part of the country (53).

The CCA began acquiring and distributing lands in 1929 (Garrido 1988). However, it purchased few large properties and often delivered them to civil servants and soldiers rather than peasants (Thiensenhusen 1995, 96). Until 1935, the CCA primarily parceled plots to colonists on state-owned land, a slow process that only placed about 100 colonists per year (Garrido 1988, 54). Most of the properties purchased by the CCA were acquired by the end of 1939, at which point negotiating the price of land with landowners started to become more difficult for financial reasons (54). There were only eight properties expropriated prior to 1958 (Garrido 1988).

Moreover, the 1925 constitution was accepted by landlords, albeit begrudgingly, after they were granted control over peasants' votes, which guaranteed that their economic interests would be overrepresented in congress (Przeworski 1991, 82–83; Baland and Robinson 2008). Similarly, the same year it promulgated the constitution, the dictatorship that replaced Chile's parliamentary system adopted a draconian labor code that centralized labor unions under government tutelage.

Indeed, it was only a series of reforms that began in the mid-1950s that truly liberalized Chilean politics in new and consequential ways. These included more liberal electoral rules. The franchise was extended to women in 1948. The ballot was made secret in 1958, which meant that landlords could no longer control the peasant vote; therefore, they lost considerable political representation in the Chilean Congress (see Baland and Robinson 2008). These reforms also included the empowering of trade unions and the legalization of rural trade unions in 1967, which opened the door to radicalization. Indeed, many of the country's peasants voted for leftist candidate Salvador Allende in his first candidacy (Thiesenhusen 1995, 95). This transformed the land issue into a major political problem as urban political parties learned that the mass rural electorate could aid them in winning elections if they could be mobilized.

Therefore, while we have argued that there are good reasons why it might be more accurate to consider Chile as a popular democracy starting in 1934, albeit one imposed from above, this discussion suggests that there are also reasons to consider the onset of popular democracy as belated. More generally, while in this book we prefer to defer to our formal coding rules in order to prevent post hoc rationalizations from influencing our descriptive statistics and quantitative analyses, we acknowledge that some of these coding decisions are noisy approximations of the actual political equilibria; in Chile between 1934 and 1963, one could argue that this is perhaps the case. While there are certainly grounds to debate when exactly popular democracy starts in Chile, there is no doubt that by the 1960s, Chile was a quintessentially popular democracy.

The March to Salvador Allende

The Jorge Allesandri administration (1958–1963) did not start its life as a paragon of popular democracy. Continued monetary and fiscal stimulus, coupled with financial repression and price controls, stoked Chilean inflation to alarming levels (Hirschman 1963). While high levels of inflation were at first masked and protracted by equally high levels of external debt (Grunwald 1970, 842), the situation soon became unsustainable. To fight inflation, Allesandri adopted several stabilization and austerity measures aimed at constraining monetary policy and reducing fiscal deficits. At first, this included a partial wage freeze, restrictions on directed credit, a transition to uniform exchange rates, budget cuts, and tax increases (Baer 1967, 15).

Alessandri's anti-inflationary policies were met with significant opposition. Organized labor mounted several nationwide strikes in response (see Braun et al. 2000, 249). These had considerable success in arresting Alessandri's austerity measures. For example, although Alessandri tried repeatedly to rescind the automatic wage adjustment mechanisms that had been in place since the era of the Radical Party's hegemony (1938–1951), he ultimately failed. Moreover, his administration faced a severe balance of payments crisis in the early 1960s that culminated in a massive currency devaluation in 1962 – further stimulating inflation (see Ffrench-Davis 2002). Toward the end of his term, Alessandri revived price controls and import restrictions and rescinded credit restrictions (Furnish 1971, 482–483).

Indeed, Alessandri, who was nominally a conservative, did not really change the system's basic distributional characteristics. He retained the tax structure's progressivity. He also introduced a land reform bill that was passed in 1962. Law 15020 introduced a clause providing for the "social responsibility" of property ownership and allowed for expropriation of unproductive land.[4]

Each of Alessandri's successors then cleanly split with the old oligarchy. First, in 1964, Eduardo Frei brought the Christian Democrats to power for the first time on a progressive platform known as "Revolution in Liberty." His agenda espoused social justice, and he moved swiftly to partially nationalize

---

[4] The law, however, was complex and full of loopholes, and in cases of expropriation, it did not permit for deferred compensation, or at valuations other than determined by the market and enforced by courts.

the copper industry upon taking power. In 1965, Frei submitted legislation to the congress to replace Law 15020. While congress debated the legislation, Frei began reform on land purchased from private landholders under Law 15020. From November 1964 to July 1967, the land reform agency CORA acquired 478 large farms for a total of more than one million acres (Thome 1989, 193). Many of these were acquired through negotiated settlements of payment in installments over ten years.

Congress subsequently passed a new land reform law (Law 16640) in 1967. Law 16640 allowed CORA to transform public property for land reform purposes and to acquire private land for redistribution to peasants. Expropriation of private property was legalized for reasons of "large farm size [eighty basic irrigated hectares], deficient land use, abandonment, unauthorized subdivision of farms (to evade the large-farm provisions of Law No. 16,640), corporate land ownership, lack of compliance with the liberalized labor laws (passed just before the agrarian reforms), and public infrastructural use" (Thiesenhusen 1995, 97). CORA was also empowered to purchase property from willing sellers. However, voluntary transfers were categorized as "expropriations" in order to subject them to lower compensation rates according to the law (Thome 1989, 194).[5] About 3.5 million hectares of land, or 13 percent of the farmland in Chile, were brought into the reform sector under Frei (Thiesenhusen 1995, 98).

Salvador Allende: The Apogee of Popular Rule

In 1970, Salvador Allende won the presidency on his fourth try with a small plurality (he garnered only 37 percent of the vote) at the head of a so-called Popular Unity coalition composed of communists and socialists. Figure 7.3, which graphs Chilean taxes as a percent of GDP since its independence in 1810, suggests that Allende was the most populist leader in Chile's history. Indeed, after running on an explicitly socialist platform and a pledge to "eliminate the hacienda," Allende immediately nationalized the copper industry through a constitutional amendment, expropriating the Anaconda and Kennecott mines without compensating their North American owners. He also dramatically deepened the country's land reform, expropriating more than five million hectares of land by vigorously applying Frei's land reform law and enforcing landholding ceilings. Between Frei and Allende, 43 percent of Chile's agricultural land was expropriated or purchased from private landowners (Jarvis 1989, 243). Allende also nationalized the country's banks, as well as more than 150

---

[5] Compensation to landlords expropriated due to excess landholdings was set at 10 percent of payment in cash and 90 percent in twenty-five-year bonds, with less in cash for abandoned or poorly used properties (Thiesehusen 1995, 98). Property valuations were made based on the current appraisal of the land for tax purposes plus the market value of improvements (98). However, inflation dramatically eroded the value of bonds given to expropriated landowners.

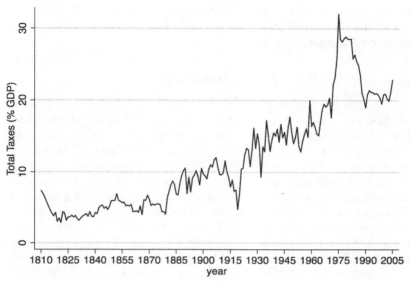

FIGURE 7.3. Historical trajectory of Chilean taxation.

Notes: This excludes government grants and revenues from mining companies. To standardize the values between 1810 and 1995 and 1996 and 2005, we discounted the latter values by a trivial amount to reflect differences in coding across sources.

Sources: Astorga, Bergés, and FitzGerald (2011); Albertus and Menaldo (2014a).

firms, including more than 50 percent of Chile's largest companies (Larraín, and Meller 1991, 188–189).

The serial violation of property rights represented by these nationalizations was then complemented by subtler ones. Wage laborers and peasants took over several privately owned factories and farms, triggering social unrest. Indeed, Allende leveraged the farm occupations to apply Article 171 of the 1967 labor law, which allowed the government to acquire private lands in the event of labor disputes.

On the macroeconomic front, Allende unleashed the printing presses like no Chilean president before him. He did this to boost wages and salaries. Price controls were also instituted. Unsurprisingly, the average inflation rate during his tenure was 152 percent; it reached a high of 362 percent in 1973.

The result was disastrous. Although in the short run these policies boosted demand and therefore economic growth, eventually they triggered an economic implosion. Real wages fell precipitously due to inflation, and economic growth collapsed.

Chile's economic catastrophe galvanized domestic support for a coup by Chile's upper and middle classes, the military, and the Nixon administration. With the help of the CIA, Allende was overthrown by the military on

September 11, 1973. That same day, a military junta composed of the heads of the armed forces, air force, navy, and national police force took over, with General Augusto Pinochet at the helm.

Making Sense of Chile's Era of Popular Democracy

With the exception of Allende, the Chilean executives who governed under popular democracy shared more in common than what set them apart. Although some were nominally on the left and others in the center or on the right, they abided by a similar set of policies that restrained – but did not destroy – the market and sought to fashion a more egalitarian society, albeit one constructed through economic distortions that created some clear losers.

A few accomplishments stand out. Educational opportunity and attainment improved steadily over several decades. By 1970, spending on education had reached more than 8 percent of GDP (Pribble, Huber, and Stephens 2009) and illiteracy had decreased from 40.7 percent in 1940 to 12.6 percent in 1970 (Braun et al. 2000, 244). Also notable is the fact that spending on health exceeded 4 percent of GDP by the end of Allende's term (Huber and Stephens 2012). Therefore, inequality decreased drastically; by 1975, the top fifth quintile of the income distribution had 54 percent of total income (Braun et al. 2000, 244) and the Gini coefficient for income inequality was in the low forties (see Figure 7.4), one of the lowest numbers in Latin America.

CHILE UNDER THE IRON FIST OF PINOCHET

Upon seizing power in 1973, the military junta led by General Augusto Pinochet declared a state of emergency and restricted civil liberties. It banned political parties and turned to massive repression and the chronic violation of human rights, including mass murders and disappearances. The regime also engaged in draconian censorship of speech and the airwaves and eventually controlled the media.

Heretofore, there has been little argument about the Pinochet dictatorship's economic policies. They have been widely considered as the instantiation of neoliberal orthodoxy, the living embodiment of the Chicago School of Economics (see, e.g., Huneeus 2000). We strongly demur from this view. While the military junta's most immediate goal upon coming to power was to restore the Chilean economy to health, and this indeed called on orthodox stabilization measures and deregulation, Pinochet also pursued policies that systematically destroyed the coalition that had been assembled and consolidated under popular democracy. He then proceeded to help his economic allies succeed, allowing his regime to lean on a new political support group that transformed the government's revenue base. In short, Pinochet executed a political playbook and used the rhetoric of neoliberalism as a legitimizing motif but ignored neoliberal prescriptions when convenient.

Pinochet set upon a concerted deindustrialization effort dedicated to weakening the coddled manufacturers and urban wage earners that had supported Chilean presidents since the 1930s (Schamis 1999; Valenzuela and Valenzuela 1986). During Pinochet's first year in power, tariffs on trade were drastically reduced and tariff dispersion was eliminated: tariffs were set at a uniform rate of 10 percent. The regime also abolished nontariff barriers. These policies succeeded in making manufacturing much costlier and in reorienting the country toward commodity exports. According to Schamis (1999),

The level of real protection in the manufacturing sector plummeted and had unequivocal distributional consequences. Exports expanded in copper and non-copper mining, fish and sea products, forestry and wood products, and agriculture. Imports, however, increased faster than exports, especially in the consumer durable, food, intermediate, and capital goods sectors, in that order. The manufacturing sector thus experienced considerable deindustrialization, particularly in traditional import-substituting activities. (247)

To put Pinochet's deindustrialization policies in perspective, consider two patterns. First, the drastic fall in manufacturing value added depicted by Figure 7.2. Second, the spectacular rise in income earned by copper exports, which became the government's chief source of revenue.

By weakening organized labor, the second leg of the coalition that had supported the elected governments under popular democracy, the regime's labor-market reforms reinforced deindustrialization. Pinochet deregulated the Chilean labor market in 1979 through a labor law that allowed for at-will firing, proscribed collective bargaining beyond the firm level, and reduced severance payments while allowing firms to replace workers on strike with scabs (Murillo 2002, 477). According to Wacziarg and Wallack (2004), Pinochet's liberalization of the labor market was consolidated by macroeconomic policies that included the elimination of the fiscal deficit and the elimination of price and interest rate controls.

After destroying the economic elites who were allied to political incumbents during Chile's popular democracy, Pinochet replaced them with a new group of economic elites. The regime accomplished this in several steps. First, Pinochet privatized the economy to benefit a few handpicked insiders. Second, he reconstituted a private banking sector that became a pillar of Chile's new, ostensibly neoliberal, globally oriented economy. This swashbuckling financial sector was generously subsidized by the country's taxpayers, however. Third, the regime revived the country's beleaguered landed elite. This further served to prop up export-oriented commodity sectors rooted in copper mining, timber, fishing, and fruits and vegetables.

The regime's privatization program was instrumental to creating a new set of economic elites. In 1973, the state owned and operated 594 companies; by 1989, this was down to only 43. Public employment was cut by more than 35 percent between 1974 and 1983 (Murillo 2002, 476). The sectors of the economy that were privatized included utilities such as telecommunications and electricity, as well as the country's banks. The privatization process was designed to create big conglomerates, so-called *grupos económicos*, which combined newly privatized banks with newly privatized nonfinancial firms.

The individuals who headed and ran these conglomerates – who controlled the lion's share of stock and sat on the boards of directors of newly privatized companies – were essentially hand-picked and groomed by the regime. They were either erstwhile business and bank owners who had wormed their way into the Pinochet administration or former government officials, including high-ranking military officers who had recently exited the regime.

Consider the newly privatized nitrate company, Soquimich. Julio Ponce-Leroux, Pinochet's son-in-law, was added to the board of directors, along with the former budget director, Juan Carlos Mendez, and the former mining minister, Enrique Valenzuela. Meanwhile, the former finance minister, Sergio De Castro, was appointed as its president (see Schamis 1999, 249).

Or consider the examples given by Murillo (2002):

The head of the Enersis group, José Yuraszeck, had been in the government planning agency and was then appointed as CEO of Chilectra before its privatization. The head of Gener, Bruno Phillipi, had led the National Energy Commission in charge of electricity privatization ... Other former government officials also joined the boards of these companies: former minister José Piñeira became the president of Chilectra, former minister Hernán Errázuriz was on the board of Enersis, and former minister Eduardo Undurraga was on the board of Entel. (482n74)

Moreover, the way in which publicly owned firms were privatized hugely advantaged Chile's new economic elites. According to Schamis (1999):

Purchases were effected with a down payment provided by a direct loan from the state agency CORFO (Chilean Development Corporation) at a preferential interest rate and guaranteed by the very assets privatized. According to some calculations, the subsidy involved in these loans amounted to 30 percent of the net worth of the firms divested. Receipts from privatization equaled $543 million, and 65 percent of those assets were purchased by eight economic conglomerates. By 1979 the four most politically involved of these conglomerates–Cruzat-Larraín, Vial, Matte, and Edwards–owned assets equivalent to 20 percent of GDP, including the largest private banks. In fact, the two largest banks (Banco de Santiago and Banco de Chile), owned by the Cruzat-Larraín and Vial groups, respectively, controlled 42 percent of credit. (247)

Similarly, according to Murillo (2002), "The subsidy implicit in the privatization of electricity distribution [was] 32 percent for Chilmetro (Enersis), 25 percent for Chilquinta, and 22 percent for Gener…for the sale of Endesa subsidies [ranged] from 7 to 20 percent for public employees, military, small investors, and company employees" (483n75).

The bank privatization process was the linchpin of Pinochet's privatization program. Chile's banks were auctioned off by the regime to the *grupos económicos* in a patently illiberal fashion, with little attention paid to optimizing the bidding process and outsized attention paid to subsidizing the purchases made by their economic allies. The *grupos* who sought to buy a state-owned bank only had to put down 20 percent toward the purchase price and were allowed to purchase it with loans made from the banks themselves at a very low interest rate; the collateral backing these loans were the shares in the banks themselves (Barandiarán and Hernández 1999; Calomiris and Haber 2014). Once the banks were bought by fledgling conglomerates at cheap prices, the conglomerates then borrowed from their newly purchased banks to make down payments on other nonbank businesses that were up for sale (Andrews 2005, 12).

This phenomenon led to a huge concentration of wealth in the hands of a few empresarios and families. According to Diaz-Alejandro (1985), "The two largest business groups in Chile by late 1982 controlled the principal insurance companies, mutual funds, brokerage houses, the largest private company pension funds and the two largest private commercial banks...By late 1982 many banks had lent one quarter or more of their resources to affiliates" (14) The *grupos económicos* were not only large and few in number; they were endowed with considerable market power, which they then exploited to extract rents from consumers. For example, "the Enersis-Endesa holding acquired property rights over 80 percent of usable water streams, including control of generation, transmission, and distribution grids" (Schamis 1999, 249).

The creation of a concentrated market where a few players could exercise market power was most prevalent in the banking sector itself. The regime's financial liberalization included the reduction of capital controls, the relaxation of interest rate controls, the elimination of directed credit to domestic industries, and fixing the exchange rate to the US dollar (in 1979). Yet certain loopholes in Chile's bank liberalization process created a segmented credit market and allowed the *grupos* to enjoy sizable rents (see Menaldo and Yoo 2015). This was the by-product of the banks being barred from taking on exchange-rate risk when they borrowed abroad – instead, their final domestic borrowers had to assume that risk. This created an incentive for arbitrage whereby the larger banks that could borrow cheaply from abroad then lent out the money in domestic currency with large spreads.[6] Alternatively, these banks engaged in related lending: they loaned money out on favorable terms to other firms within their respective conglomerates (Schamis 1999, 247).[7]

The regime's privatization scheme and monetary and financial policies encouraged risky lending at high volumes, which was abetted by financial deregulation. Chilean citizens were allowed access to unlimited amounts of foreign exchange, and restrictions on foreign borrowing were lifted. Imprudent lending practices were incentivized by the fact that the Pinochet government had eliminated interest-rate and credit-allocation controls and drastically

---

[6] This paragraph draws closely on Schamis (1999, 246).

[7] We should note, however, that foreign investors were granted unhampered, nondiscriminatory access to the Chilean banking sector (Schamis 1999, 246).

reduced reserve requirements – they reached less than 10 percent of deposits by 1980 (Diaz-Alejandro 1985, 8). This stoked unprecedented growth in the credit market: private-sector debt almost doubled between 1980 and 1982 (see Menaldo and Yoo 2015). By 1982, private firms owed more than public-sector firms (Diaz-Alejandro 1985, 13).

These policies also set the stage for a financial implosion. In 1981, international interest rates increased on the heels of the Federal Reserve's attempts to end stagflation in the United States. This meant that Chile's current account deficit, which had ballooned due to the fact that capital had poured into the country to arbitrage the spread between higher interest rates there versus the United States, became unsustainable. In turn, this precipitated the collapse of the Pinochet regime's fixed nominal exchange rate in 1982, which ushered in a sizable currency devaluation in light of serious exchange-rate overvaluation.

This proved devastating, especially considering the runaway expansion of credit outlined previously. The majority of Chile's private debt was denominated in (very expensive) dollars, which triggered a wave of defaults: "Nonperforming assets of Chile's banks rose from 11 percent of their capital and reserves at the end of 1980, to 22 percent at the end of 1981, to 47 percent at the end of 1982, and to 113 percent in May 1983" (Diaz-Alejandro 1985, 11).

It is important to note, however, that this crisis could have been averted if a prudential regulatory structure had been put in place by the Pinochet regime before financial deregulation. Such a structure could have been aimed to curb currency and credit risk, as well as insider lending. It would also have been fully compatible with neoliberal precepts. Alas, however, this would have come at the expense of the hefty profits that served to line the pockets of Pinochet's economic allies.

Unsurprisingly, the government's response to the financial crisis was as friendly to insider elites as it had been when it set up the post-Allende banking system. After Chile's devaluation, the big banks were unable to access international credit markets. The central bank then stepped in by providing ample liquidity and purchasing the private banks' nonperforming loans (Andrews 2005, 12). While three banks were ultimately closed down – depositors lost 30 percent of their deposits in those banks (Diaz-Alejandro 1985, 12) – and two banks came under the direct supervision of the state, five were bailed out by the Pinochet regime. This meant that the government had dominion over 67 percent of Chile's deposits, 57 percent of accumulated pension funds, and 70 percent of the firms that were previously privatized by Pinochet (Schamis 1999, 248).

As in most banking crises, moral hazard played a role. In 1983, the Chilean government assumed the entire foreign currency–denominated debt of the country's private banks – in essence, socializing their huge losses. This response was completely expected by both the foreign lenders and the domestic depositors who had fed the country's credit boom: in 1977, Pinochet had bailed out a large private bank (Osorno) that had gotten in trouble due to risky insider lending – despite vehement forewarnings that it would allow banks to fail, as per neoliberal ideology – setting a perverse precedent for other recently privatized banks (Diaz-Alejandro 1985, 8).

In the aftermath of the crisis, financial development cratered, and the government reprivatized the banking system after nursing it back to health to the tune of billions of dollars. After a sharp devaluation of the peso, the abandonment of the dollar peg, and a successful rescheduling of the external debt, the Pinochet regime set about returning the banking sector to its booming post-Allende growth path. The regime privatized the pension system and created individual savings and investment accounts. Millions of citizens were incentivized to increase their use of Chilean banks and money market funds and to purchase shares of Chilean firms. Chile's credit collection agencies were strengthened to allow them to better track and record borrowers' credit histories, making it cheaper for them to loan money to a greater share of the population.

The facts speak for themselves. The size of the banking sector as measured by commercial bank deposits as a percentage of GDP reached a high of 27 percent in 1989. Figure 7.1 – which along with bank deposits also includes the size of the stock market, mortgages, and public bonds – reveals the impressive size that Chile's financial system achieved during the Pinochet regime.

The final prong of Pinochet's political-economic strategy was reviving the landed elite who were expropriated under Frei and Allende during popular democracy. Upon coming to power, Pinochet annulled the land reform law and abolished CORA, creating the Office to Normalize Agriculture (ODENA) in its place. He also decreed a series of laws to guarantee tenure security on private farms – first those less than forty basic irrigated hectares in size and then those between forty and eighty basic irrigated hectares in size. A total of 1,649 farms were wholly returned to their original owners, and another 2,174 were partially restored (Thiesenhusen 1995, 109). By 1979, roughly 30 percent of the total land expropriated from 1965 to Allende's final days in 1973 had been returned to its former owners, a third was given to rural workers who could make the best case that they had lived and worked on the farm prior to expropriation and had not participated in land invasions, and the remainder was auctioned off, sold to cooperatives, or retained in the public sector for forestation projects (Lapp 2004, 81; Jarvis 1989, 245).

The cessation of the program was a boon to remaining middle-class landowners as peasants were progressively expelled from the agricultural economy.[8] The Pinochet government provided almost no technical aid or credit to the beneficiaries of land reform during the transition stage or

---

[8] We do note, however, that peasant land reform beneficiaries under Frei and Allende who received parcels of farmland under the military government only paid roughly 50 percent of its market value and financed the purchase with thirty-year loans (Thiesenhusen 1995, 110). The military had assigned most of the reform sector land by the end of 1976, with the majority taking place in 1975 and 1976 (Garrido 1988, 184). Therefore, landholding was considerably more equal in 1976, and even in 1986, than it had been in 1965 (Jarvis 1989, 253–257). Jarvis (1989), writes,

through the 1980s (Jarvis 1989, 247). As a result, many peasants faced capital shortages compounded by the necessity of selling off machinery or livestock from the *asentamientos* on which they had worked to meet the government's demands to repay past production credits (247). The ultimate result was that many peasants who received land had to sell it, increasing land transactions in the 1970s and 1980s (Thiesenhusen 1995, 110). At the same time, reconstituted medium-sized and large farms were provided with cheap capital (Jarvis 1989, 248).

GAMING DEMOCRACY: CHILE'S 1980 CONSTITUTION

Pinochet and top regime officials sought to cement the new status quo by codifying a constitution in 1980. This new constitution was intended to announce, reinforce, and legitimize the military junta's political power and restore and consolidate their allies' economic positions. Over time, as the military and its allies sought to orchestrate a return to democracy, the 1980 constitution served as a means by which the political and economic elites could preserve their interests after the transition. This is because it created an institutional architecture that muzzled the regime's economic and political foes and empowered their allies. While the constitution has been heavily amended since democratization, the fact that it still stands and serves to protect the regime's allies might be the military junta's most successful legacy.

The process that led up to the 1980 constitution was peculiar, protracted, and rife with authoritarian features. The military junta first created a constitutional (study) commission to work on a new constitution; later this committee deputized subcommittees to specialize on different aspects of the constitution and sometimes requisitioned advice from outside experts and business leaders. Composed of law professors and other attorneys, it had a purely consultative role. It could advise General Pinochet and the other members of the junta, but its meetings were secretive and its role ultimately proved to be limited. Indeed, military leaders repeatedly injected their own ideas during the crafting of the constitution's first draft (Cea Egaña 2002, 77).

The second order of business was dismantling the 1925 constitution. This occurred in a piecemeal fashion. Three executive decrees partially derogated the document: while the military junta took control of the country's constitutional, executive, and legislative functions and therefore abolished the elected parliament, the judiciary continued, for the most part, to be regulated by the 1925 constitution.

In 1978, a draft of the new constitution was released by the constitutional commission after its 417th meeting. It was then revised by the State Council over a nearly two-year period. The State Council was another consultative

"The net effect of the reform was that some 50,000 new farms had been created; this left about half of Chile's agricultural land in the hands of small farmers and minifundistas" (253).

body whose members were appointed by Pinochet and included former Chilean presidents,[9] a former head of the Supreme Court, former heads of the armed forces and the national police, and former bureaucrats and academics, plus some token members of civil society, including from the business community and unions. In revising the document, the State Council sought a modicum of input from the public, albeit in a limited and secretive manner, and made its own recommendations. It completed its modifications in July 1980 after fifty-one sessions.

The final step was for the military junta itself to modify and approve the constitution, which they did alongside a working group composed of government ministers. They reviewed it in secret for a month before approving the final draft. The regime then put the constitution up for public approval through a plebiscite organized and run by the military and held on September 11, 1980 under a state of emergency, draconian censorship, and without an organized opposition to criticize it. After the new constitution was approved by 67 percent of the vote, it was promulgated in October 1980 and made operable in March 1981.

The immediate result was a mixed bag. On the one hand, the constitution introduced a series of checks and balances that worked to constrain Pinochet (Barros 2002). On the other hand, the 1980 constitution made the president's powers formidable: endowed with an eight-year term, the president had the ability to initiate and shape legislation across several domains. Besides the exclusive right to propose legislation of various sorts, the executive could propose new items up for congressional debate, set congressional priorities and deadlines, and make comments on legislative proposals, as well as veto them. The president could also call "extraordinary" sessions of congress, make changes to constitutional amendments proposed by the legislature, and call national plebiscites regarding amendments in which it had a disagreement with the parliament. The executive also had the power to dissolve the congress.

Finally, the constitution included a timetable for a return to elected government. Consequently, the constitution later served as a blueprint for the "restricted democracy" that ensued.

Many of its provisions were aimed at politically neutering the regime's enemies, especially the Far Left. Indeed, the constitutional commission created by Pinochet to study the elements of a new constitution declared in a memorandum (dated November 1973) that one of the fundamental goals of the new constitution should be to inoculate Chilean institutions against Marxism and the dangers it posed to political order and economic stability. It later declared, in a similar memo, that the new constitution should eschew social rights because these were impractical and polarizing (see Cea Egaña 2002, 90). Similarly, a declaration of "regime principles" issued by the Pinochet regime in March

---

[9] Salvador Allende, of course, was dead, and this did not apply to him; he committed suicide during the 1973 coup.

1974 rejected politics based on class strife and valorized liberalism (75–76). Finally, the constitution itself included a ban on extremist parties, especially those that championed class warfare.

In this vein, the 1980 constitution itself stipulated that private property rights were sacrosanct. The rhetoric used to justify these rights, which made allusions to classical liberalism and individual liberty, was rooted in "natural law"; the constitution stipulated that the state was ultimately subordinate to individuals who possessed fundamental economic rights – hence the state's role was to enforce these "natural rights." This also meant refraining from targeting any economic activity for discrimination and promoting the free entry of new corporations. Eminent domain could be deployed by the state in a limited fashion, and any expropriations that were undertaken by the government had to be compensated at market value. Moreover, privatizations conducted under the military regime had to be accepted without investigations into to the privatization process. Finally, collective bargaining among workers and owners was banned at any level above the firm, and the military and national police force were empowered by the constitution to restore public order by interdicting strikes and work stoppages.

The 1980 constitution also contained several provisions that gave fiscal and monetary policy a very conservative bent. The central bank was made independent and the president of the independent central bank would be chosen by the military. The bank's purview was relegated to keeping inflation low and helping manage currency flows. Nowhere in its mandate was there a provision for boosting employment, let alone achieving full employment. In terms of fiscal policy, the executive branch was granted the exclusive right to initiate fiscal and budgetary legislation, including social welfare programs, and congress had to vote these up or down or, at maximum, *reduce* expenditures contained in projects introduced by budgetary laws. Moreover, the budgets emanating from the executive contained a sunset clause: if they were not ratified within sixty days, the entire budget would be automatically approved.

The constitution was also designed and subsequently tweaked to systematically protect outgoing incumbents and benefit their economic allies, primarily the *grupos económicos*, after elections occurred, especially in light of the possibility that the opposition might win the presidency. Indeed, as we will document in the following sections, the constitution was considerably amended in 1989 to bolster its "inoculating" powers after Pinochet lost a plebiscite about whether he should continue in power for another presidential term.

The 1980 constitution enshrined several protections for outgoing regime officials and the armed forces, which were designated as the ultimate defenders of the country's institutions. The commanders in chief of the armed forces and the national police were awarded permanent offices and could only be dismissed by the president if permission were granted by a national security council. The latter was created by the constitution and awarded broad powers to ensure "institutional stability" and make decisions about states of national emergency and states of exception tantamount to suspending constitutional rule. The council was composed of four representatives from the armed forces – the heads of the military, navy, air force, and national police – and the president of the senate and the president of the supreme court.

Other constitutional provisions also protected and benefited the armed forces. Amnesty was extended for political crimes committed between 1973 and 1978. The military was given sovereignty over defense policies, and along with the national police, power over military courts that represent a parallel judiciary system for their members. The armed forces were given autonomy over its command structure, the military budget, and the promotion of generals. The military was also given the right to name eight members of the senate, who had lifelong positions. Finally, 10 percent of copper revenues were automatically allocated to the military budget (Heiss and Navia 2007).

For all intents and purposes, the 1980 constitution transformed the Chilean senate into an authoritarian enclave. First, while it was to contain twenty-six elected senators, each of the country's thirteen regions were awarded two senators. This meant only two senators for the greater Santiago metropolitan area, which represents almost half of the country's population, and the over-representation of rural – and therefore more conservative – places (Montes and Vial 2005, 8). Second, the constitution prescribed the appointment of several unelected senators with an eight-year term. The National Security Council was allocated four senators, which could be selected from former commanders in chief of the armed forces and heads of the national police force. The Supreme Court was allocated three senators. The executive was granted two senators, who could be selected from former ministers and former provosts of state universities. Finally, ex-presidents, including Pinochet, were awarded seats in the senate for life. Unelected senators therefore represented more than 25 percent of the chamber's members.

The constitution's enforcement and amendment process also benefited outgoing elites. The charter created a constitutional court – the Constitutional Tribunal – that had the power to use judicial review to assess the constitutionality of the laws. The seven members of this tribunal were appointed by the Supreme Court, the executive branch, the National Security Council, and the senate.

To obtain constitutional reform, supermajorities of 60 percent were required across both chambers and special supermajorities of two-thirds across both chambers for issues related to the executive branch, Constitutional Tribunal, the military, and the National Security Council. Besides this very high quorum, any amendment depended on the approval of two successive congresses. Another de facto barrier to constitutional reform created by the 1980 constitution was that there was no joint commission between the two legislative chambers in regards to constitutional issues; this significantly hindered their ability to coordinate to introduce reforms and adjudicate differences (Fuentes 2015, 104).

Fine-Tuning the Constitution on the Eve of Democratization

The 1980 constitution had, under the timetable it set for democratic transition, prescribed that the junta had to nominate a presidential candidate in 1988 who had to be elected through a plebiscite. Pinochet, to his surprise, lost that plebiscite (55 percent voted against him), and acquiesced to the results. This set the stage for elections in December 1989. The regime used this period of time to unilaterally craft a series of constitutional reforms without opposition input. Despite increased pluralism engendered by now legal political parties and a freer press, the regime continued to monopolize formal institutions, ruled under a state of emergency, and employed repression. Pinochet then won support for these reforms in a plebiscite held in July 1989.

Most accounts suggest that the 1989 constitutional reforms were oriented toward legitimizing the 1980 constitution and gaining some support from the opposition (e.g., Fuentes 1996). The reforms were, after all, crafted by constitutional experts and party leaders appointed by both the regime and the opposition and appeared to be a result of negotiations between these two actors (see Montes and Vial 2005). A look under the hood of these amendments, however, suggests a more self-interested, calculated intent by the regime. A deeper look also suggests that the regime was able to impose its preferences on the opposition by controlling the terms and pace of the reform process (Heiss and Navia 2007).

The regime sought to tweak the rules of the game in favor of outgoing incumbents and their economic allies in light of its anticipation that the opposition front would win the 1989 elections and continue to achieve electoral success in the future. Therefore, its primary aims were to bolster the military's autonomy, power, and veto points; weaken the executive branch; and strengthen the legislative branch while overrepresenting conservative parties in both chambers (see Heiss and Navia 2007).

The outgoing Pinochet regime pushed through several key laws and constitutional provisions that bolstered the power of the military. First, new provisions legally prevented the president from forcing the retirement of high-ranking military officers. Second, the executive's ability to declare a state of exception was restricted. Third, Article 94 of the constitution was expanded to protect the retirement benefits, seniority, internal organizational matters, internal succession, and budgets of the military.

This and similar measures were consequential steps to deepen the article's former protection of autonomy in military appointments, promotions, and retirements. Beyond these key changes, the armed forces stipulated that the military's budget could not fall below the previous year's budget adjusted for inflation, ensuring that military resources could only expand. Relatedly, as mentioned previously, the so-called Copper Law shunted profits from annual sales by the state-owned copper giant CODELCO directly to the military, which were used largely for military hardware acquisitions. These funds were not subjected to congressional oversight, effectively granting the military an untouchable slush fund (Heiss and Navia 2007).

To top this off and stall the debilitation of military autonomy, the laws regulating the armed forces were upgraded from ordinary to organic constitutional status, rendering them subject to supermajority congressional thresholds for change. This helped counteract a reform to the supermajority threshold for changes to organic laws: from three-fifths to four-sevenths of the representatives in both houses of congress. It also softened the elimination of the provision that two consecutive congresses had to meet these supermajority thresholds for specific constitutional reforms.[10] Even so, given the regime's political allies' dominant positions in the senate (due to appointed and lifetime senators) and the role of the Constitutional Tribunal, the four-sevenths threshold remained a high bar.

Other constitutional reforms in 1989 served to further undergird the influence of the outgoing regime. For instance, the first presidential term under democracy was reduced from eight to four years. This was a bald-faced attempt to shorten the rule of what was widely expected to be a presidential victory in the 1989 elections by opposition forces. These forces were represented by a political alliance known as the Concertación de Partidos por la Democracia (Concertación), a coalition of seventeen parties opposed to the military regime that orchestrated the campaign against Pinochet in the run-up to the 1988 plebiscite and had united to oppose the regime and the 1980 constitution as early as 1980. The Concertación included the Christian Democrats, radicals, and socialists.

Other reforms likewise benefited outgoing authoritarian elites. For instance, the president's power to dissolve the lower chamber was withdrawn. Moreover, the number of elected seats in the senate was expanded from twenty-six to thirty-eight, a measure explicitly designed to overrepresent conservative parties tied to the former regime due to malapportionment.

Finally, consider the largest political albatross of them all: Chile's binomial electoral system. Unique among electoral systems worldwide, Chile's binomial electoral was engineered to favor the second-largest electoral block: the Chilean Right. Critical to understanding this electoral system is the fact that "its establishment was completed in 1989, after the October 1988 plebiscite supplied the electoral engineers with valuable information concerning both voting behavior and the structure of the electoral competition" (Rahat and

---

[10] Even after the 1989 constitutional reforms, amendments to the constitution required either a two-thirds or three-fifths majority in both chambers, depending on the part of the constitution that was to be amended.

Sznajder 1998, 430). In other words, the outgoing regime reverse-engineered a unique electoral system that would maximally favor its electoral strength given the results of the 1988 plebiscite.

The key conundrum for electoral engineers was that the Right's support generally hovered between one-third and one-half in most districts. A majoritarian electoral system therefore threatened the Right – and its constitutional bulwark – with political annihilation. A typical proportional representation system would, similar to a majoritarian electoral rule, risk the possibility that the Right would fail to garner enough seats to block constitutional reform, even with supermajority thresholds for change. The resolution of this conundrum was the binomial electoral system. At the time of Chile's democratic transition and in the wake of the 1988 plebiscite, the Center-left was expected to garner about half the vote, the Right between one-third and one-half, and the Marxist Left less than either of these blocks.

CHILE'S ELITE-BIASED DEMOCRACY

Chile's autocratically imposed constitution has had a profound impact on its politics since the return to democracy in 1990. The principal reason is that this elite-biased arrangement has been very stable. It is well documented that constitutional reforms in Chile are significantly more difficult to enact than regular legislation (Alemán and Navia 2009; Toro, Acevedo, and Matamala 2010) due to factors we reviewed above, such as required supermajority thresholds for change and the lack of a joint commission to resolve constitutional reform inconsistencies between the two houses of congress. And while there have been several amendments to Chile's 1980 constitution nonetheless, only a minority of these has adversely affected the autocratic regime's outgoing incumbents and their economic allies.

Overrepresentation of Conservative Parties

The electoral system introduced by the 1980 constitution created two coalitions. The first was composed of the political parties associated with the opposition movement under the military regime, the Concertación. The second was the political parties affiliated with the Pinochet regime, the Alianza por Chile (Alianza), which included the Independent Democratic Union (UDI), Chile's most conservative political party. The Alianza was composed of business leaders, attorneys, and advocates who fiercely supported the military dictatorship and helped craft the 1980 constitution. It is important to note that before 2005, when the constitution was amended to eliminate unelected senators, Alianza strongly relied on the senators appointed by the outgoing regime, which meant that they had a virtual veto over policy in the senate (Fuentes 2015). Before 1998, however, this was a moot point: Alianza had an outright majority in the senate; between 1998 and 2006, they had an even split of the seats with

Concertación. Over these years, they also held their ground in the lower chamber, achieving near parity with the Concertación.[11]

Why did the Right do so well under democracy? Given the binomial electoral system, the Right could obtain representative parity even against an alliance of leftist and centrist parties as long as it won more than one-third of the votes in each district. All of Chile's electoral districts are two-member districts. Candidates can join interparty alliances or run as independents. Each alliance can present at most two candidates in a district. Voters then select one representative for each chamber. The number of votes for each alliance or independent determines its seat allocation. The alliance with the highest number of votes receives the first seat, but this same alliance can only win the second seat if its votes are more than double those for the second most popular alliance. Otherwise, the second alliance wins the seat.

Chile's electoral system operates precisely as intended, therefore favoring the Right in the translation of votes to congressional seats and yielding near left-right parity despite a substantial numerical disadvantage for the Right (Rahat and Sznajder 1998). Consider the following distortions in how votes are translated into seats in the lower chamber. In 1989, Alianza received only 34.2 percent of the votes but 40 percent of the (120) seats; in 1993, it received only 36.7 percent of the votes but 41.6 percent of the seats; in 1997, it received only 36.3 percent of the votes but 39.1 percent of the seats; and in 2001, it received only 39.1 percent of the votes but 47.5 percent of the seats. Meanwhile, consider that in 1997, the Communists received 6.9 percent of the votes but no seats.

Besides giving the Right an outsized voice in crafting ordinary legislation, this electoral system has long served to make the supermajority thresholds for constitutional reform in the legislature unattainable. This is not to say that constitutional reforms were not attempted, however. The first two center-left Concertación administrations pursued and won several constitutional reforms, such as democratizing municipal elections and Supreme Court appointments and advancing some civil rights (Fuentes 2015, 104). However, none of these reforms substantially affected the interests of the Right and former Pinochet-era elites (Fuentes 2015, 109). President Aylwin (1990–1994), who was elected with 55.5 percent of the vote in December 1989, was deliberately nonconfrontational with the Right, and President Frei's (1994–2000) major reform attempts – to reduce the role of the armed forces in politics and the electoral system – failed.

Fate of Pinochet Regime Officials

The broad institutional contours of the transition agreement that guided Chile's democratization in 1990 enabled Pinochet and most top regime officials to skate free from punishment and even to flourish politically and economically

---

[11] In 2001, for example, Alianza held 47.5 percent of the seats versus Concertación's 51.6 percent.

under democracy. Table 7.1 lists the upper echelon of Pinochet regime officials, their positions in the regime, and their fates under democracy. It indicates that despite the well-documented crimes of the dictatorship, few of its top officials ever met with serious punishment. In fact, the official that faced the stiffest penalty was the secretary general of the presidency Jorge Ballerino Sanford, who was sentenced to four years in prison for corruption in 2015 related to his role in arranging secret offshore bank accounts to hide Pinochet's money.

Several other officials received almost laughably light penalties for their misdeeds, such as minor fines. Even Pinochet himself avoided any domestic convictions before his death.[12] The majority of high-level officials in the Pinochet regime avoided any punishment at all.

Furthermore, many of the Pinochet regime's top officials experienced a return to political or economic prominence under democracy. A host of these officials retained leadership positions within Chile's powerful military. Pinochet, Rodolfo Stange, and Santiago Sinclair became senators. Labbé became the longtime mayor of Providencia. Others such as Carlos Cáceres, Enrique Seguel, Hernán Felipe Errázuriz, Hernan Buchi, and Luis Larraín moved to the private sector to preside over major corporations or serve on the boards of directors of major multinational firms – some of which were the principal beneficiaries of Pinochet-era privatization. Buchi also joined the board of directors of the Banco de Chile in 2008. Minor punishments of a few of these officials for their role in the dictatorship did not jeopardize their political and economic success under democracy.

Conservative Monetary and Fiscal Policies

After the return to democracy, elected governments sustained Chile's conservative fiscal and monetary policies. This was in part due to the elite-biased measures sustained by the 1980 constitution, including extraordinary central bank independence and the fact that the Chilean legislature was prevented from augmenting budgetary policies with parochial spending measures. The facts bear this out: Figure 7.3 clearly shows the continued decline of total taxation (percent GDP) under Chile's elite-biased democracy.

Finance Continues to Blossom

As Figure 7.1 makes clear, the recovery of Chile's financial system continued to be quite robust after the 1989 democratization. The ratio of private credit to GDP increased by 67 percent (from 31.52 percentage points to 52.66 percentage points) after the transition (1990–2006), compared with the autocratic period (1973–1989). The linchpin of Chile's post-transition financial system

---

[12] As we discuss in a following section, however, Pinochet did face some legal troubles before his death.

TABLE 7.1. *Fate of Former Pinochet Regime Officials*

Elite Name	Position	Fate
Augusto Pinochet	Junta president (1973–1990); army commander in chief (1973–1998)	Commander in chief of armed forces and then senator for life after stepping down as president. Detained by British authorities in London in 1998 after Spain requested his extradition in connection with the torture of Spanish citizens in Chile during his rule. Allowed to return home in 2000 after a British court ruled that he was physically unfit to stand trial. Continued to face investigations by Chilean authorities but died before any conviction.
José Toribio Merino	Navy admiral; junta member	Stayed in the military and retired with no punishment.
Rodolfo Stange Oelckers	National paramilitary police (Carabineros) general (1985–1990); junta member	Director of the Carabineros until 1995. Elected senator in 1997. In 1994, was investigated for involvement in political murders (the *Caso Degollados*), but never found guilty.
Fernando Matthei	Air force general; defense minister (1978–1990); junta member	Remained in the air force until 1991 and then retired. Implicated in the torture and dead of General Bachelet (Michelle Bachelet's father), but the case failed.
Carlos Cáceres Contreras	Interior minister (1988–1990); finance minister (1983–1984)	Moved to the private sector and headed several companies such as the Chilean Tobacco Company and served on several private enterprise boards.
Enrique Seguel Morel	Finance minister (1989–1990); Central Bank president (1985–1989)	Became member of the directing board of the Banco Central for six years after the transition and then the director of several private enterprises such as Entel.
Hernán Felipe Errázuriz Correa	Foreign affairs minister (1988–1990)	Moved to the private sector and became director of several private enterprises such as Chilectra, Banco Security, and Detroit Chile.

(*continued*)

TABLE 7.1 (*continued*)

Elite Name	Position	Fate
Cristián Labbé Galilea	Government secretary general (1989–1990)	Became a longtime mayor of Providencia, elected in 1996, 2000, 2004 and 2008. On October 12, 2014: He was detained for ten days (and freed upon paying a fine) for his role in the activities of Pinochet's personal gaurd during the dictatorship.
Patricio Carvajal	Defense minister (1983–1990); foreign affairs minister (1973–1978)	Retired after transition and committed suicide in 1994.
Hernán Büchi Buc	Regime candidate for 1990 elections	Moved to the private sector and became president of several companies within the Grupo Luksic (e.g., the food company Lucchetti and the metals manufacturer Madeco). Became vice president of the Sociedad Química y Minera de Chile in 2000 and has been a member of the board of directors of Banco de Chile since 2008.
Santiago Sinclair Oyaneder	Army general; junta member (1988–1990)	Designated senator as a representative of the military until 1998. Also designated as institutional senator for the National Security Council. Put in preventive custody for charges of murder (1973) in February 2015 but was released with a fine the next day.
Jorge Ballerino Sanford	Secretary general of the presidency	Sentenced to four years in prison in May 2015 for a corruption case related to secret bank accounts for Pinochet that was spurred in part by a US Senate investigation.
Luis Larraín Arroyo	Development minister	Moved to the private sector and became manager of a financial company (Poderopedia); also dedicated since 1992 to a think tank he founded with Hernán Büchi (Instituto Libertad y Desarrollo), which he started directing in 2014. Appointed in 2014 to direct the company in charge of the Universidad Católica soccer team.

was stronger property-rights protections and the rule of law (Haber 2009), which were epiphenomenal to the enduring influence of the 1980 constitution. This interacted with Pinochet's privatization of the pension system, which remained intact after democratization and incentivized widespread private investment that reinforced the financial sector.

Large, Export-Oriented Agricultural Interests Continue Their Ascendance

The transition to democracy and the agricultural policies of the Concertación essentially continued the policies pursued in the latter years of Pinochet's rule, albeit with greater emphasis on peasant agriculture and social policies. Macroeconomic stability, an emphasis on agricultural exports, and insertion into international markets have remained the cornerstone of government policies (Kay 2002, 475).

To be sure, under democracy the Concertación governments introduced social policies in rural areas such as the provision of education, housing, water, and electricity. Furthermore, the Chilean government has (especially since 1993) titled indigenous communities, subsidized land purchases for these communities, and granted state-owned land to them, typically purchased from private owners. Land transfers have served to regularize ownership, amplify current holdings, and grant land to dispossessed communities. By 2005, the Corporación de Desarrollo Indígena had granted more than 200,000 hectares of land to indigenous communities (Aylwin 2005, 9–10). These policies, however, are at least as notable for what they are not: land redistribution programs have been entirely struck from the policy agenda.

Inequality

During the last quarter century, Chile's skewed income distribution has reflected the elite-biased nature of the 1990 democratic transition. As Figure 7.4 demonstrates, the Gini coefficient of income inequality climbed from the mid-forties when Pinochet took power to the low fifties on the eve of Pinochet stepping down. A decade after democratization, it had actually *risen* to above fifty-five, making the gap between rich and poor worse under the new democracy than under Pinochet. Indeed, in 2005, the income of the wealthiest 10 percent was forty-one times greater than the income of the poorest 10 percent, a figure that is closer to many Sub-Saharan African countries than Latin American ones.

This is partially due to the fact that real wages for the average Chilean worker have been in a steep decline since the 1970s and have hit unskilled workers particularly hard due to trade and financial liberalization without a commensurate increase in social insurance (see Borghi 2005). In addition, Chile has suffered from marked inequities in access to quality healthcare and education, despite the fact that targeted transfers and economic growth have helped reduce poverty. Only in the late 2000s did inequality slightly decline,

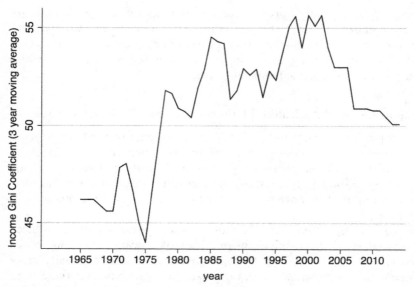

FIGURE 7.4. Chile's income inequality.
Notes: For the majority of data points, the Gini uses monetary income without reference to whether it is disposable or gross.
Source: Pribble, Huber, and Stephens (2009).

back toward the low fifties. We discuss the political underpinnings for that modest reversal in the next section.

There are deeper, more revealing, reasons why inequality has remained stubbornly higher than it was prior to Pinochet's coup. The economic elites created and consolidated during the dictatorship have fared well long after Pinochet handed over the formal reins of power to elected civilian governments because Chile's economic policies give them a leg up. While the *grupos económicos* favored by the military dictatorship continue to reap the rewards of an orthodox macroeconomic orientation rooted in trade and capital account liberalization, they also benefit from several tacit proscriptions against redistribution associated with the 1980 constitution. More concretely, they also benefit from economic policies that are hardly neoliberal: the state has promoted exports and coddled the financial sector through all sorts of subsidies, tax benefits, and financing schemes.

REFORMING ELITE-BIASED DEMOCRACY

Although Chile's last authoritarian regime constructed a transition agreement that delivered most of the outcomes it desired under democracy, key elements of the agreement have come undone. The first set of consequential constitutional reforms occurred in 2005. There were many important changes. First was the elimination of designated senators (including those designated by the National Security Council) and lifetime senate seats for former presidents. Second was the president's ability to remove the commander in chief of the armed forces and the chief of police after informing both chambers of congress. Third was the reduction of the president's term from six to four years without consecutive reelection. Fourth was a reformation of the Constitutional Tribunal that diminished the military's power over constitutional change. Fifth was a reduction in the National Security Council's powers, including its obligation to defend the constitution, and a change in its composition to include a greater number of civilians. Sixth was an increased ability for congress to create investigative commissions. Seventh was the creation of a new ministry of public safety in which the national police now reside, rather than being housed within the armed forces.

What facilitated these substantial constitutional changes? The conventional wisdom is that these changes were a reflection of civilians finally asserting their influence from below. Generational change coupled with a more assertive opposition succeeded where underground social movements in the 1980s had failed: they bucked off the yolk of the dictatorship.

This argument, however, struggles to explain at least three important puzzles. First, why did constitutional reform only come in 2005, and not in the early or mid-1990s, once Pinochet stepped down? Second, why were the 2005 constitutional reforms limited in scope? For instance, the binomial electoral system remained intact, continuing to overrepresent the Right. Third, why has public policy in Chile remained so favorable to the incumbent economic elites who thrived under Pinochet?

Our theory provides a different explanation for the 2005 constitutional changes – an explanation that simultaneously sheds light on each of these puzzles. As Fuentes (2015) argues, "The transformation of civil-military relations and, in particular, the weakening of General Pinochet's influence also facilitated [the 2005 constitutional] agreement" (110). Pinochet remained the commander in chief of the armed forces after stepping down as president and then took a designated senate seat in 1998. However, he was arrested by Interpol in London in 1998 on Spain's extradition request. Pinochet returned to Chile in 2000 and was stripped of immunity from prosecution by the Santiago Court of Appeals. In response, he resigned his senate seat and pleaded senile dementia, absolving him from prosecution until the courts reversed their position in 2004. Charges mounted and the Right began to distance itself from him just prior to his death in 2006. Pinochet's increasingly tenuous position and old age facilitated a constitutional agreement that had been in the works since early 2000 and debated in the senate for four years.

To be sure, the weakening of Pinochet-era elites did not alone set the stage for constitutional reform. Negotiations on constitutional reform began in March 2000 on the back of a negative shock to economic growth in 1998–1999 – the largest setback to hit Chile since 1982. The economic crisis enabled UDI candidate Joaquín Lavín to cast the Concertación candidate Ricardo Lagos as representing continuity with the policies responsible for plummeting growth and rising unemployment. Furthermore, trade openness spiked in the early 2000s in the wake of the recession, rising by nearly one-third between 1999 and 2004. This threatened selected urban workers (e.g., those unionized in manufacturing sectors) but was a boon to Pinochet's incumbent economic elites in mining and agriculture. Moreover, Pinochet-era economic elites appealed to beleaguered workers to threaten the Concertación's continued rule in 2000.

Why did the Right agree to constitutional reforms in 2005? The answer is not that they got steamrolled. Quite the opposite: given the way the political winds were blowing, conservative elements calculated that several key reforms were in fact in their interest. Consider one of the most important reforms: the removal of designated senators and lifetime senate seats for former presidents. With the first three presidents drawn from the center-left Concertación, these governments began to appoint designated senators, and the balance of power in the senate began to tilt away from former authoritarian elites and, absent a removal of this provision, promised to flip in the future. Both factors pushed the Right in favor of stripping these provisions from the constitution, lest their position in the senate erode further under continued Concertación rule.

A similar scenario played out regarding reforms to the legislative branch, the executive branch, and the Constitutional Tribunal. In exchange for agreeing to eliminate designated and lifetime senators, the Right requested that the powers of the presidency be diminished and those of the legislature enhanced. In particular, they sought minority powers to request ministerial accountability, enhanced powers to establish investigative commissions, and a stronger legislative veto role for the Constitutional Tribunal, which could act as a bulwark against changing the electoral system (Fuentes 2015). In short, while some of these reforms weakened former authoritarian elites' political positions in the short term, it allowed them to avoid political annihilation in the long term. In the process, they also legitimized the authoritarian legacies that were not excised from the constitution.

Viewed through this lens, it is not surprising that public policy has continued to be biased in favor of elites even after 2005. As discussed previously, few top Pinochet-era officials have been punished, inequality has barely budged, taxes remained modest, and the coddling of economic sectors such as banking and export-oriented agriculture has continued apace.

CONCLUSION

This chapter hones in on Chilean history, which has gone through pronounced and well-documented political cycles over the last century: from republican oligarchy to popular democracy to military regime and finally to elite-biased democracy. In critically examining these shifts and their political and economic consequences, we reveal broader patterns that fit our theoretical predictions from earlier chapters. Both the broad structure and the seemingly odd contours of recent Chilean history can be best understood not through the lens of ideology, political partisanship, or military concerns with national security or order but rather through the pitched battles of dueling factions of economic elites, powerful and self-interested political players, and the masses.

The struggles among these groups, and reactions to these struggles, have largely defined how the majority of citizens live. Furthermore, the military has cast dark shadows over democracy that have distorted the ability of voters to satisfy their political demands. Most prominently, the Pinochet regime left indelible birthmarks on contemporary Chilean democracy that consolidated an economy centered on crony capitalism, stunted the progressivity of public policy, and enabled regime officials to elide punishment for their misdeeds in office. Therefore, Chile remains one of the most unequal countries on the planet, despite more than twenty-five years of democratic rule.

Of course, Chilean political history continues to be written. Michelle Bachelet returned to office in 2014 in a landslide electoral victory under the banner of the New Majority coalition. With the Right knocked back on its heels and most Pinochet-era officials either dead or at an advanced age, she promised to further roll back the Pinochet dictatorship's legacy. Most prominently, Bachelet pushed through a major electoral change in 2015 that would do away with Chile's binomial electoral system and return the country to a form of proportional representation similar to what was in place before Pinochet's rise to power.

The new electoral system, which will have governed the 2017 elections slated to take place after we wrote this book, promise to empower smaller political parties, thereby opening the door to strengthening far-left parties that have hitherto been forced to moderate their positions under the 1980 constitution. But it will also likely engender greater dispersion in the vote share across parties, weakening both the center-left New Majority coalition and the conservative alliance. It therefore remains to be seen whether this electoral reform will actually be a boon to the Left.

Of similarly major political importance, though less constitutional significance, is Bachelet's overhaul of the education system. Leveraging ongoing student protests and longstanding demands for greater access to education, recent reforms passed in January 2016 guarantee free higher education for the poorest half of students admitted to state-certified universities and colleges, with the intent to eventually expand this figure to include 70 percent of the poorest students. To finance subsidized higher education and other progressive reforms, Bachelet moved the needle on taxes. In the most progressive overhaul to the tax code since Pinochet, a 2014 reform raised corporate taxes, reduced exemptions, and changed how it calculates capital gains to individuals. The goal is to increase tax revenue by 3 percent of GDP by 2018, drawing heavily from the richest Chileans.

Will these reforms finally pave the way for a return to popular democracy in Chile? Or will they be watered down by economic elites or, even worse, reversed under a return to dictatorship? The next five to ten years will be critical in providing answers to these questions.

8

Colonial and Occupier Legacies in New Democracies

The previous chapters of this book demonstrate that democracies' social contracts are often rooted in authoritarianism. The majority of countries that have transitioned to democracy since World War II have done so guided by constitutions written under authoritarian regimes. These constitutions can bring some desired degree of continuity and stability to what can otherwise be unpredictable and volatile transitions. But our analysis suggests that the authors of these deals are, more than anything else, self-interested: outgoing dictators and their political and economic allies use constitutions as a vehicle for advancing their political and material interests, despite the host of formal political changes that a democratic transition engenders.

Authoritarian constitutions, then, give us a simple, powerful window into the strength of outgoing authoritarian elites and the institutional infrastructure they foist upon new democracies. The legacies they leave behind have a potent influence on how political decisions are made in terms of the degree of participation by citizens and their influence over public policy, as well as its distributive impact.

This chapter unpacks a related phenomenon that we have not yet examined in detail: legacies from colonial rule or foreign occupying powers. Chapters 3–5 treat countries that transition to democracy with constitutions penned under dictatorship as elite-biased democracies and all other democracies as popular democracies. Yet this latter category contains two arguably quite different sets of countries: those that operate with constitutions that they write themselves upon transition (e.g., Argentina in 1983) and those that are democratic since their inception.

This latter set includes countries that split from democratic forebears, such as the Czech Republic and Slovakia's peaceful 1993 divorce, which created separate nation states out of a formerly unified democratic country, Czechoslovakia. These are straightforward cases to which our theory can clearly be extended: new democracies that split from former democracies typically inherit democratic legacies from their predecessors.

In other cases, however, such as Canada, Finland, India, Laos, Myanmar, or the Philippines, new democracies can be subject to the influences – or even dictates – of their former colonial occupier, despite starting as a democracy immediately upon gaining sovereignty. The same can be true of new democracies that win back their sovereignty from foreign occupiers, often at the end of major wars. By collapsing these cases with popular democracies as a default category in the analyses we conducted in Chapter 4, we biased our empirical tests against us. Namely, to the extent that some democracies since inception in fact have elite-biased legacies that favor former colonial or foreign occupiers, it is harder to uncover the impact of de novo democratic institutions on political and economic outcomes. Similarly, we likely underestimate the degree to which nondemocratic legacies distort public policy.

We made these previous coding decisions for theoretical reasons: authoritarian constitutions are different in kind than the legacies that might be imposed by occupiers. Authoritarian constitutional legacies presuppose a democratic transition, which itself entails one group of powerful domestic actors handing over de jure political power to another group. The former group almost always remains within the country and is subject to its rules and regulations. By contrast, occupiers who leave behind institutional legacies eventually exit the countries they occupy, even if their economic interests remain protected well after that.

This chapter unpacks the legacies imposed by occupiers in several steps. First, it classifies the countries that have been subject to such legacies. Second, it discusses the conventional wisdom on the history of colonial legacies across the world. Third, it distills this history along lines familiar to those we explored in previous chapters in the context of two prominent democracies (Canada and the Philippines) that arose from colonial occupation as well as one democracy (Ukraine) that cleaved off from a geographically larger authoritarian predecessor state (the Soviet Union). In doing so, we present a set of common "pathologies" that many newly independent democracies inherit from their former occupiers.

This exercise also provides a new lens for understanding the at times arcane and anachronistic nature of constitutions and other important institutions – as well as their political consequences – in democracies that win sovereignty from an occupier. Many seemingly unique characteristics of different countries are often assumed to reflect a country's essence and therefore some immutable permutation of singular geographic, cultural, or ideological roots. One of the major contributions of this chapter, however, is to demonstrate that many of these characteristics are instead by-products of institutions that are imposed from abroad instead of from within. Moreover, far from immutable, these characteristics often stem from an artificial and deliberate decision by an occupying power.

Our framework and approach also helps address yet another important puzzle in social science: Why do certain former colonies have systematic policies that set them apart from other former colonies that they should resemble much more closely? Take the United States and Canada, for instance. Political economy scholarship suggests that these two countries should have similar institutional and political trajectories, rooted in their early history as British settler societies where land was plentiful and disease burdens low (e.g., Acemoglu, Johnson, and Robinson 2001; Engerman and Sokoloff 2000). Yet these countries are much more different politically than theory would anticipate.

Alternatively, consider the Philippines. It inherited key extractive institutions similar to Spain's other longtime colonies in Latin America. In a host of important ways, however, Philippine politics differ from those in Spain's erstwhile Latin American colonies. Many of these differences can be accounted for by examining the subsequent legacy of the US occupation of the archipelago.

CLASSIFYING COLONIAL AND OCCUPIER LEGACIES

Table 8.1 lists two sets of countries that were democratic either at their founding or in the wake of foreign, wartime occupation. In the first set, listed in the leftmost columns of the table, countries were democratic since their inception as an independent country. Within this category are several groups of countries. The first group comprises countries that won independence from their colonial forebears, including cases such as Australia, Canada, India, Nigeria, Papua New Guinea, Sudan, and the United States. These countries are most likely to have political legacies imposed on them by their colonial forebears that resemble authoritarian legacies, especially if they did not win independence by force via revolutions. Two of the cases we examine later in the chapter – Canada and the Philippines – draw from this first group.

A second group of countries formed as modern countries from smaller territorial factions or regions not previously recognized internationally as countries. Examples in this group include Switzerland, which was founded as a federation of smaller states, and Israel, which was carved out of part of the Palestinian Mandate. Countries such as Switzerland that are formed from smaller states often create new bargains and institutions upon their founding. While these bargains might introduce institutional arrangements that favor certain elite groups from selected states in order to win their approval for a deal (especially in the context of federalism), they also create novel suprastate institutions. Similarly, in Israel, colonial legacies were not at the fore.

A third group of countries are successor states to larger countries that break up. Examples include Croatia and Macedonia, which became independent countries when Yugoslavia dissolved. The Czech Republic and Slovakia are another set of examples; these countries peacefully split after the former Czechoslovakia was dissolved in 1993. Yet another set of examples are the Soviet successor states of Estonia, Latvia, Lithuania, and Ukraine. New democracies like the Czech Republic that split from a former democracy typically inherit a legacy from their forebears. These are straightforward cases to which our theory can

TABLE 8.1. *Democracies since Independence or Foreign, Wartime Occupation*

Democracies since independence		Democracies since foreign occupation	
Country	Year of independence	Country	End of foreign occupation
Armenia	1991	Austria	1920
Australia	1901	Austria	1946
Canada	1867	Belgium	1946
Congo	1960	Czechoslovakia	1918
Croatia	1991	Czechoslovakia	1945
Czech Republic	1993	Denmark	1945
Estonia	1991	France	1946
Finland	1917	Germany	1919
India	1950	Germany	1949
Israel	1948	Greece	1944
Laos	1954	Japan	1946
Latvia	1991	Netherlands	1945
Lithuania	1991	Norway	1945
Macedonia	1991	Poland	1919
Mauritius	1968		
Moldova	1991		
Myanmar	1948		
New Zealand	1857		
Nigeria	1960		
Pakistan	1950		
Papua New Guinea	1975		
Sierra Leone	1961		
Slovakia	1993		
Slovenia	1991		
Solomon Islands	1978		
Somalia	1960		
Sri Lanka	1948		
Sudan	1956		
Switzerland	1848		
Timor-Leste	2002		
Trinidad and Tobago	1962		
Ukraine	1991		
United States	1776		
Yugoslavia	1921		

Note: Table 8.1 includes all countries that were either democratic upon independence or occupied by a foreign power for several years during wartime, and following occupation, their regime became democratic. Regime-type data span 1800–2008 and are from Cheibub, Gandhi, and Vreeland (2010).

easily be extended. Yet they are not cases of particular interest because our theory would predict continuity in their legacy, whatever that might be.

Of greater interest within this third group of countries are newly democratic successor states that split from an authoritarian predecessor. The Soviet successor states listed previously are illustrative. Newly democratic successor states can indeed inherit elite-biased legacies from their authoritarian predecessors in ways that mimic an authoritarian constitution. We investigate this further later on in the case of Ukraine.

The rightmost columns of Table 8.1 list a second set of cases distinct from the first set. This second set comprises countries that were occupied by foreign powers during wartime and became democratic upon regaining sovereignty when the foreign power retracted. These cases represent predominantly European countries occupied by other European powers or the United States in the context of World War I or World War II. Examples include France, Germany, and the Netherlands after WWII.

In contrast to colonial occupation, foreign occupation is much shorter in duration. Occupiers are less likely to invest in sending their nationals to develop the economy and impose a sophisticated, tailor-made set of favorable political institutions. Instead, occupiers tend to import "off-the-shelf" institutions from other countries. Take, for example, the case of Japan in the wake of WWII. The head of the US occupation authority, General Douglas MacArthur, charged a small US military committee with penning a new constitution in less than a week after he deemed the Japanese's proposal unsatisfactory. The result was a document that hewed closely to the British parliamentary model with some modifications to satisfy the circumstances at hand, such as Japan's prohibition against waging war.

We therefore anticipate that the strength of any institutional legacies in these cases should be, on average, weaker than those imposed by longtime colonial occupiers on new states. Furthermore, they are less likely to be tailored to a specific set of well-established indigenous elites who act as intermediaries between the occupying power (and any colonial elites they place on the ground) and citizens of the occupied society. Nonetheless, such legacies can be important. They are also likely to reflect the political institutions of the occupying power. When the occupier is a democracy, the occupied country is less likely to inherit elite-biased institutions that mimic authoritarian constitutions – though this can occur in some circumstances. Instead, elite-biased institutions are more likely to occur when the occupier is an authoritarian country.

THE CONVENTIONAL WISDOM ON COLONIAL LEGACIES

Scholarship on colonial legacies has proliferated in recent years. A host of prominent contributions to the literature have documented a pervasive and long-standing impact of colonization on subsequent political and economic development. One particularly noteworthy recent contribution is the work of

Acemoglu, Johnson, and Robinson (2001), who demonstrate a "reversal of fortune" whereby many of the richest territories that were colonized are relatively poor today and many of the poorest colonized territories are now rich. To explain this reversal, these authors point to the extractive versus inclusive colonial governance strategies exercised by powers such as the Spanish and British.[1] Although both empires essentially sought to uniformly expand their dominions and enrich their metropoles, their local governance strategies were determined by powerful geographic factors; in particular, local disease burdens and native population density. Colonial powers set up inclusive institutions where disease burdens were low and land plentiful, attracting settlers from the metropole. By contrast, they imposed extractive institutions where disease burdens were high, impeding colonial settlement, and where native populations were large, which enabled the labor-intensive extraction of valuable metals such as gold and silver and the production of labor-intensive agricultural products such as sugar.

Similarly, Engerman and Sokoloff (2000) argue that initial factor endowments such as climates, soil type, and native populations guided colonizers' settlement patterns and institutional infrastructure, which in turn determined economic and political trajectories for decades or even centuries to come after colonies won independence. Other authors similarly argue that colonial patterns have had a major – and typically adverse – impact on contemporary outcomes such as levels of corruption (La Porta et al. 1999) and democratic stability (Bernhard et al. 2004).

Take, for instance, Latin America. Colonization strongly impacted both early landholding patterns and institutional design in Latin American countries (Acemoglu, Johnson, and Robinson 2001; Engerman and Sokoloff 2002). These early patterns persisted for at least the first century of the postindependence period. Circa the early 1900s, resource-rich countries with large indigenous populations that survived the colonial period but were forced to work as indentured servants on massive plantations and in mines (e.g., Mexico, Bolivia, and Peru) were some of the most unequal countries in the world (Engerman and Sokoloff 2002). This implies that their colonial legacies endured well after colonialism ended.[2]

This chapter echoes the literature on colonial legacies in arguing that the institutions colonizers imposed on the territories they occupied were designed to benefit the colonizers as well as their key indigenous allies. A more novel contribution is our demonstration of how specific elements of institutional design, and especially constitutional design, benefited colonizers and their local allies. Rather than distinguish between inclusive and extractive or liberal and

---

[1] For a view that distinguishes between Spanish and British colonial legacies, see Lange et al. (2006).

[2] To be sure, there remains a lively debate over whether geographic factors were indeed the chief drivers of the types of institutions that colonizers built. Some authors, for instance, hold that the ideology of the colonizers is a stronger predictor of their type of colonial institution building, with liberal colonizers implanting less pernicious legacies on their colonized territories (e.g., Banerjee and Iyer 2005; Mahoney 2010; Treisman 2000).

illiberal institutions, we delve into the minutiae of how specific institutions and constitutional stipulations are carefully crafted to empower the political and economic interests of former colonizers and their local elite conduits. Furthermore, we show how these institutions persist or change over time and how they impact a country's rules, both those that govern political competition and help determine the economy's winners and losers.

We focus our attention on a specific subset of former colonies: those that gain independence as democracies. These are cases that the literature on colonial legacies would find as generally exceptional: because most colonizers imposed tight political control on their colonies and sought to maximize revenue extraction, they typically left authoritarian regimes in their wake. Societies colonized through a more "inclusive" rather than "extractive" strategy, however, are predicted by the literature to have become democracies, with public policies that were more egalitarian in nature than their authoritarian counterparts (e.g., Acemoglu, Johnson, and Robinson 2001; Mahoney 2010).

By contrast, we find that many new democracies that were erstwhile colonies or foreign territorial holdings are both unequal and prone to sharp elite biases. This is not coincidental or marginal to these newfound polities: inegalitarian social contracts were central to the new political game bequeathed by their colonizers and occupiers.

DEMOCRACY FOLLOWING COLONIAL RULE: THE CASES OF CANADA AND THE PHILIPPINES

This section examines two countries with colonial legacies under new democratic regimes that mirror the legacies of authoritarian constitutions: Canada and the Philippines. These countries were established at their founding as democracies but were saddled with institutional legacies that favored elites who were powerful under colonial rule, as well as the interests of their colonizers.

Canada

Canada is fertile ground for illustrating the form and endurance of colonial legacies imposed on new democracies. Like their colonies to the south, British holdings in northern North America enjoyed substantial political autonomy. They also had small native populations spread over large areas; expansive, fertile plains; and a climate that was devoid of malaria and favored small-scale farming of cereal crops (e.g., wheat) rather than plantation agriculture. These colonies included Newfoundland, Nova Scotia, Quebec, and the Island of Saint John at the time of the American Revolution. The territories that became Ontario and New Brunswick were settled in large part by Tories fleeing the American Revolution.

Historians, sociologists, and political scientists, however, have also long documented the dramatic and long-standing differences between Canadian and American societies. Lipset (1991), in his prominent book *Continental Divide*, summarizes:

Canada, as many of its historians and cultural critics reiterate, was formed as a counterrevolutionary monarchical society that valued hierarchy in class relations and religion and authority and deference in politics. Its leaders looked askance at the vulgar, populist, upstart new state to the south. In contrast, the United States was founded as a nation seeking to explicate a set of political and religious ideals that emphasized liberty, saw danger in concentrated government power, and increasingly stressed populism and equality of opportunity and of social relations. (10–11)

Yet the divide between the United States and Canada cannot merely be attributed to cultural differences or the shock of the American Revolution to the northern British Colonies. We instead focus on the role the British had in the founding of the Confederation that predated Canada's national sovereignty in 1867.

Canadian Independence: A British Orchestration

Several events conspired to drive Canadian independence in 1867. The most decisive factors do not evidence defiance against the British crown or the desire to renounce British ties. To the contrary, the creation of the Dominion of Canada was viewed as the most deliberate manner of creating an enduring and strong relationship with Great Britain (e.g., Lipset 1991; Smith 2008). The first event driving the timing of the reform was the US Civil War. The provinces were concerned that their individual links to the British crown might not withstand encroachment from a mobilized Union Army to the south and hoped that a centralized confederation of provinces would serve as a more potent deterrent (Lipset 1991).

A second factor was the formation and subsequent lobbying of a powerful group of British investors with large stakes in the Canadian provinces. As Smith (2008) carefully lays out, the formation of the British North American Association (BNAA) in 1862 helped catalyze the definitive push toward a Canadian Confederation. The BNAA comprised many of the most prominent and influential investors in the Canadian provinces – investors that supported colonial unification, in part because of transprovincial initiatives such as the proposed Halifax-Quebec railway. Indeed, some had close personal ties to the Colonial Secretary such as Edward Watkin, a railway executive and member of the BNAA. Whereas the Colonial Office had ignored a federation proposal by the Canadian government in 1858–1859, the formation of the BNAA gave "all provincial questions a shove": the Colonial Office switched its prior position within six months of the BNAA's founding and began actively supporting unification (Smith 2008, 62). Members of the BNAA also sat as MPs in both the Conservative and Liberal Parties within Britain's House of Commons and gave the Confederation bill strong support (Smith 2008, 112).

In terms of impacting the timing of the British vote for Confederation, rather than the vote itself, the disruptive role of Nova Scotia stands out.

Nova Scotia had eliminated its property qualification for suffrage in 1851. It then scheduled an election for late 1867, and the expectation was for a strong anti-Confederation majority, a result that would bolster its desired right to self-determination. A clutch of MPs carrying the bill for confederation sought to lock Nova Scotia in before it went ahead with the election (Smith 2008, 112).

British Colonial Legacies

Canada's confederation in 1867 was shaped fundamentally by its British colonizer. The British carefully crafted a series of institutions and laws that were intended to perpetuate the status quo distribution of power in Canada, as well as British economic access to Canadian markets. British investors and bankers linked to Canada had similar interests and views as the Fathers of Confederation – "a community of like-minded individuals on both sides of the Atlantic worked together to produce a constitutional settlement that was mutually satisfactory" (Smith 2008, 131). They agreed that Canada's subjects should remain British. They "also agreed that colonial democracy needed to be tempered by a stiff dose of aristocracy and monarchy. Yankee democracy, with its (white) manhood suffrage, elected judges, and debt repudiations, was a terrible evil that needed to be avoided" (130).

Indeed, the easy passage of the bill granting Canada independence in the House of Lords is attributed to the fact that it was "perceived as an essentially conservative document" (Smith 2008, 115–116). As Lipset (1991) writes, "'Canadian confederation was expressive of Tory values'; it was designed to 'counteract democracy and ensure constitutional liberty' and was resisted by the liberal and continentalist elements" (43).

Bicameralism was one of the institutions intended to favor British and Tory interests. As detailed in Chapter 3, bicameralism serves to reduce policy volatility and has historically entailed a more elitist upper chamber. Canada exemplifies these regularities. There was a landed property qualification for the senate, which the Colonial Secretary argued was the closest approximation to the House of Lords that could be forged (Smith 2008, 116).[3] Furthermore, senators were – and are – appointed rather than elected. The governor general was charged with appointing senators upon the formation of the Confederation. These senators had lifetime terms. Senate seats were assigned regionally rather than according to the population size of districts, empowering rural interests as an effective counterweight against more liberal population centers.

These rules constructing and guiding the senate were not without their critics, however. Take the powerful manufacturing businessmen John Bright, who

---

[3] Indeed, the property requirement remains in place today, though its impact has been effectively eliminated by inflation. Nonetheless, it periodically resurfaces as illustrated by the appointment of Peggy Butts in 1997. A Catholic nun who had taken a vow of poverty, Butts had to have a small parcel of land transferred to her name in order to be sworn into office.

sympathized with Nova Scotia's desire to remain separate from Canada, was a proponent of Manchester Liberalism, and was a principal leader of the opposition to the Confederation. He opposed the creation of an upper house during British parliamentary debates: "Bright stated that while he did not object to any people imitating British institutions if they truly desired them, the people of Canada did not want an unelected upper chamber" (Smith 2008, 118). Bright and the opposition were overruled, however.

The governor general position was a powerful post intended to serve as a conduit of continuity between the Canadian Confederation and the British crown. Aside from senate appointments, the governor general could appoint justices to the Supreme Court, most superior and county court judges within the provinces, and lieutenant governors of the provinces.

The governor general post was paired with substantial centralized policy-making power. In contrast to its neighbor to the south, centralization in Canada was favored over state's rights, especially given the evident dangers posed by reformers in provinces such as Nova Scotia. This served as a bulwark against local transgressions against property rights. Furthermore, the central government controlled power over all forms of taxation.

The franchise was also severely restricted upon independence. Although the provinces controlled franchise rules independently, they shared one thing in common: across the board, only male British subjects that were at least twenty-one years of age and met a property qualification could vote. Staggered elections and the lack of a secret ballot meant that provinces could vote on different days and that party machines had powerful patronage levers over voters casting ballots toward the end of elections.

Importantly, the creation of the Canadian Confederation was never put to a vote in Canada. Although the option was mooted by Lord Campbell in the House of Lords, it was nearly uniformly opposed. As Smith (2008) writes, "Lord Monck, the current Governor General, thought the demand 'betrayed a great ignorance' of 'the principles of the British Constitution.' ... [Colonial Secretary Lord] Carnarvon also attacked the idea of holding an election to decide the question of union as being against constitutional tradition, noting that the Anglo-Scottish union of 1707 had been accomplished without an appeal to the voting public in either country" (116).

That Canadian independence was achieved without firing a shot and without the consent of the Canadian people is noteworthy but not surprising from our perspective: this was a fait accompli that in both its timing and characteristics served the political and economic interests of the colonial elite.

The Long (but Faded) Shadow of the British Colonial Past
The British dictated the terms of the Canadian Confederation and constructed institutions to protect the interests of the crown and its allies for an enduring period. Indeed, roughly a quarter of Canada's domestic capital was owned by foreign investors from the time of independence until the 1930s, a figure

dominated by British investment in natural resources such as copper, zinc, and aluminum mines, as well as hydrocarbons (Piketty 2014, 157).[4] Britain also used its links with Canada to promote transatlantic trade and counterbalance US domination in the western hemisphere (Holloway 2006).

A number of changes have nonetheless occurred since independence. These changes did not occur easily or rapidly. To a certain extent, there was for a long time a lid on the degree of change that could be implemented because the United Kingdom retained legislative control over Canada well after 1867. Until 1949, the ability to change the British North America Acts resided with the British Parliament. The Canadian Parliament was therefore required to request amendments from the British (which it complied with in practice). Full Canadian control over the constitution was only handed over in 1982.

Perhaps most prominently, and paralleling the trend in most developed countries, the franchise became universal. This did not happen quickly, however. The adoption of the secret ballot in the late nineteenth century (1874) came much more quickly. Property qualifications continued to be manipulated until their complete abolishment in 1948. The Wartime Elections Act and Military Voters Act of 1917 selectively granted the franchise to female relatives of combatants while stripping the vote from conscientious objectors and naturalized British citizens who were born in enemy countries or spoke enemy languages. Women were granted the full right of suffrage in 1918. The Dominion Elections Act of 1920 then set a countrywide standard for franchise requirements. However, selected disenfranchisement of Asian Canadians, indigenous peoples, and selected religious groups persisted. These groups were only fully extended the vote in 1948, 1960, and 1955, respectively.

Other institutional vestiges of the British colonial legacy remain in place. Parliamentary supremacy remains intact in spite of Canada's federal structure and Supreme Court. Bicameralism has endured, as has the appointment rather than the election of senators. There is still a property requirement for holding a senate seat, though the bar is now quite low. However, the prime minister now appoints senators rather than the governor general. The governor general also appoints supreme court justices in consultation with the cabinet and prime minister. The provinces and parliament do not have formal input in this process.

In short, a number – though hardly all – of the colonial legacies intended to favor British and Canadian political and economic elites have been removed. As Chapter 5 anticipates, the removal of these legacies yielded much more egalitarian social and economic outcomes. Indeed, income inequality in Canada is now lower than in the United States, and although it increased in

[4] This contrasts with far lower foreign ownership in the American economy. As Piketty (2014) discusses, it is "difficult to find purely economic reasons" for this discrepancy; rather, "political factors played a central role" (157), particularly the longer British colonial legacy in Canada and the fact that this link was never violently ruptured.

the 1990s, it leveled out in the 2000s while inequality in the United States continued to climb steeply. Yet changes to Britain's colonial legacies generally took decades to transpire, as well as major political shocks to shake their foundations. The two world wars, the weakening of the British Empire, and technological change empowered new social actors in Canada and led to the diminished power of British investors that had been strong at the time of the passage of the 1867 British North America Act and decades thereafter (e.g., Piketty 2014).

The Philippines

Colonial legacies in newly independent democracies are not unique to the nineteenth century, when monarchies (the most prodigious colonizers) were commonplace. A host of countries that are democratic since inception have elite-biased legacies favoring former colonial or foreign occupiers, and these span the sweep of history as well as a range of colonizers and occupiers. Other former British colonies that won independence as democracies in the mid-twentieth century such as India and Myanmar were also saddled with elite biases in their constitutions and legal systems imposed by London. The same is true of countries that won independence from other occupiers, such as Papua New Guinea (colonized by the Netherlands) and the Philippines (colonized by the United States).

This section examines the legacies the United States left in the Philippines in the wake of WWII. Of course, the United States was not the Philippines' only colonizer. The United States wrested the islands in 1898 from Spain during the Spanish-American War. The Spanish had ruled the islands for more than three centuries prior to the United States. They were sparsely settled and malarious – more like Brazil and Spain's Caribbean holdings than its densely populated colonies such as Mexico or Peru. They were also at the periphery of the Spanish Empire. Yet, like in many of Spain's sparsely settled Latin American colonies, the colonial metropole had set the seeds for extractive agriculture and harshly hierarchical labor relations. Spain's immigration policies encouraged the formation of a predominantly Chinese mestizo landowning and commercial class. Sugar plantations took root, particularly in the Negros region. And, like it had done across its Latin American colonies, Spain imprinted Catholicism on the vast majority of the population.

However, twentieth-century politics and society in the postindependence Philippines was principally guided not by its Spanish colonial legacy – or by stereotypically "traditional" Filipino cultural characteristics such as personal indebtedness, shame, pity, or congeniality – but by the legacy of American rule. Indeed, the extent of Spanish territorial control was limited, the Catholic Church's role in agriculture was uneven, and commercial trade through the ports was dominated by non-Spanish European merchants (Hedman and Sidel

2000, 7). The Philippines in the twentieth century was therefore largely devoid of the working-class mobilization, corporatist policies, and autonomous military rule that characterized Spain's former Latin American colonies in this period.

Hedman and Sidel (2000) emphasize the importance of the American colonial legacy:

The broad contours of recent Philippine history are best understood not against the backdrop of "traditional" Filipino culture or Hispanicised society, but rather in the context of the state structures erected and imposed in the course of the American colonial era. For even as American troops were still "pacifying" pro-independence Filipino forces, elections to municipal office, based on highly restricted suffrage, were first held in 1901, followed by those for provincial governors (1902), representatives to the national Philippine Assembly (1907), an American-style bicameral legislature (1916), and the Commonwealth presidency (1935). The timing, phasing, and structural design of "colonial democracy" left several lasting legacies which have continued to shape Philippine politics long after independence in 1946. (7)

Filipino Independence on an American Timetable

The United States occupied the Philippines for nearly five decades, from 1898 to 1946. The Philippines was a designated US territory until 1934. Yet the intention was not to ultimately grant the Philippines statehood. Instead, as embodied in the 1916 Philippine Autonomy Act (the Jones Law), the United States sought to eventually grant independence to the Philippines. Of course, the lack of urgency toward this end inspired Filipino resistance. This resistance, however, was never sufficient to overthrow the yoke of American occupation. The United States not only reengineered the Filipino state during occupation; it also left the country on its own terms.

The wheels for independence were set in motion in 1934 with the Tydings-McDuffie Act. This act, authored in the US Congress, granted the Philippines its independence in 1946 and was ratified by the Philippine Senate. The act also ensured that the United States would maintain several military bases on the islands while retaining the ability to impose tariffs and quotas on exports from the Philippines that threatened to compete with American products. Critically for postindependence Philippine politics, the act also mandated the drafting of a new constitution as well as a ten-year transitional period of American-Philippine rule.

World War II broke out during this transitional period. The Japanese occupied the Philippines shortly after the bombing of Pearl Harbor. The Philippine government fled to Washington, DC. Despite Philippine resistance sponsored by the United States as well as direct American military engagement, the Japanese managed to control parts of the islands until 1945. The US victory over Japan in 1945 set the timetable for Philippine independence back on track. Full independence was granted to the Philippines in 1946.

Political Legacies of the American Occupation

Philippine independence hardly meant a definitive break with the past. To the contrary, the United States spent decades designing institutions and laws that were oriented toward calcifying the status quo distribution of power on the islands while also ensuring an American military and economic beachhead. These actions were anchored to the preexisting and powerful local elite in Philippine society, with whom the US occupation authorities shared an interest in stability, hierarchical social relations, and economic production (especially agro-exports such as sugar, coconut oil, and timber). Many of these local elites were significant landowners – often Chinese landed capitalists or native land-owners – or moneylenders with ties to the Catholic Church. The skewed distri-bution of large tracts of public lands and the Spanish colonial "friar lands" – lands owned by the Catholic religious orders – by the American occupation authority entrenched existing landed elites and inequality in the countryside. It did so by enabling wealthy individuals to acquire the lion's share of the friar lands and other public lands available for purchase (Escalante 2002).

American efforts at shaping Philippine politics were already bearing fruit within a decade of occupation. The Philippine Commission, a legislative body composed of Americans named by the US president and ratified by the US Senate, was the sole legislative body in the Philippines from 1900 to 1902. Its president also served as the governor general, who was vested with execu-tive control over the island until 1935. The commission created a judicial sys-tem and supreme court, wrote the legal code, and introduced a civil service. Municipal elections were held in 1901, provincial governors were elected in 1902, and representatives for a national assembly were elected in 1907 – all under restrictive suffrage rules that set requirements for literacy, property holdings, and language spoken. The mere 1.4 percent of the population that voted in the 1907 assembly elections "closely approximated the small group of Filipinos who had comprised the *principalias* in the *pueblos* during the Spanish regime" (Hayden 1942, 267). This was a rarefied group of local village- and town-level elites who were typically either large landowners or who had ties to large landowners (McCoy 1993). Meanwhile, the Philippine Commission became the unelected upper body of congress.

The limited franchise and timing of elections bolstered the Americans' local elite partners. This is because "local, particularistic, patronage-based concerns and networks would serve as the building blocks of electoral competition" and bolstered local bosses "whose discretion over state resources, personnel, and regulatory powers provided enormous opportunities for private capital accu-mulation" (Hedman and Sidel 2000, 7). Local elites then cooperated with the US occupation authorities and helped ensure the quiescence of their labor forces in exchange for the ability to pass favorable economic policies. Indeed, in 1908 the new parliament exempted the friar lands from the limitations on the amount of land an individual or corporation could buy or lease from the insular government. Large landowners – many of whom were in parliament or had connections to parliamentarians – then took advantage of this exemption to scoop up extensive tracts of land.

An elected upper house replaced the Philippine Commission in 1916 under the Philippine Autonomy Act, yielding an American-style legislature. The franchise nonetheless remained heavily restricted, which served to strengthen the hegemony of local elites who were largely sympathetic to American interests. Landowning elites in particular became even stronger starting in the late 1910s and early 1920s as an increase in commodity prices spurred growth in commercial agriculture. Notorious among these elites were the major sugar planters centered in Negros Occidental.

The next major institutional change came with the passage of the 1935 constitution. The 1934 Tydings-McDuffie Act stipulated the drafting of a constitution – which had to incorporate certain provisions and had to be approved by the president of the United States – to guide the Philippines toward independence by 1946. Constitutional convention delegates were elected in 1934. The restricted suffrage resulted in the election of a mix of traditional elites and new professionals, but ongoing patronage politics as well as pressure from well-organized sugar elites largely limited the range of interests that were likely to deviate from the status quo interests of the United States (Takagi 2016, 45–46).

The result was a constitution with a division of powers between the executive, legislature, and judiciary that largely imitated the US Constitution. One noteworthy exception was the presidency, which was vested with substantial emergency powers, powers over national commerce, and budget appropriation powers (Hedman and Sidel 2000, 16). The president replaced the US governor general in the 1935 elections and assumed principal executive authority, with the caveat that the United States still held formal possession of the territory. The 1935 constitution also established a unicameral rather than bicameral legislature, though it was amended in 1940 to create an upper house.

As a final salvo on the eve of Philippine independence, the United States passed legislation securing a host of military bases on the islands as well as trade rules such as the Bell Trade Act. The Bell Trade Act enabled the United States to slap import quotas on Philippine goods that competed with US-produced goods. It also secured equal access for American citizens and corporations to Philippine natural resources. The United States obtained these concessions by threatening to withhold funds to rebuild Philippine infrastructure and industry destroyed during WWII.

With these arrangements set, the United States granted full independence to the Philippines in 1946. This ushered in democratic elections under rules of universal suffrage. In spite of this political sea change, Hedman and Sidel (2000) conclude,

Philippine post-colonial electoralism has manifested enduring patterns of narrow class rule already discernible before independence. In fact, throughout the postwar period, a national oligarchy "essentially recruited from families of long standing economic wealth or political dominance or both" has continued to define the nature and direction of electoral politics as large landowners, commercial magnates, and their scions have filled both houses of Congress as well as the offices of municipal halls and provincial capitols throughout the archipelago…Significantly, moreover, the colonial lineages of this political class endowed it with control over a combination of clientelist structures, coercive mechanisms and monetary resources which, in turn, facilitated sustained oligarchic predominance in Philippine electoral politics. At the same time, colonial policies introduced discriminatory laws and practices against labour parties and other nonelite political organisations which, buttressed by constitutional provisions for the suppression of "insurrections," served to further strengthen the institutionalisation of oligarchy-dominated bi-factional electoral politics in the post-war period. (15–16)

The Maintenance and Modification of the American Colonial Legacy

The institutional and legal architecture imposed by the United States during its occupation of the Philippines remained stable for decades. Until the constitution was replaced in 1973, it was hardly modified. Aside from an amendment to add an upper house of parliament in 1940, the 1935 constitution was only amended again in 1946–1947 to incorporate the Bell Trade Act and to grant parity rights to American citizens in the Philippines.

In many ways, the 1935 constitution and associated legal framework was in fact too stable. On the one hand, universal suffrage enabled mass participation in elections, and the constitution enabled those elections to produce strong executives. But on the other hand, the dominant social actors – the agro-commercial oligarchy and the business class, many with economic or political ties to the United States – monopolized the seats in both houses of the national legislature (Hedman and Sidel 2000). The result was persistent economic inequality and political gridlock: "Democracy was not helping the Philippine citizenry demand more redistribution from the oligarchy; it was allowing the oligarchy to secure elected office and protect itself from state extraction" (Slater et al. 2014, 366). Citizens consequently turned to expressing their demands through extra-electoral mobilization in the form of insurgencies, street protests, and the rise of pervasive localized violence.

These tensions boiled over periodically until they produced an executive (Ferdinand Marcos) who selectively wielded sectors of popular support against the most powerful and entrenched social actors, generating a series of full-blown political crises. Marcos was elected in 1965 after holding legislative seats in both the Philippine House of Representatives and senate. The outset of his second term in office was bedeviled by a series of major protests and demonstration marches against the government as well as simmering communist and Muslim insurgencies. Economic elites simultaneously squashed Marcos's attempts to raise corporate and luxury taxes to fund his campaign promises (Slater et al. 2014, 367).

In retaliation, Marcos declared martial law in 1972. He quickly promulgated a new constitution in 1973 that abolished the upper house of congress.

Marcos then embarked on a concerted campaign to seize private businesses and public institutions and grant control over them to his family and close political allies. At the same time, he instituted a land reform program in 1972 in an effort to win the support of peasants and undermine selected landowners (Wurfel 1989). While limited in nature, it was the most redistributive land reform in the Philippines up until that time – much more so than the adulterated agrarian reforms of presidents Macapagal and Magsaysay.

Marcos was, of course, also renowned for repression, corruption, and nepotism. He was ultimately ousted from office forcibly during the 1986 People Power Revolution. The new democratic regime, headed by Corazon Aquino, appointed a constitutional commission that hammered out a new, more popular charter in 1986. This constitution was, for the first time, an outgrowth of the popular will.

Yet several vestiges of the United States' occupation of the Philippines, such as strong economic and foreign policy ties to the United States and local de facto bossism (manifested at the national level through "cacique democracy"), have continued to persist. The United States remains one of the Philippines' top trading partners and is its largest foreign investor. For instance, the archipelago is suffused with coconut plantations that help satisfy American consumers' appetite for soap, cosmetics, margarine, and other coconut oil–based products. The United States has also long maintained a series of strategic military bases in the Philippines under the Mutual Defense Treaty, which it used to police the Pacific (it also used these bases for logistical support during the Vietnam War). Though the treaty lapsed in the 1990s, new agreements resuscitated US military access. Most recently, in early 2016 the United States and the Philippines agreed to a new permanent American military presence across five bases in the archipelago.

But these lingering US ties to the Philippines have become more tenuous since the onset of more popular democracy. Indeed, the most recently elected president, Rodrigo Duterte, has repeatedly threatened to redefine the relationship with the United States. Indeed, during his first year in office he went so far as to declare that he wants American troops to eventually leave the country.

A DEMOCRATIC SUCCESSOR STATE TO AN AUTHORITARIAN PREDECESSOR: THE CASE OF UKRAINE

As with colonial or foreign occupiers, democratic successor states that are founded from the ashes of authoritarian predecessors are similarly subject to persistent institutional legacies. These legacies, however, differ from those that operate via elite-biased constitutions inherited from previous authoritarian regimes. In particular, authoritarian elites from the larger predecessor state might be much stronger outside the borders of the successor state than within them. Furthermore, these cases of transition entail changes not just in regime type but also in statehood, nationhood, and in some cases, the economic system. Therefore, key elements of the political game are changing in tandem, and not all of these changes are encompassed by our theory. Nonetheless, our theory does anticipate that to the extent there is a powerful outgoing authoritarian elite with a stake in the new successor state, then this elite will try to obtain a favorable institutional arrangement.

Ukraine exemplifies key dynamics of an authoritarian predecessor imposing legacies on a democratic successor state. In the case of Ukraine, the authoritarian predecessor was the Soviet Union, which began fraying in the late 1980s and finally dissolved in 1991. A newly independent Ukraine was one of a series of new democracies that sprung up among the former Soviet Socialist Republics. Others included Estonia, Latvia, Lithuania, and Armenia.

The new dawn in Ukraine, however, had a distinctly Soviet tinge. As D'Anieri et al. (1999) write, "Although we think of 1991 as the opening of a new era in Ukrainian history, institutionally and economically, the legacy of the Soviet Union has been powerful. The former Soviet administrative and political elite has retained great power and influence at the center of government and the economy in newly independent Ukraine" (6). Other democratic successor states of the former Soviet Union also inherited Soviet legacies, and the nature of their particular political battles and stakes led to varying institutional outcomes as well as economic and social consequences.

The Founding of Ukraine: A Bridge to the Soviet Past

The path Ukraine would take as a newly independent democracy in 1991 was already being shaped several years prior under the Soviet Union. Along with a host of major political and economic initiatives, Mikhail Gorbachev worked to change the Soviet Union's constitution in 1988. Changes to the constitution of Ukraine – mainly to allow semicompetitive elections – were subsequently adopted in 1989 after substantial debate and resistance by Ukraine's Communist Party (Harasymiw 2002, 36). One consequence was the rise of the longtime communist apparatchik Leonid Kravchuk as chairman of Ukraine's Supreme Council.

In late 1990, a parliamentary commission was established to draft a new constitution that would accommodate Gorbachev's perestroika. This commission, headed by Kravchuk, started a long-term tussle over the form of its political institutions as well as its orientation toward the Soviet Union and subsequently Russia. A broad range of major issues were on the table, from the electoral system to the form of parliament, the delineation of powers across government branches, and even the name of the country. As Harasymiw (2002) writes, "In Ukraine beginning in 1990, the drafters and decision-makers were attempting to write not only a new and long-lasting constitution but also one that would be crafted to their advantage" (36). Of the forty-seven parliamentary deputies to the commission, twenty-four were members of the communist majority. Another dozen members not drawn from parliament included insider political players such as the ministers of justice and internal affairs. Kravchuk, for his part, pushed for a strong presidency and bicameralism.

As these constitutional issues were being debated, the Soviet Union exhaled its final breath. Kruvchek resigned from the Communist Party following a Soviet coup attempt in August 1991. Ukraine then passed a declaration of independence in late August. Kruvchek won the presidency in December 1991 during an election that also included the formal vote for secession from the Soviet Union.

Soviet Legacies in Independent Ukraine

The next several years were marked by a push and pull over a new draft constitution as well as a flurry of amendments to Ukraine's older constitution (many of which favored Kruvchek and his allies). A full constitutional accord was sidelined until new parliamentary and presidential elections in 1994. A new president – Leonid Kuchma, Kruvchek's former prime minister – took power in these elections. Kuchma was a consummate insider: he had run an enormous missile factory in Dnipropetrovsk during the Cold War and profited handsomely from it following independence.

Meanwhile, a host of individuals who had powerful political and economic positions on the eve of Ukraine's independence leveraged that power to ensure that they would remain politically indispensable under democracy. Many of these were managers in state-owned firms. These so-called red directors secured around 30 percent ownership stake during insider privatizations (which were more common than voucher privatizations), giving them a controlling share of these assets (Aslund 2007, 184). Insider privatization quickly consolidated selective property rights and "transferred huge wealth to a privileged few" – the same few with the capacity to block privatization where it was not sufficiently favorable (184). The consequence was that the old Soviet *nomenklatura* "perpetuated the corruption of the former system through the persistence of clannish, highly nepotistic networks of relations, based loosely upon regional and industrial groupings" (D'Anieri et al. 1999, 6). While these *nomenklatura* were uniformly Communist Party members when Ukraine was still part of the Soviet Union, many, like Kruvchek, left the party around the time of independence and either became unaffiliated or tied themselves to ideologically unanchored (and often regionally based) centrist parties.

Indeed, these former *nomenklatura* were important players in the parliament of 1994–1998 that drafted a new constitution in 1996. Enterprise directors and farm managers comprised the third largest group in the Rada following top state officials and professionals (Puglisi 2003, 109). With the Far Left (mostly communists and socialists) and Right (market-oriented reformers from western Ukraine) deadlocked, the Center came to play an outsized role. Constituting slightly more than a third of parliamentary seats, it was composed of mainly non-party-affiliated deputies, many of whom were members of the former *nomenklatura* or worked in the executive. Consequently, "centrists were closely associated with the so-called 'party of power'" (Whitmore 2004, 69). They were the most outwardly supportive of President Kuchma.

The regional concentration of centrist deputy groups resembled Soviet-era regional groups. Those from Unity were known as the "Dnipropetrovsk clan," a prominent and long-standing elite group; Social-Market Choice was connected with the "Donetsk clan" of elites (Whitmore 2004). There was also a contingent of central government bureaucrats. Favored by the electoral law that they in part helped craft in the early 1990s, "centrist deputies were able to informally perpetuate Soviet deputy formations and base their associations on the old regional and branch forms of elite networks" (Whitmore 2004).

These groups tended to pursue narrow, sectional interests. They were open to bargaining with more ideologically oriented deputies in order to pursue these interests – an eminent example of Hellman's (1998) "partial reform equilibrium," in which the winners of partial early reforms subvert further reform attempts for purposes of private profit.

President Kuchma, however, faced truculent opponents on the ideologically far left and far right who were not easily steamrolled. Kuchma therefore engaged in a series of power plays that were intended to undermine the institutional position of his adversaries, availing constitutional engineering when necessary. Most prominently, he repeatedly threatened to hold a referendum on the constitution as an end-run around the parliamentary commissions charged with drafting the document, and he passed the controversial 1995 "Law on Power" with a simple parliamentary majority that served to subordinate the prime minister and cabinet ministers to the president.

Even though Kuchma's supporters were wary about his new presidential powers (D'Anieri 2015, 132), he carried on, repeatedly threatening public referenda until he coerced parliament into delivering him additional presidential powers. The constitution granted the president extensive powers to appoint most government, judicial, and military office holders; to initiate legislation; and to dissolve the unicameral parliament. It also gave the central administration power over local and regional administrative appointments, circumventing local-level challenges to presidential policies and initiatives (131–133).

Kuchma's strong-arm tactics during the drafting of the 1996 constitution dealt a blow to the closest ideological descendants of the Soviet-era Communist Party of Ukraine: communists and socialists. These groups were largely shut out of the final constitutional process (D'Anieri 2015), though the communists would remain a significant political force until the 2014 Euromaidan uprising. Ironically, the savviest beneficiaries of the Soviet legacy – those who divorced themselves from the Communist Party during Ukraine's independence while using their managerial positions or personal connections within the state to reap the lion's share of profits from privatization – were the ones who came out ahead.

These wolves in sheep's clothing, Kuchma included, came to tower over Ukraine's political and economic landscape and represented different regions of the country and economic sectors. Many were elected to parliament under weak or personalist party labels. And many continued to do business with the Russian government and with Russian oligarchs who had similarly come out on top during privatizations in the 1990s. This included exporting armaments (e.g., aircraft engines, ballistic missiles, and uranium) to Russia along with other goods manufactured in Ukraine. That is, until the Euromaidan popular uprising in 2014.

Wiggling in the Straightjacket: Attempts to Overhaul Ukraine's Institutions

Although the Soviet legacy cast a long shadow over Ukraine's institution building and economic reform in the 1990s, there has also been a struggle to entirely overhaul this legacy. A new group of oligarchs arose from the economic chaos of the 1990s, especially following the second wave of privatization beginning in 1997 that sold off state assets to outsiders. These oligarchs generally preferred to more tightly bind the hands of the state to protect their newfound fortunes. One prominent new oligarch is Ukraine's current president, Petro Poroshenko. Yet as with the first wave of post-Soviet oligarchs, most of this new cohort ties their interests to their firms and regions rather than to strong, ideologically rooted parties. Their abilities and interests in changing Ukraine's institutions are therefore limited.

The extensive presidential powers President Kuchma won in the 1996 constitution also came to haunt Ukraine with a "winner-take-all" style of politics in which the enormous stakes led to contestation over presidential votes and the exercise of power. The Orange Revolution was the most prominent manifestation of this conflict. Spurred by a fraudulent 2004 election between Viktor Yanukovych, Kuchma's prime minister who hailed from the pro-Russian Donetsk region, and Viktor Yushchenko, who favored European integration, the massive uprising forced a repeat runoff and handed a victory to Yushchenko. But a constitutional amendment between the first and second presidential runoffs in 2004 stripped the president's power to appoint the prime minister and most cabinet ministers.

Corruption, increasing economic inequality, and political instability continue to plague Ukraine. Yanukovych was elected president in 2010 and, much to Russia's satisfaction, rejected an EU association agreement in 2014. But the threat of a turn away from Europe and toward Russia immediately spurred the Euromaidan popular uprising, which forced Yanukovych to flee into exile to Russia. Russia then retaliated. It seized Crimea and clandestinely sent troops into eastern Ukraine to support separatist rebels. Petro Poroshenko was elected to replace Yanukovych, but he has been severely undermined by Russia's ongoing support of separatist activity in eastern pro-Russian oblasts, including Yanukovych's Donetsk.

Ukraine's political and institutional instability has generally served not to upend the Soviet legacies in Ukraine but rather to weaken the state and exacerbate a political power struggle. The consequence is that regional and sectoral elite networks – rooted in the Soviet era and renovated by individuals connected to the Soviets or otherwise benefitting from privatization – have flourished and stepped in to fill the power vacuum. Anders (2015) summarizes it well: "The problem with the Ukrainian state is that the old Soviet system remains alive and well with all its bureaucracy and centralization. Political will to pursue a fundamental reform has never prevailed. Even the Orange Revolution failed to make a dent in Ukraine's tenacious old structures" (25–26).

Our analysis of Ukraine's flawed and incomplete democracy, which we have undertaken in a similar manner as the rest of this book (i.e., through the lens of constitution making by elites who were powerful under the previous authoritarian regime), yields an important takeaway. Despite changes in the political and economic system that mattered greatly, the same cast of characters from Soviet times were able to shape and then themselves use the country's new institutions to continue to dominate Ukrainian politics and economics. Yet despite strong evidence that Ukrainian politics was distorted by a heavy dose of personalism, Ukraine's institutions have also helped oligarchs and the Russians assert their continued dominance.

CONCLUSION

In this book we have argued and shown that citizens who wrestle an authoritarian regime to its knees, and deny outgoing elites any opportunity to entrench their power beyond a democratic transition, typically reap the benefits under a new democracy. They and their representatives have an opportunity to forge a new social contract that works for them because it is by them. The result is a more even political and economic playing field.

Citizens of democracies founded in the wake of colonial or foreign occupation, by contrast, are not always so fortunate, a phenomenon that mirrors what we have documented happens in the wake of a different breed of democratizations: those dominated and engineered by outgoing authoritarian elites. While they might help run their occupiers out of town, occupiers recognize that they are in a high-stakes game. Consequently, colonizers and foreign occupiers typically invest substantial resources in constitutions and associated institutions in an effort to protect their political and economic interests, as well as those of the indigenous elites who aided their rule, long after they sail away. These investments elapse over the course of years and even decades. They are often channeled into vehicles that mimic many of the same components of holdover authoritarian constitutions: unelected ruling bodies, restrictive franchise rules, bicameral legislatures, stilted electoral rules, a judiciary constructed to serve as a bulwark for property rights protection, and tailor-made forms of centralization or decentralization that are engineered to aggrandize the power of elites linked to the occupiers.

These vehicles often deliver social and economic outcomes that are analogous to those of the holdover authoritarian constitutions we have discussed in previous chapters: an unequal economic playing field, restricted or less consequential political participation, and policy gridlock. They are frequently topped off with arrangements that align the new democracy's foreign policy with the interests of its former colonizer or occupier. This typically includes favorable trade relations, military cooperation, and even permanent military bases.

Like elite-biased constitutions inherited from authoritarian predecessors, however, colonial and other occupier legacies can fade under democracy. This rarely occurs quickly or automatically. It instead typically occurs – as with authoritarian constitutions – when an organized opposition seizes on an economic crisis or a shift in the balance of power. In the Philippines, the postindependence democratic gridlock that gave rise to Ferdinand Marcos was only broken by the People Power Revolution. In Canada, the world wars and the associated weakening of the British Empire enabled the ascendant middle classes and selected minority groups to win the franchise and eliminate property rights restrictions to voting.

But the power of former colonizers and foreign occupiers can also fade gradually, and certainly more gradually than the power of former authoritarian elites under new democracies. Colonizers and occupiers have less at stake than domestic actors: they are not subject to the same laws and often have financial and political interests spread elsewhere. Consequently, major economic shifts and technological changes can render the interests of former colonizers and occupiers less encompassing, opening a window for political renovation in the formerly occupied country without risking bloodshed or instability.

9

Conclusion

This books lays to rest the twin notions that new democracies are typically the masters of their own fates and that elected political representatives represent the average voter. Instead, we demonstrate that in terms of institutional design, the allocation of power and privilege, and the lived experiences of citizens, democracy might not reset the political game. Those who benefited under the previous dictatorship often continue to do so well after they formally step down. The price that elites extract in exchange for increased political competition and pluralism is a tailor-made set of elite-biased institutions laden with laws and procedures that shield outgoing incumbents from punishment for the crimes they committed under dictatorship and bestow their economic allies with unfair advantages that hurt regular citizens and increase inequality. Therefore, democracy can be a Pyrrhic victory: after transition, those who pine for political and economic equality are often left hungry for real change.

In this book, we show that the majority of democracies throughout history have been the product of a pact between outgoing authoritarian elites and the opposition intended to bind the latter's hands for an indefinite period after transition. From 1800 to 2006, only 34 percent of new democracies began with a constitution that they created themselves or inherited from a past episode of democratic rule in their country. Much more frequently, new democracies inherit and operate under a constitution that was designed under dictatorship and imposed by outgoing elites during the transition process. This includes not only recently minted democracies such as Chile and South Africa; many Western European countries such as Sweden, Denmark, and the Netherlands also inherited elite-biased constitutions from their autocratic pasts.

What determines whether a democracy is incarnated as elite biased? This book argues that authoritarian elites and their economic elite allies are at times threatened by groups of ascendant outsider economic elites. Incumbent authoritarian political elites and incumbent economic elites might fear that this group of outsiders will eclipse their own strength and topple them from power in pursuit of a more favorable political and economic arrangement. As the balance of power becomes more favorable to outsider economic elites, this group cannot credibly promise not to challenge the current authoritarian political and economic insiders. The result is that incumbent political and economic elites might move to strategically exit the regime together, imposing a new democratic arrangement that is favorable to their interests and cuts these outsiders out of the political deal indefinitely. The safest and most effective way to accomplish this task is by forging a pretransition deal with opposition forces that exchanges political and economic safeguards for elections, usually through a constitution penned by outgoing elites.

The upshot is that for those who captain the ship under dictatorship, democracy does not spell shipwreck. When political elites strategically exit dictatorship by engaging in careful constitutional engineering before handing over power to an elected government, they do quite well under the succeeding democracy. Powerful authoritarian elites frequently avoid prosecution for crimes perpetrated under autocracy.

For those passengers who make the journey in first class under dictatorship, the fate is equally favorable. The interest groups that had successfully lobbied for subsidies, barriers to entry, and friendly fiscal and macroeconomic policies under dictatorship do not disappear – to the contrary, they flourish under the new regime. Indeed, these actors often secure even less progressive policies than under the previous autocratic period, which contributes to the widening of inequality and a reduction in opportunities for the majority. Furthermore, they can avoid the uncertainty that sometimes accompanies life under autocracy. Consequently, institutions and policies are biased against the majority of the population even decades after a transition in a large number of democracies.

In this book we therefore suggest that researchers and interested publics reconceptualize democracy by disaggregating democracies into those that are elite biased in nature versus those that are more popular. Constitutional origins lie at the heart of this distinction: they matter for explaining the timing, scope, and pace of democratization. They also matter for explaining how inclusive, pluralistic, and representative a democracy's institutions are. To be sure, there are gradations to how elite biased a democracy can be, and even some popular democracies are flawed. Yet we can nonetheless gain analytic leverage by making a fundamental distinction between the different ways in which democracies are constructed.

As with the nature of democracy, constitutional origins determine a society's level of economic competition, allocation of capital, prices, and rates of return. They play a key role in the distribution of assets, income, and opportunities. Indeed, constitutions affect a whole host of critical public policies such as taxation, spending, agricultural and trade policy, and monetary policy.

Put simply, a popular democracy is institutionally designed to yield more economically egalitarian outcomes. To be sure, markets can at times foster massive inequality, often in conjunction with exogenous factors such as technology. But if inequality is allowed to mushroom in a democracy without offsetting policies such as social insurance and redistribution, it is usually because outgoing authoritarian elites have rigged the economy to benefit their economic allies and successors. Therefore, another contribution made by this book is to challenge the idea that capitalism is an impersonal, monolithic force that inexorably engenders inequality (e.g., Piketty 2014). If it does this, it is frequently by design.

This book also demonstrates, however, that authoritarian legacies do not always condemn democracies to an entirely bleak destiny. Some of the most monumental achievements in democracy in recent decades consist not of toppling dictatorship itself but rather of dramatically revising the terms of the social contract under democracy. We show that this has been possible because some elite-biased democracies eventually overhaul or even jettison a constitution inherited from outgoing autocratic elites as citizens and groups that were previously disenfranchised force political change on insiders who are holdovers from the previous regime.

The metamorphosis from elite-biased to popular democracy is ironic. The dismantlement of holdover institutions typically resides with "rival" economic elites who are either a preexisting group shunned during the transitional design period or a nascent group that rises after democratization. These rival economic elites spearhead democratic reforms in order to secure more liberal policies intended to strip unfair advantages from the economic elites allied with the former authoritarian regime and thus level the playing field. This has important associated effects: it ushers in a more majoritarian democracy that requires the newly empowered economic elites to finance a greater degree of redistribution to the masses. Average citizens represent both the numbers and political machinery, such as party foot soldiers, needed to change elite-biased institutions that typically require supermajority thresholds to be reformed. In short, the key to obtaining popular democracy is an alliance of convenience between ascendant economic elites and the masses.

Through extensive data collection and compilation, we have built several comprehensive datasets to support the abovementioned claims. These datasets span the globe and date back to 1800. The cornerstone of this effort is fine-grained data on constitutions. We spell out the content of these constitutions in great detail, enumerating the institutions, rights, and laws that they codify to protect outgoing incumbents and their economic allies. To name but a few examples of the commonly utilized tools, this book identifies restrictions on the franchise, bicameral institutions, electoral laws that overrepresent parties tied to the former authoritarian regime, and strong protections for the status quo distribution of private property. We also introduce variables that measure progressive taxation, social spending, spending on welfare and social insurance, and commitments to political pluralism, egalitarianism, and social justice, as well as outcomes related to the fate of former authoritarian incumbents after democratization.

Beyond our global empirical analyses, we also employ detailed data at different levels of analysis in case studies of Chile and Sweden. These case studies help demonstrate the validity of our argument as well as its nuances and manifestations. Furthermore, we show that our argument can, in the main, be logically extended to the institutional legacies left by colonizers or other occupiers of newly independent democracies – a claim we explore in the cases of Canada, the Philippines, and Ukraine.

Our data and case studies allow us to make several original contributions to the study of political regimes. First, we demonstrate how pervasive the phenomenon of elite-biased democratization has been across time and place. Second, we outline the diverse range of institutional and legal mechanisms that authoritarian elites use to protect their political and economic interests after democratic transition. Third, we explore the causes of democratic transitions, both to elite-biased democracy and popular democracy. Fourth, we explore the differential consequences of these transitions. Fifth, we document and explain the reason behind the annulments and amendments of long-standing elite-biased constitutions inherited by democracies.

The rest of this chapter addresses issues that we have only hinted at in the rest of the book. First, we discuss democratic breakdown, inspecting both old and new patterns and attempting to shine light on its causes using our theoretical framework. Second, we discuss shifts from popular democracy to elite-biased democracy: how a democracy that is created from below, or an elite-biased democracy that is subsequently reformed, can nonetheless succumb to capture by economic elites. Finally, we discuss the broad policy implications that stem from our theoretical framework and analyses and offer both democracy's advocates and would-be democrats a handbook for how to bring about meaningful political change.

DEMOCRATIC BREAKDOWN

Far from an "end of history" view in which democracy becomes the only game in town, authoritarianism is again on the rise. Examples include Putin's Russia, Maduro's Venezuela, Erdoğan's Turkey, Duterte's Philippines, and the military junta that has ruled Thailand since 2014. These reversions are seen by many, along with the rise of hard-liners in autocracies such as China and Iran who have aborted liberal reforms, as an end of the acceleration toward democracy that hastened after the fall of the Berlin Wall.

While this book focuses predominantly on the role of elites in democratization, it also has implications for how and when democracy might break down. Between 1800 and 2006, there are seventy-seven breakdowns in which a democracy reverts to dictatorship. Of course, not all of these reversions result in enduring dictatorship. Many countries in which democracy fails in this period eventually return to democracy. For example, in Chapter 7 we outlined how this occurred in Chile in 1990 after a seventeen-year authoritarian interregnum. At the extreme are countries such as Argentina, Greece, Peru, Thailand, and Turkey, which cycle several times between democracy and dictatorship. In many of these cases, democracy returned in fairly short order after an authoritarian interruption, only to succumb to dictatorship again after that.

What, if anything, can our theoretical framework say about these patterns? While only twenty-nine of the seventy-seven reversions were from elite-biased democracy, forty-eight were episodes of backsliding from popular democracy. Furthermore, of these forty-eight episodes of breakdown from popular democracy, in nineteen cases democracy was reborn with an elite-biased constitution inherited from authoritarianism. Examples include France, Spain, Poland, Guatemala, Brazil, Nigeria, Pakistan, and Turkey. And in twelve cases, democracy is defunct within our time period of analysis: no democracy returns at a later time. Examples include Myanmar and Uganda.[1] These figures are hardly surprising from our perspective. After all, elite-biased democracy is created of elites, by elites, and for elites, whereas popular democracy poses a host of threats to elites who do not participate in its inception. Sometimes the safest decision is to avoid democracy altogether.

It is the breakdown of elite-biased democracies, however, that is perhaps of most interest to students of democracy and democracy activists today. This is because these democracies are typically more subject to populism. Populist movements claim to express the will of the majority directly, unfiltered through elite actors and institutions. Yet they simultaneously ride roughshod over deliberation and consensus building and often threaten politically vulnerable interest groups and minorities. And, in general, populism undermines civil liberties. Therefore, it is not a surprise that opportunistic politicians with an authoritarian bent might try to agitate the masses in elite-biased democracies to do an end run around "corrupt" elites and their "rigged" institutions. After all, as we have shown throughout this book, hemming in the masses and protecting the wealthy and well connected is often the express purpose of these elite biases. They are therefore perfect scapegoats for populists who may themselves harbor authoritarian intentions.

A quintessential example is Turkey, where Erdoğan has used both strongman bluster and constitutional reform to gut the checks and balances and military vetoes that previously hemmed in civilian politicians. The same occurred under Chávez and later Maduro in Venezuela. Similar developments have occurred in Hungary under Orban and in the Philippines under Duterte.

Of course, our theory cannot – nor does it seek to – explain all instances and forms of democratic erosion. Consider Pakistan. Since its independence from India in 1947, it has cycled between democracy and dictatorship twice

---

[1] To be sure, some tentative, albeit small, steps towards democracy have been taken by elites in both countries.

(see Table 3.2). The reasons behind these regime changes have more to do with separatism, military autonomy, and international politics – including nuclear brinksmanship with India. Also, consider a host of sub-Saharan African reversions such as Nigeria (1983), Sierra Leone (1997), and Niger (1996). These reversions revolved not around the political and economic issues central to our theory but rather around concerns about corruption and the flagrant abuse of patronage, ethnic balance, and power sharing.

Our theory can, however, shed light on many reversions back to dictatorship. Before we explain how that is the case, consider that there are two types of reversions to dictatorship: those that arise "from below" and those that transpire "from above." Reversions "from above" entail the military stepping in via a coup to cancel democracy. The military then either retains the reins of power itself or passes governance to another appointed individual or ruling body. Examples include a host of military coups in Thailand, including the most recent one in 2014; the Pinochet coup in Chile that we explored in Chapter 7; as well as the Sisi-led coup in Egypt. Reversions from below denote the gutting of checks and balances or the suspension of elections by elected leaders who become strongmen and replace their democracies with dictatorship. Examples include Hitler in Germany, Putin in Russia, and Erdoğan in Turkey. These are often referred to as auto-coups.

Our book can account for several different types of democratic breakdown from above. For example, there are instances in which outgoing authoritarian elites seek to set up an elite-biased democracy but something goes terribly awry. First, authoritarian elites might simply miscalculate the likely effects that particular institutions or rules will have. For instance, an authoritarian regime might not conduct elections or have access to reliable opinion polls, or even censuses, that accurately reveal the political support for the regime's candidates and economic allies. For this reason, outgoing authoritarians' attempts to create electoral districts or electoral rules that are supposed to overrepresent their interests can backfire. In this case, a regime might be forced to imperfectly estimate its political support and design democratic institutions amid greater than average uncertainty.

Things can alternatively go awry for a more pedestrian reason. Outgoing authoritarian elites anticipate that once they exit the stage via a carefully orchestrated arrangement, the new incoming regime will play nice. An incoming leader, however, might not be willing or able to toe the line. On the one hand, a newly elected democratic leader might attempt to tear up the transition agreement; in doing so, he or she can simply misjudge the willingness of outgoing authoritarian elites to use their de facto power to cancel democracy. On the other hand, a newly democratic leader might be pushed beyond the bounds of what is acceptable for outgoing authoritarian elites by their constituency. The newly democratic leader in this case chooses risking a reaction by the erstwhile autocrats or the military instead of letting down his or her loyalists.

Take Egypt in 2011 after the military allowed presidential elections to occur. Muhammad Morsi was the Muslim Brotherhood candidate, running as the standardbearer of the Freedom and Justice Party. He proceeded to act boldly and decisively, firing the top two generals who had ruled under the military junta that succeeded Hosni Mubarak, and annulled the constitution – a revised version of the preexisting one – that had been bequeathed by the junta to considerably limit the powers of the elected government. Morsi also attempted to revive the Muslim Brotherhood–dominated parliament after it had been dissolved by Egypt's Supreme Constitutional Court on the grounds that it had been elected unconstitutionally. Finally, he also attempted to create a new constitution that would usher in popular democracy. All of these flagrant violations of the transitional arrangement imposed by the military unsurprisingly catalyzed them into reacting violently, toppling Morsi in less than one year. He was summarily found guilty of several crimes, including inciting deadly violence, and is slated to serve lengthy prison time.

Another problem is that a constitutional convention might get away from outgoing elites. Authoritarians seeking to exit the dictatorship often convoke a constitutional assembly that they then hope to control in order to author a document that protects their interests after democratization but has a patina of legitimacy. They do this by manipulating the composition of the constituent assembly – selecting the delegates or restricting the selection process – and concocting its agenda setting and voting rules. But these assemblies can take on a life of their own, and their members could exercise more autonomy than elites expect them to. Also, the agenda setting and voting rules that govern the constitutional assembly might simply yield unforeseen consequences: unwanted institutions, rules, and policies can find their way into the constitution.

Finally, even if outgoing authoritarian elites set up favorable institutions that protect them and their allies for several years, a "black swan" event could take place. In other words, an extremely unlikely or unforeseen event might transpire that strengthens outsider economic elites or the masses and enables them to coordinate on peeling back elite biases and forging a more popular social contract. To their chagrin, former authoritarian elites are then forced to step in and go back to the drawing board: return to autocracy and possibly reattempt democratization on better terms further down the line.

Thailand is one illustrative example. It transitioned back to democracy in 1992 after military rule (and several earlier experiments with democracy). The first five years under this elite-biased democratic spell were fairly predictable for the military and the monarchy: the long-standing, conservative, and royalist Democrat Party held office and did not seriously stir the pot. But the Asian Financial Crisis of 1997 rained down hard on Thailand, leading to high inflation and worsening poverty. It decimated the Democrat Party, generating a political vacuum that Thaksin Shinawatra stepped into.

Shinawatra set about reforming the constitution and then wantonly flaunted constraints to executive rule. He quickly became wildly popular among the rural masses, embracing populist economic appeals and winning reelection in the country's largest landslide ever in 2001 (Slater 2013). An unhinged populist was an unacceptable – and previously unforeseen – threat to the monarchy and the military, however. Shinawatra was ousted in a coup in 2006.

What all of these scenarios share in common is that they are likely to induce a serious case of buyer's remorse for former authoritarian elites. As we outlined in the previous examples, these elites might have sufficiently strong incentives to try to dial back democracy entirely via a coup. This begs the question, however: Why are former authoritarian elites strong enough to orchestrate a coup to return their countries to dictatorship? There are several reasons.

Former authoritarian elites might retain substantial de facto power after they step down. While we have argued throughout this book that authoritarian elites' enduring de facto power is not enough, on its own, to explain the strong patterns of elite bias under democracy, it can nonetheless matter in other, sometimes subtler, ways. While elite-biased constitutions and institutions might be necessary for outgoing elites to protect their interests after democratization, they are not always sufficient. De facto power, in the form of their control of important factor endowments – especially land or cash stashed abroad – is often the means by which they enforce their political will. As we explained earlier in the book, it is this de facto power that might finance political campaigns that catapult conservative politicians into elected office, buy off the support of the judiciary at critical junctures after the transition, or broadcast propaganda that legitimizes holdover institutions and venerates the military as the guardian of the constitution and democracy.

Moreover, the democracy's inherited de jure institutions bolster the de facto power of economic elites grandfathered into the new regime by ushering in economic rules that concentrate assets and rig markets to their advantage, allowing former political incumbents and economic allies to remain strong even decades after democratization. In turn, this may allow them to recruit the military to do their bidding. Or, as in the case of Chile, Pakistan, Thailand, and Turkey, former authoritarian elites may remain in positions of power as top military generals or senators for life. In this case, it is not surprising that they might orchestrate a coup against a popular democracy that threatens their interests. Indeed, as in the cases of Peru, Chile, and Egypt, the constitution itself empowers them to intervene to protect the democracy from populism. In short, because they control the levers of coercive power, they can roll out the tanks and take over the capital city's central square with alacrity.

A similar dynamic can occur even when holdover elites do not directly control the military, but are instead allied to it. For instance, in Peru, the long-standing "forty families" that constituted the country's economic elite repeatedly – and effectively – called on the military to topple unfavorable elected governments between the 1930s and 1960s (Albertus 2015).

Former authoritarian elites need not draw exclusively on the military in order to topple a democracy that goes sour, however. An extremist party could rise to power and implement a rigidly ideological policy platform that benefits only a plurality of society and poses an existential threat to segments of the middle class. A popular extremist party might seek to quickly please its supporters through procyclical macroeconomic policies that engender inflation and erode the purchasing power of groups not protected by government dictated wage increases and price controls and who cannot hedge against inflation. In turn, disaffected segments of the population might band together with former authoritarian elites and their allies to topple the government. As we saw in the case of Chile in Chapter 7, in our discussion of the coup that felled the democratically elected government of Salvador Allende, disgruntled elites were aided by disaffected elements of the middle class and the masses for this very reason. The military merely finished the job.

Our theoretical framework also elucidates the reasons behind some reversions to autocracy that stem from below. Consider the case of auto-coups. If former elites are concentrated in a veto-holding body like the senate, an elected democrat could try to abolish that body and further consolidate power by weakening other democratic institutions as well. Hugo Chávez in Venezuela is one illustrative example. Elected with substantial backing in 1998, Chávez quickly convened a constituent assembly to draft a new constitution. The new constitution strengthened executive powers and abolished the upper house of congress in 1999. Chávez then won partisan control over the National Electoral Commission in 2000 through a favorable transition council that operated between the approval of the new constitution and the August 2000 election of a new congress. The 2004 passage of the Organic Law of the Supreme Tribunal of Justice then increased the number of justices and enabled Chávez to place partisan allies on the bench. In short, Chávez dismantled democratic checks and balances in an effort to attack economic elites who had long benefited under the elite-biased Punto Fijo Pact that ushered in democracy in the late 1950s.

We can also explain examples of gradual democratic erosion in which authoritarian tendencies creep back into the political game, such as the advent of a one-party state. Take for example South Africa's 1994 transition from apartheid rule, which was guided by the elaborately constructed 1993 constitution. Among many other provisions that sought to protect the outgoing National Party (NP) from the popular African National Congress (ANC), the negotiations delineated "nine constitutionally created federal provinces with projected NP majorities in two (Western Cape and Northern Cape), an IFP majority in another (Kwazulu-Natal), and finally, an unspecified 'handshake agreement' that those provinces would have real fiscal powers" (Inman and Rubinfeld 2005, 42). Furthermore, provinces were allowed to adopt their own constitutions.

However – and serving as a powerful example of outgoing elite mistakes and unforeseen eventualities in the construction of transition deals – the NP never won in the Northern Cape. And although they won the Western Cape in 1994, they were forced to ally with the Democratic Party to keep a majority in 1999. Eventually, the NP folded in the early 2000s. Of course, this was unforeseen by the NP at the time of the democratic transition. Eventually, the ANC absorbed most NP politicians, effectively giving them new political life while also decimating a pole of political opposition. South African democracy continues to creak under the weight of a hegemonic party – the ANC – that views itself as uniquely suited to ruling and cannot conceive of life in the political opposition.

SHIFTS FROM POPULAR DEMOCRACY TO ELITE-BIASED DEMOCRACY

There is another common phenomenon that we have not taken up in this book hitherto but that our theory speaks to: elite capture under democracy. Our conception and coding of elite-biased democracy throughout the book captures instances in which outgoing authoritarian political elites and their economic allies set up an institutional architecture on the eve of democracy and subsequently benefit from it and its attendant policies after democratization. Chapter 5 details the circumstances under which such elite biases can be overturned, yielding a more popular democracy.

We do not discuss – nor do we code – potential shifts from popular democracy to elite-biased democracy. In many ways, this makes intuitive sense: Why would citizens freely choose to abandon institutions that favor their interests and replace them with institutions that favor elites? Nonetheless, this is not entirely uncommon, though such shifts tend to benefit not former authoritarian political elites but rather economic elites who were dominant under authoritarianism but lay dormant for a while, or economic elites who rose at some point after democratization.

Shifts from popular democracy toward elite bias can occur when economic elites grow strong enough and politically forsake the masses, even though the democracy remains, on paper, a fully popular one. Elites can free themselves from allying with average citizens in numerous, well-documented ways: bribing politicians for favorable policies, lobbying, providing financial backing to candidates that reciprocate with favorable policies once elected, repressing voter turnout, and even perpetuating electoral fraud (see, e.g., Stokes et al. 2013; Ziblatt 2009). The result is that elites end up with a voice in politics in a nominally popular democracy that far outstrips their numbers, akin to what one would observe in an elite-biased democracy. Unsurprisingly, they leverage this power to advantage themselves economically.

Some examples from the developing world come to mind. These include Mongolia, which transitioned to popular democracy in 1990, and the Dominican Republic, which transitioned to popular democracy in 1966.

In Mongolia, a successful transition from communism on the back of a popular and peaceful revolution created a semipresidential democracy with regular free and fair elections. Up until 2014, the country also grew at breakneck speed and, at least on the surface, seemed relatively egalitarian. Yet a small economic elite has nonetheless been able to commandeer the commanding heights of the economy through a mix of corruption and crime. It is not the country's abundant gold, copper, and uranium mines that are the underlying cause of this phenomenon, however (see Menaldo 2016). Rather, the country's democratic institutions, especially its judiciary, have been captured by gangster capitalists who amassed economic clout outside of the resource sector and marshaled it to impose their will on the political process. Sometimes aided and abetted by foreign mining firms that look to cut regulatory corners and reduce their tax bills, Mongolia's nouveau riche have extended their tentacles into the minerals sector.

In the Dominican Republic, a series of coups and countercoups swept aside long-standing dictator Rafael Trujillo. The country transitioned to a popular democracy in 1966 that brought the populist Joaquín Balaguer to power. The Dominican Liberation Party and Dominican Revolutionary Party have since dominated political life under democracy. These parties are notoriously non-ideological, shifting between left and right positions while in practice acting as the personalist vehicles of ambitious politicians. In the meantime, a rising economic elite has capitalized off of prying the country open to transnational capital and has turned to both political parties to fashion them favorable institutions and rules. The result is endemic corruption and a government that turns a blind eye to the interests of common voters, particularly when those interests conflict with those of economic elites.

Several examples from the developed world also stand out. Indeed, Piketty's *Capital in the Twenty-First Century* made a big splash in 2014 when he succinctly laid bare the troublesome but undeniable increase in inequality in a host of developed countries since the 1970s. His explanation rests on the idea that capitalism is hard-wired to increase asset inequality inexorably – a process that was only arrested by the world wars and Great Depression as major stocks of capital were destroyed. Nonetheless, the book intimates that the most recent uptick in inequality is due to institutions or, more specifically, the capture of representative bodies and the judicial system by rising economic elites.

We concur with his assessment of the symptoms, but not the diagnosis. Inequality has clearly increased throughout the developed world, but the underlying reason is not the natural reconstitution of capital after the end of World War II. Rather, it is blatant political capture, even in seemingly popular democracies.

Consider the United States. After the country was hit by the Great Depression, Franklin Delano Roosevelt (FDR) responded to the increasingly progressive tendencies of the expanding electorate, tilting the country the closest it has ever been to popular democracy. An earlier parade of reforms set the stage for FDR, including the change to direct elections in the senate and the Progressive Movement, which expanded the franchise for women and introduced trust-busting and other measures that leveled the economic playing field, such as attempts to reduce growing inequality between cities and rural areas. FDR went further still, rewriting the nation's social contract by introducing a host of new government programs and agencies during the New Deal: Social Security, unemployment insurance, the subsidization of mortgages, the Works Progress Administration, the Tennessee Valley Authority, the introduction of minimum wages and maximum hours, and the Wagner Act to bolster labor unions. At the same time, he reined in Wall Street with the Glass-Steagall Act and the creation of the Securities and Exchange Commission.

This more progressive social contract outlasted FDR's death. President Lyndon Baines Johnson (LBJ), in particular, passed landmark civil rights legislation and bolstered the social safety net. This included an end to segregation and the 1965 Voting Rights Act, which fully enfranchised black citizens. Moreover, LBJ introduced programs such as welfare transfers, Medicare and Medicaid, and public housing. Indeed, as we outlined in Chapter 4, during the "embedded liberal" international order under the Bretton Woods fixed exchange rates regime, the United States, like other industrialized democracies, used capital controls along with expansive monetary and fiscal policy to achieve full employment and deepen the welfare state.

Yet this progressive social contract began to fray in the 1970s and 1980s, a process that accelerated through the 1990s and 2000s. The financial system is perhaps the best example of a small group of economic elites capturing politicians and securing a suite of favorable fiscal, monetary, and regulatory policies since the 1980s. The end of the Bretton Woods regime of fixed exchange rates ushered in floating exchange rates and the scaling back of capital controls. In synergy with the rise of automated teller machines, which melted away interstate banking restrictions (Calomiris and Haber 2014), this helped bring financial repression to a close, bolstering the profits of banks by increasing their yields and the range of products they could offer. For instance, "bond trading [was made] much more lucrative. The invention of securitization, interest-rate swaps, and credit-default swaps greatly increased the volume of transactions that bankers could make money on. And an aging and increasingly wealthy population invested more and more money in securities, helped by the invention of the IRA and the 401(k) plan" (Johnson 2009).

The short-term winners of this major policy shift then leveraged their newfound clout to try to lock in longer-term gains. One case in point is the well-known Supreme Court decision *Buckley v. Valeo* in 1976. Spearheaded by New York Senator James Buckley of the Conservative Party – a party heavily favorable to the banking industry and business moguls more generally, and that also supported lower corporate and individual income taxes, right to work laws, low minimum wages, and an abolition of estate taxes – this decision struck down limits to campaign expenditures that were set in place earlier in the 1970s. Indeed, Buckley himself was elected after "a maze of dummy campaign committees was used to pump more than $400,000 in last-minute money" into his race (*Sarasota Journal* 1970, 12). The identity of donors was hidden by sending funds through false-front groups arranged in Washington, DC. Furthermore, "part of the Buckley donations came from loyal Republican donors in New York financial circles who didn't want to alienate the state's GOP organization by having their names tied to the third-party candidate" (12).

Bankers continue to be perhaps the most influential lobbying group in the United States and one of the top contributors to American political campaigns. Furthermore, a revolving door allows financiers to seamlessly move between government agencies charged with regulating the financial system, especially the Federal Reserve, and private banks (Adolph 2014).

It is therefore not surprising that many policies supported by both Republicans and Democrats have allowed bankers and investors to pile on risk, and thus reap huge rewards, because they anticipate that major financial institutions will be bailed out even if those risks backfire. The key deregulatory bill, the Saint Germain Act, was passed in 1982. This was coupled with the government's willingness to look the other way when new savings and loan institutions made "cash-for-trash" fraudulent loans, on high leverage, to fly-by-night commercial developers (Black 2005). These events precipitated the savings and loans crash in the early 1980s and led to major bailouts by the federal government.

The party continued to rage on for bankers in the 1990s and 2000s. Consider several key regulations that fueled the 2008 financial crash. First were policies that gutted underwriting standards and fostered the emergence of so-called liar's loans in the mortgage banking industry during the early 1990s, in which false statements about income allowed risky subprime loans to spread like wildfire (Black 2005). Next was the elimination of the Glass-Steagall Act in 1999, allowing deposit banks to merge with investment banks, thus creating institutions that were "too big to fail" and thus likely to be bailed out if their risky bets failed to pan out. Last was the government's indefatigable promotion of homeownership. Rather than invest in social safety nets that obviate the insurance functions associated with homeownership, the federal government provided large subsidies to major lenders to make subprime loans to low-income borrowers with bad credit and compromised abilities to repay their mortgage debts (Calomiris and Haber 2014). Financiers have also been able to block policies that could threaten their profits, including efforts to increase the oversight of credit rating agencies, regulate credit default swaps, impose fees on banking activities, increase taxes on capital gains, and claw back bonuses for managers incentivized to make risky loans.

Indeed, the rise of the 1 percent – and even more so the 0.1 percent – across the world can largely be explained by the blistering rise of untrammeled global finance in the wake of deregulation across the world. The United States is only the most visible example, as it has been marked by exponential growth in the profits accruing to the financial industry. According to

Johnson (2009), "From 1973 to 1985, the financial sector never earned more than 16 percent of domestic corporate profits. In 1986, that figure reached 19 percent. In the 1990s, it oscillated between 21 percent and 30 percent, higher than it had ever been in the postwar period. This decade, it reached 41 percent. Pay rose just as dramatically. From 1948 to 1982, average compensation in the financial sector ranged between 99 percent and 108 percent of the average for all domestic private industries. From 1983, it shot upward, reaching 181 percent in 2007."

The patent political capture of US institutions and economic regulation by powerful financial interests has had real consequences. The savings and loan and 2008 financial crises amounted to more than a trillion dollars in losses paid by taxpayers. The latter left a depression-like economic downturn in its wake, followed by an anemic recovery where the median income took almost a decade to return to its precrisis level. Inequality remains at historically high levels.

POLICY IMPLICATIONS: THE DEMOCRACY CURE?

In some ways, the picture of democracy we paint in this book is a bleak one. We have argued that democratization is usually timed and orchestrated by autocratic elites. Furthermore, democracy's institutions are often designed by outgoing autocrats and their allies in a nakedly self-serving manner. We have also argued that newly elected democratic leaders are constrained by this straightjacket: if they follow the rules dictated by the constitution they inherit, they end up governing in ways that benefit former autocrats and their allies long after the latter have formally relinquished power. Finally, while some democracies succeed in overturning elite biases only to be overthrown in a coup, other popular democracies are captured by elites down the road. In short, in many ways this book suggests that democracy is a false promise.

Our book nonetheless provides several insights that practitioners and democracy advocates can draw from in the quest to bring democracy to more people across the globe. First, a flawed democracy riddled with elite biases is better than no democracy at all. Democracy allows for greater popular representation, even if it is incomplete, and competition, even if constrained. It typically frees citizens from the threat of arbitrary or trumped-up detention and allows them to speak their minds. And it buys time for liberalization. Indeed, since 1950, a third of the countries that democratized with autocratic constitutions went on to shed their inherited constitutions and replace them with new social contracts.

Because some democracy is better than no democracy, democracy advocates should be open to compromise and remain pragmatic about ideology, including relaxing puritanical definitions of what democracy entails and sacrificing the notion that a radical shift toward equality and transitional justice is viable. It is not that these are not ideals to strive for. However, they are not always in the realm of possibility, and pursuing them could backfire: the price of these ideals might end up being democracy itself.

Charting a pragmatic course in which compromise prevails might entail, like in the case of Chile, that newly elected leaders eschew retaliation and extend military leaders reliable assurances that their worst fears – prosecution, forced retirement, seizure of their assets, or even death – will not materialize after a transition. Or consider Bulgaria, the punishment of outgoing regime officials for human rights violations after communist rule was scrapped even though this did violence against the strictest imperatives of transitional justice. This outcome transpired precisely because all parties abided by the consti-tution. The country's former dictator, Lukanov, was charged with corruption after democratization largely because the communists formed only a minority in parliament. Yet because the Bulgarian Socialist Party was endowed with political power beyond its numbers, it was able to push the government to drop these charges. This helped consolidate Bulgarian democracy, the quality of which has improved over time.

Portugal's 1975 transition similarly evinces the type of pragmatism that democracy advocates around the world should take heed of. There, the exclu-sion of the Communists – who threatened to expropriate businesses and land owned by former autocratic elites – from the left-wing party alliance that headed a transitional government was key to convincing the military to give democratization a green light. It also reduced the likelihood that elites would have a reason to undermine democracy later down the line. Moreover, this transition served as a model for future transitions across Latin America, yield-ing the longest democratic episodes experienced by the majority of the region's countries to date.

Democracy advocates can also take heart of the fact that, years after Portugal's transition, political reforms tied to the country's entry into the European Union increased political pluralism, allowing citizens to gradually claw back barriers to greater equality.

Long, drawn-out, and carefully constructed transitions that allow – and even protect – authoritarian enclaves are more likely to result in stable democ-racies. In these cases, generational change and economic shifts can raise new actors and topple old ones, enabling new coalitions to form that can effectively reform illiberal democratic institutions and empower citizens with a greater voice in decision-making.

Consider the meandering and protracted path that Myanmar has traveled to reach elected government. There, a constitution engineered by the generals who ruled for the past half century stipulates that one-quarter of the seats in parliament must be reserved for the military. Until 2015, much of the remain-der was held by members of the pro-government party. That year, the chief opposition party, the National League for Democracy, made major electoral inroads and now controls the country's cabinet. This agonizing path to greater democracy has been almost two decades in the making and is still in process.

Myanmar's elite-biased constitution appears likely to remain in effect for the foreseeable future, given that more than three-quarters of the parliament must vote in favor of any constitutional amendment for it to pass.

Nurturing and eventually calling on prudent statesmen and women who valorize forbearance and resilience is also paramount. Consider Nelson Mandela, who was fully aware of the tradeoffs implied by the bargain he and the African National Congress (ANC) struck with South Africa's apartheid regime, in which a host of elite biases were exchanged for an end to segregation, free and fair elections, and universal suffrage. Mandela's willingness to tolerate patently undemocratic features when bargaining over the end of the de Klerk regime was what made him the ideal person to head the South African transition. One of Mandela's chief strengths was that he was a temperate leader who had come to understand how critical it is to build trust and proceed cautiously. Had he agitated for wholesale, radical reform, it is unlikely that the apartheid regime would have been willing to hand over power to begin with. Instead, Mandela tolerated compromises such as the creation of political enclaves that extended elements of elite dominance.

Mandela captured this sentiment perfectly during his first presidential campaign when he said, "Just as we told the people what we would do, I felt we must also tell them what we could not do. Many people felt life would change overnight after a free and democratic election, but that would be far from the case. Often, I said to crowds…'life will not change dramatically, except that you will have increased your self-esteem and become a citizen in your land. You must have patience.' "

Democracy advocates should also remember that timing is of the essence. Rather than engaging in pitched battles with former authoritarian elites who remain powerful under democracy in an effort to prematurely claw out piecemeal reforms, citizens and activists should seize on focal points to push for major institutional changes when the time is right. That these focal points will come to pass is predictable; when they will transpire is not. As we made clear in previous chapters, the most effective focal points are associated with the death or serious weakening of the most powerful elements of the erstwhile authoritarian political elite. At these moments, even if some of the formerly incumbent economic elite remain strong or some political elites are still on the scene, it might be possible to galvanize elements of civil society to agitate for serious political reform.

These focal points are not enough to achieve reform on their own, however. They have to be coupled with a strengthening of opposition forces in the lead-up to critical openings. As we demonstrate in Chapter 5, those openings include events such as economic shocks that are largely out of the hands of political reformers. In other words, just because a former dictator dies does not mean that citizens can pour into the streets with impunity and topple the dictator's legacy. Only if they are well organized, well funded, and on the rise will they be able to make major reforms to the institutional architecture of democracy that will pay off in the long term. Donors and democracy advocates would do well to bide their time and concentrate their resources on bolstering reformers in the sometimes long lead-up to major focal points that allow for political reform.

Even when change is possible, however, reformers should remain prudent. Rather than steamroll over every institutional vestige remaining from authoritarianism during a window of opportunity, they should focus on first casting out the most offensive elite biases. By building a reputation for patience and prudence, they can earn the confidence of former authoritarian elites and their allies and, perhaps more importantly, give these former elites and their allies time to reinvent themselves to compete in a more popular democracy. This is far superior to backing them into a corner where their best option is to strike against the democracy itself in a bid to return the country to a friendlier dictatorship.

This points to our last piece of advice for would-be democrats, and certainly the most controversial. As much as popular democracy is a normatively preferable and a materially superior version of elected rule for average citizens, the attempt to reach this golden shore through a popular revolution is often dangerous and can backfire in a spectacular manner. While a successful revolution can pave the way to an egalitarian, popular democracy – consistent with our findings in Chapter 4 – a popular revolt might alternatively pave the road to an even worse and more long-standing dictatorship, this time on the back of a reactionary counterrevolution.

Since the end of World War II, there have been roughly fifty major revolutions that have either toppled autocratic regimes or led to significant political reform in elite-biased democracies. For those revolutions that have occurred under dictatorships, only about a third have resulted in transitions to democracy. The bulk of countries that experience a popular revolution remain authoritarian, and in some cases, usher in an even deadlier stripe than what preceded revolution. The checkered political aftermaths of postrevolutionary China, Cuba, Mexico, Russia, and Iran should make even the most fervent revolutionaries take pause.

Or consider the Arab Spring. What has happened in Libya, Egypt, and Syria since 2011 has chilled the initial burst of optimism about these revolutions. Back then, Western pundits and activists alike declared that democracy was just around the corner across the Middle East. They proved to be dead wrong.

Western-backed intervention in Libya to bolster the country's popular revolution appeared to some like a necessary step on the road to freedom. Despite repeated entreaties by Libya's neighbors and Western powers for him to step down peacefully and seek political asylum, Muammar Gaddafi was toppled during a bloody civil war after he had unleashed hell on rebels and their would-be sympathizers. The eventual result was anarchy and a vacuum filled by terrorists. Rather than democracy, the country devolved into wide-scale repression and sectarian bloodshed. Anarchy continues today.

In Egypt, although the Muslim Brotherhood's presidential candidate Muhammad Morsi won in free and fair elections and took power in June 2012, seemingly completing the promise of the revolution, he proceeded to impose an illiberal constitution and govern in an uncompromising fashion. Morsi fomented sectarian strife against Shi'ites and Christians, presided over a cratering economy, and pushed for the prosecution of activists who were charged with insulting the head of state. This led to a plunge in his popularity and mass protests. He was summarily ousted in a coup and jailed after failing to comply with an ultimatum issued by the military. Since then, the military has brutally cracked down on Morsi supporters, killing hundreds. General Sisi now rules with an iron fist and is in many ways worse than Mubarak.

In Syria, the revolutionary uprising that sought greater democracy has instead led to a devastating civil war that has dragged in the United States, Russia, and Turkey, and has served as a breeding ground for the Islamic State and Kurdish separatism. In the wake of popular protests that met with severe government repression, a number of military officers (including a few higher ranking ones), diplomats, and notable politicians defected and helped form the Free Syrian Army, which escalated matters beyond a popular revolution. Bashar al-Assad ratcheted up a brutal crackdown against rebels, feeding a ferocious cycle of violence. The death toll had exceeded 500,000 as of 2017, with more than 10 million people displaced, including almost five million refugees who fled to neighboring countries.

In fact, so many Syrians fleeing the civil war have poured into Western Europe that pundits declared, circa 2017, that this mass exodus destabilized politics in countries such as Germany, France, the Netherlands, and Denmark. Mass immigration coupled with the rise of the Islamic State seem to have fomented a reactionary backlash and buoyed right-wing populist parties. Similarly, it might have precipitated the decision by Britain to exit the European Union after a popular referendum inflamed by anti-immigrant sentiment. This is bitterly ironic. Some of the world's most popular democracies were, during the completion of this book, flirting with illiberal measures that were originally provoked by attempts to promote democracy in the most authoritarian enclave in the developing world.

In short, democracy advocates should proceed slowly and cautiously, focus on evolutionary rather than revolutionary change, and concentrate their resources and coordinate their efforts around obvious focal points in the wake of shocks such as economic crises. If this advice seems too timid to some, it is because we know much more about what can go wrong than we do about how to precisely make things go right.

This brings us to reemphasize our parting advice to those who yearn for freedom in the face of tyranny: perfection is the enemy of the good. The politics of the possible is often badmouthed as too timid and boring. But when citizens' lives and livelihoods are at stake, and powerful actors have the will and means to assure their own survival and protect their riches, an old fashioned, republican modus vivendi is preferable to bloodshed. It is also preferable to what is possibly an even worse and more unfair political and economic system under a renewed dictatorship. Dictators are often perfectly adequate founders, so long as succeeding generations of democrats never give up the hope that their flawed blueprints can be perfected later on through assiduous, yet strategically timed, activism.

References

Acemoglu, Daron, Simon Johnson, and James Robinson. 2001. "The Colonial Origins of Comparative Development: An Empirical Investigation." *American Economic Review* 91(5): 1369–1401.

2005. "Institutions as a Fundamental Cause of Long-Run Growth." In *Handbook of Economic Growth*, eds. Philippe Aghion and Steven Durlauf. Amsterdam: Elsevier, 385–472.

Acemoglu, Daron, Simon Johnson, James Robinson, and Pierre Yared. 2008. "Income and Democracy." *American Economic Review* 98(3): 808–842.

Acemoglu, Daron, and James Robinson. 2001. "A Theory of Political Transitions." *American Economic Review* 91(4): 938–963.

2006. *Economic Origins of Democracy and Dictatorship*. New York: Cambridge University Press.

2008. "Persistence of Power, Elites and Institutions." *American Economic Review* 98(1): 267–291.

Adolph, Chris. 2014. *Bankers, Bureaucrats, and Central Bank Politics: The Myth of Neutrality*. New York: Cambridge University Press.

Aidt, Toke, Jayasri Dutta, and Elena Loukoianova. 2006. "Democracy Comes to Europe: Franchise Extension and Fiscal Outcomes 1830–1938." *European Economic Review* 50(2): 249–283.

Albertus, Michael. 2015. *Autocracy and Redistribution: The Politics of Land Reform*. New York: Cambridge University Press.

2017. "Landowners and Democracy: The Social Origins of Democracy Reconsidered." *World Politics* 69(2): 233–276.

Albertus, Michael, Alberto Diaz-Cayeros, Beatriz Magaloni, and Barry Weingast. 2016. "Authoritarian Survival and Poverty Traps: Land Reform in Mexico." *World Development* 77(1): 154–170.

Albertus, Michael, and Victor Gay. 2017. "Unlikely Democrats: Economic Elite Uncertainty under Dictatorship and Support for Democratization." *American Journal of Political Science* 61(3): 624–41.

Albertus, Michael, and Oliver Kaplan. 2013. "Land Reform as a Counterinsurgency Policy: Evidence from Colombia." *Journal of Conflict Resolution* 57(2): 198–231.

Albertus, Michael, and Victor Menaldo. 2012a. "If You're Against Them You're with Us: The Effect of Expropriation on Autocratic Survival." *Comparative Political Studies* 45(8): 973–1003.
2012b. "Coercive Capacity and the Prospects for Democratization." *Comparative Politics* 44(2): 151–169.
2014a. "Gaming Democracy: Elite Dominance during Transition and the Prospects for Redistribution." *British Journal of Political Science* 44(3): 575–603.
2014b. "Dealing with Dictators: Negotiated Democratization and the Fate of Outgoing Autocrats." *International Studies Quarterly* 58(3): 550–565.
Alemán, Eduardo, and Patricio Navia. 2009. "Institutions and the Legislative Success of 'Strong' Presidents: An Analysis of Government Bills in Chile." *Journal of Legislative Studies* 15(4): 401–419.
Alesina, Alberto, and Edward Ludwig Glaeser. 2004. *Fighting Poverty in the US and Europe: A World of Difference*. Oxford: Oxford University Press.
Alexander, Gerard. 2002a. *The Sources of Democratic Consolidation*. Ithaca: Cornell University Press.
Alexander, Neville. 2002b. *An Ordinary Country: Issues in Transition from Apartheid to Democracy in South Africa*. New York: Berghahn Books.
Alm, James, Jorge Martínez-Vazquez, and Sally Wallace. 2004. *Taxing the Hard-to-Tax*. Amsterdam: Elsevier.
Anderson, Karen. 2009. "The Church as Nation: The Role of Religion in the Development of the Swedish Welfare State." In *Religion, Class Coalitions, and Welfare States*, eds. Kees Van Kersbergen and Philip Manow. Cambridge: Cambridge University Press, 210–235.
Andrews, Michael. 2005. *State-Owned Banks, Stability, Privatization, and Growth: Practical Policy Decisions in a World without Empirical Proof*. Washington, DC: International Monetary Fund.
Ansell, Ben, and David Samuels. 2014. *Inequality and Democratization*. New York: Cambridge University Press.
Aslund, Anders. 2007. *How Capitalism Was Built*. New York: Cambridge University Press.
Astorga, Pablo, Ame Bergés, and Edmund V. K. FitzGerald. 2011. *The Oxford Latin American Economic History Database (OxLAD)*. Oxford: The Latin American Centre, Oxford University.
Atkinson, Anthony. 2015. *Inequality*. Cambridge: Harvard University Press.
Aylwin, José. 2005. "Implementación de Legislación y Jurisprudencia Nacional Relativa a los Derechos de los Pueblos Indígenas: La Experiencia de Chile." Unpublished manuscript.
Baer, Werner. 1967. "The Inflation Controversy in Latin America: A Survey." *Latin American Research Review* 2(2): 3–25.
Bakke, Kristin, and Erik Wibbels. 2006. "Diversity, Disparity, and Civil Conflict in Federal States." *World Politics* 59(1): 1–50.
Baland, Jean-Marie, and James Robinson. 2008. "Land and Power: Theory and Evidence from Chile." *American Economic Review* 98(5): 1737–1765.
Banerjee, Abhijit, and Lakshmi Iyer. 2005. "History, Institutions, and Economic Performance: The Legacy of Colonial Land Tenure Systems in India." *American Economic Review* 95(4): 1190–1213.
Banks, Arthur. 2009. "Cross-National Time-Series Data Archive." *Databanks International*. www.databanks.sitehosting.net/.

Barandiarán, Edgardo, and Leonardo Hernández. 1999. "Origins and Resolution of a Banking Crisis: Chile 1982–86." Working paper no. 57. Santiago: Central Bank of Chile.

Barros, Robert. 2002. *Constitutionalism and Dictatorship: Pinochet, the Junta, and the 1980 Constitution.* New York: Cambridge University Press.

Bartels, Larry. 2005. "Homer Gets a Tax Cut: Inequality and Public Policy in the American Mind." *Perspectives on Politics* 3(1): 15–31.

Bates, Robert. 1991. "The Economics of Transitions to Democracy." *PS: Political Science and Politics* 24(1): 24–27.

Bearce, David, and Michael Hallerberg. 2011. "Democracy and De Facto Exchange Rate Regimes." *Economics & Politics* 23(2): 172–194.

Benabou, Roland, and Efi Ok. 2001. "Social Mobility and the Demand for Redistribution." *Quarterly Journal of Economics* 116(May): 447–487.

Berger, Stefan, and Hugh Compston. 2002. *Policy Concertation and Social Partnership in Western Europe: Lessons for the 21st Century.* New York: Berghahn Books.

Bernhard, Michael, and Ekrem Karakoç. 2007. "Civil Society and the Legacies of Dictatorship." *World Politics* 59(4): 539–567.

Bernhard, Michael, Christopher Reenock, and Timothy Nordstrom. 2004. "The Legacy of Western Overseas Colonialism on Democratic Survival." *International Studies Quarterly* 48(1): 225–250.

Bird, Richard, and Eric Zolt. 2005 "The Limited Role of the Personal Income Tax in Developing Countries." *Journal of Asian Economics* 16(6): 928–946.

Black, William. 2005. *The Best Way to Rob a Bank Is to Own One.* Austin: University of Texas Press.

Boix, Carles. 1999. "Setting the Rules of the Game: The Choice of Electoral Systems in Advanced Democracies." *American Political Science Review* 93(3): 609–624.

2003. *Democracy and Redistribution.* New York: Cambridge University Press.

Boix, Carles, Michael Miller, and Sebastian Rosato. 2013. "A Complete Dataset of Political Regimes, 1800–2007." *Comparative Political Studies* 46(12): 1523–1554.

Boix, Carles, and Susan Stokes. 2003. "Endogenous Democratization." *World Politics* 55(4): 517–549.

Borghi, Elisa. 2005. "Trade Openness and Wage Distribution in Chile." Unpublished manuscript, Università Commerciale Luigi Bocconi.

Brady, David, Evelyne Huber, and John Stephens. 2014. "Comparative Welfare States Data Set." University of North Carolina and WZB Berlin Social Science Center. http://huberandstephens.web.unc.edu/common-works/data/.

Braun, Juan, Matías Braun, Ignacio Briones, and José Díaz. 2000. *Economía Chilena 1810–1995: Estadísticas Históricas.* Santiago: Catholic University of Chile.

Brennan, Geoffrey, and Alan Hamilton. 2001. "Constitutional Choice." In *The Elgar Companion to Public Choice*, eds. William Shughart and Laura Razzolini. Cheltenham: Edward Elgar, 117–139.

Brownlee, Jason. 2009. "Portents of Pluralism: How Hybrid Regimes Affect Democratic Transitions." *American Journal of Political Science* 53(3): 515–532.

Buchanan, James, and Gordon Tullock. 1962. *The Calculus of Consent*, vol. 3. Ann Arbor: University of Michigan Press.

Bueno de Mesquita, Bruce, Alastair Smith, Randolph Siverson, and James Morrow. 2003. *The Logic of Political Survival.* Cambridge: MIT Press.

Bulmer-Thomas, Victor. 2003. *The Economic History of Latin America since Independence.* New York: Cambridge University Press.

Calomiris, Charles, and Stephen Haber. 2014. *Fragile by Design: The Political Origins of Banking Crises and Scarce Credit.* Princeton: Princeton University Press.

Carlsson, Sten. 1987. "From Four Estates to Two Chambers: The Riksdag in the Period of Transition, 1809–1921." In *The Riksdag: A History of the Swedish Parliament,* ed. Michael Metcalf. New York: St. Martin's Press, 165–222.

Carnes, Nicholas, and Noam Lupu. 2015. "Rethinking the Comparative Perspective on Class and Representation: Evidence from Latin America." *American Journal of Political Science* 59(1): 1–18.

Cea Egaña, José Luis. 2002. *Derecho Constitucional Chileno, Tomo I.* Santiago: Universidad Católica de Chile.

Cheibub, José Antonio. 2007. *Presidentialism, Parliamentarism, and Democracy.* New York: Cambridge University Press.

Cheibub, José Antonio, Jennifer Gandhi, and James Raymond Vreeland. 2010. "Democracy and Dictatorship Revisited." *Public Choice* 143(1–2): 67–101.

Chwieroth, Jeff. 2007. "Neoliberal Economists and Capital Account Liberalization in Emerging Markets." *International Organization* 61(2): 443–463.

Clague, Christopher, Philip Keefer, Stephen Knack, and Mancur Olson. 1996. "Property and Contract Rights in Autocracies and Democracies." *Journal of Economic Growth* 1(2): 243–276.

Cohen, Benjamin. 1998. *The Geography of Money.* Ithaca: Cornell University Press.

Colomer, Josep. 2004. *Handbook of Electoral System Choice.* London: Palgrave Macmillan.

Congleton, Roger. 2003. *Improving Democracy through Constitutional Reform: Some Swedish Lessons.* Boston: Kluwer.

2011. *Perfecting Parliament.* New York: Cambridge University Press.

Corporación Nacional de Desarrollo Indígena (Conadi). 2004. *Informe Nacional del Gobierno de Chile.* Santiago: Fondo Indígena.

D'Anieri, Paul. 2015. *Understanding Ukrainian Politics: Power, Politics, and Institutional Design.* London: Routledge.

D'Anieri, Paul, Robert Kravchuk, and Taras Kuzio. 1999. *Politics and Society in Ukraine.* Boulder, CO: Westview Press.

Dailami, Mansoor. 2000. "Financial Openness, Democracy, and Redistributive Policy." Washington, DC: World Bank.

Debs, Alexandre, and Hein Goemans. 2010. "Regime Type, the Fate of Leaders, and War." *American Political Science Review* 104(3): 430–445.

Debs, Alexandre, and Gretchen Helmke. 2010. "Inequality under Democracy: Explaining the Left Decade in Latin America." *Quarterly Journal of Political Science* 5(3): 209–241.

De La O, Ana. 2013. "Do Conditional Cash Transfers Affect Electoral Behavior? Evidence from a Randomized Experiment in Mexico." *American Journal of Political Science* 57(1): 1–14.

Desai, Raj, Anders Olofsgård, and Tarik Yousef. 2003. "Democracy, Inequality, and Inflation." *American Political Science Review* 97(3): 391–406.

Diaz-Alejandro, Carlos. 1985. "Good-Bye Financial Repression, Hello Financial Crash." *Journal of Development Economics* 19(1): 1–24.

Drake, Paul. 2009. *Between Tyranny and Anarchy: A History of Democracy in Latin America, 1800–2006*. Stanford: Stanford University Press.

Elkins, Zachary, Tom Ginsburg, and James Melton. 2009. *The Endurance of National Constitutions*. New York: Cambridge University Press.

2010. "The Comparative Constitutions Project." https://comparativeconstitutions project.org.

Engerman, Stanley, and Kenneth Sokoloff. 2000. "History Lessons: Institutions, Factor Endowments, and Paths of Development in the New World." *Journal of Economic Perspectives* 14(3): 217–232.

2002. "Factor Endowments, Inequality, and Paths of Development among New World Economies." *Economia* 3(1): 41–88.

Epifani, Paolo, and Gino Gancia. 2009. "Openness, Government Size and the Terms of Trade." *Review of Economics Studies* 76(2): 629–668.

Escalante, Rene. 2002. *The American Friar Lands Policy: Its Framers, Context, and Beneficiaries, 1898–1916*. Manila: De La Salle University Press.

Faundez, Julio 1997. "In Defense of Presidentialism: The Case of Chile, 1932–1970." In *Presidentialism and Democracy in Latin America*, eds. Scott Mainwaring and Matthew Shugart. New York: Cambridge University Press, 300–320.

Ffrench-Davis, Ricardo. 2002. *Economic Reforms in Chile: From Dictatorship to Democracy*. Ann Arbor: University of Michigan Press.

Fine, Jason, and Robert Gray. 1999. "A Proportional Hazards Model for the Subdistribution of a Competing Risk." *Journal of the American Statistical Association* 94(446): 496–509.

Fortin, Jessica. 2012. "Is There a Necessary Condition for Democracy? the Role of State Capacity in Postcommunist Countries." *Comparative Political Studies* 45(7): 903–930.

Frankel, Jeffrey, and Andrew Rose. 1996. "Currency Crashes in Emerging Markets: An Empirical Treatment." *Journal of International Economics* 41(3): 351–366.

Freeman, John, and Dennis Quinn. 2012. "The Economic Origins of Democracy Reconsidered." *American Political Science Review* 106(1): 58–80.

Freeman, d B., Robert Topel, Richar Birgitta Swedenborg, eds. 1997. *The Welfare State in Transition: Reforming the Swedish Model*. Chicago: University of Chicago Press.

Fuentes, Claudio. 1996. "El discurso militar en la transición chilena." Santiago, Chile: FLACSO-Chile.

2015. "Shifting the Status Quo: Constitutional Reforms in Chile." *Latin American Politics and Society* 57(1): 99–122.

Furnish, Dale. 1971. "Chilean Antitrust Law." *American Journal of Comparative Law* 19(3): 464–488.

Gandhi, Jennifer. 2008. *Political Institutions under Dictatorship*. Cambridge: Cambridge University Press.

Garrido, José, ed. 1988. *Historia de la Reforma Agraria en Chile*. Santiago: Editorial Universitaria.

Gasiorowski, Mark. 1995. "Economic Crisis and Political Regime Change: An Event History Analysis." *American Political Science Review* 89(4): 882–897.

Geddes, Barbara. 1999. "What Do We Know about Democratization after Twenty Years?" *Annual Review of Political Science* 2(1): 115–144.

Gerring, John, Strom Thacker, and Carola Moreno. 2005. "Centripetal Democratic Governance: A Theory and Global Inquiry." *American Political Science Review* 99(4): 567–581.

Gilens, Martin, and Benjamin Page. 2014. "Testing Theories of American Politics: Elites, Interest Groups, and Average Citizens." *Perspectives on Politics* 12(3): 564–581.

Goemans, Hein. 2008. "Which Way Out? The Manner and Consequences of Losing Office." *Journal of Conflict Resolution* 52(6): 771–794.

Goemans, Hein, Kristian Skrede Gleditsch, and Giacomo Chiozza. 2009. "Introducing Archigos: A Dataset of Political Leaders." *Journal of Peace Research* 46(2): 269–283.

Grunwald, Joseph. 1970. "Some Reflections on Latin American Industrialization Policy." *Journal of Political Economy* 78(4): 826–856.

Grzymala-Busse, Anna. 2002. *Redeeming the Communist Past: The Regeneration of Communist Parties in East Central Europe*. New York: Cambridge University Press.

Haber, Stephen. 2009. "Latin America's Quiet Revolution." *Wall Street Journal*, January 31, W3.

Haber, Stephen, and Victor Menaldo. 2011. "Do Natural Resources Fuel Authoritarianism? A Reappraisal of the Resource Curse." *American Political Science Review* 105(1): 1–26.

Haggard, Stephan, and Robert Kaufman. 1995. *The Political Economy of Democratic Transitions*. Princeton: Princeton University Press.
   2016. *Dictators and Democrats: Masses, Elites, and Regime Change*. Princeton: Princeton University Press.

Harasymiw, Bohdan. 2002. *Post-communist Ukraine*. Edmonton: Canadian Institute of Ukrainian Studies Press.

Hariri, Jacob Gerner. 2012. "The Autocratic Legacy of Early Statehood." *American Political Science Review* 106(3): 471–494.

Hayden, Joseph Ralston. 1942. *The Philippines: A Study in National Development*. New York: Macmillan Company.

Heckscher, Eli Filip. 1954. *An Economic History of Sweden*. Cambridge: Harvard University Press.

Heiss, Claudia, and Patricio Navia. 2007. "You Win Some, You Lose Some: Constitutional Reforms in Chile's Transition to Democracy." *Latin American Politics and Society* 49(3): 163–190.

Hellman, Joel. 1998. "Winners Take All: The Politics of Partial Reform in Postcommunist Transitions." *World Politics* 50(2): 203–234.

Henisz, Witold. 2000. "The Institutional Environment for Multinational Investment." *Journal of Law, Economics, and Organization* 16(2): 334–364.
   2002. "The Institutional Environment for Infrastructure Investment." *Industrial and Corporate Change* 11(2): 355–389.

Hinnerich, Björn Tyrefors, and Per Pettersson-Lidbom. 2014. "Democracy, Redistribution, and Political Participation: Evidence from Sweden 1919–1938." *Econometrica* 82(3): 961–993.

Hirschl, Ran. 2004. *Towards Juristocracy: The Origins and Consequences of the New Constitutionalism*. Cambridge: Harvard University Press.
   2009. "The 'Design Sciences' and Constitutional Success." *Texas Law Review* 87(7): 1339–1374.

Hirschman, Albert. 1963. "Inflation in Chile." In *Journeys Toward Progress: Studies of Economic Policy-making in Latin America*, eds. Albert Hirschman and August Heckscher. New York: Twentieth Century Fund, 159–223.

Holloway, Steven. 2006. *Canadian Foreign Policy: Defining the National Interest.* Peterborough, Canada: Broadview Press.

Holmberg, Erik, and Nils Stjernquist. 1996. *The Constitution of Sweden: Constitutional Documents of Sweden.* Stockholm: Swedish Riksdag.

Howard, Dick. 1991. "The Essence of Constitutionalism." In *Constitutionalism and Human Rights: America, Poland, and France*, eds. Kenneth Thompson and Rett Ludwikowski. London: Lanham, 3–41.

Huber, Evelyne, and Stephens, John D. 2012. Social Policy in Latin America and the Caribbean Dataset, 1960-2012. Dataset, University of North Carolina.

Huber, Evelyne, Thomas Mustillo, and John Stephens. 2008. "Politics and Social Spending in Latin America." *Journal of Politics* 70(2): 420–436.

Huneeus, Carlos. 2000. "Technocrats and Politicians in an Authoritarian Regime: The 'ODEPLAN Boys' and the 'Gremialists' in Pinochet's Chile." *Journal of Latin American Studies* 32(2): 461–501.

Huntington, Samuel. 1991. *The Third Wave: Democratization in the Late Twentieth Century.* Norman: University of Oklahoma Press.

Hurtado, Carlos. 1984. "La Economía Chilena entre 1830 y 1930 y sus Limitaciones y Herencias." *Colección Estudios CIEPLAN* 81(12): 37–60.

Husted, Thomas, and Lawrence Kenny. 1997. "The Effect of the Expansion of the Voting Franchise on the Size of Government." *Journal of Political Economy* 105(1): 54–82.

Immergut, Ellen. 2002. "The Swedish Constitution and Social Democratic Power: Measuring the Mechanical Effect of a Political Institution." *Scandinavian Political Studies* 25(3): 231–257.

Indrayana, Denny. 2008. *Indonesian Constitutional Reform, 1999–2002: An Evaluation of Constitution-Making in Transition.* Jakarta: Penerbit Buku Kompas.

Inman, Robert, and Daniel Rubinfeld. 2005. "Federalism and the Democratic Transition: Lessons from South Africa." *American Economic Review* 95(2): 39–43.

Isaacs, Anita. 1993. *Military Rule and Transition in Ecuador, 1972–92.* Pittsburgh: University of Pittsburgh Press.

Iversen, Torben. 1996. "Power, Flexibility, and the Breakdown of Centralized Wage Bargaining: Denmark and Sweden in Comparative Perspective." *Comparative Politics* 28(4): 399–436.

Iversen, Torben, and David Soskice. 2006. "Electoral Institutions and the Politics of Coalitions: Why Some Democracies Redistribute More than Others." *American Political Science Review* 100(2): 165–181.

Jarvis, Lovell. 1989. "The Unraveling of Chile's Agrarian Reform, 1973–1986." In *Searching for Agrarian Reform in Latin America*, ed. William Thiesenhusen. Boston: Unwin Hyman, 240–275.

Justman, Moshe, and Mark Gradstein. 1999. "The Industrial Revolution, Political Transition, and the Subsequent Decline in Inequality in 19th-Century Britain." *Explorations in Economic History* 36(2): 109–127.

Karl, Terry. 1990. "Dilemmas of Democratization in Latin America." *Comparative Politics* 23(1): 1–21.

Kaufman, Robert, and Alex Segura-Ubiergo. 2001. "Globalization, Domestic Politics, and Social Spending in Latin America." *World Politics* 53(4): 553–587.

Kaufmann, Franz-Xaver. 2013. "Variations of the Welfare State: Great Britain, Sweden, France and Germany Between Capitalism and Socialism." In *German Social Policy*, vol. 5, ed. Lutz Leisering. New York: Springer, 23–239.

Kay, Cristóbal. 2002. "Chile's Neoliberal Agrarian Transformation and the Peasantry." *Journal of Agrarian Change* 2(4): 464–501.

Keefer, Philip. 2007. "Clientelism, Credibility, and the Policy Choices of Young Democracies." *American Journal of Political Science* 51(4): 804–821.

Keefer, Philip, Eric Neumayer, and Thomas Plümper. 2011. "Earthquake Propensity and the Politics of Mortality Prevention." *World Development* 39(9): 1530–1541.

Korpi, Walter. 1983. *The Democratic Class Struggle.* London: Routledge and Kegan Paul.

Krugman, Paul. 1979. "A Model of Balance-of-Payments Crises." *Journal of Money, Credit and Banking* 11(3): 311–325.

Kuznets, Simon. 1955. "Economic Growth and Income Inequality." *The American Economic Review* 45(1): 1–28.

La Porta, Rafael, Florencio Lopez-de-Silanes, Andrei Shleifer, and Robert Vishny. 1999. "The Quality of Government." *Journal of Law, Economics, and Organization* 15(1): 222–279.

Laeven, Luc, and Fabian Valencia. 2008. "Systemic Banking Crises: A New Database." International Monetary Fund. Washington, DC: IMF Working Papers.

Lake, David, and Matthew Baum. 2001. "The Invisible Hand of Democracy: Political Control and the Provision of Public Services." *Comparative Political Studies* 34(6): 587–621.

Lange, Matthew, James Mahoney, and Matthias vom Hau. 2006. "Colonialism and Development: A Comparative Analysis of Spanish and British Colonies." *American Journal of Sociology* 111(5): 1412–1462.

Lapp, Nancy. 2004. *Landing Votes: Representation and Land Reform in Latin America.* New York: Palgrave Macmillan.

Larraín, Felipe, and Patricio Meller. 1991. "The Socialist-Populist Chilean Experience, 1970–1973." In *The Macroeconomics of Populism in Latin America*, eds. Rudiger Dornbusch and Sebastian Edwards. Chicago: University of Chicago Press, 175–221.

Leonhardt, David, and Kevin Quealy. 2014. "The American Middle Class Is No Longer the World's Richest." *New York Times* A1, 14.

Levi, Margaret. 1989. *Of Rule and Revenue.* Berkeley: University of California Press.

Levitsky, Steven, and Lucan Way. 2010. *Competitive Authoritarianism: Hybrid Regimes after the Cold War.* New York: Cambridge University Press.

Levy-Yeyati, Eduardo, and Federico Sturzenegger. 2005. "Classifying Exchange Rate Regimes: Deeds vs. Words." *European Economic Review* 49(6): 1603–1635.

Lewin, Leif. 1988. *Ideology and Strategy: A Century of Swedish Politics.* New York: Cambridge University Press.

Lindberg, Staffan, Michael Coppedge, John Gerring, and Jan Teorell. 2013. "V-Dem: Codebook." Unpublished manuscript.

2014. "V-Dem: A New Way to Measure Democracy." *Journal of Democracy* 25(3): 159–169.

Lindert, Peter. 1994. "The Rise of Social Spending, 1880–1930." *Explorations in Economic History* 31(1): 1–37.

2004. *Growing Public: Social Spending and Economic Growth since the Eighteenth Century*, vol. 1. New York: Cambridge University Press.

Linz, Juan, and Alfred Stepan. 1996. *Problems of Democratic Transition and Consolidation: Southern Europe, South America, and Post-communist Europe*. Maryland: Johns Hopkins University Press.

Lipset, Seymour Martin. 1991. *Continental Divide: The Values and Institutions of the United States and Canada*. New York: Routledge.

Lizzeri, Alessandro, and Nicola Persico. 2004. "Why Did the Elites Extend the Suffrage? Democracy and the Scope of Government, with an Application to Britain's 'Age of Reform.'" *Quarterly Journal of Economics* 119(2): 707–765.

Lodin, Sven-Olof. 2011. *The Making of Tax Law: The Development of Swedish Taxation*. Amsterdam: Lustus Förlag.

Lott, John, and Lawrence Kenny. 1999. "Did Women's Suffrage Change the Size and Scope of Government?" *Journal of Political Economy* 107(6): 1163–1198.

Lust-Okar, Ellen. 2006. "Elections under Authoritarianism: Preliminary Lessons from Jordan." *Democratization* 13(3): 456–471.

Mahoney, James. 2010. *Colonialism and Postcolonial Development: Spanish America in Comparative Perspective*. New York: Cambridge University Press.

Mahtani, Shibani, and Richard Paddock. 2015. "Cronies of Former Myanmar Regime Thrive despite U.S. Blacklist." *Wall Street Journal*, August 12, 2015. www.wsj.com/articles/cronies-of-former-myanmar-regimethrive-despite-u-s-blacklist-1439433052.

Mainwaring, Scott, and Aníbal Pérez-Liñán. 2014. *Democracies and Dictatorships in Latin America: Emergence, Survival, and Fall*. New York: Cambridge University Press.

Marfán, Manuel. 1984. "Políticas Reactivadoras y Recesión Externa: Chile 1929–1938." *Colección Estudios CIEPLAN* 81(12): 89–120.

Marx, Karl. [1848] 1998. *The Communist Manifesto*. New York: Signet Classic.

McBride, George McCutchen. 1936. *Chile: Land and Society*. New York: American Geographical Society.

McCoy, Alfred. 1993. *An Anarchy of Families: State and Family in the Philippines*. Madison: University of Wisconsin Press.

Metcalf, Michael. 1987. *The Swedish Riksdag: A History of the Swedish Parliament*. New York: St. Martin's Press.

Meltzer, Arthur, and Scott Richard. 1981. "A Rational Theory of the Size of Government." *Journal of Political Economy* 89(5): 914–927.

Menaldo, Victor. 2012. "The Middle East and North Africa's Resilient Monarchs." *Journal of Politics* 74(3): 707–722.

2016. *The Institutions Curse*. New York: Cambridge University Press.

Menaldo, Victor, and Daniel Yoo. 2015. "Democracy, Elite Bias, and Financial Development in Latin America." *World Politics* 67(4): 726–759.

Michels, Robert. [1911] 1962. *Political Parties: A Sociological Study of the Oligarchical Tendencies of Modern Democracy*. New York: Free Press.

Montes, Esteban, and Tomás Vial. 2005. "The Role of Constitution-Building Processes in Democratization: Case Study Chile." Working paper, International Institute for Democracy and Electoral Assistance, Stockholm, Sweden.

Moore, Barrington Jr. 1966. *Social Origins of Dictatorship and Democracy: Lord and Peasant in the Making of the Modern World*. Boston: Beacon Press.

Murillo, Victoria. 2002. "Political Bias in Policy Convergence: Privatization Choices in Latin America." *World Politics* 54(4): 462–493.

Myerson, Roger. 2008. "The Autocrat's Credibility Problem and Foundations of the Constitutional State." *American Political Science Review* 102(1): 125–139.

Nalepa, Monika. 2010. *Skeletons in the Closet: Transitional Justice in Post-communist Europe*. New York: Cambridge University Press.

Negretto, Gabriel. 2006. "Choosing How to Choose Presidents." *Journal of Politics* 68(2): 421–433.

   2013. *Making Constitutions: Presidents, Parties, and Institutional Choice in Latin America*. Cambridge: Cambridge University Press.

Nelson, Joan. 2007. "Elections, Democracy, and Social Services." *Studies in Comparative International Development* 41(4): 79–97.

O'Donnell, Guillermo, and Philippe Schmitter. 1986. *Transitions from Authoritarian Rule*. Baltimore: Johns Hopkins University Press.

Palma, Gabriel. 1984. "Chile 1914–1935: De Economía Exportadora a Sustitutiva de Importaciones." *Colección Estudios CIEPLAN* 81(12): 61–88.

Perotti, Roberto. 1996. "Growth, Income Distribution, and Democracy: What the Data Say." *Journal of Economic Growth* 1(2): 149–187.

Piketty, Thomas. 2014. *Capital in the Twenty-First Century*. Cambridge: Harvard University Press.

Posner, Daniel, and Daniel Young. 2007. "The Institutionalization of Political Power in Africa." *Journal of Democracy* 18(3): 126–140.

Pribble, Jennifer, Evelyne Huber, and John Stephens. 2009. "Politics, Policies, and Poverty in Latin America." *Comparative Politics* 41(4): 387–407.

Przeworski, Adam. 1991. *Democracy and the Market: Political and Economic Reforms in Eastern Europe and Latin America*. New York: Cambridge University Press.

   2009. "Conquered or Granted? A History of Suffrage Extensions." *British Journal of Political Science* 39(2): 291–321.

Przeworski, Adam, Michael Alvarez, Jose Antonio Cheibub, and Fernando Limongi. 2000. *Democracy and Development: Political Institutions and Well-Being in the World, 1950–1990*. New York: Cambridge University Press.

Puglisi, Rosaria. 2003. "The Rise of the Ukrainian Oligarchs." *Democratization* 10(3): 99–123.

Rahat, Gideon, and Mario Sznajder. 1998. "Electoral Engineering in Chile: The Electoral System and Limited Democracy." *Electoral Studies* 17(4): 429–442.

Remmer, Karen. 1990. "Democracy and Economic Crisis: The Latin American Experience." *World Politics* 42(3): 315–335.

Riedl, Rachel Beatty. 2014. *Authoritarian Origins of Democratic Party Systems in Africa*. New York: Cambridge University Press.

Rodden, Jonathan. 2011. "The Long Shadow of the Industrial Revolution: Political Geography and the Representation of the Left." Unpublished manuscript.

Rodríguez Weber, Javier. 2009. "Los Tiempos de la Desigualdad: La Distribución del Ingreso en Chile, entre la Larga Duración, la Globalización y la Expansión de la Frontera, 1860–1930." Thesis. Montevideo, Uruguay.

Rodrik, Dani. 1998. "Why Do More Open Economies Have Bigger Governments?" *Journal of Political Economy* 106(5): 997–1032.

Roemer, John. 1998. "Why the Poor Do Not Expropriate the Rich: An Old Argument in New Garb." *Journal of Public Economics* 70(3): 399–424.

Rogowski, Ronald. 1989. *Commerce and Coalitions: How Trade Affects Domestic Political Alignments.* Princeton: Princeton University Press.

Rokkan, Stein. 1970. *Citizens, Elections, Parties: Approaches to the Comparative Study of the Process of Development.* Oslo: Universitetsforlaget.

Ross, Michael. 2006. "Is Democracy Good for the Poor?" *American Journal of Political Science* 50(4): 860–874.

Rueschemeyer, Dietrich, Evelyn Huber Stephens, and John Stephens. 1992. *Capitalist Development and Democracy.* Chicago: University of Chicago Press.

Salmon, Patrick. 1997. *Scandinavia and the Great Powers: 1890–1940.* New York: Cambridge University Press.

Samuels, David, and Richard Snyder. 2001. "The Value of a Vote: Malapportionment in Comparative Perspective." *British Journal of Political Science* 31(4): 651–671.

Sandalow, Terrance. 1971. "Local Government in Sweden." *American Journal of Comparative Law* 19: 766–785.

Sarasota Journal. 1970. "False Fronts Conceal Donors." December 28, 1970, 12.

Schamis, Hector. 1999. "Distributional Coalitions and the Politics of Economic Reform in Latin America." *World Politics* 51(2): 236–268.

Shapiro, Ian. 2002. "Why the Poor Don't Soak the Rich." *Daedalus* 131(1): 118–128.

Sisk, Timothy. 1995. *Democratization in South Africa.* Princeton: Princeton University Press.

Slater, Dan. 2013. "Democratic Careening." *World Politics* 65(4): 729–763.

Slater, Dan, Benjamin Smith, and Gautam Nair. 2014. "Economic Origins of Democratic Breakdown? the Redistributive Model and the Postcolonial State." *Perspectives on Politics* 12(2): 353–374.

Slater, Dan, and Joseph Wong. 2013. "The Strength to Concede: Ruling Parties and Democratization in Developmental Asia." *Perspectives on Politics* 11(3): 717–733.

Smith, Andrew. 2008. *British Businessmen and Canadian Confederation: Constitution Making in an Era of Anglo-Globalization.* Montreal: McGill-Queen's University Press.

Snyder, Richard, and David Samuels. 2004. "Legislative Malapportionment in Latin America." In *Federalism and Democracy in Latin America*, ed. Edward Gibson. Baltimore: Johns Hopkins University Press, 131–172.

Steinmo, Sven. 1993. *Taxation and Democracy: Swedish, British and American Approaches to Financing the Modern State.* New Haven: Yale University Press.

Stepan, Alfred. 1973. "The New Professionalism of Internal Warfare and Military Role Expansion." In *Authoritarian Brazil: Origins, Policies, and Future*, ed. Alfred Stepan. New Haven: Yale University Press, 47–65.

Stephens, John. 1979. *The Transition from Capitalism to Socialism.* London: Macmillan 1979.

Stiglitz, Joseph. 1998. "Central Banking in a Democratic Society." *De Economist* 146(2): 199–226.

Stjernquist, Nils. 1987. "From Bicameralism to Unicameralism: The Democratic Riksdag, 1921–1986." In *The Riksdag: A History of the Swedish Parliament*, ed. Michael Metcalf. New York: St. Martin's Press, 223–303.

Stokes, Susan. 2001. *Mandates and Democracy: Neoliberalism by Surprise in Latin America.* New York: Cambridge University Press.

Stokes, Susan, Thad Dunning, Marcelo Nazareno, and Valeria Brusco. 2013. *Brokers, Voters, and Clientelism: The Puzzle of Distributive Politics*. New York: Cambridge University Press.

Sunstein, Cass. 2001. *Designing Democracy: What Constitutions Do*. Oxford: Oxford University Press.

Sutter, Daniel. 1995. "Settling Old Scores: Potholes along the Transition from Authoritarian Rule." *Journal of Conflict Resolution* 39(1): 110–128.

Svolik, Milan. 2012. *The Politics of Authoritarian Rule*. New York: Cambridge University Press.

Takagi, Yusuke. 2016. *Central Banking as State Building: Policymakers and their Nationalism in the Philippines, 1933–1964*. Singapore: National University of Singapore Press.

Thelen, Kathleen. 2014. *Varieties of Liberalization and the New Politics of Social Solidarity*. Cambridge: Cambridge University Press.

Thiesenhusen, William. 1995. *Broken Promises: Agrarian Reform and the Latin American Campesino*. Boulder, CO: Westview Press.

Thome, Joseph. 1989. "Law, Conflict, and Change: Frei's Law and Allende's Agrarian Reform." In *Searching for Agrarian Reform in Latin America*, ed. William Thiesenhusen. Boston: Unwin Hyman, 188–215.

Tilly, Charles. 1992. *Coercion, Capital, and European States, AD 990–1990*. Cambridge, MA: Wiley-Blackwell.

Tilton, Timothy. 1974. "The Social Origins of Liberal Democracy: The Swedish Case." *American Political Science Review* 68(2): 561–571.

Toro, Sergio, Carolina Acevedo, and Kimberling Matamala. 2010. "Quebrando Paradigmas en Contextos Presidencialistas: Un Examen Sobre la Capacidad Legislativa en Chile." *Revista Ibero-Americana de Estudos Legislativos* 1(1): 102–110.

Treisman, Daniel. 2000. "The Causes of Corruption: A Cross-national Study." *Journal of Public Economics* 76(3): 399–457.

Truex, Rory. "The Myth of the Democratic Advantage." *Studies in Comparative International Development*, forthcoming.

Tsebelis, George, and Jeannette Money. 1997. *Bicameralism*. New York: Cambridge University Press.

Upchurch, Martin, Graham Taylor, and Andrew Mathers. 2016. *The Crisis of Social Democratic Trade Unionism in Western Europe: The Search for Alternatives*. New York: Routledge.

Valenzuela, Julio Samuel, and Arturo Valenzuela. 1986. *Military Rule in Chile: Dictatorship and Oppositions*. Baltimore: Johns Hopkins University Press.

Vernby, Kåre. 2013. "Inclusion and Public Policy: Evidence from Sweden's Introduction of Noncitizen Suffrage." *American Journal of Political Science* 57(1): 15–29.

Verney, Douglas. 1957. *Parliamentary Reform in Sweden, 1866–1921*. Oxford: Clarendon Press.

Wacziarg, Romain, and Seddon Wallack. 2004. "Trade Liberalization and Intersectoral Labor Movements." *Journal of International Economics* 64(2): 411–439.

Walsh, Katherine. 2012. "Putting Inequality in Its Place: Rural Consciousness and the Power of Perspective." *American Political Science Review* 1(1): 1–16.

Wang, Chen, and Koen Caminada. 2011. "Disentangling Income Inequality and the Redistributive Effect of Social Transfers and Taxes in 36 LIS Countries." Research memorandum, Leiden University Department of Economics.

Weingast, Barry. 1997. "The Political Foundations of Democracy and the Rule of Law." *American Political Science Review* 91(2): 245–263.

Whitmore, Sarah. 2004. *State Building in Ukraine: The Ukrainian Parliament, 1990–2003.* London: Routledge.

Wintrobe, Ronald. 1990. "The Tinpot and the Totalitarian: An Economic Theory of Dictatorship." *American Political Science Review* 84(3): 849–872.

Wood, Elisabeth. 2000. *Forging Democracy from Below.* New York: Cambridge University Press.

World Bank. 2012. "World Bank Development Indicators." Washington, DC: World Bank Publications.

Wright, Joseph. 2008. "Do Authoritarian Institutions Constrain? How Legislatures Affect Economic Growth and Investment." *American Journal of Political Science* 52(2): 322–343.

Wurfel, David. 1989. "The Development of Post-war Philippine Land Reform: Political and Sociological Explanations." In *Second View from the Paddy*, eds. Antonio Ledesma, Perla Makil, and Virginia Miralao. Quezon City: Institute of Philippine Culture, Ateneo de Manila University, 1–14.

Zeitlin, Maurice. 1984. *The Civil Wars in Chile.* Princeton: Princeton University Press.

Ziblatt, Daniel. 2009. "Shaping Democratic Practice and the Causes of Electoral Fraud: The Case of Nineteenth-Century Germany." *American Political Science Review* 103(1): 1–21.

2017. *Conservative Political Parties and the Birth of Modern Democracy in Europe.* New York: Cambridge University Press.

Zingales, Luigi. 2012. *A Capitalism for the People.* New York: Basic Books.

Index

governance and material outcomes under
democracy, 57–58
egalitarian democracy variable, 117
equal distribution of resources variable, 117
percentage of population with suffrage
variable, 117
range of consultation variable, 117
redistribution measures, 118–20
representation of disadvantaged groups
variable, 117, 118
statistical strategy for explaining by regime
type, 122–24
Great Britain, 7
Great Depression
in Chile, 217–19
Guatemala
revolution and popular democratic
transition in, 105

Haggard, Stephan, 17
health
in Chile under popular democracy, 224
in democracies vs. dictatorships, 6
of dictators, 61
Hitler, Adolf, 131
Hungary, 107

illiberal institutions, 9
income inequality. *See also* redistribution
in Chile, 210, 224
in Chile under elite-biased
democracy, 241–42
under democracy, 2–3, 6–7, 11–12
democratic transitions and, 56, 57
elite-biased transitions and, 56
in Spain under democracy, 15
in Sweden during the 1900 to 1910
period, 175
in Sweden during the 1950s to 1960s
period, 203
Swedish policies reducing, 199–200
in the U.S., 283
incumbent economic elites, 32–33, *See also*
economic elites; outsider economic elites
effect of proximate factors and structural
underpinnings on and political regime
outcomes, 51–53
Great Depression in Chile and, 217
vs. outsider economic elites, 33–35
reaction to liberalization in
Sweden, 182–84

in Sweden under dictatorship, 177–80
volatile dictatorships and, 37–39
Indonesia, 20, 50
constitutional reform in, 143
industrialization, 109
informal institutions, 29
Iran, 50
iron law of oligarchy, 66
Italy, 90

Kaufman, Robert, 17
Kenya
elite-biased constitution of as furthering
elite bias, 155
Kirchner, Christina and Nelson, 119–20
Kyrgyzstan, 19

land reform and redistribution, 2, 20, 105
in Chile, 221–22, 229–30
in Philippines, 263
Latin America, 5
elite-biased constitutions and, 95–96
leftwing party bans
elite-biased constitutions and, 80–90, 93
legislature under dictatorship
elite-biased democratic transitions and, 102,
112–16
elite-biased democratic transition in Mexico
and, 103–04
forestalling popular initiation of legislation
and, 80–90
popular democratic transitions and, 102,
112–16
legislatures, 49, 61, *See also* bicameralism
elite-biased transitions and, 46–47
measurement of as variable in democratic
transitions, 107
Libya, 286

Malaysia, 20
Mandela, Nelson, 285
Marcos, Ferdinand, 262–63
Marx, Karl, 4
masses, the
assumptions on preference for
democracy, 15–16
consolidated dictatorships and, 36–37
constitutional amendments and annulments
and, 155–58
governance outcomes for in democratic
transitions, 58

popular democracies (*cont.*)
  current state of in Sweden, 207–08
  effect of proximate factors and structural
    underpinnings on elites and the masses
    and, 51–53
  effects of in Sweden, 205–06
  governance outcomes under, 57–58
  impact of on governance and material
    outcomes, 120–21
  impediments to popular rule from elite-
    biased constitutions, 80–90
  median voter and, 36
  as more inclusive, pluralistic, and egalitarian
    than elite-biased democracies, 142
  outsider economic elites and the masses
    and, 42–43
  in Philippines, 263
  progressive taxation and, 118–20
  question of start of in Chile, 219–21
  shifts from to elite-biased
    democracy, 279–83
  social and political factors in Sweden's
    development from elite-biased to popular
    democracy, 175–77
  transitions to from elite-biased
    transitions, 44
popular democratic transitions, 42–43
  constitutions and, 74
  defined, 106
  distributional outcomes following, 61–62
  earthquakes and, 112–14
  economic inequality and, 57
  economic shock and collapse as proximate
    factor in, 50–51, 102, 116
  economic shock and collapse in Argentina
    and, 105–06
  elite-biased constitutions and, 74
  endogenous sources of change in, 109
  legislature under dictatorship and, 102,
    112–16
  the masses as actors in, 35–36
  modernization theory and, 56
  redistribution after, 58–60
  revolution in Guatemala and, 105
  revolutions and, 49–50, 102, 114–15
  statistical results of determinants of, 112–16
  statistical strategy for estimating, 110–11
  transitional justice for outgoing political
    incumbent elites and, 60
Portugal, 19, 284
  elite-biased constitution of, 73

poverty, 3
power resources theory, 6
progressive taxation, 118–20
property rights
  protection of under elite-biased
    constitutions, 80–90, 94
proportional representation, 154, 155
  elite-biased constitutions and, 80–90,
    92–93
  in Sweden, 188–91, 201–02
Przeworski, Adam, 72

redistribution, 10, *See also* income inequality
  in elite-biased democracies, 118
  fixed exchange rate measure, 119–20
  forms of, 118
  of land under dictatorships, 20
  as measure in governance and material
    outcomes under democracy, 118–20
  outcomes after democratic transitions, 4–5,
    58–60
  progressive spending measure, 118
  progressive taxation measure, 118–20
  total size of government measure, 118
revolutions, 29, 286–87
  defined, 109
  economic growth in historically
    underdeveloped nations and, 20
  measurement of as variable in popular
    democratic transitions, 109
  outsider economic elites and, 19, 108
  percent of under dictatorships resulting in
    democracy, 19
  popular democratic transition in Guatemala
    and, 105
  popular democratic transitions and, 49–50,
    102, 114–15
  reasons for rarity of democratic transitions
    after, 19–20
  Sweden's transition from elite-biased to
    popular democracy and, 197
Romania, 90
  constitutional reforms in, 145
Russia, 20

Salazar, António (Portuguese President), 73
Samuels, David, 20
Scandinavia
  and successful democracies, 99
Sein, Thein (President of Myanmar), 64
Senegal, 90

unions, 6, 119
  in Chile, 220
  in Sweden, 176, 199, 202, 206
United States, 7, 9, 90, *See also* Philippines and
    American colonial legacies
  income inequality in, 283
  political capture of institutions and
    economic regulation by powerful financial
    interests in, 280–83
  suffrage in U.S. South during the Jim Crow
    era, 124
Uruguay, 20

Venezuela, 90, 103
volatile dictatorships, 26, 36, 37–39, 42
  distributional outcomes under, 61–62
  transitions between consolidated and,
    43–44

World War I
  effect of on elite-biased institutions in
    Sweden, 193–97
  manufacturing in Chile during, 216–17

Zimbabwe, 20